The Battle of Shiloh in Color

A Step-by-Step Account of One of the Greatest Battles of the American Civil War

By Jack Kunkel

Copyright

PEPPER PUBLISHING

The editorial arrangement, analysis, and professional commentary are subject to this copyright notice. No portion of this book may be copied, retransmitted, reposted, duplicated, or otherwise used without the express written approval of the author, except by reviewers who may quote brief excerpts in connection with a review. Any unauthorized copying, reproduction, translation, or distribution of any part of this material without permission by the author is prohibited and against the law.

DISCLAIMER AND TERMS OF USE

No information contained in this book should be considered as financial, tax or legal advice. Your reliance upon information and content obtained by you at or through this publication is solely at your own risk. Neither Pepper Publishing nor the author assume any liability or responsibility for damage or injury to you, other persons, or property arising from any use of any product, information, idea, or instruction contained in the content or services provided to you through this book. Unless specifically stated otherwise, the author has no financial interest in and receive no compensation from manufacturers of products or websites mentioned in this book.

US COPYRIGHT REGISTERED: TX0009436777

PEPPER PUBLISHING/JACK KUNKEL

Table of Contents

Copyright ii
Table of Contents iii
Forward iv
About the Pictures, Drawings & Maps v
1 The Road To Shiloh 1
2 The Union Encampment 15
3 The March to Shiloh 25
4 First Clash 33
5 Prentiss Reinforces 37
6 Breaking Peabody's Brigade 41
7 Breaking Miller's Brigade 47
8 Breaking Hildebrand's Brigade 55
9 Buckland's Brigade Holds 67
10 McClernand Joins the Fight 73
11 Collapse of the Union Right 79
12 Union Counterattack 89
13 Hurlbut Draws a Line 95
14 The Hornet's Nest 101
15 Struggle on Union Left 111
16 Johnston Cracks the Union Line 121
17 Surrender at Hell's Hollow 133
18 Grant's Last Line 139
19 Lew Wallace Finally Arrives 153
20 Buell Advances 159
21 Confederate Counterattacks 167
22 Grant Attacks 173
23 Final Attacks & Withdrawal 179
24 Aftermath 187
Appendix A - Order of Battle 195
Appendix C - Army Organization 201
References 203
Index 205

Forward

The Battle of Shiloh was fought deep in the Tennessee woods, far away from the intensely-reported, intensely-documented, intensely-visited Civil War battlefields in the East. It lacked the neatness and precision of many of the later battles. All battles are chaotic, but Shiloh was more so than most. And though the combatants were North against South, they were all considered "Westerners" by the folks back East. Today of course they would be considered Mid-Westerners. But at the time, the western combatants often had more in common with each other than they did with their eastern cousins, including the fact that they all hailed from a more remote, wilder region, nearer to the edge of what was then the American frontier.

By the time the soldiers in the East got around to fighting their bloody battles at Antietam and Gettysburg, most of them at least had some training under McClellan and Lee. By contrast, with the exception of a few West Point graduates at the top of the command structure, the vast majority of the men on the field at Shiloh were complete amateurs at the business of war – mostly local lawyers and politicians leading tens of thousands of their hometown boys into the gates of hell.

Because of their inexperience, combined with a typically straight-forward, Midwestern way of doing things, it's only a mild exaggeration to say that the tactics of the battle of Shiloh boiled down to 80,000 country boys loading their newly-acquired high powered rifles, lining up facing each other, and blasting away. What's amazing is the absolute fury and tenacity with which these citizen-soldiers fought, and the astounding courage most of them displayed.

For those who survived the inferno without an emotional breakdown and without losing important body parts, Shiloh served as an excellent proving-ground for future military leaders in the West. But their confused, on-the-job training session certainly left a mess for us writers to explain. Possibly for that reason, many books on the subject tend to shy away from the actual battle, instead focusing heavily on the politics and battles leading up to the fight, so that it's often not until page 100 before anyone takes a shot at anybody at Shiloh.

But in this book I've confined the political foreplay to the first chapter. After that we get down to the tactics and the battle itself. I've dispensed with footnotes, since this work is not intended to be a scholarly treatise, though I can back up the book-quotes if needed – most of them came from the books listed in the References section. I consider myself a "splainer," rather than a "true" historian. For one thing I've never been to historian school, and for another I haven't spent decades doing in-depth research, pouring over newspapers, letters and journals. I admire those who do, and in my next life I might join them, but right now my object is to synthesize their collective findings and explain things in an interesting manner that readers can understand - taking full advantage of any maps, photos and/or illustrations I can create or lay hands on.

A pet peeve of mine with battle-books is their lack of maps relating to the text. I *hate* thumbing through 20 pages trying to figure out which map belongs to the text I'm reading! For that reason I've included maps in almost every chapter, both close-up and big-picture maps, most big enough to be visible from Pluto.

But the participants at Shiloh weren't just pins on a map. So I've tried to include lots of their personal recollections. And since there weren't many photos taken of the field after the battle, and Shiloh's empty fields of today aren't terribly photogenic, I've settled for including numerous illustrations throughout the book, most of them drawn by artists of that time period, some of whom may have actually witnessed the battle.

I've also included refurbished photos of as many of the participants as I could lay hands on, about 125 of them - which is probably a world record for any book on Shiloh.

My goal is for you to come away with a better understanding of how the battle unfolded, step by step, and more importantly, what it was really like for the men and boys who fought in the terrible Battle of Shiloh.

Jack Kunkel

About the Pictures, Drawings & Maps

About the Pictures & Illustrations

The main benefit of reading this book in color, at least in my opinion, is that it makes the maps clearer. But as a bonus, all of the period photos and drawings have also been colorized. There are about 125 photos of the participants included in this book. Nearly all of the images came from either the Library of Congress or the National Archives. Many of them are in rough shape due to age and rudimentary photography equipment of the time, so I've attempted to restore them to the best of my ability, with varying degrees of success. Also, at the bottom of each photo, I've included the subject's rank at the time of the battle, but note that many of the photos show the subjects with higher ranks since the pictures were taken later, when the individuals had achieved a higher rank.

Most of the illustrations in this book came from a four-volume series of books written in the 1880s, called *Battles and Leaders*. The series covered the entire Civil War, but it did include a section on the battle of Shiloh.

There were no photos taken during the battle and only a couple immediately afterwards, so these illustrations are the closest we can come to seeing what the field actually looked like during the battle. Presumably, some of these artists either witnessed the battle themselves, or at least they collaborated with veterans who did witness the battle.

Anyway, in the interest of history, I've included a number of these drawings, and I've also colorized them, which I think is an improvement. However, since there are no subtle gradations of color and shade in a drawing like exist in a photo, the colorization of a drawing is not as accurate as it is in a photo.

About the Maps

Maps are essential to understanding battles. But books present some challenges in displaying maps, so I thought I'd take, a moment to explain how they're set up in this book.

First of all, there are two general kinds of maps used here - book maps and Google maps.

A. Book Maps

You will find three types of book maps within this text.
1. Close up maps
2. Location maps
3. Overall maps

Almost every chapter contains a "Close-up" map that pertains to the subject being discussed. But to give you an idea of where that close-up section of the battle fits into the rest of the battlefield, I've also included a smaller, "Location map" somewhere near the Close-up map. The small square in the Location map shows where the Close-up map fits into the entire battlefield.

Finally, because there were usually several battles going on at Shiloh at the same time, I've included an "Overall map" at the end of most chapters that shows you where all the units on the field were at this particular time.

Samples of all these maps are shown on the following pages.

B. Google Maps

You can also view the modern location of various sites using Google maps. The links are stored on my Google Cloud account, which you can access for free. Each chapter contains a set of links to the locations discussed in that chapter.

The actual URL link is a monster, too big to type. So I've created an online "short URL" which is easier to type. Just type the short URL into your cell phone, then bookmark the link for later use.

The link is: **bit.ly/4iKcLun**

Sample Maps

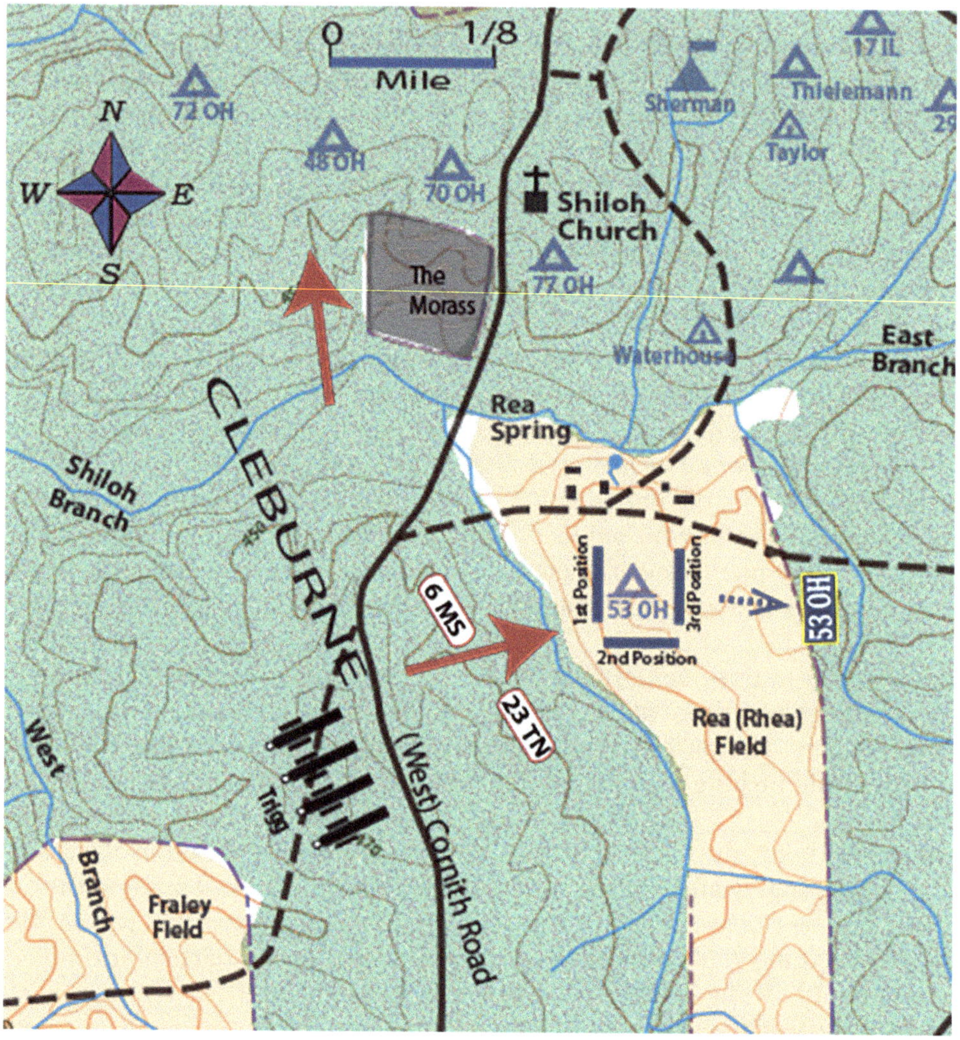

1. A sample *Close-up or Chapter map*, displaying the locations of the units discussed in a specific chapter.

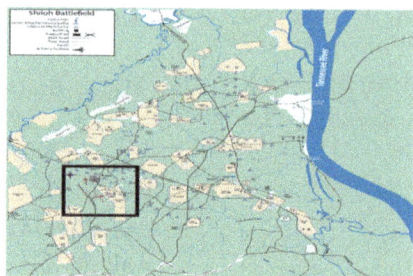

2. A sample *Location map*, displaying the battlefield location of the Close-up map shown above

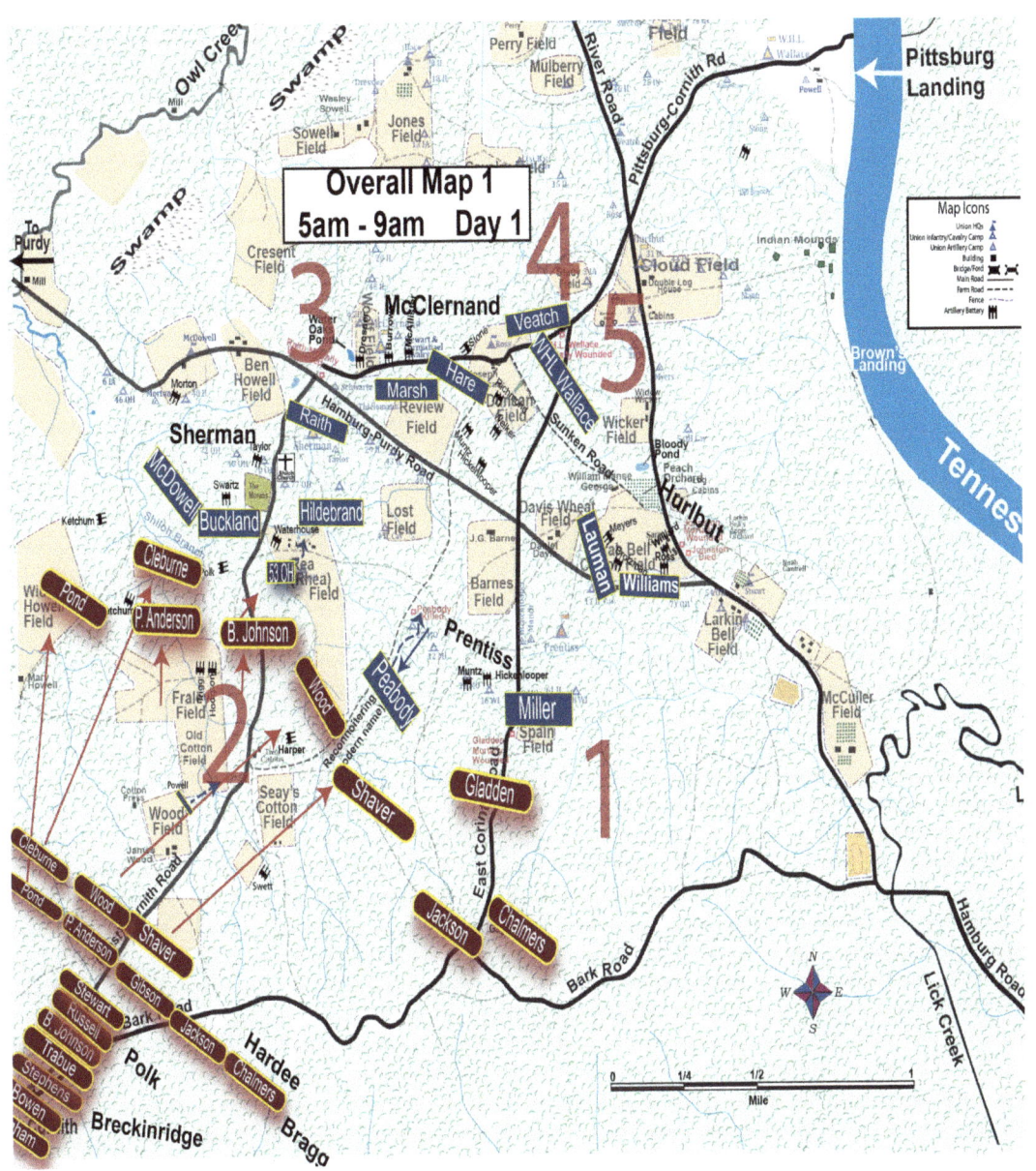

3. A sample *Overall map,* which is usually included at the end of each chapter to display the entire battlefield situation at a certain time.

Understanding Army Organization

Since I know the subject very well, I constantly throw around terms like *regiments, brigades, divisions*, and *corps*, like everybody knows what they are. But of course not everyone *does* know what they are. If you're one of the benighted, I'd recommend that you take a quick glance at the Appendices, which briefly outline Civil War army organizations, so we'll all be on the same page. And once your familiar with using it, you can quickly refer back to the Appendix as you read the book.

1 The Road To Shiloh

Few nations were as unprepared for war, least of all a civil war, as were the combatants in April 1861 when the Slavery-State Rights powder keg exploded at Fort Sumter. At that time the U.S. Army numbered about 16,000 "regulars." The Confederacy possessed no army at all except for the few hundred U.S. Army officers who resigned their commissions and joined the South. Within months, both sides would be training and arming tens of thousands of citizen-soldiers.

Both sides built their armies via a state volunteer system, and both Presidents, Abraham Lincoln and Jefferson Davis, called on their respective states to provide quotas of troops organized into companies – theoretically 100 men per company – and these companies would be combined into regiments – theoretically 10 companies per regiment.

Off to See the Elephant

For the eyeball-to-eyeball business of forming the companies, state governors relied on local politicians and community leaders to recruit volunteers in thousands of towns and villages. For young men who had never set foot outside their county, the prospect of going to war like their revered Revolutionary War forefathers was the thrill of a lifetime – much more exciting than milking cows or clerking at the dry goods store. Tens of thousands raced to sign up in recruiting drives packed with hometown parades, bands, cheering crowds, absolutions & blessings by clergy, and stirring speeches by town fathers. The women joined in the excitement by sewing flags and uniforms of every color and design. If their town was big enough to support a photographer, the recruits lined up to have their picture taken. The boys were embarking on a tremendous adventure "to see the elephant," which meant seeing something wondrous – in this case, battle. Few of them had ever seen a battle except maybe in a colorful painting of the Revolutionary War or the Battle of Waterloo, where war always looked glorious and smoky.

Finally, the proud companies tramped off to war through their town's streets, hopelessly out of step, past the cheering crowds of mothers and fathers, aunts and uncles, and above all, the girls, while being relentlessly serenaded by local bands. Excited young boys raced up and down the sides of the column. The recruits, if they had weapons, were usually armed with shotguns, old muskets, various calibers of squirrel guns, and evil-looking hunting knives. Their officers were local community leaders – usually lawyers and politicians, but sometimes school masters and preachers.

These companies would eventually rendezvous at large camps where things were only slightly less festive, with lots of speeches, singing and harrahing. The first order of business was to merge the companies into regiments, regiments into brigades, brigades into divisions, and divisions into corps. The fancy company flags, so lovingly sewn by the hometown women, were packed up and shipped home; only regiments would carry flags, usually two - a national flag and a regimental flag. The officers of the various companies in each regiment gathered and elected a regimental colonel and other field officers from among their number. Few of these officers had any military experience.

It would be a massive understatement to say this recruiting system was imperfect. The North's system was even more imperfect because the legal enlistment-term established by the Uniform Militia Act of 1792 limited the military term of volunteers to 90 days. So when Lincoln called up 75,000 volunteers after Fort Sumter, their terms had expired by the end of summer 1861. Some of these three-month volunteers reenlisted for three years, and some didn't.

But this hometown method of building armies had one major advantage: it created tremendous cohesion. Almost every soldier knew his comrades from childhood because they were all from the same community. Each soldier's performance on the battlefield would be relayed to that man's family, neighbors, and community, and remembered forever. And back then in America, physical cowardice was not considered a virtue.

Throughout the fall, winter and spring of 1861-1862 the North raised armies and funneled them to jump-off points for a southern offensive. In the western theater, that point was Cairo, Illinois where the Ohio and Mississippi Rivers converge.

Militarization got off to a slightly smoother start in the South due to giddy war fever that gripped Southerners at the time; plus Confederate President Jefferson Davis had the legal ability to summon volunteers for twelve months, not three. Also, due to the Nat Turner slave rebellion of 1831 and John Brown's attempted slave revolt of 1859, many Southern communities had already organized local militias, convenient for quick conversion into military units.

Initially, the lion's share of organized regiments in the Southern states, which included most of those with military training or Mexican War experience, were shipped to Virginia for the defense of Richmond.

By the beginning of 1862, the eighth month of the Civil War, many battles had been fought but few were of consequence, except of course to the participants, with the exception of the First Battle of Bull Run in Virginia and, to a lesser extent, the Battle of Wilson Creek in Missouri. The South had won almost all the significant clashes, with less than 5,000 war casualties so far. By January of 1862, the South had become accustomed to constant victories.

Both sides, while still hoping knock each other out in a short war, were girding for a long one. And what both sides didn't yet know about conducting wars could have filled volumes.

The South's Kentucky Shield

Soon after war was declared, Kentucky, a critical border state, proclaimed its "neutrality," and forbade troops from either side from crossing its borders. The Federals had to respect Kentucky's prohibition since Lincoln was determined to avoid any act that might tilt the state into the waiting arms of the South. Kentucky's neutrality was a boon to the Confederacy since it shielded Tennessee's long northern border without the need to station troops there.

But the South threw away its Kentucky shield when, in September 1861, Maj. Gen. Leonidas Polk, the commander of Confederate forces in the Mississippi Valley, took it upon himself to occupy the Mississippi River town of Columbus, Kentucky thus violating Kentucky neutrality. Polk's move was logical from a tactical standpoint – Columbus stood on a high bluff which dominated the river for miles, making it a wonderful fortress. But from a strategic and political standpoint, his move was a disaster because it drove most Kentuckians straight into the arms of the Union (Kentuckians went Union four to one); worse, Tennessee's long, nearly undefended northern border was now fair game for a Union invasion, a fact that would quickly be taken advantage of by a little known Union general named Ulysses S. Grant.

Chapter 1 - The Road to Shiloh

The Federals

Through the winter of 1861-1862, the fiercest fighting in the western theater occurred between Union Maj. Gen. Henry W. Halleck in St. Louis and his Ohio rival, Maj. Gen. Don Carlos Buell, in their competition to win overall western command. Eventually, in March of 1862, Halleck won and Buell's army was consolidated into Halleck's Department of Mississippi, which now included all Union forces in the Mississippi and Tennessee River valleys.

Maj. Gen. Henry W. Halleck 1815 - 1872

Forty-seven-year-old Henry W. Halleck, "Old Brains" came with a brilliant resume – besides being offered a prestigious Harvard engineering professorship, he was a Phi Beta Kappa, third in his class at West Point, a prolific military author, bilingual, and had once headed a successful law firm. But though he was an intellectual giant, he was not a field officer. Bookish, and bug-eyed with a sly, devious demeanor, Halleck was a plodding officer who was far more comfortable mounted on a chair in the office than on a saddle in the field, particularly given his constant battle with hemorrhoids. In short, he was a natural-born bureaucrat, not a field officer, but no one knew that yet.

In November of 1861, before Halleck assumed command, the border area was under the command of Gen. John C. Fremont, who was known as "The Pathfinder" for his conquest of California 15 years earlier. But Fremont was a flop as a Civil War commander; among other problems, he isolated himself in his palatial headquarters in St. Louis and refused to communicate with his generals in the field.

Maj. Gen. Ulysses S. Grant 1822 - 1885

But before he was cashiered, Fremont did make one outstanding decision: for some reason, probably due to the lack of any better candidates, he appointed a rather shabby officer, with a reputation as a drinker, to command the Union forces in Cairo, Illinois.

That officer was 39-year-old Ulysses S. Grant. Just over a year earlier, Grant, a failure in every enterprise he attempted, had been feeding his family by peddling firewood on the streets of St. Louis while living in a log cabin. Quiet and unpretentious, always looking somewhat troubled he was ill at ease in public and always seemed to be alone even in a crowd. The great puzzle about Grant would always be that he seemed so *damned ordinary.*

As is true of many shy people, he had an uncommon ability with animals, especially horses. At a tender age he was riding horses while standing on their backs. And, not with harshness, but with gentleness, he could break, train, and ride horses that other men couldn't. As a boy he had worked in his father's tannery where he developed a life-long aversion to blood; he wouldn't eat meat unless it was cooked "charred gray." He eschewed military pomp, and wore a plain private's jacket unadorned except for his general's stars. He graduated from West Point in 1843 in the bottom half of his class. He excelled at math and horseback riding, but not much else. As such, he was relegated to the infantry because the elite Army Corps of Engineers didn't want him and there was no room in the cavalry. His hidden talents would only blossom in war.

One of Grant's best friends at West Point was James Longstreet, who would become Lee's second in command, and who attended Grant's wedding.

During the Mexican War, Grant was assigned to the normally non-combatant role of supply and logistics, which he excelled at, but he always found a way to get into the middle of every big fight. Longstreet would say of him, "*You could not keep him out of battle ... [He] was everywhere on the field.*" In war, it would turn out that Grant had a healthy dose of Midwestern common sense and a logical mind, combined with three extraordinary talents: a surprising aggressiveness, a bulldog determination, and an uncanny ability to remain calm in situations that would drive most sane men to hysteria.

His reputation as a drunkard follows him to this very day. The reputation was and is overblown. There never seems to have been any issue with his drinking throughout the Civil War, or during his Presidency, or in his retirement. He did drink, and he was known to be unable to hold his liquor. But he didn't drink excessively, at least by army standards, unless he was bored and his wife wasn't around.

At one point before the war he had been stationed in a gloomy and rainy army post on the wilderness coast of what is now Oregon; he dearly missed his wife whom he adored and hadn't seen for over a year, as well as their baby he had never seen. This was during the Gold Rush era and everyone in California seemed to be getting rich. Hoping to make enough money to bring his wife out to his post, he invested in several enterprises that all failed.

Bored and without much to do, he started drinking heavily. The facts are a bit murky, but apparently the commander gave him a choice of resigning from the army or a court martial. Grant chose the former.

But now, in 1861, even with his reputation, he commanded thousands of men. Soon he would be commanding tens of thousands, and eventually hundreds of thousands. He was now the commander of the important Federal garrison in Cairo, Illinois, at the confluence of the Mississippi and Ohio Rivers. Just across the rivers were the slave states of Missouri and Kentucky, both of which had divided loyalties. As already discussed, initially Kentucky tried to stay neutral but its 'neutrality" had been violated by the Confederates on September 3, 1861 by Polk's occupation of Columbus, Kentucky on the Mississippi River. So, the next day, having learned from one of Fremont's scouts that the citizens in the nearby city of Paducah, Kentucky, were eagerly awaiting the arrival of Confederate Gen. Gideon Pillow and his troops, Grant decided to occupy Paducah, 36 miles east of Cairo. Paducah sat at the important confluence of the Ohio, Tennessee, and Cumberland Rivers. Grant sent his boos, Fremont, a couple of telegrams, suggesting the town be occupied. As usual, Fremont didn't respond. Taking that as a "yes", Grant loaded two regiments and a battery on riverboats and sailed for Paducah, surprising the hell out of Fremont, not to mention the Paduchians, who had been planning a joyous, flag-waving welcome for the Confederates, only to be serenaded by a blue-coated, damn-Yankee band blasting out "*Hail Columbia"* as Grant and his troops marched into town.

This quick, bloodless coup was exactly the type of action Lincoln longed for. It was a refreshing change from the situation back east, where he was awash in strutting generals who talked tough but who rarely fought, and lost when they did.

Then, in November of that year, Grant loaded 3,100 troops – infantry, artillery, and two companies of cavalry – aboard transports, and sailed 25 miles down the Mississippi River to attack a Confederate stronghold at Belmont, Missouri. The idea was to clear the Mississippi River of Confederates, cleaving

Chapter 1 - The Road to Shiloh

clear the Mississippi River of Confederates, cleaving the Confederacy in two, and restoring Union commerce from the Midwest to the Gulf of Mexico. Belmont today no longer exists - it was flooded out by the Mississippi River. But at the time it was a town just north and across the river from Polk's Confederate fortress at Columbus, Kentucky.

Two timberclad gunboats – the Lexington and Tyler - accompanied Grant and his little flotilla. These two boats would play important roles in many of Grant's later battles.

Upon landing near Belmont, Grant completely surprised the Confederates. In a vicious little battle, Grant was winning for the first part of the day, but his troops dawdled to loot Confederate tents, giving the surprised Confederates in Columbus time to recover and reinforce, and by the latter part of the day they had the Federals surrounded and in serious danger of being annihilated. Grant's raw troops began to panic. But he kept his cool and told them, *"We've cut our way in here, and we'll cut our way out."* The Federals managed to re-embark and escape by the skin of their teeth, with Grant being the last man to trot his horse up a narrow gang plank with the pursuing Confederates in sight. His operation a failure and suffering 500 casualties, Grant was roundly criticized in the press. He down-played the whole affair as a mere raid.

But one thing the "raid" did accomplish was that it sealed Grant's partnership with the US Navy and its brown-water navy. The navy's cooperation, along with its gunboats and transports, would be critical in Grant's, and later Sherman's, future advances in the West.

Meanwhile, back in St. Louis, Fremont, besides being totally incompetent and corrupt, had started making proclamations about freeing the slaves, which is the last thing Lincoln wanted in the volatile border states, where many citizens were slaveholders. Lincoln ordered Fremont to rescind the proclamation. Fremont refused. Lincoln fired him. No sooner had Grant returned to Cairo than Lincoln replaced Fremont with Henry Halleck, and also consolidated General Buell's Ohio army under Halleck. And Lincoln made it clear to Halleck that he expected action.

Like everyone in the regular army, Halleck had heard the rumors about Grant's drinking. He sent one of his staff – Col. James McPherson – to serve as Grant's engineer at Cairo and parts south, and also to spy on Grant and inform Halleck at the first sign of Grant's drinking. But as it would turn out, the highly competent McPherson – first in his class at West Point – became one of Grant's, and later Sherman's, most trusted officers, and they served together until McPherson was killed in Atlanta in 1864. It would be McPherson who first suggested the idea of attacking Fort Henry, which launched Grant to national fame.

Halleck also sent Grant the unwelcome addition of Col. John A. McClernand, a lawyer with no military experience but politically important because he was a rare Democrat who supported Lincoln. He would be awarded a politically-based, undeserved promotion to brigadier general and would quickly become a constant thorn in Grant's side.

In any case, with Halleck now in command, the Federals in the west were finally unified under a single commander. And now, with Halleck's full approval, in early 1862 Grant was on the move again, with some critical assistance from the U.S. Navy in the form of a squadron of gunboats commanded by Flag Officer Andrew H. Foote. Majestic ships of the line might rule the seas, but drab gunboats - called "turtles" or "turtle-backs" - ruled the rivers. These ungainly brutes were initially just civilian river steamers protected with 2 inches of oak ("timberclads"). But the later ones were built from the ground up to be gunboats, and they were protected by an inch of oak covered by two and a half inches of iron plate ("ironclads").

About 200 feet long - or about two-thirds the length of a modern football field - the ironclads must have seemed cavernous on the inside. They were floating artillery platforms, manned by a crew of 150 sailors and armed with far bigger guns than anything the army could drag into the field. Whereas the army's standard field gun was a 6-pounder (later, 12-pounder) cannon, the gunboats could carry 32, 42 and even 64-pounder cannon. The Union had built eight ironclads by early 1862.

They would turn out to be one of the Union's most effective weapons of the war in the West. But how they would fare against Confederate forts was still untested.

The South couldn't build and maintain these massive boats; pitifully, the best they could do was use cotton bales to protect their boats ("cottonclads"). So the Confederacy placed its bet on river fortresses, which were to become Grant's chief targets in his western campaigns.

the Confederacy in two, and restoring Union commerce from the Midwest to the Gulf of Mexico. Belmont today no longer exists - it was flooded out by the Mississippi River. But at the time it was a town just north and across the river from Polk's Confederate fortress at Columbus, Kentucky.

Two timberclad gunboats – the Lexington and Tyler - accompanied Grant and his little flotilla. These two boats would play important roles in many of Grant's later battles.

Upon landing near Belmont, Grant completely surprised the Confederates. In a vicious little battle, Grant was winning for the first part of the day, but his troops dawdled to loot Confederate tents, giving the surprised Confederates in Columbus time to recover and reinforce, and by the latter part of the day they had the Federals surrounded and in serious danger of being annihilated. Grant's raw troops began to panic. But he kept his cool and told them, *"We've cut our way in here, and we'll cut our way out."* The Federals managed to re-embark and escape by the skin of their teeth, with Grant being the last man to trot his horse up a narrow gang plank with the pursuing Confederates in sight. His operation a failure and suffering 500 casualties, Grant was roundly criticized in the press. He down-played the whole affair as a mere raid.

But one thing the "raid" did accomplish was that it sealed Grant's partnership with the US Navy and its brown-water navy. The navy's cooperation, along with its gunboats and transports, would be critical in Grant's, and later Sherman's, future advances in the West.

Meanwhile, back in St. Louis, Fremont, besides being totally incompetent and corrupt, had started making proclamations about freeing the slaves, which is the last thing Lincoln wanted in the volatile border states, where many citizens were slaveholders. Lincoln ordered Fremont to rescind the proclamation. Fremont refused. Lincoln fired him. No sooner had Grant returned to Cairo than Lincoln replaced Fremont with Henry Halleck, and also consolidated General Buell's Ohio army under Halleck. And Lincoln made it clear to Halleck that he expected action.

Like everyone in the regular army, Halleck had heard the rumors about Grant's drinking. He sent one of his staff – Col. James McPherson – to serve as Grant's engineer at Cairo and parts south, and also to spy on Grant and inform Halleck at the first sign of Grant's drinking. But as it would turn out, the highly competent McPherson – first in his class at West Point – became one of Grant's, and later Sherman's, most trusted officers, and they served together until McPherson was killed in Atlanta in 1864. It would be McPherson who first suggested the idea of attacking Fort Henry, which launched Grant to national fame.

Halleck also sent Grant the unwelcome addition of Col. John A. McClernand, a lawyer with no military experience but politically important because he was a rare Democrat who supported Lincoln. He would be awarded a politically-based, undeserved promotion to brigadier general and would quickly become a constant thorn in Grant's side.

In any case, with Halleck now in command, the Federals in the west were finally unified under a single commander. And now, with Halleck's full approval, in early 1862 Grant was on the move again, with some critical assistance from the U.S. Navy in the form of a squadron of gunboats commanded by Flag Officer Andrew H. Foote. Majestic ships of the line might rule the seas, but drab gunboats - called "turtles" or "turtle-backs" - ruled the rivers. These ungainly brutes were initially just civilian river steamers protected with 2 inches of oak ("timberclads"). But the later ones were built from the ground up to be gunboats, and they were protected by an inch of oak covered by two and a half inches of iron plate ("ironclads").

About 200 feet long - or about two-thirds the length of a modern football field - the ironclads must have seemed cavernous on the inside. They were floating artillery platforms, manned by a crew of 150 sailors and armed with far bigger guns than anything the army could drag into the field. Whereas the army's standard field gun was a 6-pounder (later, 12-pounder) cannon, the gunboats could carry 32, 42 and even 64-pounder cannon. The Union had built eight ironclads by early 1862.

They would turn out to be one of the Union's most effective weapons of the war in the West. But how they would fare against Confederate forts was still untested.

The South couldn't build and maintain these massive boats; pitifully, the best they could do was use cotton bales to protect their boats ("cottonclads"). So the Confederacy placed its bet on river fortresses, which were to become Grant's chief targets in his western campaigns.

Chapter 1 - The Road to Shiloh

The Rivers and the Forts

Today, we forget that rivers were the super highways of the 19th century. Boats, powered by steam, some paddle-wheel and some propeller-driven, chugged up and down these waterways delivering heavy loads faster and cheaper than wagon transport. (Railroads were still something of a novelty, especially in the West. The first operating railroad in the US was constructed back East in 1827.) Rivers were also important economically because factories and towns tended to cluster along rivers due to the ease of shipping product and receiving raw materials. Rivers would freeze in the North during the winter, but rarely in the South, where river traffic operated throughout the year.

In the West, there were three major rivers, along with their many tributaries, that wriggled like arteries deep into the Confederacy's body - the Cumberland, the Tennessee, and the Mississippi Rivers. If the Union could seize control of these arteries, in a matter of days it could send soldiers, supplies and armaments flowing south into Tennessee, Mississippi and Alabama, and quickly metastasize into the Confederate heartland. And once the Federal army landed, it was easy to supply by river, at least until the troops advanced too far inland.

Coincidentally, all three of these rivers converged, or nearly converged, within 40 miles of each other at the southern tip of Illinois near Cairo, Illinois and Paducah, Kentucky.

The Cumberland River

The Cumberland River begins somewhere in the Cumberland Valley of Kentucky, not far north of Knoxville, Tennessee, and flows generally west through part of Kentucky, before dipping south into middle Tennessee, and then turning north and converging near Paducah, Kentucky with the Ohio River, which in turn empties into the Mississippi River at Cairo. Critically, the Cumberland River runs through Nashville, Tennessee, an important Confederate city, second only to New Orleans in size in the western Confederacy.

The South protected this waterway with Fort Donelson, near Dover, Tennessee.

The Tennessee River

The Tennessee River begins somewhere near Chattanooga, Tennessee and flows west though Alabama before turning north into Tennessee and, like the Cumberland, empties into the Ohio River near Paducah, Kentucky. If the North could take the Tennessee River, its boats could steam all the way south though western Tennessee to Florence, Alabama. From there, the boats couldn't go any farther due to rapids near Florence at a place called Muscle Shoals.

To protect this river, the South built a fort, Fort Henry, on the eastern side of the Tennessee River in what is now Stewart County, Tennessee. (In later years, the fort's location was submerged when the river was widened). It was only about 11 miles east of Fort Donelson, which guarded the Cumberland River as already mentioned.

Brig. Gen.
John B. Floyd
1806 - 1863

The Mississippi River

By far the biggest of the rivers was and is the Mississippi, which runs 2,400 miles from northern Minnesota. Besides Missouri and Kentucky, it flows through three Southern states - Arkansas, Mississippi, and Louisiana - all the way to the Gulf of Mexico at New Orleans. If the North could seize this river, it would cut the Confederacy in half.

Brig. Gen.
Gideon J. Pillow
1806 - 1878

To guard this vital river, the South initially built a fort at Columbus, Kentucky, as already discussed. But if and when Forts Henry and Donelson fell, the South would be forced to abandon Columbus and fall back to another fortress at Island No. 10, where the Mississippi River corkscrews in a hairpin turn near the town of New Madrid, Missouri.

But at the moment, because Polk's Columbus fortress on the Mississippi River was too formidable, all the important Union commanders in the West, including Halleck, agreed that the lowest hanging fruit were Fort Henry on the Tennessee River, and Fort Donelson on the Cumberland River. The advance on these forts was not, as often thought, solely Grant's idea.

Brig. Gen.
Simon Bolivar Buckner
1823 - 1914

Nor was it Lincoln's idea. The President was anxious for an advance into the eastern Tennessee mountains, where there were few slaves and much Union sentiment, but Halleck, Buell, and possibly McClellan, who was the Commander of the Army at that time, prevailed on him to accept an advance on the South's river highways.

Fort Henry

So, in early February 1862, Grant loaded 15,000 soldiers on transports, escorted by Foote's four ironclads and two timberclads, and sailed south in what would be one of the first, and certainly the largest, joint amphibious operation in American history up until that time. The armada's trailing smoke painted the sky with a dark, ominous cloud "*as far as the eye could see.*" The first target on Grant's list was Fort Henry, a poorly situated and incomplete fortification on

the Kentucky-Tennessee border, guarding the Tennessee River and manned by 3,400 Confederates. The overall Southern commander in the West, Gen. Albert Sidney Johnston, stationed more or less in the center of the Confederate defensive line at Bowling Green, Kentucky, had ordered his subordinate, Maj. Gen. Leonidas Polk, to complete the fortifications along the Tennessee River, including Fort Henry, but for whatever reason Polk neglected to do so. The fort's new commander, Gen. Lloyd Tilghman, a West Pointer, wrote Johnston that the fort was placed in a location "*without one redeeming feature.*" And just to be certain he was clear, he added, "*The history of military engineering records no parallel in this case.*" And if that wasn't enough, the river was 14 feet higher than normal due to heavy rains, with water nearly reaching the mouths of the Confederate cannon and threatening to flood the ammunition magazines.

The Union gunboats attacked the fort on February 6th and quickly pulverized it. Meanwhile, Grant's army was approaching by land. But the fort surrendered to the gunboats, allowing Grant to march in unopposed without firing a shot. Tilghman and most of his men managed to escape to Fort Donelson.

The untested Union ironclads had won their first victory against a Confederate fort. Ominously, however, even in its decrepid state, the fort managed to knock out one of the four ironclads, hitting the boat's boiler and scalding 30 sailors to death.

Fort Donelson

Well! That seemed easy enough. So Grant marched his men 11 miles to the east to attack Fort Donelson on the Cumberland River. Foote's gunboats sailed back north on the Tennessee River, then east on the Ohio River, and then south down the Cumberland River to do to Ft. Donelson what they had done to Ft. Henry.

Grant and his scouts assumed Fort Donelson was as weak as Fort Henry. Grant even sent a message to Halleck, stating that he planned to take Donelson

Chapter 1 - The Road to Shiloh

Gunboat Atttack on Ft. Donelson

"*within a day*." Grant simply surrounded the fort and waited for Foote's gunboats to sail down and blast the fort into surrender.

But in this Grant was wildly overly optimistic. Ft. Donelson was a whole different ball game than Ft. Henry. The fort was a well-placed earthen fort on a 130-foot bluff, manned with 17,000 troops, plus a separate command of 1,000 cavalry under Nathan Bedford Forest. And it had 11 large cannon facing the Cumberland River.

But unfortunately for the Confederacy, the fort was commanded by two military imbeciles: Maj. Gens. John B. Floyd and Gideon Pillow. The senior of the two, Floyd, was a politician, not a military man. The second in command, Pillow, was so incompetent that he was the only Confederate general that Grant held in total contempt, having known Floyd during the Mexican War.

Appointing these two incompetents to command such a vital position would be Confederate General Albert Sidney Johnston's first and greatest mistake in his short tenure as commander of the Confederates' western army.

Third in command was Brig. Gen. Simon Bolivar Buckner, a West Point classmate of Grant. Because of his military background, Buckner probably would have been the best choice to command the fort. Even better would have been an experienced general like William Hardee. But Johnston put Floyd and Pillow in charge. Why he entrusted so critical a post those two is a mystery. In Floyd's case, Johnston may have chosen him as a favor because Floyd was a prewar political ally of Johnston, and he had also brought Johnston a number of Virginia regiments. In any case, it was a disastrous mistake. One of Johnston's greatest weakness seems to have been his lack of ruthlessness in choosing and directing subordinates. He was by nature too trusting.

At 3pm on February 14th, Commodore Foote and four ironclads abreast chugged confidently toward the fort, their stacks belching smoke at full steam, followed as usual by the two timberclads, the Lexington and Tyler.

At about 3:30 pm, within a mile of the fort, they opened fire with their big 64-pounders. The problem was that the fort had 128-pounders, and the Confederate gunners had the ranges precisely sited, using landmarks along the river banks.

It was a massacre. The Confederates blasted the ironclads to pieces, with sailors dismembered or scalded by hot steam from exploding boilers.

The captain of one of the gunboats, the *Carondelet*, described the carnage:

"We heard the deafening crack of busting shells, the crash of solid shot, and the whizzing fragments of shell and wood as they sped through the vessel. A shot hit the pilot house, killing one of the pilots. They came harder and faster, taking flag staffs and smoke stacks and tearing off the side armor as lighting tears off the bark from a tree."

Then a port gun exploded. One of the gunners described it:

"It knocked us all down, killing none, but wounding over a dozen men and spreading dismay and confusion among us. Then the cry ran through the boat that we were on fire and my duty as pumpman called me to the pumps. While I was there, two shots entered our bow-ports and killed four men, and wounded several others. They were borne past me, three with their heads off."

Meanwhile, Foote had been standing in the wheelhouse of his flagship, the *St. Louis*, when a shell slammed in, killing the pilot and severing the Commodore's foot.

Three of the gunboats drifted down river, back north, completely out of control, while the fourth, the *Carondelet*, managed to retire under its own steam after taking 54 direct hits.

So much for the theory that gunboats were a match for river forts!

Clearly, if Grant was going to take the fort, it would have to be by siege with his infantry. A thousand miles away, Lincoln, whose 11-year-old son Willie lay dying in an upstairs bedroom in the White House, was anxiously watching affairs at Donelson and literally begging Halleck to take that fort, telegraphing him, *"Our success or failure at Fort Donelson is vastly important, and I beg you to put your soul into the effort."*

Back inside the fort, Floyd and Pillow had correctly concluded that the fort couldn't be defended from a long siege; but they also felt they were too outnumbered to face the Federals on open ground. So they decided to break out the next morning and force open a route to Nashville. That night, in a howling wind with temperatures in the teens and 3 inches of snow blanketing the ground, 10,000 Rebels slipped outside the fort and deployed to attack Grant's right wing, which was commanded by McClernand, now a newly appointed major general and division commander.

Many of Grant's troops were suffering heavily from the cold. This was February. But the weather had been unusually warm, and on the hot march from Ft. Henry to Ft. Donelson, many of the troops had foolishly discarded their coats. Now, suddenly the weather changed, and the soldiers were freezing. The Federal soldiers' struggle to keep warm no doubt distracted them.

The Confederate Sortie

The Confederates struck at daybreak, catching Grant totally by surprise, and not for the last time. Grant knew both Floyd and Pillow and considered them to be dolts who would sit tamely inside the fort and await his siege. He was not even on the field when the attack began, and not for the last time. The wounded Commodore Foote couldn't leave his boat, and he requested Grant meet him there for a conference on what to do next. Grant was riding back from that conference, making slow progress over the icy and rutted road, when a frantic messenger reached him with the news that the Confederates were attacking McClernand, and his division was in big trouble.

Another of Grant's division commanders, Maj. Gen. Lewis "Lew" Wallace, a 35-year-old lawyer and politician from Indiana who would later achieve fame as the author of the novel, *Ben-Hur*, witnessed the attack. His vivid description demonstrates his writing chops:

> "The wood rang with a monstrous clangor of musketry, as if a million men were beating empty barrels with iron hammers ... The roar never slackened. Men fell by the score, reddening the snow with their blood. Close to the ground the flame of musketry and cannon tinted everything a lurid red. Limbs dropped from trees on heads below, as if shorn by an army of cradlers ..."

Wallace ordered part of his division to assist McClernand, saving McClernand's division from total collapse.

Now Grant reached the field. Shown haversacks of dead Confederates which contained extra rations, he concluded correctly that the attack was actually a retreat, and that the trapped Confederates were trying to break out. He told everyone in sight, *"The one who attacks now will be victorious!"*

He decided that since the Confederates' were trying to break out on his right flank, they must be weak on his left flank. So, he ordered a counterattack on that flank, which was held by 55-year-old division commander, Maj. Gen. Charles F. Smith. Over six-feet tall with a flowing white mustache, Smith was a highly esteemed general who had been commandant of West Point at the time Grant attended. They got on well, but Grant was slightly embarrassed to be Smith's senior in rank.

Grant ordered Smith to strike the Rebels hard on the left. Smith replied, "*I will do it.*" *How* he did it became a legend in Grant's army. Again, here's Lew Wallace's vivid description:

> "The air about him twittered with minie-bullets. Erect as if on review, he rode on, timing the gait of his horse with the movement of his colors. He never for a moment doubted the courage of volunteers; they were not regulars – that was all. If properly led he believed they would storm the gates of His Satanic Majesty. A soldier said, 'I was nearly scared to death, but I saw the old man's white mustache over his shoulder, and went on.'
>
> "On to the abatis [wooden defensive stakes] the regiments moved, leaving a trail of dead and wounded behind. There the fire seemed to get trebly hot, and there some of the men halted, whereupon, seeing the hesitation, General Smith put his cap on the point of his sword, held it aloft, and called out, 'No flinching now, my lads! – Here – This is the way! Come on!"

Dr. John H. Brinton, Grant's surgeon, picks up the story in a letter to a fellow physician:

"You ought to have heard old C. F. Smith cursing as he led his storming regiments. 'Damn you gentlemen, I see skulkers! I'll have none of that here. Come on you volunteers! This is your chance. You volunteered to be killed for love of country, and now you can be! You are damned volunteers! I'm only a soldier, and don't want to be killed, but you came here to be killed, and now you can be!"

Now, back to Lew Wallace:

"He picked a path through the jagged limbs of trees, holding his cap all the time in sight; and the effect was magical. The men swarmed in after him – not all of them, alas! Up the ascent he rode, and up they followed. At the last moment the keepers of the rifle-pits clambered out and fled."

Smith's counter-attack completely unglued Floyd and Pillow, who had just sent Johnston a telegram stating, "*The day is ours,*" meaning the breakout had succeeded. And indeed, their morning attack had broken the Union line on the right and the way was still open for the Confederates to escape, regardless of the Federal counter-attack on the Union left. But the two Confederate generals proceeded to snatch defeat from the jaws of victory. For some reason, never adequately explained, they ordered their troops back *in* to the fort, trapping them in what was now a prison. Only Nathan Forrest and about 500 cavalry and some infantry escaped, with Forrest saying, "*I did not come here for the purpose of surrendering my command.*"

If that wasn't bad enough, Floyd and Pillow absconded, leaving the unpleasant duty of surrendering the fort to the hapless Simon Buckner. Floyd had a special reason not to be captured. Prior to start of the war, he was the US Secretary of War, and after he resigned it was discovered that he had been using his position to quietly authorize the shipment of US weapons to Southern armories. He had committed treason and was a good candidate for the gallows.

As mentioned earlier, Grant and Buckner were classmates at West Point. Shortly before the war, Grant was desperate for money and he traveled to Washington in a futile attempt to collect an old debt. So broke that he couldn't even pay his hotel bill, and on the verge of being evicted, Grant called

Chapter 1 - The Road to Shiloh

upon an old army buddy – Buckner – who came to his rescue and guaranteed the debt. (He didn't actually loan Grant money, as has often been reported.) Now Buckner was perhaps hoping Grant would be a gentleman and allow him to march off with his 15,000 troops, as had happened with the Federals at Fort Sumter and during the Revolutionary War.

Brig. Gen. Charles F. Smith 1807 - 1862

No Terms

The next morning, February 15th, Buckner sent Grant a message asking for terms, given the "*present state of affairs.*" A Rebel party delivered Buckner's message to the first Federal commander they encountered, which was C. F. Smith. Smith carried the message to Grant, who was sleeping on a mattress in an old farmhouse. After handing the message to Grant, Smith said he was half frozen and needed a drink. Grant's surgeon gave Smith a flask, and while he toasted his feet near the fireplace and nursed his drink, Grant read the letter aloud. "*No terms to the damn Rebels,*" said Smith. Grant chuckled as he wrote out his reply: "*No terms except an unconditional and immediate surrender can be accepted. I propose to move immediately upon your works.*"

Buckner sent Grant back an indignant response, referring to "*the ungenerous and unchivalrous terms which you propose.*" But the next morning he was compelled to surrender the fort with all its artillery and munitions, and costing the South and Johnston 15,000 irreplaceable troops, along with control of the Cumberland River. Due to the policy of prisoner exchange, most of these troops would be back in service within seven months, but that would be far too late to be of any assistance at Shiloh. Those captured troops might well have changed the outcome of the future battle, where Johnston would go into battle with 40,000 troops, instead of 55,000.

Grant's victory hadn't come without cost; the Federals suffered 5,000 casualties in taking Donelson. Nonetheless, the loss of the two forts was a catastrophe for the South, opening an enormous gash in its western defenses from which it never recovered; many historians mark these twin defeats as the beginning of the end of the Confederacy - the turning point of the war. Now Federal armies, via boat, had free range up the Tennessee River, allowing penetration into northern Alabama as well as eastern Tennessee; and along the way, the Federals could destroy factories and cut vital bridges. Also, command of the Cumberland River gave the Federals access to Nashville, the capital of Tennessee, which surrendered without a fight on February 25th. Also, Polk's bastion at Columbus – the one he violated Kentucky sovereignty to seize – was now effectively cut off since Federal forces could easily blockade the river and fort from the south. So, Columbus had to be abandoned, much to Polk's chagrin. Within a few days, Union gunboats were steaming down the Tennessee River as far as Florence, Alabama, happily blasting Southern river traffic, bridges, and factories along the way.

Last but not least, the capture of the two forts effectively cemented the state of Kentucky into the Union. Besides its potential man-power, Kentucky, along with Tennessee, would have been one of the biggest suppliers of grain and horses to the South.

All of this brought Grant national acclaim and promotion to major general. With loss after loss in the East, suddenly, seemingly out of nowhere, here were two smashing victories in the West! These were the first major Union victories of the war, and Lincoln was thrilled (although he was also burdened and in mourning over the death of his 11-year-old son, Willie). Captured Rebel flags from the two forts were rushed to Washington where they were given a public viewing in the House of Representatives. That night all government buildings were illuminated. The media hailed U. S. Grant as "Unconditional Surrender Grant." (One or more of the newspapers mentioned that Grant had smoked a cigar during the heat of the battle. Admirers now sent him so many boxes of cigars that he gave up smoking a pipe and switched to more expensive cigars – a habit that would eventually kill him with throat cancer).

The Federals Push South

The downside to Grant's celebrity was that he incurred the intense jealousy of his boss, Halleck, who was soon sniffing Grant's trail, looking for excuses to undercut this upstart rival. (Hearing of Grant's victory at Fort Donelson, Halleck was amazed that "*a drunkard*" could win such a prize). And Halleck found a sympathetic ear with *his* boss, Gen. George B. McClellan, who also had concerns about Grant's drinking, and who no-doubt was also jealous of Grant's fame.

(Before war, McClellan had visited the Oregon post where Grant was stationed, apparently in the middle of his drinking bout, leaving McClellan with a bad impression of Grant. As soon as the war started, Grant had traveled to Washington to request a command from McClellan; McClellan had refused to even see him.)

Halleck ordered Grant's army (which we'll now call the Army of Tennessee, although it didn't officially acquire that name until months after the battle of Shiloh) to proceed up the Tennessee River to Savannah, Tennessee, just north of the Mississippi border. (The Tennessee River, as well as the Cumberland River, flow south to north in this region so, sailing "up river" means sailing south). Meanwhile, Grant would await Halleck's arrival from St. Louis, as well the arrival of another Union army commanded by Maj. Gen. Don Carlos Buell, now also under Halleck's command.

Buell's army, the Army of Ohio, marched from central Kentucky into Tennessee. Buell, a competent but not brilliant commander with a reputation as a stern taskmaster, was ordered to take Nashville, which, with its 30,000 residents was the second largest city in the western Confederacy after New Orleans. It was also a critical industrial base with warehouses packed with military supplies and beef, and it contained important iron foundries.

Maj. Gen. Don Carlos Buell 1818 - 1898

The cautious Buell was taking his time. But Lincoln was intensely concerned about capturing Ft. Donelson, and at his suggestion, Halleck had previously ordered Buell to send one of his divisions commanded by Brig. Gen. William Nelson to reinforce Grant at Fort Donelson. The division arrived too late to be of use, but it was still temporarily under Grant's command. Hearing that Nashville had been abandoned by the Confederates and was wide open, Grant didn't hesitate. He promptly ordered Nelson to sail upriver on transports to seize Nashville, which Nelson did. So, Grant had captured Nashville, Buell's objective, with Buell's own men! The enraged Buell wrote to McClellan, his good friend, that "*My troops are being filched from me!*"

By now, Grant was on the wrong side of three powerful generals – McClellan, Halleck, and Buell. Halleck lost no time in spreading manufactured allegations that Grant was drinking again, and also that he was not properly communicating with Halleck in St. Louis. (It would turn out that a telegraph operator stationed in Cairo, Illinois between the two Union headquarters, was a Southern sympathizer who, before deserting to the Confederate army, destroyed a number of Grant's cables to Halleck). With McClellan's approval, Halleck relieved Grant and turned over command of the Army of Tennessee to Grant's senior division commander, Charles Smith. So, on March 13th, Smith sailed down to Savannah, Tennessee to take charge of the soon-to-be-arriving Union forces there, while Grant was sent into exile at Fort Henry.

Now Buell would march south from Nashville to join Smith and his army at Savannah on the Tennessee River. And there was yet a third Federal army in eastern Kentucky, commanded by Maj. Gen. John Pope, which was now also under Halleck's command, and which would also soon be joining Grant and Buell. Once Halleck arrived, his combined armies – nearly 125,000 strong – would march south to Corinth, Mississippi, a vital military objective.

But in the meantime, Lincoln ordered Halleck to either bring formal charges against Grant or return him to command. Grant, after all, had won a battle – something precious few other Union generals had done. Also, nine of Grant's senior officers, including even McClernand, and also Charles Smith, came to Grant's defense, signing a letter deploring his removal. So Halleck grudgingly restored Grant to command of the new Army of Tennessee in late March. Grant was immensely grateful to Halleck, whom he considered to be a friend and "*one of the greatest men of the age*," completely unaware that it was mainly Halleck who was slipping knives into his back. Grant didn't discover Halleck's treachery until after the war when he read Halleck's dispatches.

With Grant back in command, Smith was effectively demoted back to commanding Grant's 2nd Division. However, shortly after assuming command of the division, Smith badly scraped his leg while entering a row boat, causing a serious infection that forced him to bed and would eventually kill him. While he was incapacitated, Brig. Gen. W. H. L. Wallace (no relation to Lew Wallace) replaced him as commander of the 2nd Division.

So while Grant busied himself with his growing Army of Tennessee, and Buell's Army of Ohio made a leisurely march from Nashville to join Grant, Halleck prepared to sail down from St. Louis to take charge.

Chapter 1 - The Road to Shiloh

Importantly, Halleck gave strict orders to Grant, Smith, Buell, and everyone else, that under no circumstances were they to trigger any confrontations with the enemy until Halleck reached the scene.

Corinth - The Backbone of the Confederacy

Today, except for Civil War buffs, few people outside the state have ever heard of Corinth, Mississippi, a sleepy little town on the northeastern edge of the state, with a pre-Civil War population of 1,200. But in its day Corinth was almost as important to the Confederacy as Atlanta or Richmond.

This is not to say that visitors were fond of the place. Federal lieutenant and author, Ambrose Bierce, who would later occupy the town, described Corinth as "*a wretched place – the capital of a swamp.*" The Confederates who drilled there prior to the battle weren't impressed either. One Louisiana soldier described their encampment as "*a slough ... full of mud and surrounded by water.*" The white tents appeared to "*be floating about through the mist and rain.*" A Tennessee soldier wrote, "*The place where we are camped now is heavily timbered with oak and hickory with swamps around us in every direction and altogether, I think this is just about the poorest country I ever saw.*"

While Grant's victory at Fort Donelson threw open the Tennessee River to invasion as far south as Muscle Shoals, Alabama (near the city of Florence, Alabama), the primary objective was always Corinth. The town's strategic importance stemmed from the two major railroads that crossed there – the Mobile & Ohio and the Memphis & Charleston. The latter, called the "Confederacy's Backbone" or "The Vertebrae of the Confederacy," was especially critical to the South since it was the only direct line of communication between the eastern seaboard and the Mississippi River region. Also, if the Federals took Corinth, they could then easily much 100 miles directly west to the large Mississippi River port in Memphis, Tennessee.

Albert Sidney Johnston

The man assigned to stop the Union invasion was Gen. Albert Sidney Johnson, commander of all Southern forces in the west. A charismatic and highly respected West Pointer with a stellar reputation in the pre-war U.S. Army, Johnston was practically a legend in the South. He *looked* like a hero – handsome and "*powerfully made,*" over six feet tall with wavy gray hair and mustache. One story had him supposedly wading into a fight between a mountain lion and his pack of hunting dogs, and bashing the beast to death with his rifle butt. He commanded the 2US Cavalry, a famous unit that fought numerous Indian battles in Texas and the Great Plains. The regiment was remarkable for the number of prominent Civil War generals it spawned, including Robert E. Lee, who served as Johnston's second in command in the cavalry unit.

Back in 1837 Johnston had been appointed to command the army of the Republic of Texas. The appointment nearly got him killed when a jealous rival, Felix Huston, challenged him to a duel. At the appointed time, Johnston simply fired his pistol in the air, but Huston, who was supposed to be a crack shot, fired for real, but missed. The pistols were reloaded, and again Johnston fired in the air, and again Huston fired for real, but missed. This deadly game continued until finally, on the sixth attempt, Huston hit Johnston in the right hip, ending the duel. Oddly, Huston then apologized.

This wound would have repercussions a quarter of a century later at the battle at Shiloh, as we shall see.

In 1860, as a brigadier general, Johnston was appointed U.S. Commander of the Department of the Pacific. He and his family sailed to his new post on Alcatraz Island in San Francisco Bay. But they barely arrived when Texas, Johnston's adopted state, seceded. The Lincoln administration was well aware of Johnston's value; Winfield Scott, the then U.S. Army Commander, considered Johnston "the finest soldier he had ever commanded." When Texas seceded, the administration tried to entice Johnston to stay with the Union by promoting him to major general. But before the promotion even arrived, Johnston submitted his resignation on April 3, 1861.

Pvt. Phillip Stephenson of the 13th Arkansas, hung around Johnston's HQ one day and caught a glimpse of the general. "If ever a man looked the 'great man' Albert Sidney Johnston did. A martial figure, although dressed in civilian clothes. I saw him but once, a black felt 'slouch' hat shaded his features as he walked with head down as though buried in deep thought. He looked like an old Viking king!"

The only ships leaving San Francisco sailed for New York City. Fearing he would be arrested if he landed in New York, Johnston decided to travel by horse to Texas. After packing his family on a ship to New York, the 58-year-old Johnston and a dozen officers undertook an incredible two-month, 1,500 mile journey – a trip that would merit a book in itself – across the toughest and hottest deserts on the American continent, dodging U.S. Army patrols and Comanches and almost dying of thirst before finally reaching San Antonio, Texas. From there Johnston traveled by train and ship to Richmond, where Jeff Davis appointed him commander of the Confederate's Department of the West.

Whereas Lee's theater of operations would remain almost exclusively in the state of Virginia, with the only two brief and disastrous excursions into Pennsylvania and Maryland, Johnston's assigned territory stretched three or four times as far - all the way from eastern Kentucky to Indian territory in what is now Oklahoma. He hadn't nearly enough troops to cover this vast territory.

Gen.
Albert S. Johnson (k)
1803 - 1862

The Confederates Prepare

While the Federals prepared to invade, the Confederates weren't asleep. After the debacles at Forts Henry and Donelson, along with the fall of Columbus, Kentucky. Johnston, once the darling of the fickle and slightly hysterical Southern media, now became the medias' anti-Christ, and not without cause, Whereas the Southerners had become accustomed to victories, now suddenly they were being hit with defeat after defeat in the West.

And that wasn't all the bad news. In fact, since the beginning of the year, when the South seemed invincible, bad news from the west was suddenly flooding Richmond. On the 21st of January, Confederates under Brig. Gens. George B. Crittenden and Felix Zollicoffer suffered a defeat in eastern Kentucky near Knoxville at the Battle of Mill Springs, threatening to open up Johnston's eastern flank. Zollicoffer was killed and Crittenden was rumored to be drunk. A month and a half later, in early March, Confederates under Brig. Gen. Earl Van Dorn were defeated at the Battle of Pea Ridge in Arkansas.

Johnston was under tremendous pressure to *do*

Page 13

Chapter 1 - The Road to Shiloh

something. But while the press screamed for his head, Jefferson Davis stood by Johnston, stating, "*If Sidney Johnston is not a general, I have none.*" But for his own sake, as well as the sake of the Confederacy, Johnston had to find a way to halt the massive Union tide rolling into the Southern heartland.

The Union advance up the Tennessee River had split the Confederate defenders, with Johnston retaining command of the forces east of the Tennessee River. From Bowling Green, Kentucky, he led his army in a retreat southwest through northern Alabama to the southernmost bend of the Tennessee River.

In Grant's memoirs, he said he felt Johnston had "*lost heart*" after Donelson, and that he had abandoned Nashville too hastily, causing a panic there and the loss of precious materials. Grant felt there was no reason Johnston couldn't have made a stand on the east side of Cumberland River right there at Nashville, Also, after reading Johnston's reports after the war, Grant felt Johnston was too "indecisive and vacillating," and was "over-rated."

In any case, the Confederate forces west of the Tennessee River were now under the command of Gen. Pierre Gustave Toutant Beauregard, though Beauregard answered to Johnston.

"The Great Creole," born in Louisiana, was currently a darling of the Richmond press, for commanding the bombardment and surrender of Fort Sumter, which in fact wasn't much of a military achievement.

Gen. Pierre G. T. Beauregard
1818 - 1893

Also, he received undeserved credit for the victory at the First Battle of Bull Run.

But once in Richmond, he soon made himself a pest to Davis by spouting off to the newspapers about how the war should be run, and by extension, what Davis was doing wrong, infuriating Davis. Beauregard also had a habit of drawing grandiose and elaborate military plans that were unworkable because they had too many moving parts. With his French background, Beauregard adored Napoleon, and he had attended a high school in New York run by two of Napoleon's former generals. Beauregard never did anything militarily without Napoleon in mind.

Meanwhile, Johnston had been pleading for reinforcements. So, delighted to get Beauregard's mouth out of Richmond, Davis shipped him off to the beleaguered Johnston as a one-man reinforcement. (Federal General Halleck heard of Beauregard's transfer, along with a rumored, but non-existent, 15 regiments, which prompted Halleck to ship his army to Savannah, Tennessee.)

On Beauregard's arrival, Johnston put him to work supervising Polk's withdrawal of the western segment of the Southern forces from Columbus, Kentucky, leading the troops southward through west Tennessee into Mississippi. Although gaunt and emaciated from a recent throat operation, Beauregard took charge and did excellent work, and above all he kept a tight rein on Polk, which Johnston had failed to do.

The debacles at Forts Henry and Donelson were not solely Johnston's fault. With the loss of the Kentucky shield, he was defending a 400 mile front with just 57,500 troops, and facing double that number of Yankees. He had been pleading for reinforcements. But, partially due to meeting the hysterical demands of governors in Florida, Alabama and elsewhere, and partially because he felt that a young nation had to prove its viability to Europe by protecting its borders everywhere, Davis initially made the critical mistake of scattering troops around the South's coasts in a vain attempt to defend its entire territory at all points. Now, given the debacles in the West, Davis finally relented and agreed, a bit late, to concentrate and consolidate the western forces into a single, mobile army under Johnston.

And so, along with Johnston's army in Tennessee, more Southern troops were streaming to Corinth from Pensacola, Florida, from Columbus, Kentucky, and from Mississippi. All of these were temporarily under the command of Brig. Gen. Braxton Bragg. His troops had yet to see combat but they were the best trained Southern troops in the western theater since they had little to do in Florida but drill, and Bragg drilled them until they despised him. Bragg's troops rode to battle on boxcars of the Mobile & Ohio Railroad, arriving in Corinth before either Johnston or Beauregard, and securing the critical rail junction, at least for the moment.

Everyone it seemed was heading to Corinth, Mississippi.

2   The Union Encampment

March 17 – April 5

As discussed, the fall of Forts Donelson and Henry opened a route via the Cumberland and Tennessee Rivers through which Union gunboats and troops could quickly flow into the Confederate heartland. Anxious to capitalize on the situation, the Federals initially planned a simple raid up the Tennessee River to wreck some Rebel railroad iron. But once Halleck was appointed commander of the Department of Missouri in November of 1861, and after the fall of Forts Henry and Donelson, the raid idea mushroomed into a plan for a full-scale invasion to seize and hold Corinth and its vital railroad junction. Fully aware of the threat, Confederates began massing forces in Corinth.

On March 13th, while Grant remained in limbo at Fort Henry, Halleck's choice to command the expedition, Maj. Gen. C. F. Smith, organized 57 transports with 25,000-30,000 troops, escorted by the timberclads *Tyler* and *Lexington*. These two trusty boats would accompany the army throughout its early campaigns along both the Tennessee and Cumberland Rivers.

Smith then sailed deep into the Confederacy, arriving at the river town of Savannah, Tennessee, a village of about 800 strongly pro-Union residents. The transports, packed with troops four or five decks deep, anchored on both sides of the river. Corinth, the ultimate target, was now only about 30 miles south. Significantly, Savannah was on the opposite (east) side of the river from Corinth, which afforded the fledgling Union force some protection from any Confederate surprise attack.

While waiting for more troops, Smith ordered two raids: first, he sent Brig. Gen. Lew Wallace and his 2nd Division to Crumps Landing, about four miles south of Savannah but on the west side of the river, to seize the landing as a beachhead for future inland raids on Confederate railroads. Secondly, Smith ordered Brig. Gen. William T. Sherman to steam south 22 miles up the Tennessee River and wreck some important railroad bridges near the small village of Eastport, Mississippi – about 20 miles east of Corinth, after which Sherman and his men would sail back to Savannah.

So on March 14, Sherman and his 5th Division sailed south in 17 transports. Along the way, only about nine or ten miles south of Savannah, Sherman noticed a small landing on the west side of the river, which the ship's captain explained was the usual landing spot for river travelers heading to Corinth. It was called *Pittsburg Landing*. It wasn't much to look at; just "*three log cabins and a pig sty*," according to one traveler. A road, the Pittsburg-Corinth Road, cut through a bluff down to the river there. Near the edge of the bluff on the north side of the road stood a log cabin, with another about 100 yards back across a ravine. A third cabin was about 200 yards south of the road. A cotton field about 200 yards wide and a half mile long ran along the back of the bluff; behind the field was thick forest. The landing had been settled back in 1848 by the family of the late Pittser Tucker, whose nickname was "Pitt." He set up a trading post there, selling among other things, liquor, serving as sort of a river-based 7/11 convenience store, making the landing a popular stopover for thirsty steamboat crewmen. The landing became known locally as "Pitts Landing," and eventually, "Pittsburg Landing."

The locals were hardscrabble cotton and corn farmers living in log cabins – about three dozen families scattered throughout the future battlefield. There were few slaves here. This whole area was a hard, mean country surrounded by thick forest and swamps, and the farther south one traveled across the border into Mississippi, the harder and the meaner the country became. Water was everywhere - in the swamps, the river, the creeks and, as we shall see, pouring from overhead. The swamps must have been breeding grounds for mosquitos and all kinds of diseases, and were no doubt packed with moccasins and rattlers. Economically, the area is no paradise even today, but at least most of the swamps have been drained.

The Landing was located in Hardin County. In the 1861 Tennessee referendum on secession, the majority of residents, mostly on the eastern side of the river, voted to stay in the Union. But on the western side, where the Landing was, most young males had been drilling to fight for the Confederacy.

Sherman sent back word to Smith, suggesting that troops be posted at this Landing. Smith complied by sending Brig. Gen. Stephen A. Hurlbut to anchor, but

Page 15

not disembark, his 4th Division next to the Landing.

Meanwhile, around 7pm that same evening, Sherman and his men landed at the mouth of Yellow Creek near Eastport, Mississippi, and he set off looking for trouble. He found plenty, though not the kind he expected. Sheets of icy rain churned the roads into muddy quagmires, turning creeks into raging rivers impossible to ford. Two or three men drowned. The cannons had to be dragged underwater through the creeks. Sherman and his troops were forced to make a soggy retreat back to the transports without so much as even having seen a railroad track.

Drenched but undaunted, the general and his little armada sailed back north, still looking for another spot within easy march of some Rebel railroad iron. Remembering that small landing he had passed on his way south - Pittsburg Landing - Sherman decided it just might fit the bill. When he reached the Landing, Hurlbut's division was already anchored there to guard the place, though his men remained aboard the transports. So Sherman and his division, nearly 8,000 strong, disembarked on the 15th. But the incessant rain followed Sherman like a curse, causing the usual problems with overflowing creeks blocking his march. The whole raid, grandly called the "Yellow Creek expedition," was a bust. Sherman's cavalry did manage to reach a railroad bridge and burn it, but the Confederates repaired it within a day. One Ohio officer wrote of the whole affair,

"A very silly expedition under the circumstances and adding hundreds of weakly men to the sick list."

But while at Pittsburg Landing, Sherman noticed that it was an ideal camping location with space to accommodate 100,000 men or more – about the size of Halleck's army once Pope's and Buell's forces reached the area. The location's flanks were protected from both the north and southeast by large creeks – the Owl and Snake Creeks to the north, and Lick Creek to the southwest. Creeks around Shiloh were not the benign, idyllic creeks that exist throughout most of America. Instead, these creeks had carved out gorges of heavy underbrush, sometimes with banks 40'-60' high; and during the rainy season, the water could be 30' or more deep, and fast moving. They were nearly impassable during the rainy season, except at fords which usually included crude bridges. And so, with these creeks on each side, and the river protecting their backs to the northeast, the Federal camp would have natural protection from all sides, except one – a three-mile

Chapter 2 - The Union Encampment

opening to the southwest.

Sherman reported all the advantages of the Landing to his superior, Brig. Gen. Smith. Seizing Corinth would require an initial base of operations somewhere on the western side of the Tennessee River anyway, and Pittsburg Landing seemed as good a spot as any. So on March 15, Smith selected it as the concentration point for Union forces. And he now ordered Hurlbut to disembark his 4th Division there, following Sherman's 5th Division. By March 17th, both divisions were camped at the Landing.

But just prior to that, due to pressure from the Lincoln administration, Halleck was forced to reinstate Grant as commander of the Army of Tennessee, relegating Smith back to commander of the 2nd Division. But on March 12th, while conferring with division commander Lew Wallace aboard a transport at Crumps Landing, Smith badly scraped his leg while transferring from one boat to another, causing an infection which incapacitated him and which would kill him within a month. Brig. Gen. W. H. L. Wallace (no relation to Lew Wallace) replaced Smith and now assumed command of the 2nd Division.

Grant's First Mistake

When Grant arrived in Savannah on March 17th and assumed command, he was concerned about how dangerously divided the army was, with two completely green divisions at Pittsburg Landing, one at Crumps Landing, and two divisions on the east bank at Savannah, plus another division on the way from Cairo, Illinois.

He personally inspected the Landing on the day he arrived and approved of Smith's choice as the best location for the army's advanced base. This turned out to be his first major decision and his first major mistake. Though the creeks and river provided the Landing with good natural protection, it was still on the west side of the river – as were the Confederates just 22 miles south at Corinth.

But history is perhaps too harsh on Grant on this point. Yes, had Grant located his army back at Savannah on the *east* side of the river and waited for Buell to arrive, his men there would have been much safer from Confederate surprises. But the logistics weren't quite that simple. When Grant assumed command he was presented with the reality that two totally green divisions were already camped at Pittsburg Landing, and one veteran division camped six miles north at Crumps Landing. Individually, either of these camps would have been toast had

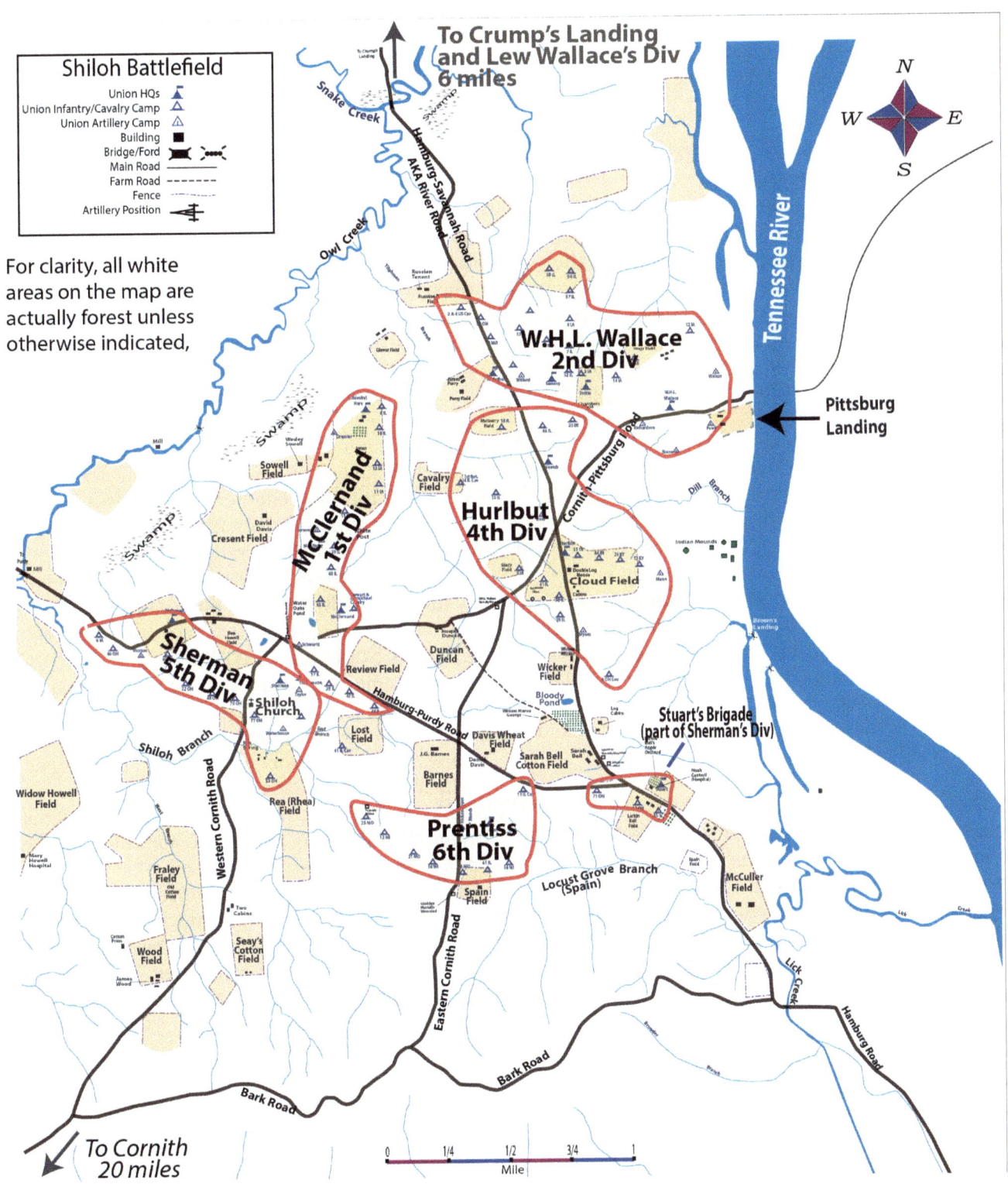

The locations of the division camps at Pittsburg Landing.

Johnston struck them.

Buell had been expected to arrive on March 24, but his march had been delayed for an unknown time due to a swollen river in his path - the Duck River - where the bridges had been destroyed by the Confederates. (Buell would later be criticized for not having brought pontoons with him). Ultimately, it would take him 10 days to cross that river, and so now he was still over two weeks away from Savannah. But Grant didn't know that.

So what was he supposed to do with the three divisions at the landings while he waited for Buell in Savannah? Loading and unloading boats – thousands of troops and horses, artillery, ammunition, food, wagons, medicines, tents, rations, etc. – was not a trivial process; it was a probably at least a full-day operation just to load a single division, and we know from Sherman's expedition that a single division required 17 transports. Should he load these divisions back on transports, just days after they had unloaded and pitched camp, then unload them back at Savannah, only to have to reload them days later when Buell arrived, and then ship and unload these 60,000+ troops again back at Pittsburg Landing? Not only would the troops think he was crazy, but it's a question whether there enough transports available for all this loading and unloading. Many of the transports were busy making round trips back and forth to Cairo for supplies. And how long would this process take? And what if the Confederates struck while any of these divisions where half loaded and half unloaded?

These are the types of annoying, mundane issues that arm-chair Napoleons tend to ignore, but no doubt Grant, a former quartermaster, was keenly aware of these problems.

Right or wrong, he decided that the best option was to concentrate his remaining army in one place – Pittsburg Landing – by moving *two* divisions *from* Savannah, rather than *three* divisions *to* Savannah and then shipping them right back to the Landing. In fact, that was probably the best option; his real mistake was not being more vigilant once the troops were camped there.

Also, the new commander was thinking offensively, and deploying his army on the west side of the river at Pittsburg Landing made it easier for him to get at the Confederates. Neither he nor anyone else seemed to give any thought to the possibility that the Confederate Army might strike *them*.

Chapter 2 - The Union Encampment

So, the following day, March 18, more Union troops descended upon the once-sleepy Landing. With transports now arriving daily, the muddy river bank was soon a hive of activity, crammed with off-loading transports docked five deep. By the end of March, Grant had six divisions in the area – five divisions of 37,500 men at Pittsburg Landing, and a sixth one of 7,300 men at Crumps Landing five miles downstream (north). Supporting Grant's infantry were 21 artillery batteries of 102 guns, plus three cavalry regiments.

As poorly as Johnston's Rebels were armed, Grant's troops weren't much better off. Most of them were armed with smoothbore muskets altered to percussion. Confederates who picked up these guns up during the battle usually discarded them because the barrels were as large as gas pipes and the hammers difficult to cock. Only a few Union regiments were fully equipped with the excellent British Enfield or the US Springfield rifle-muskets, though a few other regiments had one or two companies armed with Enfields, or the more cumbersome and less desirable Austrian rifle-muskets. A few Confederate units also had Springfield and Enfield Rifles.

But on balance, both sides would be about equally, and mostly poorly, armed in the coming battle.

Grant's Second Mistake

Grant steamed down to Pittsburg Landing nearly every day. But because there seemed to be no hurry, and because it was a convenient point to meet Buell who was expected momentarily, Grant maintained his headquarters at Savannah in a house called the Cherry Mansion, about eight miles north of his troops at the Landing and on the opposite side of the river. This was his second mistake.

However, he was planning to move his headquarters on the 6th, the day of the attack, not because of any concern about an attack but because one of his division commanders – Brig. Gen. John A. McClernand – had just be promoted to major general, outranking Sherman at the Landing. Grant distrusted McClernand, a political appointee without military training, and so he needed to be on the scene to prevent McClernand from taking control. Also, while Grant was inspecting the Landing in the rain a couple of nights prior to the battle, his horse slipped in the mud and fell on the general, spraining his ankle so badly that his boot had to be cut off and putting him on crutches throughout the coming battle and on a cane for some time after that. This

A modern photo of the Cherry Mansion in Savannah, TN, about 8-10 miles north of Pittsburg Landing. This house served as Grant's HQ prior to the battle. His room was on the second floor on the right. Later, two senior Union generals, W. H. L. Wallace and Charles F. Smith, died at the house.

may have contributed to his decision to remain in Savannah a while longer.

McClernand, an ambitious Illinois politician, commanded the 1st Division, now also camped at Pittsburg Landing. His division had done much fighting at Fort Donelson, and so was considered a "veteran" division.

Camped next to McClernand's men was another "veteran" division, the 2nd Division. Initially commanded by Charles Smith, but because of Smith's subsequent leg injury, it was now under the command of a man Grant had great faith in – Brig. Gen. William H. L. Wallace.

The final veteran division, the 3rd, was commanded by Brig. Gen. Lew Wallace (no relation to W. H. L. Wallace). The 3rd Division commander from Indiana is today best remembered as the author of the novel, *Ben-Hur*, which he wrote after the war. It was Lew Wallace's division that was camped five miles north of Pittsburg Landing at Crumps Landing. Like McClernand, he was a political appointee, and therefore suspect by professional soldiers like Grant and Sherman. But he had performed well at Ft. Donelson, saving McClernand's division from collapse.

The other three divisions at Pittsburg Landing – the 4th (Hurlbut's), 5th (Sherman's) and 6th (Prentiss') Divisions – couldn't have been much greener. The former two were organized just two weeks earlier, just prior to the army's departure up the Tennessee River; and the third one, Brig. Gen. Benjamin Prentiss' 6th Division, was actually formed at the Pittsburg Landing encampment.

Sherman's 5th being one of the first two divisions to disembark at the Landing, the then commander, Charles Smith, had ordered Sherman to push farther inland from the Landing to allow room for the later-arriving divisions. Then, because the spots close to the Landing were already taken by the time it arrived, Prentiss' just-formed 6th division had to pitch its tents on the outskirts of the encampment next to Sherman's greenhorns, but with a dangerous 650 yard gap between the two camps.

The end result was that the two greenest divisions in Grant's army – the Sherman's 5th and Prentiss' 6th – not much more than armed civilians wearing uniforms, would be smack on the army's front line in the coming battle.

Sherman

Forty-one-year-old, six foot Brig. Gen. William T. Sherman (his family called him "Cump" for his middle name of "Tecumseh") was under a cloud. To begin with, he was at war with journalists (*"...dirty, irresponsible, corrupt, malicious, a shame and a reproach to a civilized people; the most contemptible race of men that ever existed"*) for, among other reasons, they kept writing that he was demented. And for that reason he attracted reporters like flies on molasses. And who could blame them? Even in a formal photograph he couldn't keep his red hair from spiking out like a wet chicken. As fidgety as a thoroughbred race horse, profane, sarcastic, always talking, bubbling with ideas – some harebrained and some not.

All of this, plus his bluntness, almost got him kicked out of the army back in

Brig. Gen. William T. Sherman (w) 1820 - 1891

1861, when he started making shocking statements about the carnage there would be in this war. At a time when almost everyone on both sides expected a short war, Sherman, who knew the South better than most Southerners, scared hell out of everyone by claiming that it would take at least 200,000 troops just to subdue the Rebels in the Mississippi Valley alone. (Ultimately that was a vast underestimate).

But throughout his career before the war, important men saw something special in Sherman. For example, Winfield Scott, the Commanding General of the US, chose Sherman as his aide. Prior to California achieving statehood, when it was under military control, Sherman was selected as the aide to the colonel who governed the future state. He later became Superintendent of a school in Louisiana that eventually became Louisiana State University. He was president of a bank in California. And just prior to war being declared, he was hired as president of a railroad in St. Louis. When the war came he commanded a regiment as a colonel in the First Battle of Bull Run. And after the Federal defeat, Lincoln took a buggy ride out to view the troops near Washington. The only formation he found in good order was Sherman's, who was then invited to ride around with Lincoln in the buggy as Lincoln gave pep talks to Sherman's regiments.

Once war was declared, Sherman had been put in charge of the Union forces in Kentucky by accident. Strangely, Sherman never liked being in senior command. He always wanted to be the wing-man, as he would later be with Grant. He only accepted the command in Kentucky, if he was second in command. So, Robert Anderson, who had commanded at the surrender of Ft. Sumter, was given the senior post. But the pressure was too much for Anderson, and he soon requested to be relieved, leaving Sherman in charge of Kentucky.

Sherman soon worked himself into a frazzle with worry about the Confederates launching an attack on his command.

A reporter once said of him, "*When I first saw him in Missouri, his eyes had a half-wild expression, probably the result of excessive smoking ... Sherman was never without a cigar ... Sometimes he works for twenty consecutive hours. He sleeps little; nor do the most powerful opiates relieve his terrible cerebral excitement.*"

Sherman was particularly frustrated that most new regiments were being sent to either McClellan in Washington or Fremont in St. Louis.

Chapter 2 - The Union Encampment

When in October of 1861, Lincoln's Secretary of War, a corrupt politician named Simon Cameron, Lincoln would remove four months later, visited the area, Sherman saw his big chance. He induced Cameron to stay an extra day to meet with Sherman, which Cameron reluctantly agreed to do. Unfortunately Cameron insisted that his companions, mostly reporters, attend the meeting.

Sherman, determined to impress Cameron with the danger of the Kentucky situation, over-did it. He dramatically closed and locked the doors and then proceeded to tell Cameron he needed 60,000 troops just to defend Kentucky and 200,000 troops to take control of the Mississippi Valley.

These troop numbers were unheard of at the time, although they would ultimately prove conservative, and the newspapers began daily lashing Sherman as being crazy. It was humiliating. Sherman was commanding troops who were reading that he was crazy.

Halleck, who was friends with Sherman and knew him well, didn't believe the media, and he gave Sherman a 2-week leave of absence. Some historians think Sherman had a nervous breakdown - supposedly there was insanity in his family.

No doubt he was severely depressed, as anyone would be, but most likely nothing happened. He just stayed out of the limelight for awhile and rested under the care of his wife. The break seemed to help. When he came back, he was once more ready for duty. Nothing like that happened again, but he never got over his hatred of the press. Later in the war, a reporter printed information on Sherman's army movements; Sherman wanted to have the reporter court-martialed and shot for treason, but he couldn't sell Grant on it. But the reporter was banned from Sherman's army.

But there's no question he was high-strung. One general described him as "*a splendid piece of machinery with all the screws a little loose.*"

With the newspapers calling him crazy, it was only due to his powerful political connections – including his step father and his brother, John, both U.S. Senators from Ohio – that his career was salvaged. Despite his step father and brother, Sherman disliked politicians almost as much as journalists.

Besides his insanity-problem, Sherman (along with Halleck) was unlucky in that he had been stuck in California, missing the Mexican War, which served as a post-graduate course for most senior Civil War generals.

Nonetheless, with all his baggage, there was clearly something special about Sherman. As already mentioned, just prior to the war, he had been appointed Superintendent of the future Louisiana State University, where he got on well with the students, faculty, and Louisiana politicians from the governor on down. But he was adamantly opposed to secession. One night at a dinner with some of the university faculty, he delivered a surprisingly prophetic sermon:

> "You, you people of the South, believe there can be such a thing as peaceful secession. You don't know what you're doing ... The country will be drenched in blood. You mistake the people of the north. They are a peaceable people, but an earnest people, and will fight too, and they are not going to let this country be destroyed without a mighty effort to save it ... The North can make a steam-engine, a locomotive or a railway car; hardly yard of cloth or shoes can you make. You are rushing to war with one of the most powerful, ingeniously mechanical and determined people on earth – right at your doors. You are bound to fail!"

Sherman resigned his position at the college once Louisiana seceded from the Union.

Although Grant had entered West Point as a plebe during Sherman's last year there, the two hardly knew each other. But once Grant headed south to tackle Forts Henry and Donelson, Sherman took over Grant's old job back in Cairo, though without an army. His main job was to keep Grant and his troops supplied, and he did an excellent job of it. Although Sherman was still senior to Grant, he offered to waive rank if Grant needed him in the field. The two gradually developed a long-distance friendship, and soon Grant promoted him to division commander.

A professional soldier, Sherman had a low opinion of volunteer troops – writing that they had "*as much idea of war as children*" – and it greatly irritated him having to baby-sit amateurs, who could barely pitch a tent, and who constantly spooked themselves spotting phantom Rebels behind every tree. (Volunteers had preformed poorly during the Mexican War - often being more trouble than they were worth due to drinking and carousing. Most West Pointers held a low opinion of them.)

For all these reasons, plus Halleck's strict order not to engage the enemy before his arrival, Sherman kept his mouth clamped tightly shut, and relentlessly portrayed himself as a model of calm and restraint, serenely unconcerned about reports of nearby enemy forces. His brigades, and their regiments, which would be on the front line of the attack, where deployed along a front stretching a mile, and so irregularly that they couldn't form in a prolonged line if the division was called out. Sherman had given orders to face all camps west and to have no more than 22 paces between regiments. But his order was largely ignored as the regiments fronted in all directions, mainly based on access to water. As one writer said, Sherman and his green troops had camping in mind, not fighting.

Sherman pitched his tent headquarters next to a shady stream, Shiloh Creek, that ran near a tiny Methodist meetinghouse called Shiloh Church. Until formal notification of McClernand's promotion to major general (it arrived April 5th, the day prior to the coming battle), Sherman was senior officer and unofficial camp commander at the Landing in Grant's absence.

One Union private wrote home that "*There is no end to the tents. We can see them scattered in all directions as far as we can see.*" Another private of the 52IL thought the place reminded him of a religious camp meeting, but much bigger. By the end of March, Sherman was handling the daily activities of five divisions of about 37,000 troops, which included about 34,500 trigger-pullers and 3,000 support troops – medical staff, cooks, teamsters, etc.

> *Neither Grant nor Sherman voted for Lincoln in 1860, for fear it would lead to war.*

If Sherman gave little thought to a possible enemy attack, he certainly wasn't alone on that score. Even though the Confederates were massing in Corinth, all the Union brass – Grant and Halleck among them – were supremely confident that the recent Confederate defeats in the West had crippled the Southern army, and just one more battle should finish this ridiculous rebellion, at least in the West.

Grant's Third Mistake

Once he deployed his army at Pittsburg Landing, Grant neglected to construct even the skimpiest defensive fortifications to shield his inexperienced troops. At this stage of the war, most officers frowned on the use of defensive structures. Sherman's opinion was typical: "*Such a course would have made our raw men timid.*"

Chapter 2 - The Union Encampment

Also Grant, thinking offensively, wanted to use the time to train his raw troops, rather than using them as laborers felling trees and digging ditches. So, even though troops had been arriving at the Landing for nearly two weeks prior to the battle, the Union encampments sat casually scattered about in the woods like a Boy Scout jamboree, as ill prepared to receive a major attack as if the Confederates were a 1,000 miles away, rather than 20 miles. This would be Grant's third and greatest mistake. While the Pittsburg Landing encampment was indeed well protected by swamps, creeks, and the river, these barriers could also trap the Federals if they left their front door open – that three-mile gap to the southwest. But the Federal commanders completely convinced themselves that Johnston and his army were gathering in Corinth strictly to defend the town.

On April 5th, the day before the attack, as Johnston's 40,000 troops eased into position just a mile south of Sherman's camp, Sherman sent Grant a message in response to Grant's inquiry about enemy activity, stating: *"I have no doubt that nothing will occur today other than some picket firing. The enemy is saucy, but got the worst of it yesterday and will not press our pickets far. I do not apprehend anything like an attack on our position."*

> Grant did have a highly competent chief engineer, James McPherson, and it's unknown what if any input he had on the lack of fortifications.

That evening, no doubt relying on Sherman's message, Grant sent a telegram to Halleck: *"The main force of the enemy is at Corinth and points east. I have scarcely the faintest idea of an attack (general one) being made on us, but will be prepared should such a thing take place."*

Grant would rue those words for the rest of his career.

Shiloh Church, for which the battle was named, was a rough 25 x 30' log cabin with a clapboard roof built around 1854 by a congregation that was part of the Southern Methodist Episcopal Church. Like many denominations in prewar years, the Methodist Episcopal Church split into Northern and Southern branches, largely over the issue of slavery. The name "Shiloh" came from 1 Samuel and referred to a religious center to which the Hebrews annually made pilgrimage. It roughly translated to "peace," or "house of peace."

The original building is long gone, torn apart by Federal soldiers looking for souvenirs or firewood. But the church was rebuilt and is the subject of this modern photo.

Transports at Pittsburg Landing just days after the battle. At far right is the Cincinnati Sanitary Commission's *Tyconn*, loaded with medical supplies, and next to it is the *Tigress*, Grant's floating HQ.

Modern photo of the Landing.

Chapter 2 - The Union Encampment

THE CREEKS

Note the dense, almost jungle-like vegatation.

Bridge over Snake Creek

Owl Creek

Lick Creek ford
(Presumably during the dry season)

3   The March to Shiloh

April 3 - 5

The Confederate Command

When the Confederate armies converged at Corinth in late March, Johnston commanded about 40,000 soldiers. In the Southern armies, troop counts usually included non-combatants – medical, teamsters, etc. – so he probably had about 37,000 trigger-pullers, as well as five senior officers, as described below:

PIERRE G. T. BEAUREGARD

The Southern army in the west had a peculiar command structure. Though Beauregard was technically second-in-command, Johnston effectively appointed him co-commander with the responsibility of organizing the newly concentrated army. Sometimes Johnston was in charge; sometimes Beauregard was in charge. At one point Johnston even offered Beauregard command, which the latter refused.

Gen. Pierre G. T. Beauregard
1818 - 1893

Beauregard was in bad health as he was recovering from recent throat surgery he'd had done in Richmond, and as a result he was now plagued with high fevers and chronic bronchial infections. Often, he could hardly speak. The doctors thought he should be in bed. But he pressed on, outfitted in a tailored uniform lavishly adorned with gold braid and a spiffy red cap with a flat brim covered with more gold spaghetti as worn by French army officers. As a flamboyant Louisianan fiercely proud of his French heritage, Beauregard was more French than the French.

Though 40,000 troops actually only amounted to four divisions, on March 29th, Beauregard divided the army, now designated the *Army of Mississippi*, into four "corps," hoping to fool the Yankees into thinking the Southern host was twice its actual size (Traditionally a corps, modeled on European military, numbered about 20,000 soldiers, so four Confederate "corps" would appear to be 80,000 troops).

The First Corps was commanded by Leonidas Polk; the Second by Maj. Gen. Braxton Bragg, and the Third by Maj. Gen. William J. Hardee. The fourth corps, designated a "Reserve", was initially under the command of Maj. Gen. George B. Crittenden. But after the Confederate defeat in January at Mill Springs, Kentucky, Crittenden was relieved of command due to allegations of intoxication – a common problem in all armies at that time. He was replaced on the eve of the approaching battle by former U.S. Senator and Vice President, John C. Breckinridge of Kentucky, now a Confederate brigadier general.

Bragg's corps was the largest with approximately 13,000 men; Hardee's was the smallest with about half that number.

BRAXTON BRAGG

A 42-year-old West Pointer and Mexican War veteran, Bragg was a man who always seemed to live under a black cloud. He had a well-deserved reputation as a strict disciplinarian – so well deserved that, while in the regular army, some of his troops tried to kill him on a couple of occasions by slipping explosives near his tent. He was a sour, irritable man, no doubt partially due to his numerous health issues, including rheumatism, dyspepsia, nerves, and severe migraine headaches. His temperament probably wasn't improved when his Louisiana plantation was confiscated by the Federals later in 1862. A by-the-book soldier with little imagination, he was almost universally detested, and he fought with his fellow officers nearly as much as he fought with the Yankees. He really had only one supporter, but it was the one who mattered – President Jefferson Davis.

Maj. Gen. Braxton Bragg
1817 - 1876

Chapter 3 - The March to Shiloh

William Hardee

A 46-year-old, former Commandant of West Point and a Mexican War veteran, Maj. Gen. William Hardee published a book before the war with the snappy title of *Rifle and Light Infantry Tactics for the Exercise and Maneuvers of Troops When Acting as Light Infantry or Riflemen."* Better known simply as *Hardee's Tactics*, both sides used his book as their primary drill manual throughout the war, although Grant would later say the book was nothing more than common sense. Hardee, a Georgian, was a steady though not brilliant officer who would serve the Confederacy throughout the war, earning the nickname "Old Reliable." He would serve under Albert Sidney Johnston, Bragg, Hood, and finally under Joseph Johnston until the end of the war.

Brig. Gen.
William J. Hardee (w)
1815 - 1873

Leonidas Polk

Maj. Gen. Leonidas Polk, 55 years old, owned a Tennessee plantation with 200 to 400 slaves, and was a second cousin of James Polk, the former U.S. President. He attended West Point but resigned his commission immediately after graduation to enter, of all things, a theological seminary, where he would eventually became a bishop in the Episcopal Church. Now known as "The Fighting Bishop," Polk achieved his high military position without prior combat experience because of his friendship with President Davis as well as with Johnston. Though personally brave and popular with his troops, he was barely competent as a military officer and often dangerously insubordinate, as he had amply demonstrated by seizing that fort in Columbus, Kentucky, breaking that state's neutrality. He had been a bishop most of his adult life, and bishops are not accustomed to taking orders from mere mortals. He and Braxton Bragg detested each other, even at this early stage of the war.

John Breckinridge

A former U.S. Vice President and member of a prominent Kentucky family, 41-year-old Brig. Gen. John C. Breckinridge had served in the Mexican War.

Maj. Gen.
Leonidas Polk
1806 - 1864

He wasn't a West Pointer, but rather a Princeton man and a successful lawyer. In his mid-30s he ran for U.S. President against Lincoln and Stephen Douglas, coming in second in the electoral vote and third in popular vote.

Shortly before the battle Breckinridge was selected to command the "Reserve Corps," replacing Maj. Gen. George B. Crittenden who, as mentioned earlier, was dismissed on charges of alcoholism. Breckinridge developed into a competent general who would go on to serve the Southern cause throughout the war, both in the west and in the east.

The Objective

Johnston arrived in Corinth the night of March 22nd. Within a couple of days, he made up his mind to strike Grant at Pittsburg Landing. His spies kept him current on the progress of Buell's Army of the Ohio as it tramped south to join Grant's Army of Tennessee. Even with his newly consolidated and larger force, Johnston couldn't just sit back and allow the Yankee army to mass at its leisure, swelling into Goliath that obviously would march 20 miles down the road and besiege him at Corinth. Boldness was required if he was going to stem the series of Confederate reverses in the West, not to mention resurrecting his career. His best hope was to seize the initiative and strike Grant at Pittsburg Landing before Buell could join him. The catch was that he couldn't attack any sooner than absolutely necessary. His army was literally only days old; what he really had was a mob of 40,000 citizens, many only armed with scatter guns and squirrel rifles.

Brig. Gen. John C. Breckinridge
1821 - 1875

"Some wore uniforms, some half uniforms, some no

uniforms at all," noted a Louisianian. Many of them wore a butternut-colored cotton uniforms called "Kentucky jeans." The Washington (Louisiana) Artillery and the Crescent Regiment from New Orleans wore Yankee-blue coats and pants. Just days before the battle, the 2TX were issued white, undyed cotton uniforms, prompting one Texan to ask, "*Do these generals expect us to be killed and want us to wear our shrouds?*"

Confederate small arms consisted of a mixed bag of squirrel rifles, shotguns, percussion muskets, and even flintlocks. But in truth they were not much worse off than the Federals when it came to weapons. About 10,000 of Johnston's troops had the excellent British Enfield rifle-muskets, some being issued as late as April 3rd, and some even had US Springfield rifles, seized from former US armories. But a third of the cavalry had no weapons at all; the other two-thirds were mostly armed with shotguns and maybe revolvers. And as would be true throughout much of the war, except for captured Federal cannon, most of the Confederate cannon were sort of homemade, meaning they were manufactured in iron foundries that didn't specialize in making cannon, and their cannons' metal was inferior to that produced by the industrial North.

Like Grant, Johnston needed every precious minute to organize his force and provide his raw troops with at least some semblance of training. So Johnston remained in Corinth, hastily drilling his troops until the very last minute when he was to be notified that Buell's column was about to reach Grant.

In modern armies, drill and marching is mainly used to instill discipline and teamwork. There's not much other use for marching except for parades and ceremonies. But in the 1800s, since the invention of the musket, guns were very slow to load, requiring the men to fire as a group in order to achieve fire superiority. So drill was a vital and deadly serious business, requiring companies, regiments and brigades to be able to load and fire three rounds per minute and be capable of instantly changing formation and responding to commands - "*forward, about face, shoulder arms, right oblique, column right, ready aim,*" etc., etc. If a unit, or even a few members of that unit, became confused and jumbled in the mist of a battle, the entire unit could be slaughtered by an opposing formation.

Finally, late in the evening of April 2nd, Johnston received a message that Buell's troops were nearing Pittsburg Landing. The time to strike had arrived.

Johnston ordered Beauregard to have the army ready to march at daybreak. The idea seemed straight forward – simply march the 20 miles to Pittsburg Landing on April 3rd, and strike Grant's sleeping encampment at dawn, Friday, April 4th. But there were a lot of devils in the details.

The Confederate Attack Plan

President Davis later claimed that Johnston sent him a telegram on April 4th, outlining a plan of attack with Polk's Corps on the left, Hardee's in the center, and Bragg's, the largest corps, on the right nearest the river and the Landing. There, Bragg would crush the Union left and drive Grant's army to its destruction in the Owl and Snake Creek swamp bottoms.

The plan did have the disadvantage of putting Johnston's main striking force next to the river, which would surely be in range of Yankee gunboats. But other than that, it wasn't a bad plan had he stuck to it. But apparently he left the details of drawing up the official orders to Beauregard, who in turn assigned the task to his adjutant, Col. Thomas Jordan, who in turn drew up the orders based on Napoleon's battle plan at Waterloo – which in turn resulted a disaster known as Special Order Number Eight. One of the greatest criticisms of Johnston is that he left too many important decisions to subordinates, and failed to check on their progress.

Jordan and the French-worshipping Beauregard, both ardent Napoleon admirers, completely changed the battle formation. Instead of attacking with the three corps left, right and center, the new plan called for an attack in waves, with each corps attacking in succession, one behind the other, like Napoleon apparently did at Waterloo, where the battle was fought in open fields.

The problem was that, in the dense terrain of Shiloh, the corps commanders couldn't *see*, let alone control, their mile-long battle lines. And unlike the gentle, rolling plains of Waterloo, Shiloh was a rugged, hilly jungle packed with swamps, steep gullies and creeks with exceptionally dense underbrush, occasionally interspersed with a few corn and cotton fields.

One mundane item that was critical in the Shiloh

Col. Thomas Jordan 1818 - 1895

battle, though seldom discussed, was the underbrush. There are probably few areas in the United States that possessed the jungle-like foliage that seems to grow especially thick in the deep, semi-swamp creek beds that interlaced the Shiloh battlefield. But the underbrush wasn't limited to creek beds. It would be a major factor in the fighting along the Sunken Road, which we will soon be discussing.

So, Napoleon's Waterloo plan, which incidentally didn't even work for Napoleon, was a sorry model for the coming fight at Shiloh. If Waterloo resembled a carefully choreographed gentleman's duel, Shiloh would be more like a gun fight in a dark room.

Special Order Number Eight guaranteed that once the battle commenced all Confederate organization above the level of brigade, and sometimes even at the regimental level, would dissolve in the rugged terrain as the successive battle lines pancaked into the preceding ranks.

We don't know why Johnston allowed the change. It may have been simply too late to change it once he found out about it. But as overall commander, we do know that the change was his responsibility.

The March

"Well, on Thursday morning [4am, April 3rd] I was awakened by the long roll that was sounded throughout the camp," wrote one Louisiana soldier. *"Everybody was in motion ... Drums were beating, trumpets sounded, fifes blowing, brass bands playing and men hurrying."* They had been ordered to strip down for action – 100 rounds per man (40 in their haversacks and 60 in the company wagons), two hundred rounds per field gun, and five days' rations (three in haversacks and two in the wagons).

In truth, no one really knew how to move 40,000 troops at this stage of the war. And so the Confederates' march from Corinth to Shiloh was almost as traumatic as the battle itself. Aside from Bragg's trained soldiers, these were civilians with guns. And while about half of Grant's troops had at least some combat experience at Forts Donelson and Henry, *none* of Johnston's troops, except for a few senior officers, had ever fired a shot in anger.

And there was yet another flaw in Special Orders Number Eight: the order gave insufficient attention to the limited road network between Corinth and Pittsburg Landing, resulting in overcrowding and massive traffic jams. There were in fact just two

Chapter 3 - The March to Shiloh

roads – Ridge Road and Monterey Road. Both roads were bad, but Monterey Road was the worst. The order of march put Polk and Hardee on the Ridge Road, and Bragg and Breckinridge on the Monterey Road. A reporter traveling with Bragg's troops on Monterey Road described the road as *"very rough and hilly, with numerous mud holes, and occasional swamps."*

As soon as his army was on the march, Beauregard's and Jordan's Napoleon-marching-plan collapsed. In the first place, there was no way Johnston's raw troops were going to cover 20 miles in one day. Many of these recruits had not even left Corinth until after the time they were supposed to be attacking at Pittsburg Landing. In the regular army Johnston served in prior to the war, infantry was expected to march in full gear 20 miles in a 10 hour day (2 mph). But this wasn't the regular army. Due to the near-complete inexperience of officers and men, combined with the incessant rain, it took three days to cover 20 miles – about 6.7 miles per day.

Secondly, Beauregard's marching orders were too complicated, with regiments, brigades and even corps winding in and out of columns at various road intersections, often blocking other units. Even experienced troops would have had difficulty keeping up with such a march schedule. One of Bragg's soldiers wrote of the confusion: *"I could see thousands of soldiers moving in different directions marching and countermarching ... Sometimes we marched very slow and sometimes at the double quick."*

> Confederate rations on the march usually consisted of a combination of flour and grease, sometimes with molasses. Prior to a march they would fry bacon and use the grease mixed with flour to make biscuits which they wrapped in cloth and stored in their haversacks. They claimed the concoction was "tougher than a mule's ear."

Last but not least, the Confederates were no sooner on the road than they encountered the same problem that had plagued Sherman – rain. When the march began on April 3rd the sun was out and troops were complaining about the heat. But about 2am on April 4th, the sky opened up, pouring down rain, rain, and more rain like a biblical curse. Steams swelled over their banks, covering bridges

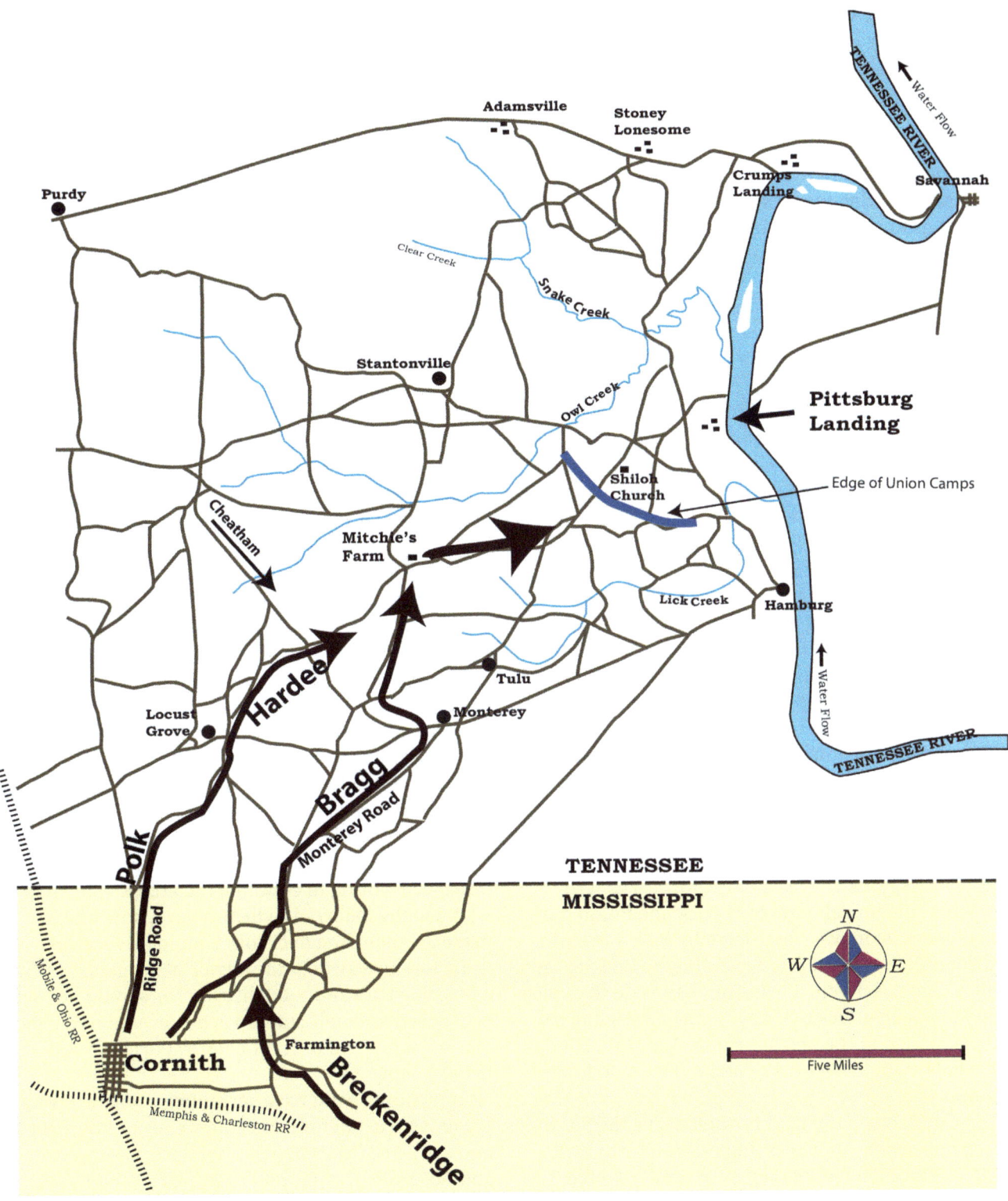

Confederate marching routes to Shiloh

Chapter 3 - The March to Shiloh

and washing away roads. Forty or so thousand infantry, plus hundreds of horse-drawn ammunition and supply wagons, plus horse-drawn artillery (115 cannons), plus 4,300 cavalry, soon churned the roads into a sticky, gooey mess, bogging the march down to a snail's pace. And the rain was bone-chilling, sometimes turning to hail, soaking the troops in their cotton clothing as they stood or sat for hours up to their ankles in water with their shoes filled with mud, waiting for crossroads to clear, or lying on the wet ground, wrapped in a soaked blanket.

The delays caused Johnston to postpone his attack from April 4th to April 5th. But April 5th wasn't any better. When the troops were forming up at 3am, according to one soldier, "*One of the hardest rains fell I ever saw in life and wound up in considerable hail.*" A Tennesseean wrote, "*We were drawn up on the edge [of the road]. As we stood there, troops tramped by in the mud and rain and darkness ... To us who were simply standing in line in the rain it was bad enough, but those men who were going by were wading, stumbling and plunging through water a foot deep.*" Another said, "*It was so dark we can't see to move, so we had to stand under arms in a pelting rain until daylight.*"

Adding to their misery, the men were soon famished. The raw troops weren't accustomed to rationing food, and they gobbled up their five days' rations within a couple of days. By the time they reached Shiloh, the rain-soaked rookies would be fighting on empty bellies.

Mercifully, Johnston and Beauregard finally arrived a mile and a half in front of Grant's camp early on April 5th, expecting to attack. But Bragg was still missing one of his divisions (Ruggles') and nobody could find it. After waiting most of the morning, Johnston exploded, "*This is perfectly puerile! This is not war!*" He himself now rode back and found that Ruggles' division was obstructed by Polk's troops. By the time this was sorted out, and the Ruggles' and Polk's troops arrived, it was 4pm – too late to deploy and launch an attack that day. So the attack had to be postponed to the next morning, April 6th, Sunday. This delay would eventually doom the Confederate attack.

The problems in the march would leave the Southern troops exhausted and hungry, with many sick with pneumonia before they even fired a shot at Shiloh.

And there were even greater problems. By now Beauregard was certain that all surprise had been lost, and he had excellent reason to believe it. Among other items, such as earlier clashes around Grant's camp, the raw Rebel troops – including an entire regiment of Texas Rangers – kept shooting off their guns to make sure their powder still worked after constant rain. And they persisted in raising hearty cheers every time a general rode by. Bands kept striking up tunes. Bugles kept sounding. Hardee's troops gave a thunderous cheer when a deer was shot in front on the battleline. Grant's army, only a mile and a half away, would have to be not only asleep, but comatose not to have heard the Confederate approach. But it didn't.

On the other hand, the day before – April 4th– Johnston did get one encouraging report, assuming the source could be believed. Hardee's men had captured several Federals in a skirmish. Without any prompting, one of the prisoners, Maj. LeRoy Crockett of the 72OH, blabbed that "*... They [the Federals] don't expect anything of this kind back yonder.*" He also helpfully mentioned that the Federals had not built earthworks, something Johnston had been greatly concerned about. As he was led away, the helpful Maj. Crockett said, "*Why, you seem to have an army here; we know nothing of it!*"

Late in the evening of April 5, Beauregard arrived at Bragg's headquarters and the two generals discussed the bleak state of affairs. The two agreed that the attack should be canceled. Then Polk arrived. Bragg accused him of causing the delay of Ruggles' division, and the two, who already hated each other, got into a heated argument. Now Johnston happened by, soon joined by Breckinridge. In what had become an impromptu war council, Beauregard, seconded by Bragg, urged Johnston to call the whole thing off and wade back to Corinth. Polk and Breckinridge disagreed, voting to continue the attack. Johnston, who usually deferred to Beauregard, now had to make an agonizing decision: Should he send his army forward against the advice of his generals, into a possible trap and total disaster; or should he turn his soaked and half-starved army around in the face of the enemy, and order it back to Corinth without firing a shot?

But by now he did have second piece of encouraging news - just before this conference on the afternoon of April 5th, a bewildered Federal surgeon and his orderly, out for an evening ride, had been captured and taken to headquarters where they were interrogated by both Johnston and Beauregard. "*Practically speechless with astonishment,*" the prisoners stated that Grant had returned to Savan-

> *On the approach march, the 6,500 men of Hardee's Corps advanced two abreast up the road at dawn on April 5th, heading toward Shiloh.*
>
> *Only about three miles from the Federal position, the corps experienced its first challenge. A lone rider emerged from the brush, blocking their path with his weapon, likely a shotgun, cradled across his saddle. The stranger shouted "Halt! Who are you?" The startled officers replied that it was Hardee's Corps. "Well then," demanded the picket, "advance and give the word." Having no clue of the password, the officers studied the stranger through their field glasses. Seeing he was wearing butternut britches – the uniform of half the Confederate army – they requested he meet them halfway for a pow-wow. He agreed. Finally face-to-face with the tenacious sentry, the officers convinced him that he was holding up the advance of a quarter of Johnston's army.*
>
> *Eventually he relented, but he still didn't like it. "Well, I suppose you can go; but it's agin' orders."*

nah, Sherman was in charge, and no one expected an attack.

No doubt fortified with that piece of good news, Johnston stiffened and made his decision, stating, *"Gentlemen, we shall attack at daylight tomorrow. They can present no greater front between those two creeks than we can, and the more men they crowd in there, the worse we can make it for them."* As he was walking away, he muttered to one of his officers, *"I would fight them if they were a million."*

The attack would proceed.

(Later that night, after more discussions with Johnston, Bragg also agreed that the attack should continue. But apparently Beauregard never changed his mind.)

The night was clear, damp, and cold, but strict orders were given that no fires could be lit, not even a cigar. Decades later one private from the 16LA vividly remembered that night before the battle, hungry, wet and shivering in the darkness as he listened to a Yankee band in the distance playing *Home Sweet Home.*

During the battle, Johnston would be at the front while Beauregard would remain at the rear, funneling troops and supplies where needed. For this and other reasons, many historians would criticize this arrangement, saying that it was another example of Johnston acting too much like a corps commander, rather than the overall army commander.

At 4am on the 6th, the troops were quietly awakened all along the line and given a welcome but hasty breakfast of biscuits and cold bacon. Then the hundreds of companies formed hollow squares where their captains read an address from Johnston:

> "Soldiers: I have put you in motion to offer battle to the invaders of your country ... you can but march to victory over the mercenaries sent to subjugate you and despoil you of your liberties, your property and your honor ... The eyes and hopes of eight millions of people rest upon you; you are expected to show yourselves worthy of your lineage, worthy of the women of the South ... and with the trust that God is with us, your generals will lead you confidently to the combat – assured of success."

"I would fight them if they were a million."

> **Where was the Federal cavalry?**
> How on earth could an entire Confederate army approach without being detected by patrolling Federal cavalry? It turns out that there **was** no patrolling Federal cavalry! Sherman's division, on the front line of the camp, was in the mist of an artillery and cavalry reorganization that began on April 2nd and wasn't completed until late on April 5th. Thus, precisely during those crucial three days of the Confederate approach, no Federal troopers were guarding the front door of the camp.
> For leaving the doors to the camp unlocked and unguarded in enemy country while his men were asleep in their tents, Sherman was very lucky he didn't face a court-martial after the battle.

> Just prior to the outbreak of war, Beauregard accepted the post of Commandant of West Point. He did so knowing that his home state of Louisiana was just days away from seceding from the Union, and that he would follow his state. He obviously only accepted the appointment because it would look good on his resume when he joined the Confederate army.
> When it became clear that he would go with his state, the West Point administration fired him, refusing to pay his fare back to Louisiana. Beauregard filed a suit for damages, and he continued to pursue the suit even after he was a general in the Confederate army.

4 First Clash

3am - 6:15am

Fraley Field, April 6

On the afternoon of April 4th, Union Col. Everett Peabody, a 240-pound, six-footer with a fiery temper, reviewed his brigade in Spain Field on the south side of the encampment.

Col. Everett Peabody (k)
1830 - 1862

His was one of two brigades in Brig. Gen. Benjamin Prentiss' 6th Division. Forced to cancel his review due to heavy rain, Peabody was informed that some of his men had spotted a squad of Rebel cavalry casually observing them from the woods at the south end of the field. Enemy soldiers allowed so close to a Federal encampment? This seemed odd to the Union recruits and also to Peabody; but the higher command – Sherman – remained unconcerned. In fact, Sherman, who had almost lost his job by getting too animated back in Kentucky, was sick of hearing about the jumpy recruits' sightings of the enemy. He even threatened to arrest anyone who brought him annoying reports like that.

Clearly, the new soldiers had a lot to learn about military matters.

The next afternoon, April 5th, back on the same Spain Field, division commander Prentiss reviewed his brigades – Peabody's and Col. Madison Miller's. During the proceedings, Maj. James E. Powell of the 25MO, part of Peabody's brigade, noticed a group of enemy riders again boldly observing the Federals from the southeastern edge of the tree line. Powell reported this to Prentiss, who ordered a 4pm patrol comprised of companies from the 21MO and 25MO of Peabody's brigade, led by Col. David Moore.

Moore and his men marched cautiously down the road a mile and a half to Seay Field, on the southwest edge of the encampment. (Sixty-four-year-old Lewis Seay was a Union sympathizer, related to Wilse Wood, a Southern sympathizer who farmed the adjoining field. Seay's cabin on the southern edge of the cotton field would be one of the few structures to survive the battle.)

On the northwest corner of Seay Field, Powell's party encountered several Negro slaves who claimed that earlier in the day they had seen as many as 200 Rebels in the area. But it was getting dark, and the patrol saw nothing, though some of the men claimed they heard thrashing in the woods. Still, they hadn't actually *see* anything, so when the patrol returned and reported, Prentiss was unimpressed, and told Peabody to forget it.

Meanwhile, less than a mile away, Johnston's 40,000 man army deployed into successive lines of battle, each about two miles long, one corps after the other, 800 yards apart – Hardee's corps, then Bragg's, then Polk's as soon as it came up, and finally with Breckinridge's in the rear in reserve.

Powell's Reconnaissance
3 AM – 6:15 AM

But Peabody *couldn't* stop fretting about those Confederates peeping around in the woods. He laid awake staring at the tent ceiling, conjuring up images of Rebels lurking nearby in those dark woods. Finally, around midnight he just couldn't stand it! With or without Prentiss' permission, Peabody intended to find out just what in the hell was going on in those woods. He rousted awake Maj. Powell, ordering him to take out another patrol before daylight and make another reconnaissance of Seay Field, hoping to surprise any Rebels lurking at that early hour.

So in the chilly, damp darkness of 3am, Maj. Powell spent an hour or so forming up about 250 grumbling soldiers from five companies of the 25MO and 12MI. They marched down the same farm lane Col. Moore

Maj. James E. Powell (k)
1819 - 1862

had taken the previous evening. (Today that road is named Reconnaissance Road) It led toward Seay Field, and beyond that, to another field called Fraley Field. (The latter was a 40-acre cotton field owned by a farmer named James Fraley, a Confederate sympathizer who had quickly departed with his wife and two children on the advice of Confederate officers.)

It was spooky out there under the dim light of a crescent moon. At one point, two nervous Union squads almost blasted each other, which would have

Page 33

Chapter 4 - First Clash

required a lot of explaining from Peabody as to why he sent out an unauthorized patrol.

As the sleepy Federals reached Seay Field, they were surprised by Confederate cavalry pickets who, equally surprised, fired off three quick shots before vanishing like phantoms into the darkness. Powell's men were now wide awake as he formed them into a long skirmish line and advanced warily into Fraley Field. About 200 yards in, the Federals collided with two, seven-man outposts of enemy sentries. These belonged to Maj. Aaron Hardcastle's 3MS Battalion of Wood's Brigade, Hardee's Corps. Hardcastle had been a lieutenant in the regular army and had accompanied Johnston on his epic trek across the desert. He had his regiment arrayed about 300 yards behind the pickets on a slight rise on the edge of an adjoining field owned by farmer named Wilse Wood.

Maj. Aaron B. Hardcastle
1836 - 1915

The Confederate sentries cranked off a volley and raced back to Hardcastle's main line, where his 280 men were now fully alert. One of Powell's Federals remembered: "*When we halted the first streak of daylight had appeared. As we watched, we noticed something white moving through the brush and in another moment we spied a horseman whose movements we made out to be those of the enemy,*" he said. Then came "*the crack of several muskets, and bullets were soon whizzing after us.*"

Powell's men continued advancing. When they got within 200 yards, the Mississippians opened fired in earnest. The Federals responded. In the half light of dawn, both sides blazed away at muzzle flashes for a half hour, from about 5:45am to 6:15am. By now Powell had taken an unknown number of casualties; Hardcastle had four dead and 20 wounded. In the growing light of dawn, Powell spotted Rebel cavalry trying to curl around his left flank. (Actually it was an escort company, the Jefferson Mounted Rifles, searching for a route through the woods to bring up artillery).

Powell and his men were the first Federals to get a clue of what they were really up against when part of Hardee's 7,000 man battle line loomed on the opposite side of Fraley Field, with the Rebels marching shoulder to shoulder in the standard two-rank battle order, bands playing *Dixie*, and heading straight at Powell and his men. Powell ordered his bugler to sound retreat. Their mini-battle had at least given Prentiss' troops some warning of storm that was about to hit them.

> **"Tonight we will water our horses on the Tennessee."**

Earlier that morning, back at the intersection of Corinth and Bark Roads at Johnston's headquarters, the Confederate generals gathered around a small fire for a breakfast of coffee and crackers. Beauregard, Bragg and Hardee resumed the previous night's discussion about whether they were walking into a trap. Johnston was "*mainly a listener*" according to one of his aides. In the middle of their debate, they heard the crash of musketry at Fraley Field. After listening a few moments, Johnston simply declared, "*Gentleman, the battle has commenced. It's too late to change our dispositions*" Wearing a big soft hat with a black plume, Johnston mounted his bay thoroughbred, Fire Eater, vowing, "*Tonight we'll water our horses on the Tennessee.*"

At around 5:14am, he rode off to the sound of the guns.

And the Battle of Shiloh was on.

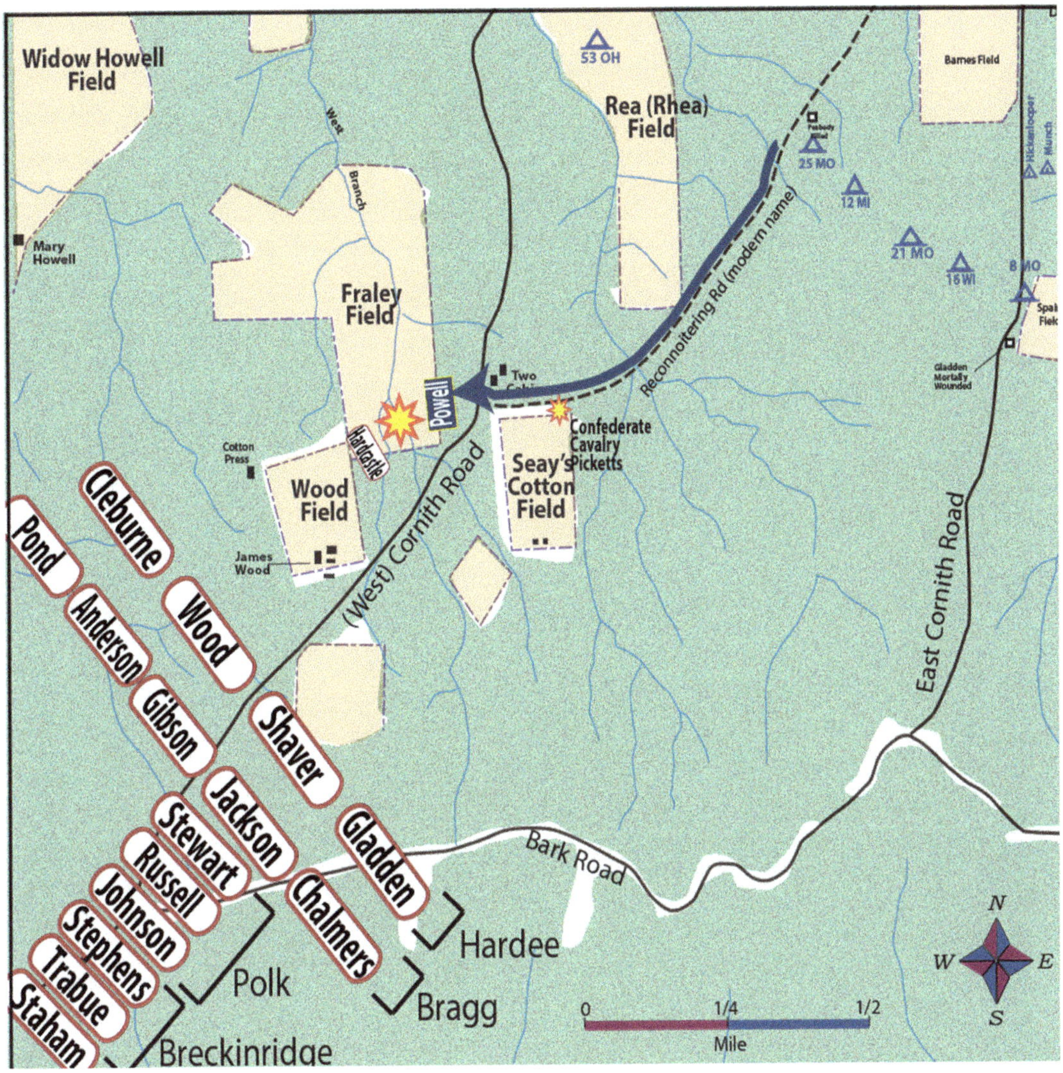

Map of First Clash

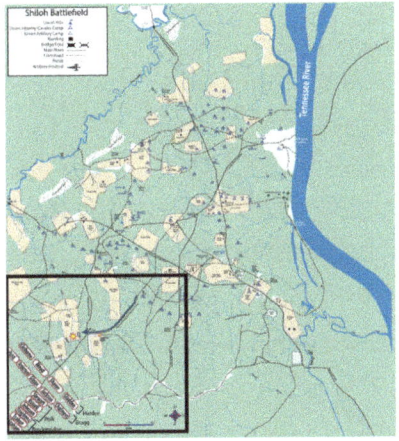

Map's Location on the Battlefield

Chapter 4 - First Clash

5 Prentiss Reinforces

7am - 7:30am

Hearing the firing in Fraley Field, 6th Division commander, Brig. Gen. Prentiss, rode into Peabody's camp around 7am, demanding to know what all the shooting was about. Prentiss, a 41-year-old Missouri rope-maker and Mexican War veteran, was yet another Illinois lawyer who dabbled in politics, reportedly with ties to Lincoln.

Brig. Gen. Benjamin M. Prentiss (c)
1819 - 1901

Prentiss had feuded with Grant back in Cairo, Illinois, and a least one newspaper quoted Prentiss as stating that he wouldn't serve *"under a drunkard."* Grant must have read it, but he still had enough confidence in Prentiss to give him command of the 6th Division.

When Peabody confessed that he had sent out a patrol, Prentiss exploded, accusing Peabody of triggering a major engagement and threatening to hold him responsible for his actions. Peabody said nothing, and instead walked over and sat down on his camp chest to eat his breakfast, jamming his spoon into his gruel and muttering that he was always responsible for his actions.

About this time a messenger arrived from Maj. Powell, reporting that he was being driven back by an enemy force of 3,000. Prentiss dispatched five companies from the 21MO commanded by Col. David Moore to reinforce Powell. As these reinforcements headed out, a company of the 16WI, just returning to camp from picket duty, volunteered to join Moore's detachment, probably now amounting to 400-500 men in total.

Col. Everett Peabody (k)
1830 - 1862

Around 6:30am Moore and his men encountered Powell's retreating force. Col. Moore, A 45-year-old hog farmer from Missouri, was said by one acquaintance to *"get madder and swear longer than any man I ever saw."* And right now Moore was madder than hell, and he ripped into Powell for cowardice. Powell tried to explain that there were a *lot* of Graybacks out there, but Moore wasn't buying it. He ordered all of Powell's able-bodied men to join his force, and sent Powell back to camp with the wounded. Moore also sent back a courier to Prentiss, requesting the five additional companies of the 21st be brought up, promising that with reinforcements he could *"lick 'em."*

Col. David Moore (w)
1817 - 1893

Back at camp, Peabody could hear the firing intensity growing ever louder. Finally, springing to his feet, he ordered his drummer boy to sound the "long roll"– the signal for battle. As Peabody sat on his mount on the right side of the line, a furious Prentiss rode up and again accused Peabody of inciting a battle. Peabody responded that it seemed to be the Rebels who were inciting the battle. He gave Prentiss a snappy salute, saying, *"If I brought on the fight, I am to lead the van."* He then posted the 25MO and 12MI on a low ridge facing south toward the firing. These men were soon joined by the remaining companies of the 16WI.

> "If I brought on the fight, I am to lead the van."

Meanwhile, Moore's column never made it to Fraley Field. Marching four men abreast about 300 yards down the same road he and Powell had used on their reconnaissances the day before, Moore and his men had almost passed Seay Field around 7am when they took heavy fire from the fence row on the south end of the field. Moore rashly ordered a charge from the western side of the field which, given the Confederate numbers, would certainly have been suicidal. But the charge didn't happen; just as Moore waved his sword to advance, he shrieked as a bullet shattered his right shin. Along with thousands of others, he would lose his right leg to amputation that night on a transport. Three months later, he would be back in the army, presumable on a cane and peg leg, and end the war as a breveted brigadier general.

An officer raced back to Powell shouting, *"For God's sake, Major, take command quick, the Colonel's wounded."* But the firing had died down momentarily and Powell, one of the few Federal officers with no illusions about the size of the enemy force, ordered all the men to back to camp.

Grant Departs for the Landing

At just about this time, around 7am, nine miles away back at the Cherry Mansion in Savannah, Grant was just sitting down to breakfast. According to Mrs. Cherry, Grant had just raised his coffee cup to his mouth when the dull rumble of cannon was heard coming from the south. The room froze. There was a pause, then more rumbling. Everybody rushed to the windows and doors to listen. *"Where is it, at Crumps or Pittsburg Landing?,"* someone asked. *"I think it's at Pittsburg,"* said Grant. Then he announced to his staff, *"Gentlemen, the ball's in motion; let's be off."*

Grant's personal steamboat, the *Tigress*, was docked at the nearby wharf. In 15 minutes, he, his staff and horses were aboard. As the boat crew fired up the boilers, Grant, still on his crutches, took a chair on the boiler deck, from which he dictated two messages. One was to Nelson, with orders to obtain a guide and somehow march his division along the east bank of the river to Pittsburg Landing, which Grant had stated was impossible just the day before. Once across from the Landing, Nelson's men would be ferried by steamboat across the river. The other message was to Buell, alerting him to the situation. Apparently unknown to Grant, after a grueling ride Buell had arrived on the outskirts of town during the night or early morning with an advance party. He would spend much of the early morning wandering about Savannah looking for Grant, only to find that he had departed, which did not improve his fondness for Grant.

Now the *Tigress* and Grant steamed south. It was now around 7:30am. It would take over an hour to steam the nine miles upstream to the Landing.

At about 8:30am, the *Tigress* approached Crumps Landing, where it slowed and pulled alongside another transport where Lew Wallace was standing on the hurricane deck. The crews listened as the two generals conversed. Wallace thought the firing was *"undoubtedly a general engagement."* Grant wasn't so sure, believing that Pittsburg Landing was perhaps a diversion, with the real attack coming at Crumps Landing. He ordered Wallace to keep his division in readiness and wait for Grant's further orders. Wallace's staff, surprised that they had to remain on standby, broke into a murmured discussion. Wallace raised his hand to quiet them, but reiterated to Grant that his brigades had already been concentrated at Stoney Lonesome and that the men were *"ready now."* Grant merely repeated his order to remain on standby. Then the *Tigress* slowly pulled away and steamed on upriver.

They hadn't traveled far before another steamer, the *John Warner*, came racing downstream with stacks billowing smoke at full speed. The boat hailed the *Tigress* and pulled alongside. A plank was dropped across, and a lieutenant came aboard with a message from W. H. L. Wallace, stating that the army was under a general attack and that the right and center wings had been driven back. The lieutenant added that the enemy was in great force. Grant, still sitting in his chair, simply muttered that when he got there he would surround the enemy.

The *Tigress* then hurried on toward Pittsburg Landing.

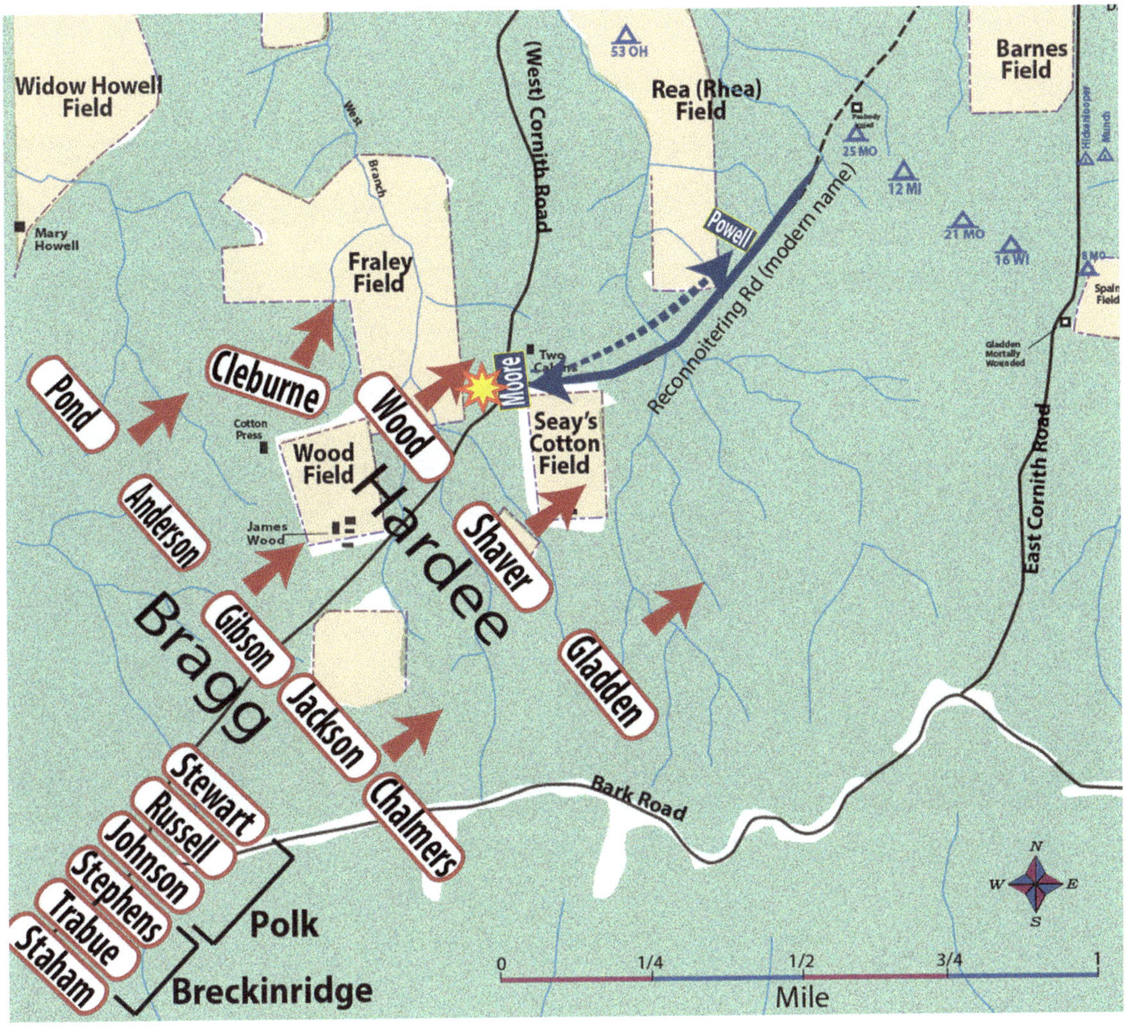

Col. Moore's detail replaces Maj. Powell's, but is soon forced to retreat.

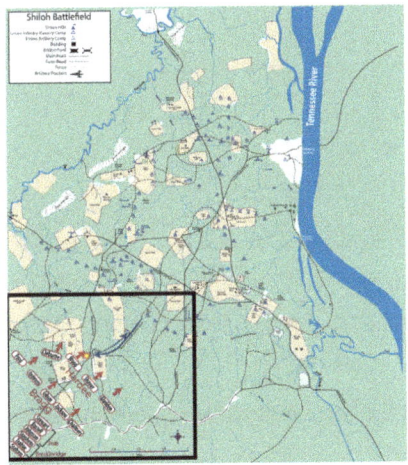

Map's Location on the Battlefield

Chapter 5 - Prentiss Reinforces

Crumps Landing

6 Breaking Peabody's Brigade

8am - 9am

Brig. Gen. Prentiss and his two brigade commanders, Col. Peabody and Col. Madison Miller, were uncertain as to whether Peabody's men had just fought a large skirmish that was now ended, or whether there was more to come. Peabody and his four regiments would be the first to be enlightened. Their tent camps, on the southern edge of the Union camp, stretched roughly east to west along Hamburg-Purdy Road, directly in the path of the approaching Confederates.

Peabody, a successful engineer and a Harvard man from a prominent Massachusetts family, had been seriously wounded back in 1861 in a scrap at Lexington, Missouri. Many of the men in his brigade had also been in that fight. At 240 pounds, Peabody was an intimidating presence. Had it not been for him sending out the 3am patrol that triggered the clash with the Confederates at dawn, it's possible that the men of both Prentiss' and Sherman's divisions would have been attacked while sleeping in their tents.

> *"[It was] a sublime but awful scene, as they advanced slowly, steadily and silently till within about 125 yards."*

But by 7:30am the remainder of Peabody's regiments not involved in the early morning skirmish stood at parade-rest in front of their tents, consisting of the 25MO, 12MI, 21MO and 16WI. Suddenly the troops noticed something strange – dozens of terrified rabbits scampering into the troops' formation. Presently they noticed something even stranger – a battleline of several thousand Confederates marching toward them – blood-red banners flapping, bayonets glistening, ,and drums beating. These were Brig. Gen. S. A. M. Wood's and Col. Robert Shaver's brigades – part of Hardee's mile and a quarter attack wave. One Union private from the 25MO described it: *"A sublime but awful scene, as they advanced slowly, steadily and silently till within about 125 yards."* Another stated: "*We were dumbfounded at seeing an enormous force of Confederate troops marching directly toward us."* For an unknown number of moments, the Federals simply gaped, not quite believing their eyes as Shaver's Confederate brigade and four regiments of Wood's brigade approached them in a tight formation of perhaps 2,200 men.

But the 25MO was composed largely of trained soldiers discharged from the regular army, and they kept their nerve as their commander, Lt. Col. Robert Van Horn, steadied them.

Wood's two right flank regiments, the 55TN and 3MO advanced somewhat ahead of the rest of the Confederate line, to about 125 yards in front of the Union line. On Van Horn's command, the 25MO blasted the two Rebel regiments, staggering them and sending them flying for the rear, yelling "*Retreat!, Retreat!*" They crashed into the 7AR, stampeding that unit as well. It was all Confederate officers, including Gen. Johnston himself, could do to herd the green troops back into a line of battle. It was a rather inauspicious start to the Confederate's main attack, but the officers managed to get their men moving forward again.

The Confederates closed to within 75 yards before opening fire. Peabody's brigade held its ground and the volume of the firing increased in tempo as casualties piled up on both sides. The Federals shouted to the Rebels to come on ahead, while the Confederates jeered back, "*Bull Run*"!

The Confederates were aided by the arrival of Capt. Charles Swett's Mississippi Battery of four 6-pounders and two 12-pounders, which formed on the right of Shaver's men. But the battery was within Federal rifle range, and the gunners were soon dropping.

A Mississippi cavalryman described the initial clash from his high vantage point: "*The roar and rattle of musketry, the belching of cannon, the screaming of shells, the whistling bullets, all united to beget emotions which words cannot be described. The deafening sounds, the stunning explosions, and the fiery flames of battle seemed to pass along the line in great billows from right to left.*"

But Peabody's brigade was outnumbered and S. A. M. Wood's Confederate brigade managed to curl around Peabody's unsupported flanks and force him back. The Federals began drifting to the rear.

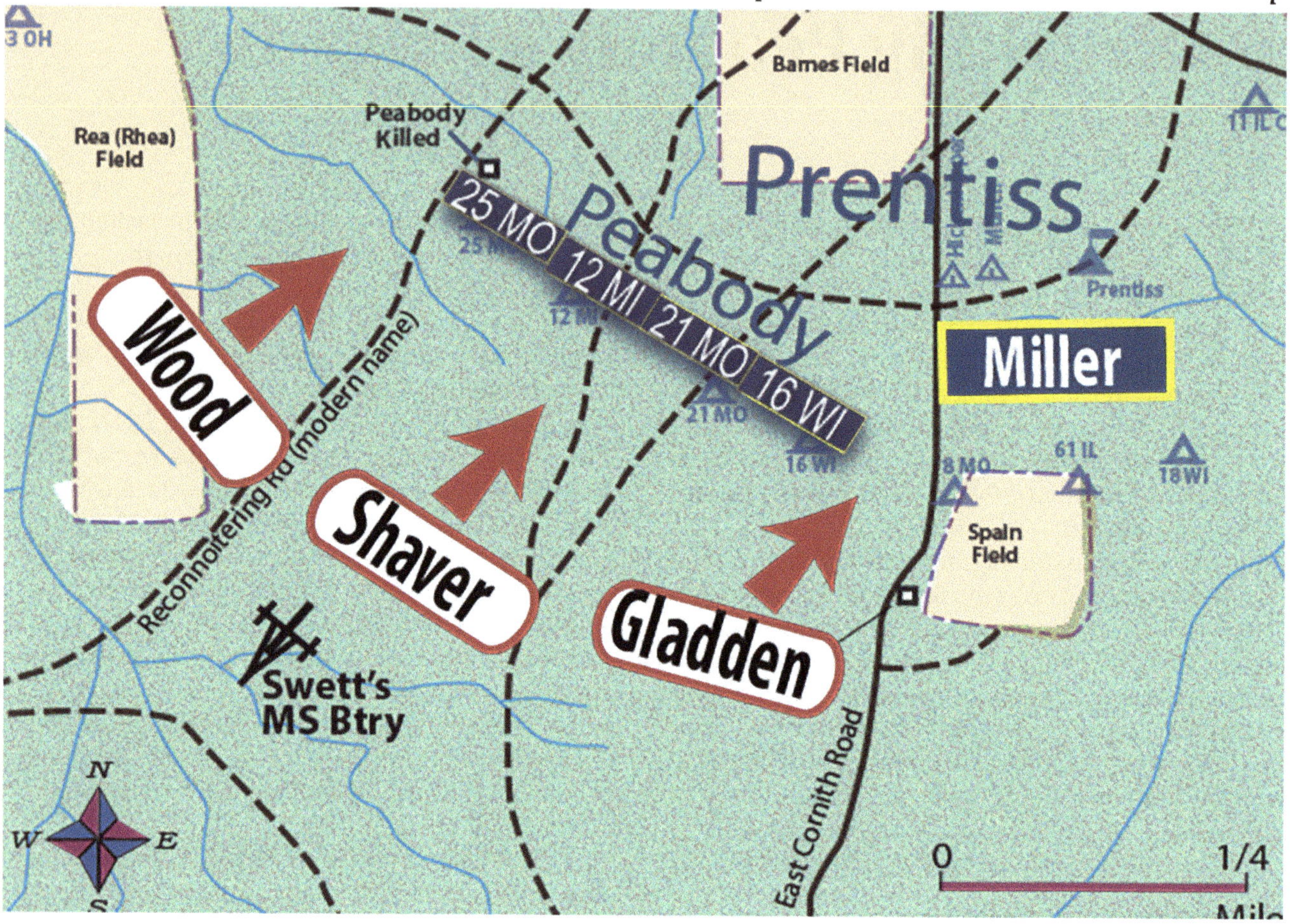

Chapter 6 - Attack into Prentiss' Camp

Attack on Prentiss' Camp

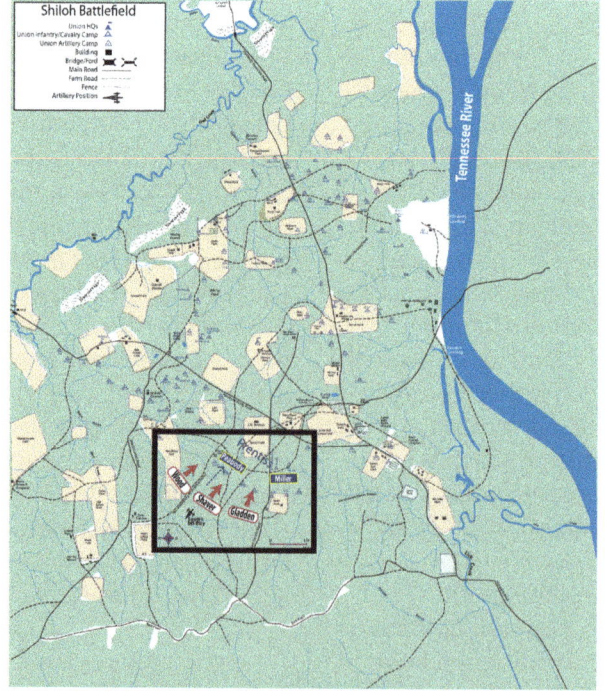

Map's Location on the Battlefield

Peabody Falls

Peabody had been away, fruitlessly searching for Prentiss, and he returned just in time to find his brigade falling apart. He desperately tried rallying his men, riding to and fro, shouting, "*Remember Lexington!*" In the process he was wounded four times, but remained mounted. Finally, at around 8:45am, seeing his brigade disintegrating, he shouted above the din of battle, "*The 25th Missouri is disgraced!*" Suddenly, his head snapped back and he hurled his sword into the air as a fifth bullet found its mark, striking him in the upper lip and passing through the back of his head. He crashed dead to the ground with his legs sprawled over a log, while his horse galloped wildly towards the Confederate lines, stirrups flapping in the air.

The Federals began falling back among their camp tents. Maj. Powell, who had earlier been accused of cowardice by Col. Moore, briefly took command of one sector before he was killed while trying to rally the men. The commander of the 16WI, Col. Ben Allen, had his horse shot from under him and, as he tried to mount another horse, that one was shot as well.

By 8:30am, Peabody's brigade was shattered, and most of its survivors now fled toward Pittsburg Landing.

The Confederates took possession of Peabody's camps, and in theory, nothing now stopped them from charging straight northeast toward Pittsburg Landing. However, the Confederates stopped to loot the camps. Also, due rough terrain, they probably didn't know quite where they were.

Though the Confederates were successful in driving whatever was in front of them so far, they were dangerously behind schedule. Johnston expected his battle line to slam into the Federal encampment at 6am. But here it was 8:30am before they even reached Peabody's camps. They had wasted over an hour skirmishing in Seay and Fraley Fields, and that precious time would be dearly missed later in the day. And even more time was lost as the Confederate troops stopped to pillage the Federal tents.

The Union encampments, packed with thousands of tents – teepee-like Sibley Tents for the troops, and wall tents for the officers – had a disorganizing effect on both sides. They broke up the cohesion of the Union ranks as the Federals retreated back through the camps, with many soldiers not stopping until they reached Pittsburg Landing. But the tents also broke up the lines of the attacking Confederates, mainly because of looting by the famished Rebel soldiers, who stopped to pillage the tents and their treasure trove of booty. Lt. Liberty Nixon of the 26AL noted that the "*Yankees... left everything they had... corn, oats, pants, vests, drawers, shirts, shoes, and a great many other things in great abundance and of the finest quality*."

At about this time, the steamer *Tigress*, with Grant on board, was just pulling into the Landing.

It was 9am. The battle had been going on for three hours.

Sibley tents were designed by former U.S. Capt. Henry Hopkins Sibley (by 1862, a Confederate brigadier general), and patterned after the teepees of the Plains Indians. A regulation Sibley tent was a large cone of canvas, 18 feet in diameter, 12 feet tall, and supported by center poll, with a circular opening at the top for ventilation and a cone-shaped stove for heat. It could fit 12 men in comfort or, more commonly, 20 men in considerably less.

Each company usually had five Sibley tents, and at the head of the row was a wall tent for the officers. Some ten to fifteen feet separated the companies to allow room for washing and cooking. The quartermaster and hospital tents were located nearby. There were some 5,000 tents crammed on almost every open, muddy field around Pittsburg Landing. In the middle of the coming battle, they were an impediment to both attacker and defender.

Surprisingly, also intertwined with these Union camps were sutler wagons, which were mobile civilian commissaries selling products the soldiers wanted but the army didn't supply - tasty snacks, playing cards, writing paper, envelopes, postage stamps, photos of naked women and, for enough money, maybe even a shot of Tennessee whiskey. Some of the sutlers traveled down on their own boats, while others apparently rented space aboard some of the troop steamers.

On the Line with the Dixie Grays

One of the Confederate soldiers in the very center of the first attacking line was 21-year-old Pvt. Henry Morton Stanley, who had been born in Wales. He never knew his father and his 18-year-old mother abandoned him as a baby. His birth certificate labeled him a "*bastard,*" which was a great stigma at the time. He was passed around by various relatives before finally being sent to one of the dreaded workhouses. Somehow, when old enough, he immigrated to America and ended up in the Confederate army in Arkansas.

He was a future journalist–adventurer who, nine years later, would locate and resupply the famed English missionary David Livingstone in central Africa and utter the famous phrase, "*Dr. Livingstone, I presume?*" But on this morning the Welshman found himself a rifleman in the 6AR, "the Dixie Grays," in Shaver's Brigade.

He described the approach:

Pvt. Henry M. Stanley
1841 - 1904

"As we tramped solemnly and silently through the thin forest, and over its grass, still in its withered and wintry hue, I noticed that the sun was not far from appearing, that our regiment was keeping its formation, that the woods would have been a grand place for a picnic, and I thought it strange that a Sunday should have been chosen to disturb the holy calm of those woods.

"A dreadful roar of musketry broke out from a regiment adjoining ours. It was followed by another further off, and the sound had scarcely died away when regiment after regiment blazed away and made a continuous roll of sound."

Beyond a thicket the regiment overtook its skirmishers when suddenly someone shouted, "*There they are!*" The captain shouted, "*Aim low men!*"

At first, Stanley saw nothing. But as the advance continued:

"I at last saw a row of little globes of pearly smoke streaked with crimson, breaking out, with spurtive quickness, from a long line of bluey figures in front; and, simultaneously, there broke upon our ears an appalling crash of sound, the series of fusillades following one another with startling suddenness, which suggested a mountain upheaved, with huge rocks tumbling and thundering down a slope. Again and again the loud, quick explosions were repeated with increased violence until they rose to the highest pitch of fury. All the world seemed involved in one tremendous ruin!

"We… loaded, and fired, with such nervous haste as though it depended on each of us how soon the fiendish roar would be hushed. My nerves tingled, my pulses beat double-quick, my heart throbbed loudly, almost painfully… I was angry with my rear rank [the soldier directly behind him], because he made my eyes smart with the powder of his musket; and I felt like cuffing him for deafening my ears!… We continued advancing, step-by-step, loading and firing as we went. To every forward step, they [the Federals] took a backward move, loading and firing as they slowly withdrew… After a steady exchange of musketry, which lasted some time, we heard the order: "Fix bayonets! On the double-quick!

"There was a simultaneous bound forward … The Federals appeared inclined to await us; but, at this juncture, our men raised a yell, thousands responded to it, and burst out into the wildest yelling it has ever been my lot to hear. It served the double purpose of relieving pent-up feelings and transmitting encouragement along the attacking line…

"They fly!" was echoed from lip to lip. It accelerated our pace, and filled us with a noble rage… It deluded us with rapture, and transfigured each Southerner into an exulting victor. At such a moment, nothing could have halted us. Those savage yells, and the sight of thousands of racing figures coming towards them, discomfited the blue-coats, and when we arrived upon the place where they had stood, they had vanished. Then we caught sight of their beautiful array of tents.

"I had the momentary impression that with the capture of that first camp the battle was well-nigh over; but it was only a brief prologue of the long and exhaustive series of struggles that day."

Meanwhile, Back at Savannah

At about this time back in Savannah, Brig. Gen. William "Bull" Nelson's 4,500 man division, the vanguard of Buell's army, had been preparing for inspection after having reached the town the previous afternoon, Bull Nelson, a 21-year Navy veteran, also known as "Big Buster", was a rotund, 300+ pound, six-foot-something Kentuckian and Annapolis graduate who Grant had sent to take Nashville after the fall of Fort Donelson.

He was popular with many of his men because of his pugnacity, but just as many considered him a tyrant, "*A cruel and foulmouthed man.*" Navy captains could be not only profane but also brutal, and Nelson didn't mind laying hands on anyone who displeased him, which was not hard to do. (He weighed twice as much as most Civil War soldiers, who averaged 147 pounds). When mounted on his massive but long-suffering black stallion, Ned, and wearing a hat with a large black ostrich feather, no one could fail to notice Bull Nelson.

Back in Kentucky, when his home state was teetering between joining the North or the South, Nelson violated Kentucky's razor-thin neutrality by blatantly opening a Kentucky recruiting depot for Union soldiers. This action triggered an entire chain of profound events, since it was used by Confederate Gen. Polk as an excuse to occupy Columbus, Kentucky, which ended Kentucky's neutrality, which allowed Grant to occupy Paducah, Kentucky, which led to the attack on Ft. Henry, etc., etc. All triggered by Big Buster.

In those chaotic times, when leaders were desperately needed and with Lincoln's help, Bull smoothly made the transition from a navy captain to army brigadier general, and a tailor even managed to locate enough yards of cloth to sew a snappy army uniform to wrap around Bull's massive girth.

Oddly, this ex-sailor seemed to be the only Federal army officer who realized that Grant's army was in serious danger. Several days earlier, while on the march from Nashville, Buell's army was halted for days by the rain-swollen Duck River near Columbia, Tennessee. Nelson exclaimed, "*By God, we must cross the river at once, or Grant will be whipped!*"

In the lead of Buell's army, Nelson finally reached Savannah at around 1pm on April 5th, where he reported to Grant at the Cherry Mansion, requesting permission to push on immediately to Pittsburg Landing. Grant told him to camp at Savannah for the moment. Nelson asked whether Grant wasn't concerned about an enemy attack, saying "*The wonder to me is that he has not done so before.*" Grant confidently explained that he had more troops than he did at Fort Donelson and he could handle any attack. C. F. Smith, who was also present, reassured Nelson, saying, "*They [the enemy] are all back at Corinth, and, when our transportation arrives, we have got to go there and draw them out, as you draw a badger out of a hole.*"

Brig. Gen. William Nelson
1824 - 1862

But Nelson remained fidgety that day, and seemed to have a premonition of a Confederate attack.

(Later that day, Grant visited an old friend, Col. Jacob Ammen, one of Nelson's brigade commanders. Ammen also asked if they shouldn't be pressing on to Pittsburg Landing. Grant told him there were no transports readily available, and that it would be impossible to march through the swamps on the east bank of the river.)

Now, on Sunday morning, April 6th, the Bull was slumbering fitfully when he was roused by the dull rumble of cannon. He "*sprang from his couch. He called for Lt. Southgate ... and ordered him to have the brigade commanders to have their men in readiness to move at any moment.*" He also sent an aide to see if any transports were available.

"*Still awaiting Grant's orders,*" Nelson "*chafed like a lion caged. He ate no breakfast, paced up and down before his tent, could not be pacified, and would not be pleased with anything or anybody.*"

Finally, "*unwilling to endure his torturing suspense, he mounted his horse and galloped to Grant's headquarters,*" only to be told that Grant had departed. But soon after that, probably around 8am, he received Grant's orders to march his division along the east bank of the river "*to a point opposite Pittsburg,*" confidently stating, "*You can easily find a guide in the city.*"

Nelson went hunting for a guide.

Chapter 6 - Attack into Prentiss' Camp

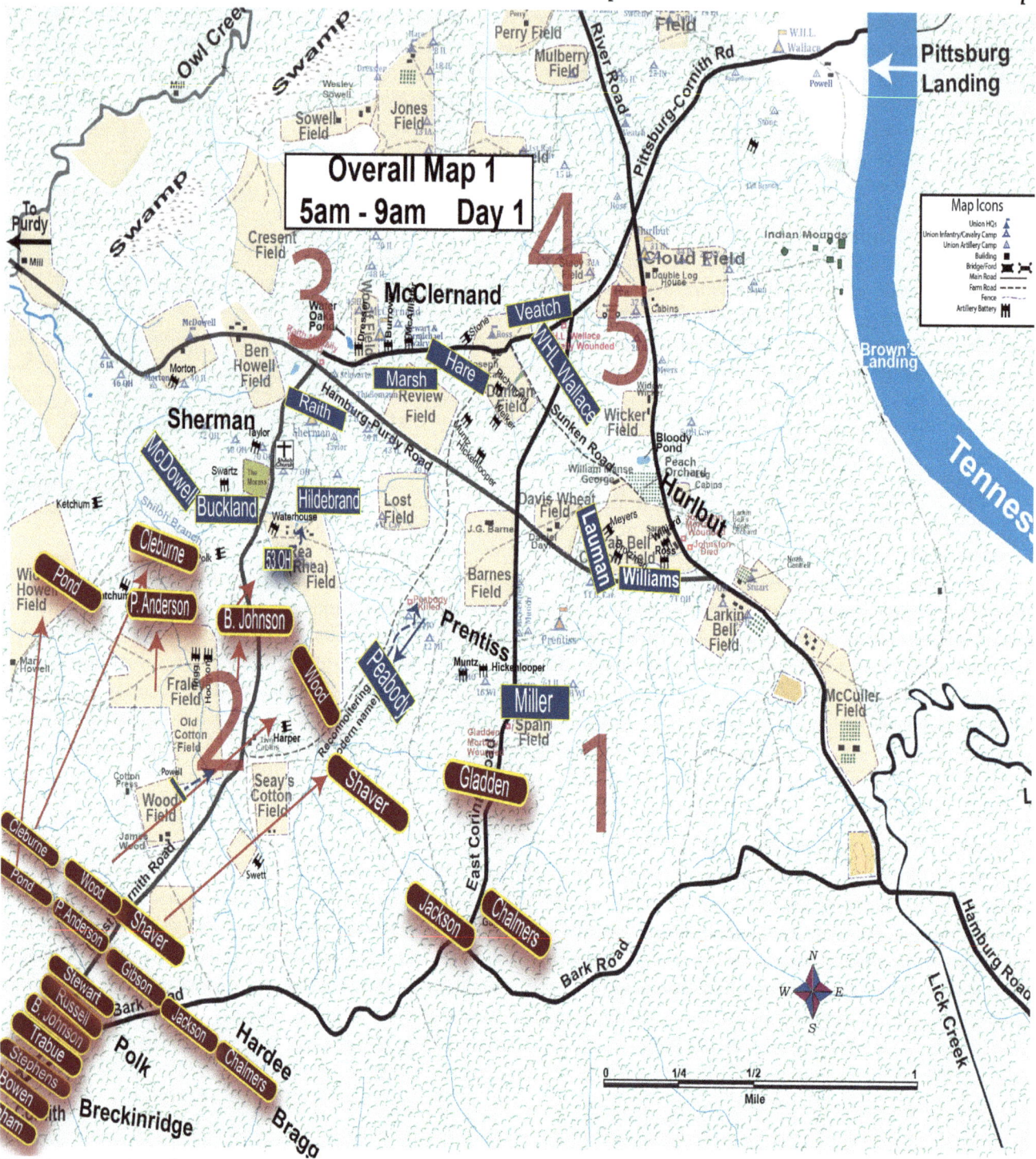

In this same time frame,
1. Confederates were attacking both brigades (Peabody's and Miller') of Prenstiss' division,
2. And also attacking both brigades (Buckland and Hildebrand's) of Sherman's division.
3. Farther north, McClernand was moving his brigades toward the sound of battle, and,
4. Hurlbut had sent one of his brigades (Veatch's) to aid McClernand & Sherman, while marching to the Peach Orchard area with his other two brigades, while
5. WHL Wallace was moving his division toward what would be known as the Sunken Road.
(Note that this same map will be shown for all chapters in this 5am-9am time frame).

7 Breaking Miller's Brigade

Miller Deploys on Spain Field
7:30am - 8am

Once Peabody's brigade was fully engaged at 7:30am, Prentiss galloped over to his other brigade, Col. Madison Miller's, yelling: *"Colonel, get out your brigade! They're fighting on the right!"* The 51-year-old Miller, a Mexican War veteran, hastily ordered the 18MO into a line of battle at the north end of Spain Field, facing timber. But Prentiss didn't like the position and wisely ordered Miller to redeploy back across to the south end of the field where the regiment, as well as the rest of Miller's 1,700-man brigade, faced a ravine and would have a clear field of fire to their front.

This new location served as a base for a solid Union battle line. Several companies of the 16WI of Peabody's brigade joined Miller's four regimens and extended the line westward across Eastern Corinth Road. Meanwhile, the 18WI and 61IL rushed up to extend Miller's line to the east.

Col. Madison Miller 1811 - 1866

On the far right of the line, the just-arrived 15MI formed up, having just marched down from the Landing to report for duty. But the 15th had a slight problem – no ammunition. Trying to make the best of a very bad situation, the 15th's commander ordered his bewildered men to fix bayonets.

By 8am Miller's battle line was as complete as it was going to get. The nervous green troops probably said some prayers as they waited their turn, listening to the crash of battle grow closer from the direction of Peabody's brigade to the west. Pvt. Edgar Embly of the 61IL remembered, *"We were drawn up in line of battle. I was looking as anxious for the Secesh as I ever did a squirrel, but I did not look long before I seen their guns glittering in the brush."*

Then, *"like the sweep of a midsummer thunderhead rolling across the stubble field,"* the battle rolled east and engulfed them. Soon thousands of men dressed in butternut emerged from the woods in line of battle, their rifles at right shoulder shift, topped off with foot-and-a-half bayonets.

Obviously, this was particularly distressing to the 15MI, which was sans bullets.

> Like the "sweep of a midsummer thunderhead rolling across the stubble field," the battle engulfed Miller's brigade.

According to 16-year-old Pvt George W. McBride, the regiment was standing at ease and order arms as they watched several long lines of men in brown and gray pouring down the opposite slope. *"The first line moves down the hillside, crosses the little creek, enters the clearing, halts, and fires into us. Not a man in our company has a cartridge to use. A few men fall. We are ordered to shoulder arms, about face, and move back, which we do."*

But at least the Federals soon had some artillery support from Capt. Andrew Hickenlooper's six-gun Ohio battery, which had literally just disembarked at the Landing. Hickenlooper dropped trails in the northwestern corner of Spain Field, east of the Eastern Corinth Road. And he was joined by Capt. Emil Munch's 1MN Battery, which unlimbered astride and to the west of the road, protecting Miller's right flank.

Gladden's Brigade Strikes
8:30am - 9am

Storming Miller's position on a northeastern slant was Brig. Gen. Jones M. Withers' division, which consisted of three brigades under Brig. Gens. Aldey Gladden, James Chalmers, and John Jackson. These men were part of Bragg's Corps and therefore part of the second wave of the Confederate assault force. A Confederate cavalryman watching from a rise later wrote, *"We could see the lines of our army for long distances, right and left as they advanced with marvelous precision, with regimental colors flying, and all the bands playing 'Dixie.'"*

Waiting to receive the Confederate assault, 18-year-old Cpl. Leander Stillwell of the 61IL, watched as, *"suddenly to the right there was a long,*

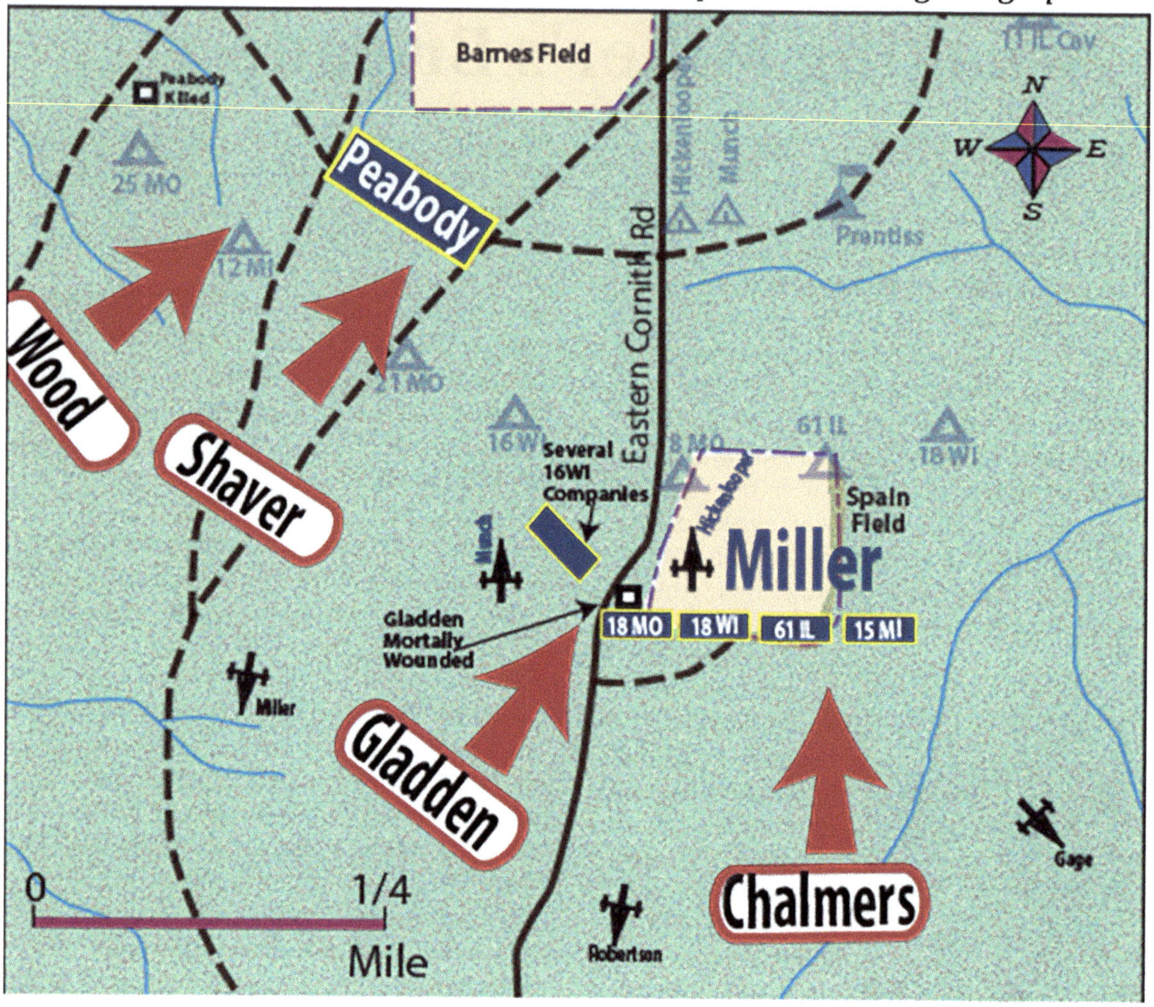

Chapter 7 - The Fighting Spreads East

The fighting spreads east into Miller's Brigade

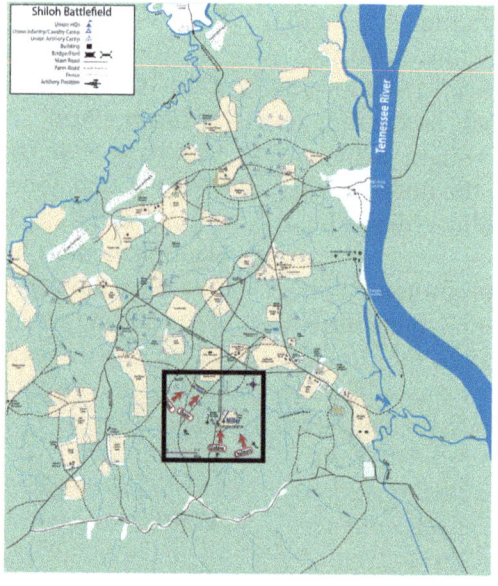

Map's Location on the Battlefield

wavy flash of bright light, then another, and another! It was the sunlight shining on bayonets – and – they were here at last! A long brown line with muskets at a right shoulder shift, in excellent order, right through the woods they came."

He also remembered that once the order to fire was given, *"from one end of the regiment to the next leaped a red sheet of flame."* But Stillwell, obviously a perfectionist, was bending down, looking for a target under the smoke. Someone behind him yelled, *"Shoot! Shoot! Why don't you shoot?"* Stillwell looked around to see one of the second lieutenants *"fairly wild with excitement, jumping up an down like a hen on a hot griddle."* Stillwell replied that he couldn't see anything to shoot at because of the smoke. The lieutenant yelled, *"Shoot! Shoot anyhow!"* Stillwell did, thinking *"that it was ridiculous to fire into a cloud of smoke."*

The lieutenant was "fairly wild with excitement, jumping up and down like a hen on a hot griddle."

Gladden's brigade had actually been advanced by Johnston to the east flank of the first wave line (Hardee's Corps), so as to extend the Confederate right flank and secure it along Lick Creek and the Tennessee River. But by 7:30am, Johnston realized that Hardee's attack was veering too far west, and so ordered Chalmers' brigade to fill the gap, once again extending the Confederate right flank so that it remained connected with Lick Creek.

The end result was that Gladden's brigade confronted Miller's Union line thirty minutes before Chalmers arrived to support him. Gladden ordered his Alabama regiments into the fray anyway. Gladden's men would have to advance across a shallow branch of Locus Grove Creek and then advance up a gentle slope of open ground about 150-200 yards from the Yankee line.

Col. Adley H. Gladden (mw) 1810 -1862

But before his attack was even launched, his troops encountered a devastating fire from Miller's infantry and Federal artillery. The Confederate line faltered. Gladden needed artillery support.

Capt. Felix Robertson's four-gun Florida battery raced up to support Gladden. And not long after, Capt. Charles P. Gage's Alabama battery from Chalmers' brigade also galloped up, dropping trails within 200 yards of Miller's line. Both Confederate batteries took heavy infantry fire, but they helped pave the way for Gladden's infantry assault.

It was now around 8:45am. Gladden ordered a charge.

The portly, 51-year-old Gladden, a Mexican War veteran and New Orleans merchant, was conspicuously mounted on horseback as he led his men forward into the ferocious fire of Yankee infantry and artillery. At least one of the Federal batteries switched to canister, and almost immediately Gladden was struck by a canister ball, nearly tearing his left arm from its shoulder socket. *"Scott,"* he yelled to his aide, *"I'm struck, but let's go on."* But after moving a few more steps, he admitted, *"It's a serious hurt, help me down, Scott."* An ambulance carried the

Canister is basically a tin can containing anywhere from 26 to 30 one-inch iron balls packed in sawdust. About two-and-half pounds of gunpowder is first rammed down the cannon barrel, followed by the canister can. When ignited, the canister balls spew out like a shotgun blast with 26 to 30 iron golf-balls flying into densely packed infantry lines. It was said that just one of these balls could cut a man in half at 500 yards.

Civil War canister, dug up and placed in a basket.

Page 49

"It was a kind of flag I had never saw before; a gaudy sort of thing with red bars."

mortally wounded colonel to the rear, where a correspondent noted that he was *"pale, faint, but still smiling."*

With the loss of their leader, the Alabamians fell back again. Command passed to the brigade's senior colonel, Daniel Adams of the 1LA, a former lawyer who had never seen combat except once when he killed a Vicksburg newspaper editor in a duel because the editor had questioned the political views of Adam's father, a federal judge. Adams grabbed the 1LA flag and rode slowly through the retreating troops, yelling, *"Will you come with me?,"* and called for the men to make another attack. The brigade rallied and surged forward, supported by a two-gun section of Robertson's cannoneers, who pushed their guns almost into point blank range of Miller's line.

Union Cpl. Stillwell saw "*men in gray and brown clothes running through the camp on our right. I saw something else too, that sent a chill all through me. It was a kind of flag I had never seen before; a gaudy sort of thing with red bars. The smoke around it was low and dense and kept me from seeing the man who was carrying it but I plainly saw the banner. It was going fast, with a jerky motion, which told me that the bearer was at the double quick."*

Veteran troops might have withstood Adam's assault, but Miller's men were not veterans. Gradually his brigade began leaking men as they drifted to the rear.

Miller's Line Collapses
8:30am - 9am

While Prentiss's right brigade, Peabody's, was collapsing. Prentiss' left brigade, Miller's, was facing the storm of Adams' attack. To protect Miller's right flank, Prentiss ordered Miller's men to *"change front to the right."* This was the wrong order to give raw troops in the middle of a battle; worse, at just that moment Adams renewed his assault, putting the Federal recruits under heavy fire and creating even more confusion in their ranks.

Brig. Gen. Daniel W. Adams (w) 1821 - 1872

Prentiss' order also doomed Capt. Andrew Hickenlooper's Ohio battery. "Changing front to the right" meant turning the guns 90 degrees, which was hard to do under fire, "*in woods filled with dense undergrowth, horses rearing and plunging and dropping in their tracks.*" Worse, it exposed the left flank of the battery, which the Confederates immediately attacked.

To cap things off, at around 8:30am, Chalmers' men finally appeared. Chalmers gave the order to attack. At first, only the 360 men of the 10MS heard the order, and the regiment charged alone. But it was soon followed by the 7MS and 9MS. The Confederates poured out of the wooded ravine on Adam's right and slammed into the 18WI, shrieking "*with a Rebel Yell that caused an involuntary thrill of terror to pass like an electric shock through even the bravest heart,*" according to Capt. Hickenlooper. After about 20 minutes, the Wisconsin troops broke and fled, creating a fatal gap in the middle of Miller's line. Immediately Confederate troops flooded into this gap, shattering Miller's entire line.

Pvt. George McBride of the 18WI described the moment: "*There was the crash of musketry, the roar of artillery, the yells, the smoke, the jar, the terrible energy. At intervals we can see the faces of the foe, blackened with powder, and glaring with demonic fury, lost to all human impulses, and full of the fiendish desire to kill.*"

"[The] Rebel Yell ... caused an involuntary thrill of terror to pass like an electric shock through even the bravest heart."

Prentiss and Miller desperately tried to rally the troops to a new position at the north end of Spain Field.

The order came,"*for some reason - I never knew what,*" Cpl. Stillwell said, to fall back across the field to their original positions on the north side of the field in front of their tent camps, where some of the fiercest fighting of the battle erupted. Stillwell fell back and jumped behind a tree, thinking they must have disturbed a nest of bees, because of an "*incessant humming above our heads,*" Then he realized those were bullets. Then he saw his first man killed, as the man next to him fell stone dead. "*I stared at his body, perfectly horrified,*" he said. "*The man had been hit square in the head. Only a few moments ago that man was alive and well.*" Stillwell admitted that "*it came near to upsetting me.*" But he said he got used to such scenes during the course of the day.

Union Pvt. McBride described the collapse of Miller's defense: "*The enemy flank us and are moving*

Chapter 7 - The Fighting Spreads East

Capt. Andrew Hickenlooper
1837 - 1904

to our rear; someone calls out 'Everybody for himself!' The line breaks, I go with others, back and down the hill, across a small ravine, and into the camp of the 11IL Calvary with the howling, rushing mass of the enemy pressing in close pursuit... The striking of shot on the ground threw up little clouds of dust, and the falling of men all around me impressed me with the desire to get out of there... I felt sure that a cannonball was close behind me, giving me chase as I started for the river... I never ran so fast before."

Prentiss' division was mostly, but not totally, demolished. Of the 5,400 men in his division, only about 600 continued fighting as Prentiss fell back. Hickenlooper's battery was hit by terrible fire that cut down 59 of its 80 horses, still in their harnesses and "all piled up in their death struggles."

According to Hickenlooper, *"Each man and officer takes his assigned position, then the minies buzz and sing about their ears. When a gunner drops from his place, another fills the gap; and thus the work goes on with a system and regularity marvelous in its perfection."* But now Confederate artillery had joined in, and it was time to get out. Hickenlooper had just given the order to limber up *"when there comes a crashing volley that sweeps our front as with a scythe, a roar that is deafening, and the earth trembles with the shock."* The blast killed most of the men and every horse near one gun, including the horse Hickenlooper was on. Now the Federal infantry guard rose up and fled, *"in wild dismay."*

When the Federals retreated, two of Hickenlooper's guns fell directly into Confederate hands. Somehow, his men extricated the other four guns by hand and with the few horses that remained. His teams hauled the guns and caissons, *"bounding through underbrush, over ditches, logs, each driver lashing his team."* What remained of the battery raced north to a line where Prentiss had planted his colors, intending to make a stand near a peach orchard along an old wagon track, soon to be known as "'The Sunken Road." But the loss of the horses would seriously hinder the battery's mobility for the remainder of the day, which is why attacking infantry always targeted the enemy's artillery horses.

"At intervals we can see the faces of the foe, blackened with powder, and glaring with demonic fury, lost to all human impulses and full of the fiendish desire to kill."

By 9am, after driving back Prentiss' division, the jubilant Rebels pursued them through their tent camp shouting "*Bull Run!,*" before breaking off. As was the story throughout the day, the victorious Confederate attack stalled while the attackers stopped to plunder the Union camps, sparing the fleeing Federals from even greater destruction. In one tent vacated by the 18WI, a beaming young lieutenant emerged with an armful of trophies. But his smile froze as he looked up to see Gen. Johnston himself, mounted on his steed, Fire-Eater, and surrounded by his glittering staff. Johnston, intent on stopping the pillaging, must have looked like Jesus and his Apostles to the astonished lieutenant. *"None of that, sir,"* the general bellowed, *"we are not here to plunder!"* The young officer was horrified; to be chewed out by the commanding general for stealing pots and pans in the middle of a battle was never helpful to a lieutenant's career.

Realizing he had been too harsh, Johnston softened the scold by smiling and doing something silly; he leaned over to pick up a tin cup off a table, announcing to all, *"Let this be my share of the spoils today."*
He would carry that cup for the rest of his life.

Chalmers & Jackson Redeploy
9am - 10am
After destroying Miller's brigade and pausing to raid the Federal camp, the jubilant men of Adams and Chalmers continued surging north to the Hamburg-Purdy Road, where they were reinforced by Jackson's brigade of Wither's division. There they would briefly encounter Hurlbut's Union division at Sarah Bell's Old Cotton Field, before Johnston pulled Jackson's and Chalmers' brigades off and sent them farther east to deal with the threat of another Union division, which would turn out to be non-existent. But in this ad hoc way, more by accident than design, Johnston was shifting more attacking power to his right flank, resurrecting his original plan to launch a powerful sweep on the Confederate right toward Pittsburg Landing.

But as we shall see later, removing Jackson and Chalmers to the far right caused the Confederates to miss an opportunity to break through Sarah Bell's Field and possibly advance straight up the River Road to Pittsburg Landing.

Grant Takes Charge

Between 8:30am and 9am, Grant's steamer, the *Tigress*, approached Pittsburg Landing. The din of battle steadily increased the nearer the boat got to the shore. By the time the boat docked the roar was so great that the sailors thought the battle was raging just on the other side of the bluff.

There was already great confusion at the Landing, with "stragglers" already beginning to converge there – about 3,000 by that time, according to one eyewitness. But there were also some recently-arrived regiments - the 23MO, 15IA, and 16IA - basically standing around, awaiting orders from somebody.

Grant ordered the 23MO to reinforce Prentiss, wherever he was, and form up with his division. The regiment's commander, Col. Jacob Tindall, who would be dead within the hour, immediately moved his men out.

A bit farther up the bluff, Grant encountered the commander of the 15IA, Col. Hugh T. Reid, and ordered him to draw ammunition and to form across the Landing road to halt stragglers. Col. Reid looked confused; Grant was wearing his usual private's jacket, and Reid didn't know who he was. Grant had to inform him, *"I am General Grant."* Reid understood and proceeded to order his men to secure the road; in the process he also gathered the 16IA to help. (Sometime during the day, Grant switched to his formal dress uniform, complete with saber and sash).

Brig. Gen. James R. Chalmers 1831 - 1898

With assistance, Grant mounted up, his crutch strapped to his saddle. He attempted to bring some order to the Landing, giving a short pep talk to some of the stragglers standing around, but with little effect. Meanwhile, his staff officers fanned out across the battlefield, notifying the division commanders that Grant was on the field. Other members of his staff were put to work dealing with supply issues, especially moving ammunition to the front.

Brig. Gen. John K. Jackson 1828 - 1866

Chapter 7 - The Fighting Spreads East

The general then rode a half mile up Corinth Road, where he encountered W. H. L. Wallace, who briefed him on the gravity of the attack. Now realizing that the main attack was indeed at Pittsburg Landing, Grant ordered his aide, Capt. John Rawlins, to send a messenger to Crumps Landing with orders for Lew Wallace to bring up his division. Another message was sent to Nelson back in Savannah to speed up his division.

Those tasks completed, Grant, along with his staff, including his chief engineer, Col. James McPherson, rode on toward the battleline to meet with his division commanders. He remained amazingly poised, partially because he was expecting Lew Wallace's division of 7,300 men by early afternoon. One of his aides, Capt. William Rowley said, *"General, this thing looks pretty squally, doesn't it?"* Grant replied, *"Well, not so very bad. We've got to fight against time now. Wallace must be here very soon."*

Around noon, he spotted some Federal troops approaching from the right, and he exclaimed, *"Now we're all right! There's Wallace."* But it *wasn't* Wallace.

As the general and his party crossed the northern edge of Duncan Field, a Rebel battery spotted them and its four or so guns opened on them. A shell exploded in front of Grant's horse. He spurred his horse, saying, *"We've must ride fast here!"* The party dashed behind a cabin but shells crashed through the building, showering them with shingles and splinters. As the group rode on, a shell fragment hit Grant's scabbard, knocking his sword to the ground. When they finally got out of range, McPherson's horse was panting and about to drop; a cannonball had completely passed through the animal's back.

> *The Mississippi cavalryman watching the fighting from a distant hill was under artillery fire* "Many solid shot we saw strike the ground," *he said,* "bounding like rubber balls, passing over our heads, making a hideous music in their course."
>
> *But one of the cannon balls struck the tail of his horse, Bremer. The horse was holding his tail high in the air due to the excitement and the cannonball* "cut away about half of it, bone and all."
>
> *From then on Bremer was known as "Bobtail Bremer."*

One casualty in the 21AL of Gladden's brigade was Lt. George E. Dixon, who was wounded in the leg. But the force of the bullet was partially stopped by a $20 gold coin in his pocket, said to be given to him by his girlfriend. The wound was still serious and he walked with a limp for the rest of his 23 years of life. After the battle, he was transferred to Mobile, Alabama and, probably unable to serve in the army due to his wound, he became involved with submarines. After some trial runs, a submarine, the CSA H. L. Hunley was shipped or built in Charleston, South Carolina. On Feb 17, 1864, the Hunley sallied out of Charleston harbor to sink a Yankee ship, with Dixon serving as the captain. The submarine sank the ship, but the force of the blast also sunk the Hunley, drowning all the occupants.

In 2000, the Hunley was discovered and raised. Dixon's bones were identified and the gold coin was found near his hip. The coin has the dent from a bullet and an inscription and his initials:

Shiloh
April 6th 1862
My life Preserver
G. E. D.
(Photo from Hunley.org)

Chapter 7 - The Fighting Spreads East

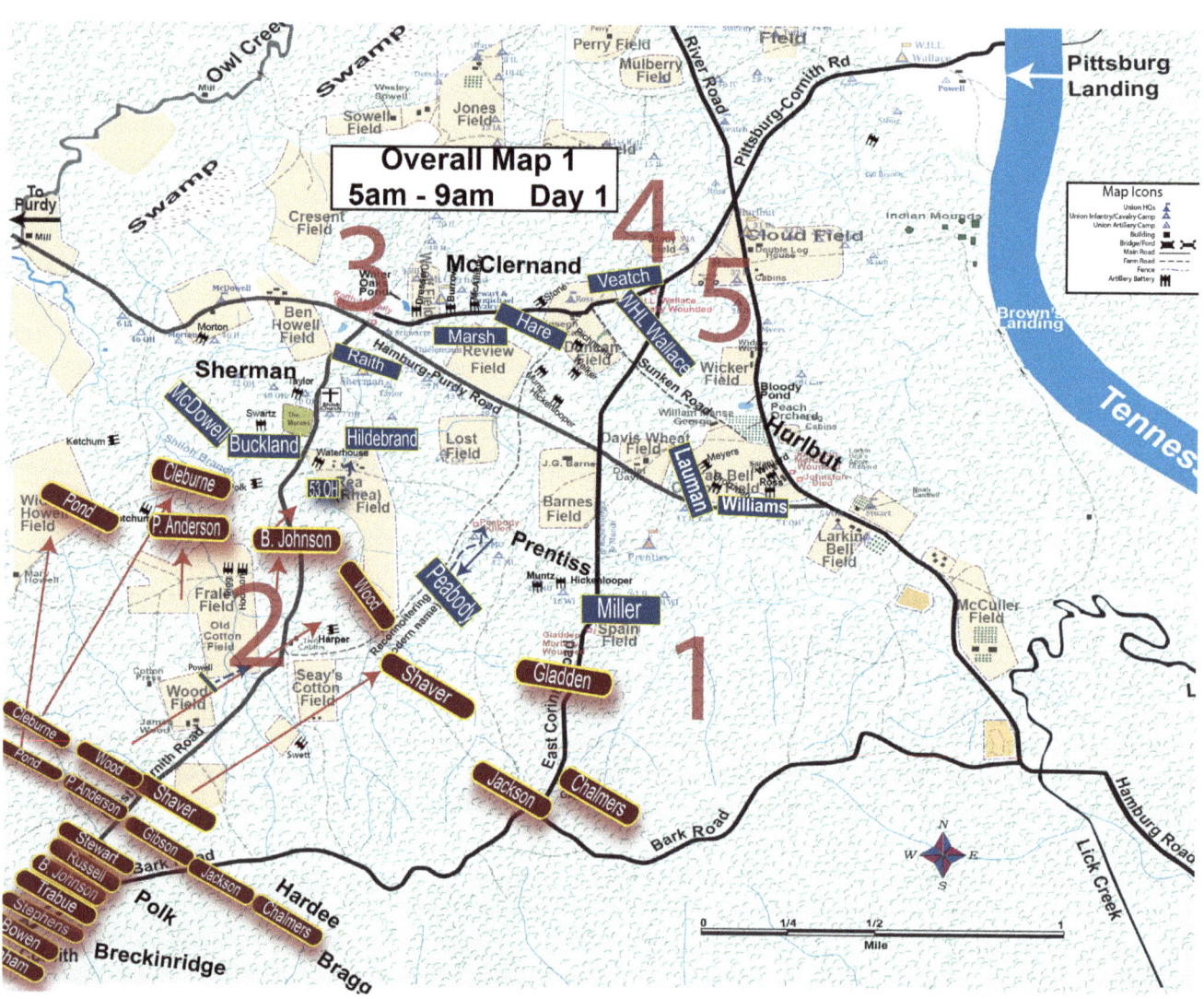

In this same time frame,
1. Confederates were attacking both brigades (Peabody's and Miller') of Prenstiss' division,
2. And attacking both brigades (Buckland and Hildebrand's) of Sherman's division.
3. Farther north, McClernand was moving his brigades toward the sound of battle, and,
4. Hurlbut had sent one of his brigades (Veatch's) to aid McClernand & Sherman, while marching to the Peach Orchard area with his other two brigades, while
5. WHL Wallace was moving his division toward what would be known as the Sunken Road.
(Note that this same map will be shown for all chapters in this 5am-9am time frame).

Page 54

8   Breaking Hildebrand's Brigade

6am - 10am
53rd Ohio Attacked in Rea Field

Both Prentiss and Sherman were under nearly simultaneous attack. We've discussed the attack on Prentiss' division to the east in the previous chapters. For the next couple of chapters, we'll discuss the attack on Sherman's division.

Sherman had two of his four brigades - Hildebrand's and Buckland's - camped on either side of Shiloh Church. Although the two brigades were fighting simultaneously, in this chapter, we'll focus only on Hildebrand's brigade on the east side of the church, while discussing Buckland in the next chapter. Note that these two brigades were also separated by the Western Corinth Road (aka Pittsburg-Corinth Road.).

Col. Jesse Hildebrand's brigade on the east side of the road consisted of three regiments - the 77OH, 57OH, and 53OH. The regiment camps ran in a southeasterly direction with the 77OH being near Shiloh Church, then the 57OH and finally the 53OH, with the latter's camp being on the south side of Shiloh Branch in Rea Field, some distance from its two sister regiments. The 53OH would be the first regiment in the path of the Confederate attack on Sherman's division.

But the day before the attack, around 4pm on Saturday afternoon, April 5th, the 53rd's commander, Col. Jesse R. Appler - a 31-year-old former Ohio probate judge and auditor - received a report that Rebel cavalry had been spotted snooping around the south end of Rea Field. Appler continued drilling his troops, but he sent a platoon to investigate.

> **"There's Rebs out there thicker'n fleas on a dog's back!"**

Suddenly shots rang out from the platoon's vicinity. An officer came racing back, yelling that they had been fired on by a line of men in butternut clothes. *"There's Rebs out there thicker'n fleas on a dog's back!,"* he exclaimed. Appler instantly ordered the long drum-roll sounded to form his men into ranks, and sent a messenger galloping to Sherman.

The colonel was standing at the head of his regiment when the courier promptly returned and announced in a sarcastic, twangy voice, loud enough to be heard by all, *"Colonel Appler, General Sherman says: 'Take your damn regiment back to Ohio. There ain't no enemy closer'n Corinth!'"* The regiment roared with laughter. A humiliated Appler dismissed his regiment.

> **"Take your damn regiment back to Ohio. There ain't no enemy closer'n Corinth!"**

Sherman had scornfully dismissed several warnings of the enemy proximity in the past two days, and he'd soon have to eat his words, being particularly mortified to see them printed in newspapers by dirty reporters.

Like Col. Peabody in Prentiss' division, Appler remained uneasy about an enemy wandering so close to his camp, regardless of Sherman's sneering, so he prudently established a small outpost near the south end of Rea Field. Early the next morning, Sunday, April 6th, these pickets came racing back to the camp, breathlessly reporting Rebel troops on the Western Corinth Road just west of the field. Then Appler heard firing from Prentiss' division to the southwest in Fraley Field. The colonel was still digesting this news when a wounded soldier of Prentiss' division to the east limped into camp, shouting that there was fighting on Prentiss' front.

Sherman or no Sherman, the harried Appler ordered the drum roll again, and the 53rd fell into line directly in front of its camp, facing west toward Fraley Field. No sooner was this done than someone spotted Confederate troops advancing across the south end of Rea Field, toward the regiment's left flank. The soldier yelled, *"Colonel, look to your left!"* Appler now pivoted his line to the left, facing south, ordering his men forward just beyond the camp. But now one of his officers, still hitching on his boots, yelled that Confederate skirmishers were in the woods around Shiloh Branch, directly to the *east*. Enemy were approaching on three sides of Appler's regiment. The whole place was *infested* with Rebs!

"This is no place for us," muttered the increasingly rattled Appler, who pivoted his regiment back through its camp and withdrew into the edge of the woods, now facing his men east. Helping buck up Appler and his frightened men, a 2-gun section of Capt. Allen Waterhouse's battery rolled into position at the edge of the woods on Appler's right.

In the midst of all this pivoting, Appler again dispatched a courier to Sherman, reporting the enemy sightings. Incredibly, especially given the level of firing he must have been hearing, which had been going on for over an hour, Sherman scoffed at the 53rd's courier, *"You must be mighty scared over there."*

But now, finally, around 7am, Sherman and his staff rode over to Rea Field to deal with this troublesome regiment, but first they trotted into the field about 200 yards south of Appler's camp. Sherman studied the south end of the field with his field glasses, trying to identify the soldiers advancing east across it. Just then, one of his aides called out to look to the right.

What Sherman saw to his right were troops of Brig. Generals S. A. M. Wood's and Patrick Cleburne's Confederate brigades, currently in the process of shooting him. Sherman instinctively threw up his arm in a defensive motion as the Rebels fired. A bullet, or more likely buckshot, struck Sherman's upraised hand. Another bullet, likely meant for Sherman, cracked open the head of his orderly, Sgt. Thomas Holiday, killing him. *"My God, we're attacked!,"* Sherman exclaimed as he beat a hasty retreat back to Appler's camp. There he ordered the colonel to hold his position, promising to support him. With that, Sherman galloped off to direct the rest of his division. On the way, he encountered Maj. Samuel Bowman of the 4IL Cavalry. His hand wrapped in a handkerchief, Sherman yelled, *"Major, give me some extra men for orderlies, one of mine has been shot already."* Before riding on, he said, *"The devil's to pay, sure enough!"*

Finally, the scales had dropped from Sherman's eyes!

In Hindsight

Sherman's reckless disregard of enemy movements until his ride into Rae Field was probably the lowest moment of his career. Had he been killed in that initial salvo, history would have remembered him as a buffoon. What saved his career and possibly Grant's army, besides the Confederates' poor aim, was Sherman's outstanding performance throughout the rest of the battle. He went from being a total fool to a brilliant commander in just one day.

The 53rd Ohio Fights & Retreats
7:30am – 8am

Soon after Sherman's departure, the 53OH suffered the full fury of the Confederate attack, which occurred about the same time Prenstiss' division was being attacked. The 53rd was facing two Confederate regiments of Confederate Brig. Gen. Patrick Cleburne's brigade - the 6MS and 23TN. The Confederates were supported by Capt. John T. Trigg's Arkansas battery of two 6 pounders and two 12 pound howitzers.

The 53rd was isolated from the rest of the brigade by the Shiloh branch and by about 200 yards of fairly open ground.

But at least some companies of the 53rd were protected by hastily erected breastworks formed by throwing additional fence rails on the five-foot high snake-rail fence bordering the field. They also used bales of hay and perhaps a few logs to bolster their line. Lt. Ephraim Dawes of the 53rd described the chaos, *"From the rear of all the camps, hundreds of men were hastening to the rear. These were the sick, the hospital attendants, the teamsters, the cooks, the officers' servants, and some who should have been in line. There was a sharp rattle of musketry far to the left on General Prentiss's front."* [This was the beginning of Gladden's and Woods' attack on Peabody].

Lt. Ephraim C. Dawes
1840 - 1895

Well to the north, the long roll was now beating in McClernand's camp. As Cleburne's men charged through the line of Union officers' tents, Col. Appler gave the order to fire, as did the 57OH and 77OH, and there was an enormous crash of musketry along the whole front of Col. Hildebrand's brigade. *"The battle was fairly on,"* said Lt. Dawes.

Also now zeroing in on Appler's men from the high ground across Shiloh Branch, 800 yards to the southwest, was Maj. Frances Shoup, commander of a 12-gun Arkansas artillery battalion. In a deafening explosion Shoup's guns opened fire on the Buckeyes as well as other Union positions around Shiloh Church.

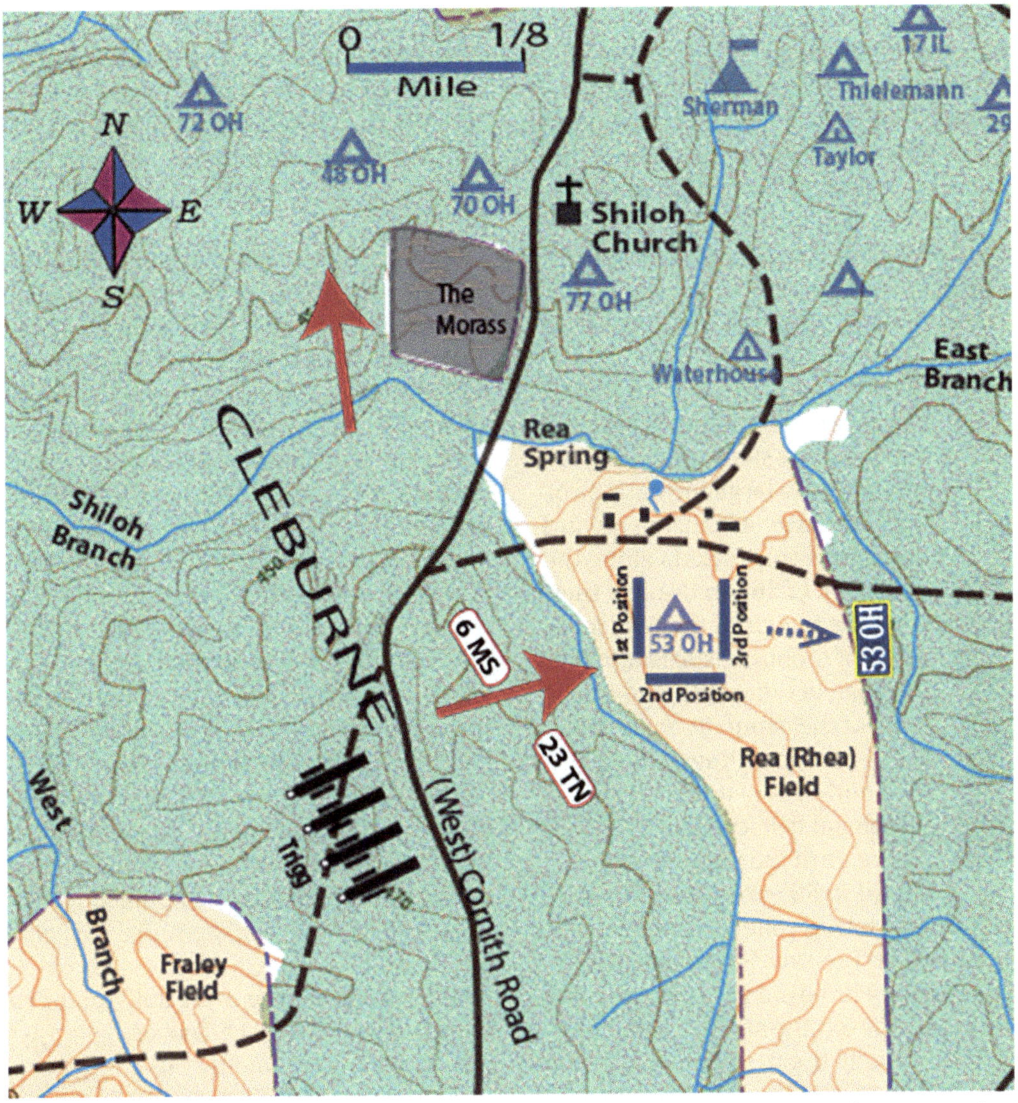

The 53rd Ohio shifts position three times in the face of Confederates attacking, seemingly from every direction.

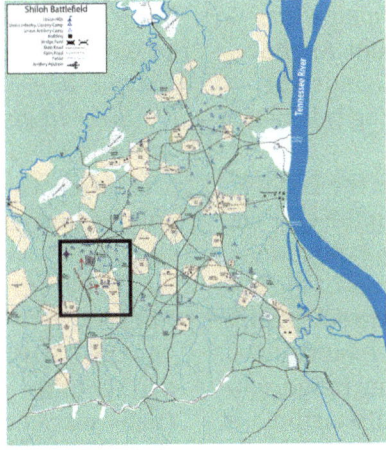

Map's Location on the Battlefield

Chapter 8 - Fighting East of Shiloh Church

Capt. Allen C. Waterhouse's Chicago battery, which had only received its battery horses 10 days prior, was in the area with its six James rifled-cannons. Waterhouse rushed up to support Hildebrand's men. One section of two guns rolled up in a clump of woods to the right of the 53OH and opened fire. But after firing only two rounds, the 2-gun section, acting on orders from Sherman's Chief of Artillery, Maj. Ezra Taylor, limbered up and raced off to join the rest of the battery farther north, on the high ground on the other side of Rea Springs and the east fork of Shiloh Branch.

Capt. Allen C. Waterhouse 1833 - 1912

Even as they watched their artillery protection racing for the rear while enemy shells rained in, the Ohioans saw large formations of Rebel infantry advancing toward them from the thickets along the main fork of Shiloh Branch; these were the troops of the 6MS and 23TN of Cleburne's brigade. But the obstructing brush and the tents of the camp disorganized the Confederate lines, causing the Southerners to attack in a piecemeal fashion. The 53rd held its fire until the two regiments closed to 50 yards, then blasted them with such a devastating volley that it broke the 23TN for the entire day. The raw Tennesseans fell back in disorder about a hundred yards to the ravine from which they had started the attack. Cleburne rode over and tried to rally them, saying "*Boys, don't be discouraged; this is not the first charge that was repulsed; fix bayonets and give them steel!*" But even with those encouraging words, staff officers only managed to round up about 20 percent of them.

But the 6MS rallied on its own, re-formed with about a 100 men less, and attacked again, As the Tennesseans lay down, licking their wounds, the 6MS charged through their ranks, yelling "*Make way for Mississippi!*"

Soon there was a tremendous blast as the Federals, including Union artillery around Shiloh church, opened on the attackers. Cannon balls, explosions, canister and bullets rained into the ranks of the Mississippians, who faltered, but somehow reformed, though they were no longer attacking. A more sustained firefight now raged at murderous range, with even more devastating results to the Mississippians, who finally broke and fled. As they scrambled back through the 23TN ranks, the Tennesseans jeered, "*Make way for Mississippi!*"

The 6MS left the ground littered with 300 dead and wounded out of its initial muster of 425 - a 70.5% casualty rate. The 6MS and 23TN would be among the first of many Southern units that day to discover that whipping Yankees was a lot easier in theory than in practice.

Union casualties were minor - the 53OH lost only two men in the entire battle. The men, the ones who remained, had stood their ground. They had some barricade protection. The Confederates weren't attacking at the moment. All and all, the green 53OH seemed to be more than holding its own. But suddenly, for no apparent reason, Col. Appler's nerve cracked. Shouting "*Fall back and save yourselves,*" he led a race to the rear, the regiment following in a disorderly retreat. Actually, only the left and center of the 53rd retreated. The right side of the line - Cos. A and F - refused to retreat. Capt. Wells Jones, the senior captain, took command and tried to rally what remained of the 53rd, though with limited success. But the ones he did rally were the best of the regiment – those still willing to fight.

By now, Confederate bullets were snapping in from all points of the compass. One soldier was hit in the shin. Capt. Jones ordered him to the rear. The man hobbled off. Presently he hobbled back, disgusted. "*Cap'n, give me a gun,*" he said, "*This blame fight ain't got no rear!*"

Somewhere nearby, after Col. Appler called for a retreat of the 53OH, Lt. Dawes, ran "*to where the colonel [Appler] was lying on the ground behind a tree, stooping over.*" Dawes cried, "*Colonel, let us go and help the fifty-seventh. They're falling back.*" According to Dawes, Appler "*looked up; his face was like ashes; the fear of death was upon it; he pointed over his shoulder in an indefinite direction and squeaked out in a trembling voice: 'No, form the men back here.'*" The order was ridiculous. The lieutenant cursed the colonel and refused the order. At which point Appler "*jumped to his feet and literally ran away.*" And that was apparently the last the regiment ever saw of Col. Appler.

> "Cap'n, give me a gun. This blamed fight ain't got no rear!"

As the 53OH broke into a disordered retreat, Dawes and six other men wandered about the smoke-filled chaos searching for the Union lines. At one point in their odyssey they happened upon a mounted artilleryman, who was crying; the brass cannon he was pulling had jammed between two trees. Dawes and his small group helped free the cannon, making the cannoneer feel better, and then they moved on. "*All around was the roar of musketry, but immediately about us was literally the silence of death. The ground was strewn with the slain of both armies,*" Dawes remembered.

Soon Dawes' group encountered a sergeant major of the 77OH, and they called to him to ask where his regiment was. The sergeant said he had no idea, as he was captured this morning and had just escaped. Dawes invited him to join them. "*No,*" said the sergeant, "*I'm going with this regiment,*" pointing to "*a regiment in full ranks, marching through a field on lower ground uniformed in blue, marching smartly by flank to a drum beat.*" Dawes couldn't believe there could be any intact Federal unit nearby. He took a closer look and grabbed the sergeant major's arm, hissing, "*They're Rebs!*" The sergeant didn't believe it. But just then "*the wind lifted the silken folds of their banner,*" said Dawes, "*It was the Louisiana State flag!*" The regiment was the illustrious Orleans Guards Battalion (*Gardes d'Orle'ans*), composed of upper-class French-Creoles from New Orleans. They went into battle wearing their prewar blue Federal militia uniforms, which at one point would cause them to be fired upon by their own side. Later in the day they would turn their coats inside out.

Dawes and his group continued wandering across the surreal, smoke-cloaked battlefield. Eventually they spotted a mounted man wearing a duster (a long coat, sort of like a rain coat), about 200 yards distant. Thinking it was a major from their unit, Dawes waved his hat to catch his attention and approached him. Saluting, Dawes asked, "*Major, where is our brigade?*" The man glumly answered, "*I don't know where anybody is.*" As he turned toward him, Dawes was shocked to see the man's uniform under that duster was gray.

"*At just that moment,*" Dawes said, "*a stand of grape [canister shot] came whirring through the air and struck just under his horse, the horse ran away and I never heard the rest of the story.*"

Later, Dawes learned that he had reported to Confederate Brig. Gen. Thomas Hindman.

Still looking for their lines, Dawes and his little band spotted a Confederate battery. They hid and watched which direction the battery was firing, and walked in that direction until they finally found their unit, or at least their army.

Most of Hildebrand's Brigade Collapses

Shortly after the 53OH was struck that morning, the 57OH formed, fronting nearly west, with its right about 300 years south of the church. To the 57OH's right, the 77OH faced south, about 150 yards north of Shiloh Branch.

Brig. Gen. Thomas C. Hindman Jr. (w) 1828 - 1868

Once the 53OH broke, the 57th was doomed, or at least many of its men thought so. "*They poured in on us like blackbirds into a cornfield,*" according to one 57th Ohioan. Another looked back toward their abandoned camp and saw nothing but Rebels and a "*confused mass of smoke.*"

Commanded by Lt. Col. A. V. Rice, the 57th fell back north through its camp toward a slight ridge near Waterhouse's guns. But upon reaching the ridge, half the regiment continued running toward Pittsburg Landing; the other half remained on the line for some unknown amount of time.

Both the 53OH and 57OH were severely criticized after the battle by the media, not to mention by Sherman. He would contemptuously state that the 53rd broke without having lost any officers and only two men, while the 57th lost only two officers and seven men.

A trooper of the 4IL Cavalry to the rear of Hildebrand's brigade described the chaos of the infantry retreat:

"*The pickets were running in every direction but our camp was so close to the lines that wee had to leave everything that wee had but our horses and sadels and our arms. The teams were running in every direction. Some of the drivers was scart so bad that they cut the horse loos from the wagons and mounted them and put spurs to them.*"

Later, when the 77OH broke, artilleryman T. M. Blaisdell of Barrett's battery watched the 77OH "*run like sheep. The Col. of the 77th [Lt. Col. Willis De Hass] sat down on a log near me and cried like a child at the cowardice of his men, whom he was unable to rally.*" Some of the gunners drew pistols on the fleeing infantrymen, but it did no good.

To the chagrin of his remaining men, brigade commander Hildebrand simply attached himself to McClernand's staff when the latter's division arrived.

Chapter 8 - Fighting East of Shiloh Church

Union Artillery Battery. in retreat. Note the Sibley tents in the background.

Although there's no question that the rear of the Federal line was chaotic, DeHass, Hildebrand and the artilleryman were premature. Not all the Federals were running. About half the men in the 57OH remained on the line, along with at least a couple of companies of the 53OH. And the 77OH, now commanded by Maj. B. D. Fearing, was still mostly intact.

What we know for sure is that *somebody* in Hildebrand's brigade was making life hell for the Confederates because it would take another hour and the better part of four brigades from three Confederate corps to totally crack Hildebrand's three regiments, or at least the fragments of those regiments, on the eastern side of Shiloh Church.

Also, along with the terrible terrain and the inexperience of the Confederate troops, great credit for Hildebrand's stand also goes to the Federal artillery. There's no question that the defense of Rea Field would have collapsed much sooner had it not been for Waterhouse's and Capt. Samuel Barrett's Chicago batteries, slamming iron into the Confederate attackers in that field.

For some time after Appler's 53OH fled the fight, the Federal gunners here put the Confederates in Rea Field under a devastating fire, giving the Confederates their first taste of canister. (In 1862, unlike today, the timber was sparser, and Sherman and his cannoneers could easily see the Rebel infantry advancing across Rea Field).

Hardee was supposed to be swinging his corps to the east in conformity with Johnston's plan to drive for Pittsburg Landing, but in the face of stubborn Federal resistance he was simply attacking straight ahead, and his attack was stalling, with his units being decimated.

He needed help!

Bragg's Corps Joins the Attack

Even though the 53OH was broken, Cleburne's exhausted and decimated brigade of Hardee's Corps was no position to advance farther. The corps following, Bragg's and Polk's, were supposed to be maintaining a 800-1000 yards distance behind Hardee, but their lines were now beginning to pancake up against his stalled line.

8:30am As Bragg's line came up, Bragg dispatched Gibson's brigade to the east toward Seay Field to assist Hindman's division in the center of the Confederate line. To close the gap left by Gibson's departure, at probably around 8:30am, Bragg ordered up Brig. Gen. Patton Anderson's 1,478 men from their reserve position to assist Hardee.

Looking south into Rea Field. At the time of the battle, this field extended over twice as far as that tree line. Most of this upper area would have been packed with the tents of the 53rd Ohio. Farther south where the trees are today, is where Sherman rode out and was struck in the hand by a Confederate bullet. About where you see that monument in the distance is one of the five Confederate mass graves marked by the Park Service.

Like Cleburne before him, Anderson was compelled to split his brigade in two, sending two regiments to the west side of Western Corinth Road to face Buckland's brigade(which we will discuss in the next chapter), and three small regiments of about 745 men - the 1FL Btn, the Confederate Guards, and the 17LA to the east side of the road, facing Rea Field and the remainder of Hildebrand's brigade.

More cautious than Cleburne, Anderson called for artillery support in his attack. Presently, on the east side of Western Corinth Road and about 800 yards south of the church, the Confederates brought up a powerful array of artillery, consisting of Shoup and his 12-gun Arkansas Battalion, along with four guns of Capt. Irving Hodgson's (Louisiana) Washington Artillery. They opened fire on the Federal batteries of Waterhouse and Barrett.

But even with this covering fire, as Anderson's three small regiments advanced into the southwest corner of Rea Field, Federal artillery opened up a blistering fire on them, sending many of them flying back to James Wood's cotton shed far in the rear.

Anderson worked furiously to get his three regiments back in line and moving forward. They slowly climbed up the Shiloh Creek bank and advanced into Rea Field, where they were again blasted by Waterhouse's six guns. That was all it took to send them running back to the creek embankment, where they remained, regardless of Anderson's cursing.

8:45am Now, behind Bragg, came Col. Robert M. Russell's 2,440-man brigade of Polk's corps. Russell's brigade was part of the division of Brig. Gen. Charles Clark.

Even though Clark's division belonged to Polk, Bragg ordered Clark to send a regiment to capture Waterhouse's battery, which was causing the Confederates so much misery. Clark dispatched the 11LA of Russell's brigade to do the job. As the 550 men of the regiment struggled through the undergrowth of Shiloh Branch they became separated, with

Brig. Gen. James P. Anderson 1822 - 1872

Page 61

Chapter 8 - Fighting East of Shiloh Church

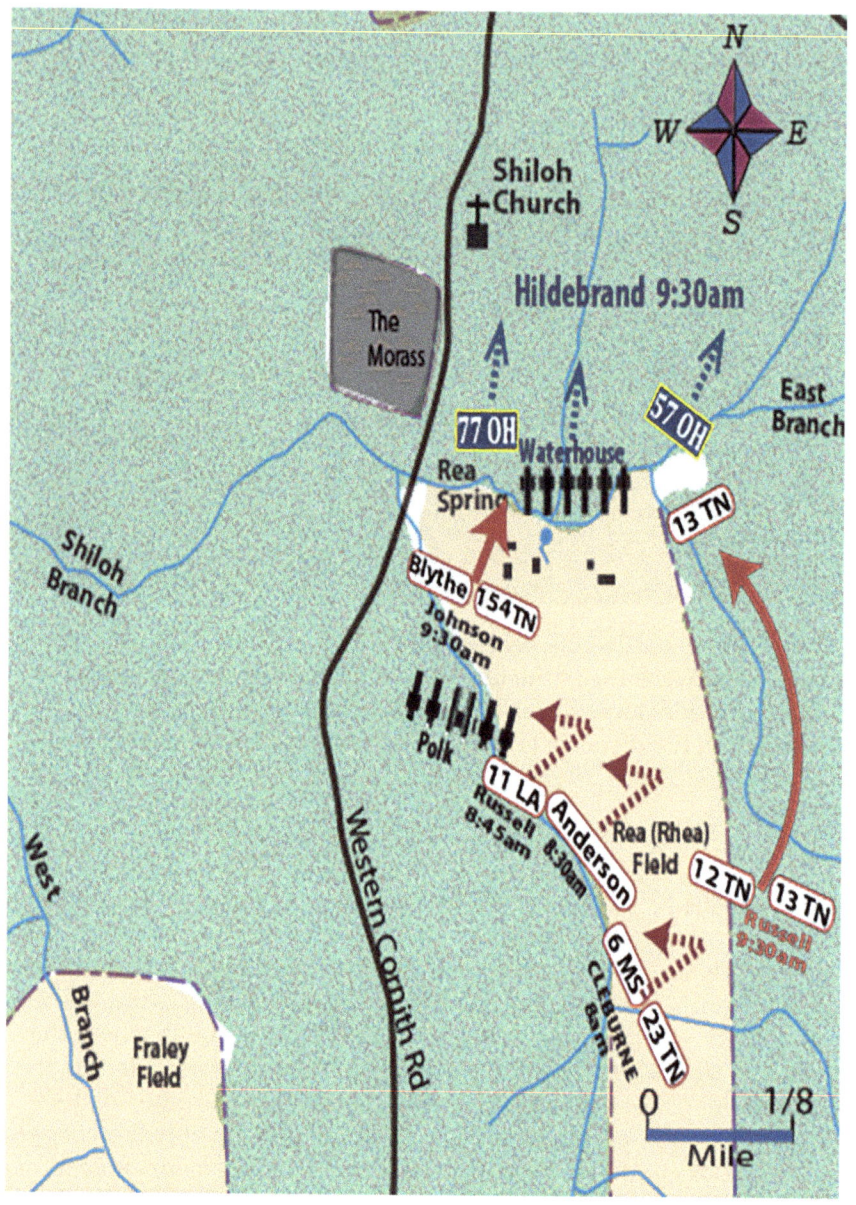

Changes in Rea Field

Running through the north end of Rea Field (sometimes spelled Rhea Field) is a ridge that composed part of the first position of Sherman's 5th Division at the start of the battle. The Rea cabin stood just north of the road. Farther in that northern direction, in the ravine, are Rea Springs and the east fork of Shiloh Branch. The 53OH, on what would soon be the left flank of Sherman's division, made its camp along the northern section of Rea Field, just south of the farm lane that cut through the field.

Looking down the length of Rea Field in 1862 the open field extended much farther south than it does today. The far tree-line was then about 900 yards from the farm lane instead of the 200 or so yards today.

Under fire from Confederate Cleburne's men, a private in the 77OH, John McInerney of Hildebrand's brigade, was struck by a bullet just over his right eye. With the wound spurting a mass of blood that covered his face, McInerney casually walked back to the file-closer, Lt. Jack Henricle and inquired, "*Lieutenant, do you think that went in deep?*" The shocked lieutenant waved McInerney to the rear.

It turned out to be only a glancing wound, and McInerney managed to survive the war.

only four companies emerging on the north side of the bank to conduct the attack into Rea Field. But they were caught in a murderous fire from both infantry and artillery, this time on their left flank, mainly from Barrett's Federal battery opposite the church. The Louisianians apparently put up a fight, but they were soon sent scurrying back behind the creek bank, with the regimental colonel reporting a *"considerable loss"* in killed and wounded.

Bragg, observing the 11LA's flight, later wrote to his wife that *"They belonged to Polk's mob."* Meanwhile, Bragg's horse was killed, falling on the generals right leg, but not seriously injuring him.

Russell rallied the bewildered 11LA and prepared the entire brigade for another assault. Because of the thick underbrush, division commander Clark directed Russell to lead the two left regiments – the 11LA and 22TN – while Clark himself commanded the right, consisting of the 12TN and 13TN.

The wings became disjointed in the thickets, and only seven of Russell's 20 companies actually made it into the camp of the 53OH. The 11LA and 22TN stormed to the west of Rea cabin, stepping over a blanket of dead and wounded comrades, which must have been disconcerting. Then the vicious fire caused them to break and flee, causing chaos in Anderson's brigade, which had been following obliquely in the rear. The 17LA, though torn in two by the fleeing 22TN, got off several volleys before retiring.

Meanwhile, Clark's right wing, slowed by tents and picket ropes, finally emerged into the 53OH camp, just in time to see the 11LA fleeing in wild disorder.

Nonetheless, in a 15 minute firefight, in which Clark was severely wounded in the shoulder, the 12TN and 13TN succeeded in driving what was left of the 57OH 500 yards to the rear. (Clark would become the wartime governor of Mississippi).

Exhausted and bleeding, the Confederates had finally "won" Rea Field. But just north of the field, around Shiloh Church, Waterhouse and Barrett's cannons, supported by the 77OH and remnants of the other two regiments, were still blasting the Confederates who at the moment could proceed no farther.

Col. Robert M. Russell 1825 - 1893

9am Now, Brig. Gen. Bushrod Johnson's brigade of Polk's Corps approached Rea Field. Although they were initially advancing toward Barrett's six guns, Bragg redirected the right two regiments – Col A. K. Blythe's MS Reg and the 154TN – against the 77OH and Waterhouse's battery. A hillock created a gap between the attacking regiments.

Col Preston Smith's 650-man 154TN closed to within 300 yards of the Federals, where they were met by a murderous fire. Lt. Col. R. C. Tyler drew his revolver on some of his own men when they began to falter.

To support the infantry, Capt Marshall T. Polk's Tennessee Battery from Memphis unlimbered near the Rea cabin. A single gun was wheeled forward for close-in work – a favorite Napoleonic tactic – but the horses quickly were shot down by the Federals and the gun had to be abandoned. The battery lost 24 of 102 men, 30 of 81 horses, and all six caissons. Young Polk was badly wounded in the leg and would later be captured.

Taken by surprise, the green troops of Hildebrand's brigade, at least some of them, had put up a surprisingly stubborn fight. The bloody fight for Rea Field was now in its second hour. Parts or all of four Confederate brigades, at least 5,300 rookies, and been thrown into the struggle against Waterhouse's battery and fewer than a 1,000 Yankee infantry, most presumably from the 77OH. Approximately seven Rebel assaults, all frontal and piecemeal, had been bloodily repulsed with hundreds of casualties.

But Bragg was determined to break that Union line.

9:30am So now Bragg ordered renewed assaults from several directions. He ordered the 154TN and Blythe's MS Reg, supported by Anderson's and Russell's brigades and perhaps 350 of Cleburne's survivors, back into the fray.

Under heavy fire, the 154TN and Blythe's regiment charged diagonally across Rea Springs and into the bloody Rea Field, straight at the 77OH, Waterhouse's battery, and probably remnants of the 57OH.

The Federals spewed out a withering fire, and Blythe was soon knocked dead off his horse. Against the protests of his men, Lt. Col. D. L. Herron of the same regiment mounted Blythe's horse to continue with the attack, but within minutes he was mortally wounded. Meanwhile, a shell fragment hit Brig. Gen. Bushrod Johnson, severely wounding him.

But somehow the two Confederate regiments pressed on. The 77OH and what remained of the 57OH eventually collapsed from the onslaught.

Chapter 8 - Fighting East of Shiloh Church

Waterhouse, wounded in the thigh, retired his battery, leaving only a single caisson. But believing every inch of ground should be contested, Sherman's Chief of Artillery, Maj. Ezra Taylor, ordered that the guns again be unlimbered only 300 yards from the previous position, dooming the battery.

Brig. Gen. Bushrod R. Johnson 1817 - 1880

Meanwhile, as the 154TN and Blythe's regiments were attacking directly across Rea Field from the southwest, Russell's 12TN and 13TN swept around the east side of the field, concealed by thickets but also getting lost in the same thickets.

Where the 12TN ended up is unknown, but the 13TN divided, with only six companies still following regimental commander, Col. Alfred J. Vaughn Jr. They made a wide sweep around the camp of the 53OH, before wheeling left into a ravine, which masked their movement. Finally, they charged Waterhouse's battery from the left flank from only 150 yards away. Waterhouse didn't have time to react, and his battery was forced to break and run. Three of Waterhouse's guns had to be abandoned, the horses being dead, and a further disabled piece was later ditched.

After celebrating their victory over those hated guns, the men of the 13TN then surged toward Shiloh Church, barely 100 yards distant. There was nothing now stopping the surging Confederates but a thin screen of Federal troopers of the 4IL Cavalry. The cavalrymen prepared to resist with sabers and carbines, but their commander saw it was hopeless against infantry, and ordered them to retreat.

10am. *Finally*, exhausted and bloodied, the Confederates had managed to sweep Rea Field and north of it, costing the Confederates two precious hours from the time Cleburne's two regiments had attacked the field at 8am until it was finally captured at 10am. Furthermore, they had expended time and blood attacking the west side of the Yankee line, when Johnston's plan was to attack the east side near the river.

Also, Hildebrand's troops, or some of them, had stalled the Confederates long enough to allow McClernand's division to form behind them, so that now the Confederates would be facing a fresh veteran Federal division, and without the advantage of surprise.

Even in their confused, disordered and unprepared state, Hildebrand's troops and the batteries of Waterhouse and Barrett had presented Grant with the gift he needed most - time.

Maj. Ezra Taylor 1819 - ?

The Phantom of Shiloh

At some point during the confusion of the morning fighting, Confederate Randal Gibson's brigade was following behind and slightly east of Alexander Stewart's brigade. Both units came under Federal artillery fire, inflicting some casualties and rattling the nerves of both green brigades.

Suddenly, Pvt. A. V. Vertner, a former member of the 4LA but now attached to Gen. Hardee as an orderly, came galloping toward Gibson's 4LA with a US flag wrapped around his waist and wearing a Yankee cap, anxious no doubt to show off his trophies to his buddies.

A Louisianan yelled, "There's your Yankee!," and a hundred rifles opened fire before the officers could stop them, riddling Vertner and his horse.

Some of the 4LA's over-shots hit the 13AR of Stewart's brigade, killing and wounding several men. Thinking they had been outflanked, the 13AR blasted the 4LA, killing or wounding 27 Louisianans. Gibson's horse was shot from under him. "It was a terrible blow to the regiment; far more terrible than any inflicted by the enemy," according to Gibson.

The enraged Louisianans, mostly French Creoles who didn't speak English, raised their guns to fire back at the 13AR, which was in the process of firing again.

Suddenly, in the middle of the two lines, came a woman wearing a sunbonnet and a long dress. In a scene both comical and eerie, the amazed soldiers held their fire while the woman, seemingly oblivious to her surroundings, walked purposely across the field as if on some vital mission, before finally disappearing into the smoke on the opposite side.

No one knew who she was, or where she was going, or what happened to her. One possible theory, as good as any other, comes from Elsie Duncan in a letter written decades after the battle. Elsie, nine years old at the time, was one of the many Duncans and others who had houses around Duncan Field, all of which were destroyed or appropriated as hospitals. In her letter Elsie describes her mother, who also had a son in the battle, trying to comfort a hysterical woman in "a house filled with wounded and dead men and the floor covered with blood." The woman was "screaming and wringing her hands" because her two sons had joined the battle on opposites sides. Possibly that woman went looking for her sons.

In any event, the mystery woman prevented the two Confederate units from destroying each other, though she never knew it.

Chapter 8 - Fighting East of Shiloh Church

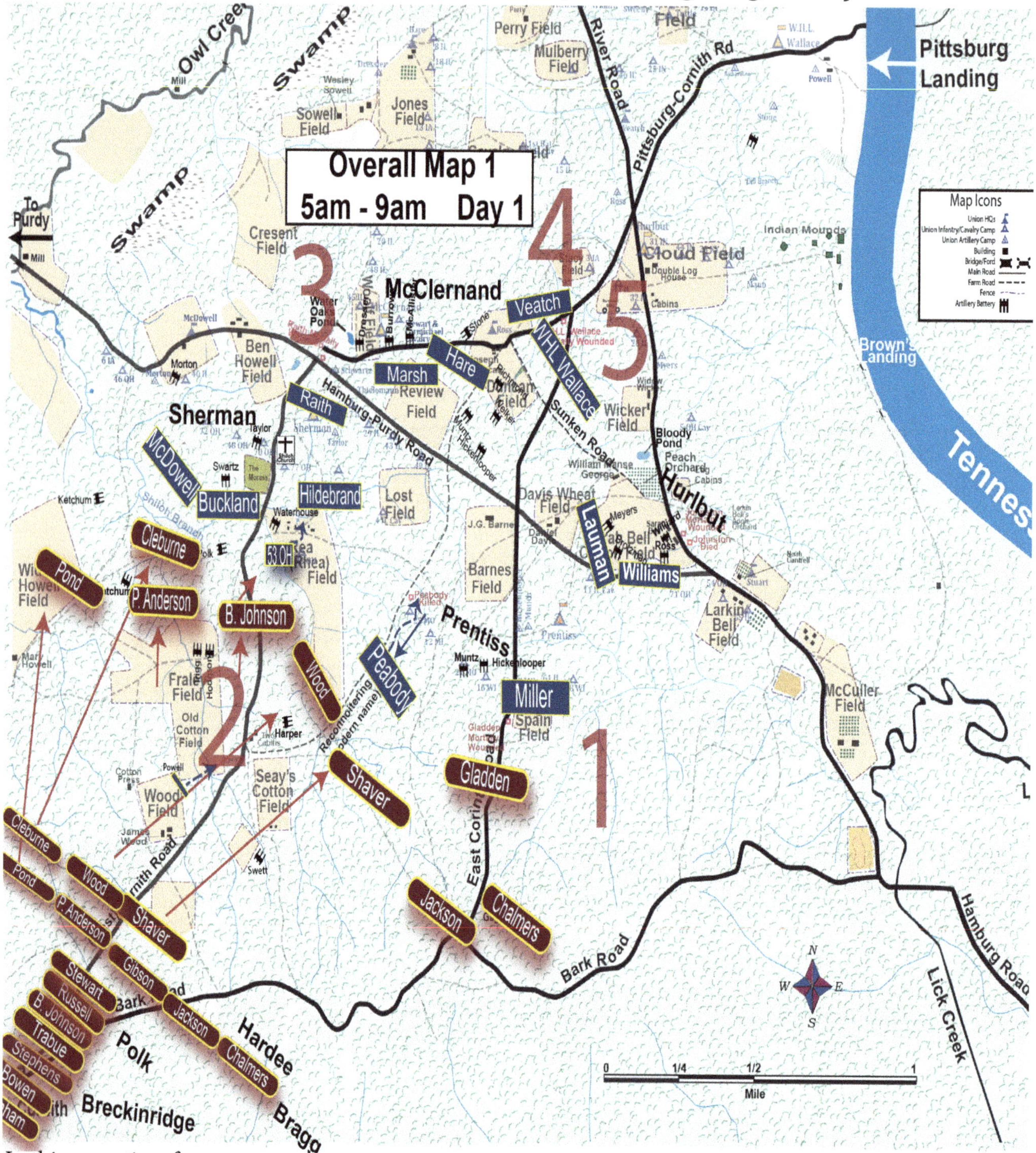

In this same time frame,
1. Confederates were attacking both brigades (Peabody's and Miller') of Prenstiss' division,
2. And attacking both brigades (Buckland and Hildebrand's) of Sherman's division.
3. Farther north, McClernand was moving his brigades toward the sound of battle, and,
4. Hurlbut had sent one of his brigades (Veatch's) to aid McClernand & Sherman, while marching to the Peach Orchard area with his other two brigades, while
5. WHL Wallace was moving his division toward what would be known as the Sunken Road.
(Note that this same map will be shown for all chapters in this 5am-9am time frame).

Page 66

9 Buckland's Brigade Holds

8AM - 1ST ASSAULT ON BUCKLAND

In this chapter we'll be discussing Sherman's brigade, Buckland's, on the west side of Shiloh Church. The fighting here was going on simultaneously with the fighting on the east side of the church by Hildebrand's brigade, as discussed in the last chapter.

Brig. Gen. Pat Cleburne's Confederate brigade was the left flank of Hardee's first attack wave. The 33-year-old officer, an Irishman who had served in the British army, was a prominent Arkansas attorney before the war. Incredibly bashful around women, he was a fierce fighter and a rising star in the Confederate army.

His men would strike the Yankees at Shiloh Branch – a creek just south of Shiloh Church. Initially the wild, broken woods and ravines helped conceal Cleburne's approach. But when he and his men reached the creek, they encountered the "Morass"– a marsh or swamp that was virtually impassable. Cleburne proved it when he plunged into the swamp at the head of his troops. His horse soon became mired up to its belly in something like quicksand; it reared and flung Cleburne off his back, sinking the general deep into the stagnant muck.

His dignity dented – this was not how battles looked in the paintings – and his clothes and boots packed with slime, the determined Cleburne slithered out of the mud "*with great difficulty*" and slid back on his mount. But the best he could do with the Morass was divide his brigade, with the two halves passing around the swamp on opposite sides. On the right side, the 6MS and 23TN attacked Hildebrand's brigade on the east of Western Corinth Road, advancing through Rea Field against the 53OH (as discussed in the previous chapter), while the 15AR, 24TN, 2TN, and 5TN - about 1,500 men - worked their way around the quagmire west of Western Corinth Road. Meanwhile, the mud-caked Cleburne galloped back and forth through the brush between the two sides of the swamp, desperately trying to lead both sections of his brigade. But the two sections never again rejoined tactically that day.

As the four Confederate regiments advanced against Buckland, "*It was a beautiful and dreadful sight,*" Sherman later admitted, "*to see them approach with banners fluttering, bayonets glistening, and lines dressed on centre*."

But things didn't seem that beautiful to the Confederates charging through the swampy thickets of Shiloh Branch.

Just prior to the Confederate assault, Buckland had formed up his regiments near Shiloh Church and advanced them south about 200 yards onto a small ridge. His three regiments - the 72OH, 48OH and 70OH - consisted of about 2,200 men, giving them the numerical advantage over the Confederates, plus, their right overlapped Cleburne's left. Furthermore, the terrain was perfect from the Federals' point of view, since they manned a bushy slope with a bend in the ridge that gave the 70OH on the east of the line an enfilading fire (ie the ability to fire into the flank or side of an attacking enemy).

And on the west of the line, the 72OH was also pushed forward toward a narrow ravine to form another angle to give them an enfilading fire on advancing enemy's left.

> Back in Helena, Arkansas, Cleburne was a prominent lawyer and friend of another Helena attorney, Thomas Hindman, who we discussed briefly in a previous chapter. The two of them were attacked one day be political enemies of Hindman. Both Cleburne and Hindman were seriously wounded, but Cleburne still managed to kill one of the attackers and chase off the other three. The legal profession in Helena, Arkansas was apparently quite vibrant back in the day!

Chapter 9 - Buckland's Brigade Holds

Before the Southerners could even reach the Yankees, they had to negotiate the swampy thickets of Shiloh Branch. *"A worse place could not have been selected for men to go through, wading creeks, going through thick underbrush & swamp land in mud & water up to our waste [sic],"* explained one of Cleburne's men.

The four Confederate regiments, one at a time, charged up the thicket-covered slope, only to be beaten back in bloody repulses.

Col. William "Old Grits" Bate led the 2TN. Although he initially advanced en echelon, Bate shifted his regiment over to Cleburne's left flank. His skirmishers unknowingly bounded into the angle of the 72OH, where the Yankees lay in the underbrush with cocked muskets. *"Immediately a brigade of the enemy rose as one man about thirty yards in front of us from ambush and poured a most terrific fire upon us,"* noted Robert Smith of the 2nd. From atop his stallion Black Hawk, Bate charged his men three times into the *"murderous cross-fire,"* each time being checked. Humphrey Bate, William's younger brother, fell mortally wounded as the colonel lit his cigar. For the remainder of his life, William would chew a cigar but never light one. The 2TN, originally 365 strong, retired to the creek, leaving thirteen officers and nearly one hundred men dead and wounded, including four of Bate's relatives besides his brother.

Col. William B. Bate 1826 - 1905

In Cleburne's center, the 24TN and 15AR met a similar fate. The 15th lost many men, including its major, J. T. Harris, who moved to within pistol range before being shot. Stocky, full-bearded Lt. Col. Thomas H. Peeples of the 24th continued to ride his horse up and down the line. Although his clothes became riddled by bullets and his horse was killed, Peeples survived. He later came up to a friend, threw his arms around him, declaring that *"Providence protected him.".* On the right of Cleburne's line, Col. Benjamin Hill's 5TN (later designated 35TN) advanced against the 70OH, which was supported by Barrett's battery right behind or right next to it. *"After a heavy volley (which wounded several of our horses) they dashed across the ravine and right up the hill at us,"* declared a Union gunner. The Tennesseans broke under the vicious blasts of canister and scrambled back to the creek.

The 5TN included 15-year-old Pvt. John Roberts, who was knocked down twice by spent bullets as he charged far ahead of his company. Another private, Pvt. Samuel Evans, who had a minee-ball pass through his cheeks, refused to leave the field and cheered on his comrades. On the other hand, a private, a sergeant, and three officers were singled out for skulking in the rear, including a captain whom Colonel Hill threatened to shoot for hiding.

The 5TN fell back. But, determined to silence Barrett's battery, Bate moved the 2TN from the west to the east side of the line, replacing the 5TN, and resumed the attack against the 70OH and Barrett's guns. In the process of performing a personal reconnaissance, the colonel received a bullet in his lower left leg, penetrating to the horse. Several men caught him before he slipped from his animal. Surgeons insisted upon amputation, but Bate kept them at a distance with his pistol. He would use a crutch from then on, but he kept his leg.

But Cleburne's men had rammed into a wall. They couldn't budge Buckland's line.

9AM 2ND ASSAULT- ANDERSON'S BRIGADE

Finally, Cleburne's exhausted regiments fell back, to be replaced or at least assisted by troops arriving in the second attack wave – Brig. Gen. Patton Anderson's 1,478-strong brigade of Bragg's Corps, Ruggle's division. Like Cleburne, Anderson was forced to split his brigade in half because of the rugged terrain. Two of his regiments - the 20LA and 9TX - got the assignment of attacking Buckland's brigade on the west side of the Western Corinth Road. They quickly ran into the same fire-storm that had stopped Cleburne's men. But Anderson's fresh troops benefited from increased artillery support. About 800 yards south of the church, Shoup's 12-gun Arkansas Battery had been shelling Buckland since before 7am. And by 8:15am he was joined by the Washington Artillery and eventually Capt. Smith P. Bankhead's Tennessee 6-gun battery at around 9am.

With this increased artillery support, plus some support from Cleburne's battered regiments, Anderson's two fresh regiments gradually pushed Buckland's line back north, almost even with Shiloh Church.

But Buckland's green troops remained stubborn, holding

Brig. Gen. James P. Anderson 1822 - 1872

Page 68

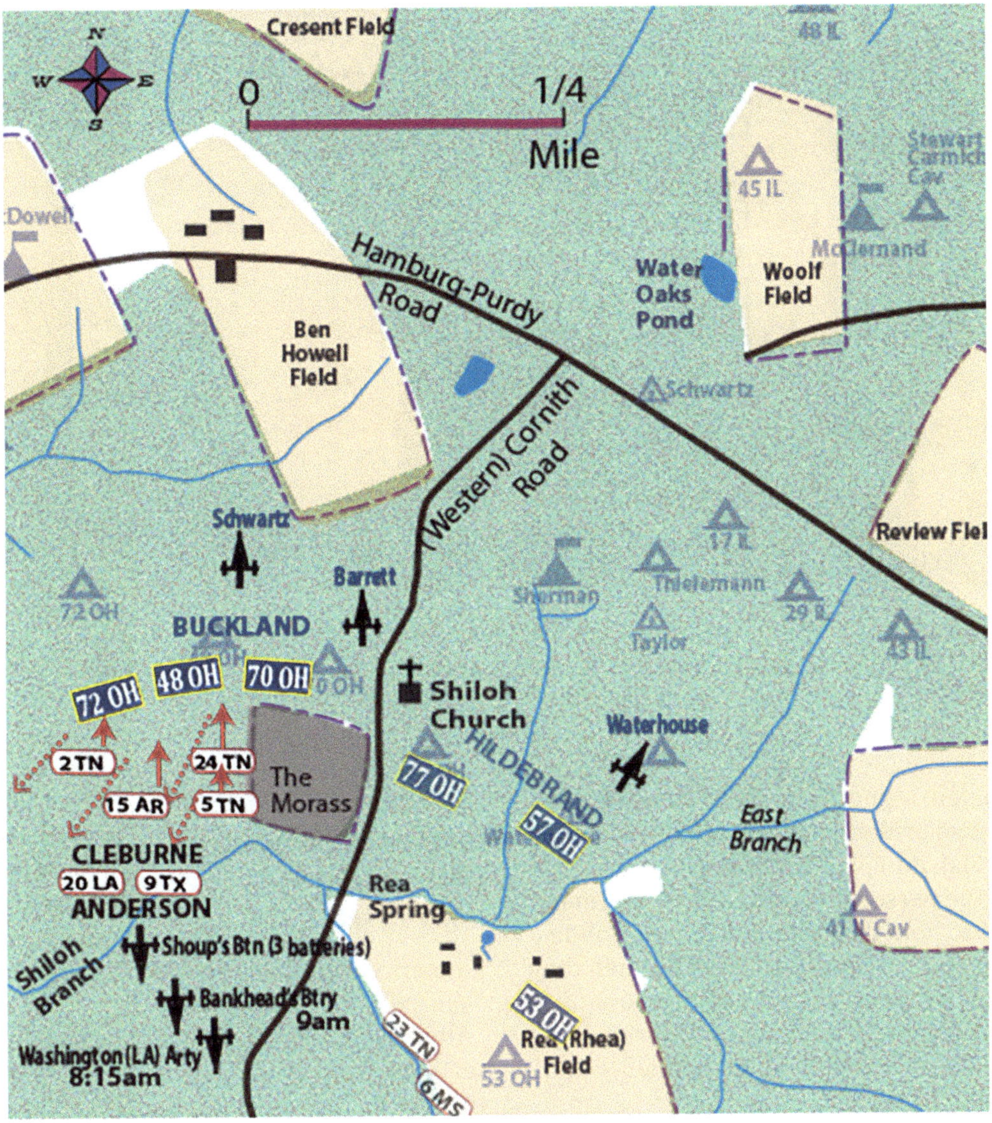

Confederates Attack Across Shiloh Branch

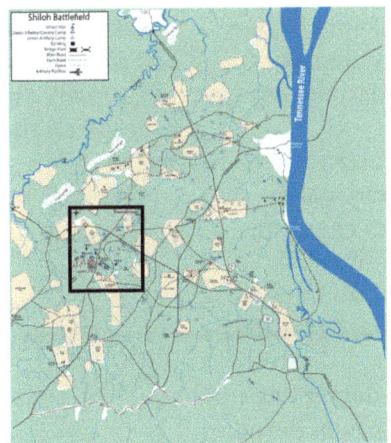

Map's Location on the Battlefield

Chapter 9 - Buckland's Brigade Holds

This is an illustration of "Waterhouse's battery's first position." If so, that may be the 53OH camp in the far right distance, and the 57OH on the near left. It looks rather serene, as many battlefields do after they've been policed up.

an excellent defensive position, and they were ably supported by two artillery batteries (Capt. Samuel Barrett's and Maj. Adolph Schwartz's).

Often under the personal supervision of Sherman, they managed to hold their position for two solid hours, beating back assault after assault. When they finally retreated, it wasn't because of pressure on their front, but due to the collapse of the brigade across the Western Corinth Road to their left – Col. Jesse Hildebrand's brigade.

As discussed in the previous chapter, Hildebrand's Federals began their fight at Rea Field where they were badly mauled; then they made a fighting retreat north directly past Shiloh Church, more or less forming in line to the east of Buckland's men, with their right flank theoretically connected to the left flank of Buckland's line.

The Union gunners of Barrett's and Waterhouse's batteries on the north side of Shiloh Church alternately blasted the surging Rebel infantry charging up on the ridge to their front and simultaneously dueling with Shoup's Battery (and other Confederate batteries arriving later) on the rise on the opposite side of Shiloh Branch.

One Union soldier, watching the Confederate lines storm forward into almost certain death, wondered, *"If they were willing to do that to themselves, what would they have done to us?"* The Union gunners

"If they were willing to do that to themselves, what would they have done to us?"

kept blasting cannister at the attackers, driving the Confederates back; each time the gunners cheered, tossed their hats in the air, and "*danced about like madmen.*"

After the battle, 85 dead Rebels were found in the ravine in front of the 72OH, and 68 more in front of the 48OH. The rule of thumb is that for every dead soldier, there's probably two or three wounded. If so, the Confederates probably suffered at least 450 total casualties in front of Buckland's line.

Buckland's brigade, on the other hand, only suffered 150 casualties in killed and wounded.

As already discussed, it was the collapse of Hildebrand on the left flank that unraveled Buckland's brigade.

10AM - SHERMAN FALLS BACK TO CROSSROADS

His line crumbling, Sherman ordered what remained of his division – the artillery, Buckland's brigade, fragments of Hildebrand's brigade, and the still-fresh brigade of Col. John D. McDowell – to fall back about 600 yards to an area known as *The Crossroads*, where the Western Corinth Road and the Hamburg-Purdy Road intersect.

At some point, Sherman sent Grant a message: "*Tell Grant if he has any men to spare I can use them. If not, I'll do the best I can. We're holding them pretty well just now, but it's hot as hell.*"

As Sherman fell back, Barrett's battery pulled back as well. Waterhouse's battery was in the process of following when Sherman's Chief of Artillery, Ezra Taylor, galloped up and demanded that every inch of ground be defended as long as possible. He ordered the battery to unlimber and deploy just 100-200 yards from its previous location. Waterhouse followed orders, but the maneuver was suicidal in the face of the Confederate onslaught. Finally, after Waterhouse and a lieutenant were sufficiently wounded and the battery had lost three more guns, Taylor allowed Waterhouse and his remaining guns to withdraw.

Federal Lt. Dawes (the same one who cursed Col. Appler for cowardice as discussed in the previous chapter), watched as the Southerners of the 13TN *"swarmed around them [Waterhouse's guns] like bees. They jumped up on the guns and on the hay bales in the battery camp, and yelled like crazy men."*

Barrett's and Waterhouse's batteries, like Buckland's infantry, performed heroically and deserve great credit for prolonging Sherman's stand here. It's all the more amazing considering the inexperience of Waterhouse's men. The Chicagoans received their horses only 10 days prior to the battle and drilled with them only three times.

> "They jumped up on the guns and on the hay bales in the battery camp, and yelled like crazy men."

In Hindsight

Although the Confederate attack plan was supposed to be a "right wheel," ultimately focused on driving back the Federals' *left* flank, Hardee's attack, the first wave of the Confederate assault, had quickly degenerated into a brutal frontal assault against a strongly-positioned defensive line on the Federal *right* flank. And then part of Bragg's corps was sucked into the same hopeless assault.

Also, Cleburne's problem at the Morass illustrates the bigger problem with the Confederate's attack deployment, where each of three corps stretched across the entire battlefield. This deployment meant that Cleburne's brigade also had to stretch out some 1,500 yards wide, in a line too long for Cleburne to control, especially in the thick underbrush.

Had the three corps instead been attacking side by side, per Johnston's original plan, Cleburne's men could have advanced along a much narrower front in battalion column (each regiment in line of battle, one behind the other), or possibly with a couple of regiments deployed side by side and each of the other four in a compact column behind, ready to be brought up and deployed as needed.

Another problem was that Beauregard should have been funneling the bulk of his reinforcements to the Confederate right, in compliance with Johnston's plan of crushing the Union line next to the river. Instead, he shoveled reinforcements toward the sound of the heaviest firing (a Napoleon tactic), and Buckland's well-defended line provided lots of heavy firing. Rather than throwing more troops against the stoutly defended Federal line at Shiloh Branch, Beauregard would have been wiser to send troops to the quieter sections, since the latter might indicate the areas of weak resistance, or maybe *no* resistance.

Sherman's stubborn two-hour defense with two brigades near Shiloh Church on the Federal right against four Rebel brigades, not only bought precious time for Grant, but it also caused the Confederates to overreact and commit troops to the wrong flank, deviating from Johnston's master plan of focusing on the Federal left near the river.

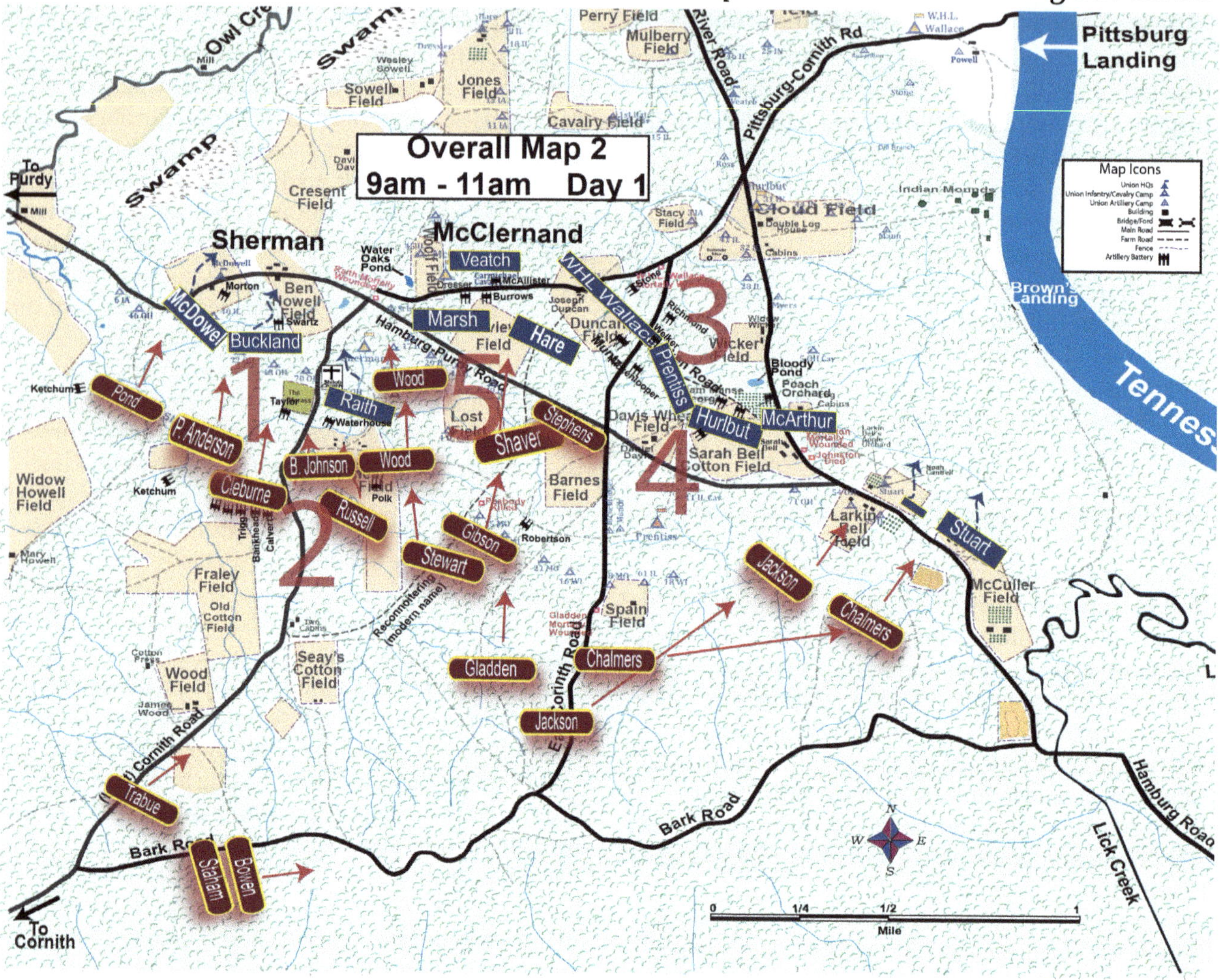

Chapter 9 - Buckland's Brigade Holds

Overall Map 2 9am - 11am Day 1

In this same 9am - 11am time frame,
1. Confederates still hadn't broken Buckland's brigade, but they were driving it back.
2. But the Confederates had broken Hildebrand's brigade and Prenstiss' division.
3. Prentiss and what remained of his division had fallen back to the Sunken Road, joining WHL Wallace's line there.
4. Hurlbut had fallen back to a better position on the north end of the Sarah Bell cotton field.
5. Meanwhile, the Confederates were attacking McClernand's division around Review Field.

Google Links to Chapter Locations

The Morass	Rea Field	The Crossroads
goo.gl/maps/4B6yL	goo.gl/maps/7q39m	goo.gl/maps/nHLFz

10   McClernand Joins the Fight

10:30 AM – 11:30 AM

One of the major problems for the Union army during the morning's fighting was that Sherman's 5th Division never tied into its closest neighbor to the east, Prentiss' 6th Division. Instead there was a dangerous 650 yard gap between the two divisions. Fortunately for the Federals, the Confederates failed to notice on this vulnerable gap for some time because it remained hidden in the dense timber.

Neither Sherman nor Prentiss were in any position to address the gap-issue as they were fully occupied just holding the lines to their front. Sherman, for example, already hit in the hand at the start of the battle, had received another painful wound when a bullet bounced off one of his metal buckles; still another bullet cut his horse's rein as he held it with his good hand; and before the day was out he would be on his fourth horse – the previous three having been shot from under him.

One Federal described Sherman at this time, on his mount with his injured hand wrapped in a handkerchief stuck inside his tunic, sitting *"ramrod straight,"* facing the Confederate fire.

Sherman's Missing Brigades

Sherman had been fighting all morning with just two of his four brigades. A day or two prior to the battle, Sherman had ordered his third brigade, Col. David Stuart's, far to the east next to the river, to guard Lick Creek. In Sherman's present predicament, Stuart's brigade might as well have been on the moon. But Sherman's fourth brigade, Col. John McDowell's, was positioned to the right of Buckland. It was facing Confederate Col. Preston Pond's brigade, but due to the terrain, Pond hadn't yet been able to attack McDowell, and so McDowell's troops had seen little action.

When Sherman fell back to the Crossroads and the Hamburg-Purdy Road line around 10am, he ordered McDowell to fall back to the same line and close up on Buckland's right flank. But so far, McDowell hadn't appeared and Buckland's right was unprotected, ie it was "hanging in the air."

McDowell had attempted to comply with the order, but he discovered that skirmishers from Anderson's and/or Cleburne's brigade had already penetrated the road between himself and Buckland about one-third of a mile west of the Crossroads. Rather than try to fight his way through to the Crossroads, McDowell decided to march his regiments back northeast across Crescent Field and into Sowell Field before swinging around to the south and linking up with McClernand's division, and then marching back south to join Sherman, which he accomplished at about 11:30am.

But in the meantime, Sherman had no idea where McDowell was, which just added to the general confusion and chaos.

McClernand Joins the Fight

McClernand's 1st Division, camped north of Woolf Field, was the obvious candidate to plug the gap in the Federal line between Sherman and the remnants of Prentiss' division. While Buckland's brigade on Sherman's right made a fighting retreat back to new positions along the Hamburg-Purdy Road, and Hildebrand's brigade on Sherman's left was retreating in disorder, McClernand's division marched from its camps and deployed along Hamburg-Purdy Road in a line that extended west to Sherman's left at Western Corinth Road, and to east, where it connected with the right side of W.H.L. Wallace's just-forming line at Duncan Field.

McClernand, a lawyer and contemporary of Lincoln back

Maj. Gen. John A. McClernand
1812 - 1900

in Illinois, owed his commission to Lincoln, who appointed him mainly because McClernand was a rare gem - a powerful Democrat in southern Illinois who supported the war. Lincoln, an Illinoisan, was fully aware that southern Illinois contained many Confederate sympathizers, and it bordered the slave states of Missouri and Kentucky, which contained even more Confederate sympathizers. But the end result was that McClernand was a political appointee with little military experience in a senior military command.

This presented problems militarily because McClernand considered himself answerable mainly to Lincoln and not to his direct army commanders, who were mostly West Pointers, and McClernand hated West Pointers, who weren't too fond of him either.

For example, if he felt his division wasn't getting enough supplies or the Federal commanders were doing something wrong, he would simply fire off a letter, complaining directly to Lincoln and bypassing his military commander. He was also extremely vain. By the luck of the draw, of Grant's five divisions, McClernand's division happened by numbered the "1st Division." So, he insisted that all his mens' return addresses include "1st Division," which was otherwise unnecessary.

Grant and his other division commanders, mostly West Pointers and/or Mexican War veterans, saw McClernand as an unctuous politician and an insufferable schemer who weaseled his way into command because of his Lincoln-connection.

Although Grant, Sherman and other West Pointers found plenty of reasons to criticize McClernand - Grant would eventually fire him at Vicksburg - McClernand seems to have performed reasonably well at Shiloh, cooperating side by side with Sherman on this chaotic first day of fighting. And technically, McClernand was senior to Sherman. We don't know what the interplay was between the two during the battle, but there seemed to be no complaints from either of them.

7am. Hearing the firing on that Sunday morning, probably around 7am, McClernand sent a messenger to Sherman asking what was happening. Sherman sent the messenger back with a request for cavalry to assist with a morning reconnaissance. McClernand sent the cavalry, but before the troopers could even reach him, Sherman himself galloped back to McClernand's camp, saying he needed support, especially to fill that 650 yard gap between Sherman and Prentiss' divisions.

Chapter 10 - McClernand Joins the Battle

McClernand rushed to fill the gap, but his camps were poorly aligned for the task since they were arranged in a north-south direction. So, although the all-Illinois 3rd Brigade was encamped along the Hamburg-Purdy Road, directly in the path of the enemy, the other two brigades stretched north for over a mile, from Woolf Field to the northern portion of Jones Field.

The 3rd Brigade commander was away on leave due to the death of his wife. The second in command was sick. So brigade command unexpectedly fell to Col. Julius Raith (pronounced 'right'). Raith was a Mexican War veteran, but otherwise had limited military experience.

Raith and his brigade had also heard the firing as early as 7am, but it was dismissed as just another picket spat. McClernand's order to assemble reached Raith around 7:30am, and Raith then called his brigade to the color line. But even then, many of the men weren't taking things seriously. The 49IL, for example, near the southeast corner of Review Field on Hamburg-Purdy Road, was slow to respond. The commander of the 43IL frantically rode over to the 49IL to warn them, but even then his words were generally ignored.

8am. It was 8am before Raith's brigade finally moved up to support Sherman's hard-pressed left flank, reaching the line of battle just in time as the Confederates were driving what remained of Hildebrand's brigade. Raith's troops initially formed near the base of a hill in the rear of the 57OH camp. Raith's right was some 350 yards behind Waterhouse's battery, and his left probably on Hamburg-Purdy Road just north of the Lost Field.

But the brigade was poorly positioned, being too far east to protect Sherman's left, and too far advanced from its own division to have its own flank protected. So McClernand soon ordered Raith's brigade to retire to the northwest and form McClernand's right flank on the Western Corinth Road, near, but not on, the Crossroads - a vital intersection where the Western Corinth and the Hamburg-Purdy Roads intersect.

Just north of the Hamburg-Purdy Road, the Western Corinth Road took almost a right-angle turn near a pond called Water Oaks. McClernand's line lacked the terrain advantages of Sherman's first position, but the road, now running nearly east-west, followed a slight ridge and provided a logical second defensive position for the Federal right.

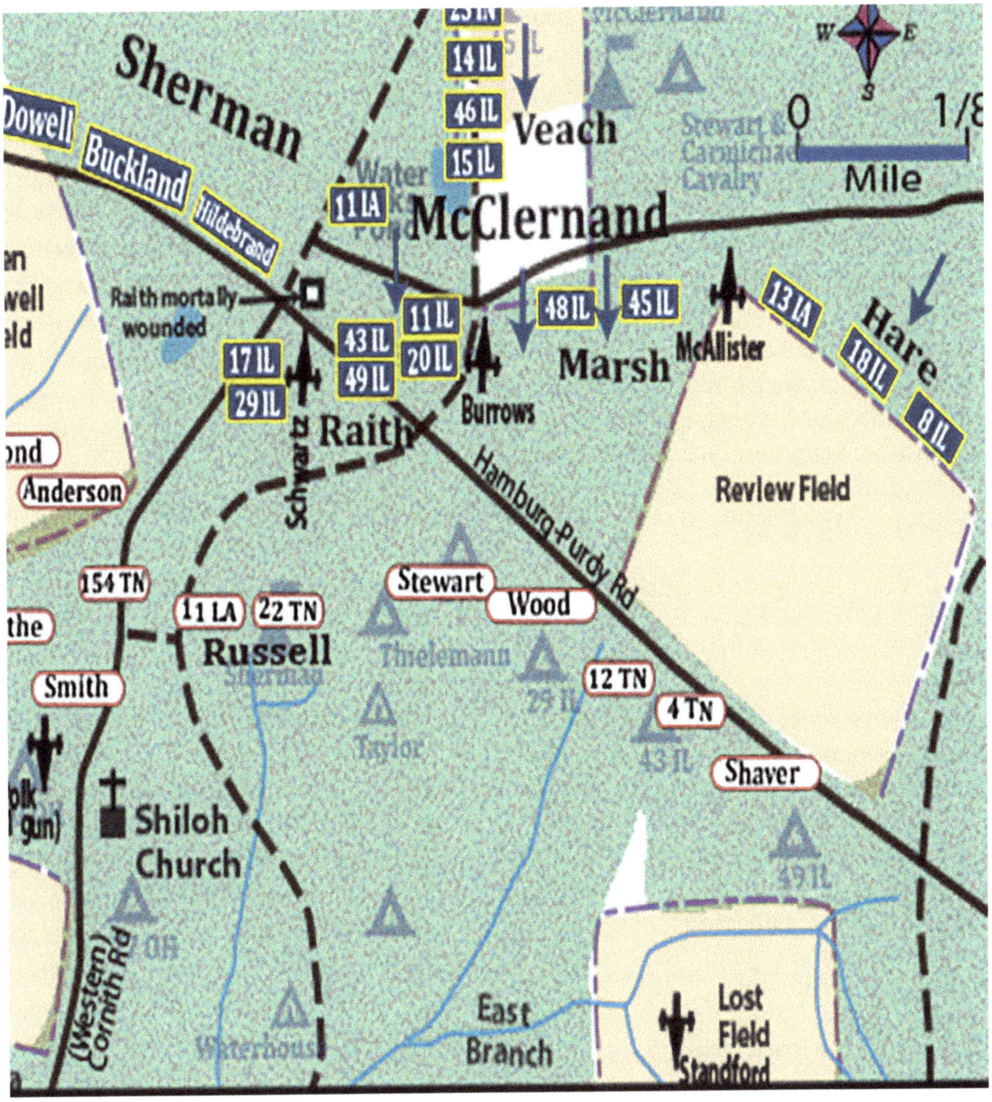

McClernand's Division joins Sherman in attempting to stop the Southern onslaught

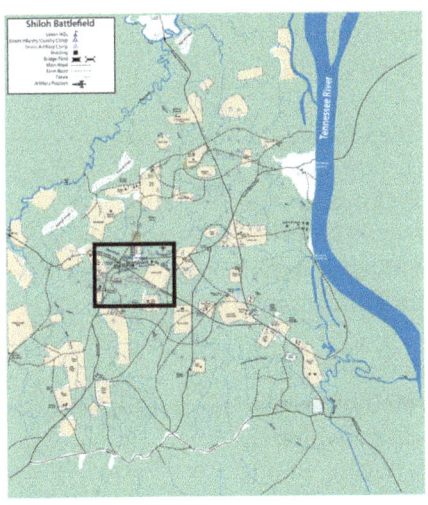

Map's Location on the Battlefield

McClernand ordered his second brigade, Col. Abraham Hare's, to form the division left. This brigade, consisting of two Iowa and two Illinois regiments, came into line about a 100 yards south of Western Corinth Road and north of Review Field.

McClernand ordered his center to be held by his third brigade, commanded by Col. C. Carroll Marsh and his 1,500 Illinois infantry, which deployed in the dense timber between Review Field and Pittsburg-Corinth Road.

Capt Edward McAllister's Battery D, 1st IL Light Artillery and its four 24-pounder howitzers rolled up to support the infantry, unlimbering in the apex of Review Field between the Hare and Marsh. At around the same time, Capt. Jerome Burrow's six-gun battery dropped trails between Marsh and Raith's brigades.

Also, Col. James C. Veach's brigade of Hurlbut's division arrived in response to Sherman's earlier plea for reinforcements and formed in line behind Marsh as a reserve.

Sherman held the sector west of the Crossroads. Specifically, Buckland's brigade, under attack, had extended along the Hamburg-Purdy Road toward Ben Howell Field. As already discussed, Buckland's right was in the air, as McDowell's troops had fallen back to Crescent Field.

The 13MO of W H L Wallace's division had earlier been ordered to guard the crucial Crossroads intersection. A remnant of Hildebrand's brigade, including the greater portion of the 77OH and some companies of the 53OH and 57OH, formed on the left of the 13MO.

This new Federal line, consisting of Sherman and McClernand's divisions, would serve as Grant's right wing, and it stretched for three-fourths of a mile and probably contained at least 12,000 infantry and 25 guns, excluding McDowell's brigade.

On paper this new line should have been formidable. Most of McClernand's men were veterans of Fort Donelson, although of course Fort Donelson was nothing like this. Also, unlike Sherman's and Prentiss' men, many of whom had never loaded their rifles, McClernand's troops had been in uniform long enough to receive some training.

But the bad news was that, unlike Sherman's defensive line perched atop a steep ravine, McClernand's line rested on flat ground with no terrain advantage. In fact it was at a terrain disadvantage, facing woods directly to its front.

Chapter 10 - McClernand Joins the Battle

Grant's Presence

Meanwhile, Grant continued visiting his divisions, lending encouragement, hastening up ammunition and supplies, and *"sending his aides flying over all parts of the field"* with orders or requests for information. One of his aides that day was Capt. Douglas Putman, normally a paymaster.

According to Putman, Grant was, for once, wearing his full general's uniform, *"complete with buff sash, making him 'very conspicuous,'"* and causing both Rawlins and McPherson *"to remonstrate with him for so unnecessarily exposing himself."* But Grant paid no attention.

He visited Sherman on at least one occasion, finding him bloody and grimy, his wounded hand tucked in his shirt, and his collar pulled around sideways, *"so that the part that should have been in front rested under one of his ears,"* according to Putman. It was a short, grim meeting, with Grant asking questions and Sherman vowing to continue fighting.

After Sherman, Grant next visited Prentiss, whose line had been pushed back a mile to what would be called the "Sunken Road." Grant told him to hold his position *"at all hazards,"* and that he would be sending him reinforcements – Lew Wallace's division – as soon as it arrived. Prentiss took to heart Grant's order to hold at all hazards.

In fact, Grant told everyone to keep fighting, and that Wallace was near at hand.

As the 1TN of Maney's brigade marched to the front, General Johnston halted the regiment to give the men a pep talk. Informing them that he had personally selected them for this post of honor, he explained the importance of defeating Grant's army before Buell's reinforcements arrived. He directed the Tennesseans to hold their positions no matter the price. Winding up his speech, he cautioned the soldiers to check their ammo pouches to be sure they had their required 40 rounds. In this solemn moment, most of the soldiers just patted their ammo pouch. But Pvt. David Adams, deeply impressed with the gravity of the situation, carefully counted all his bullets. Alarmed, he piped up, "General, I ain't got but 38!"

Johnston smiled and sent him back to the quartermaster to get two more bullets.

"The Crossroads" This modern photo on Western Corinth Road looks NE toward the intersection with the Hamburg-Purdy Road. Shiloh Church is about 200 yards behind the camera. Sherman's tent location is off the photo to the right about 150 yards. On the right just across the intersection where you see what look like blurry black triangles (they're cannon balls) which mark the location where Col. Raith was wounded. Out of view in this photo, on the right across the road, is Water Oaks Pond and Woolf Field.

Chapter 10 - McClernand Joins the Battle

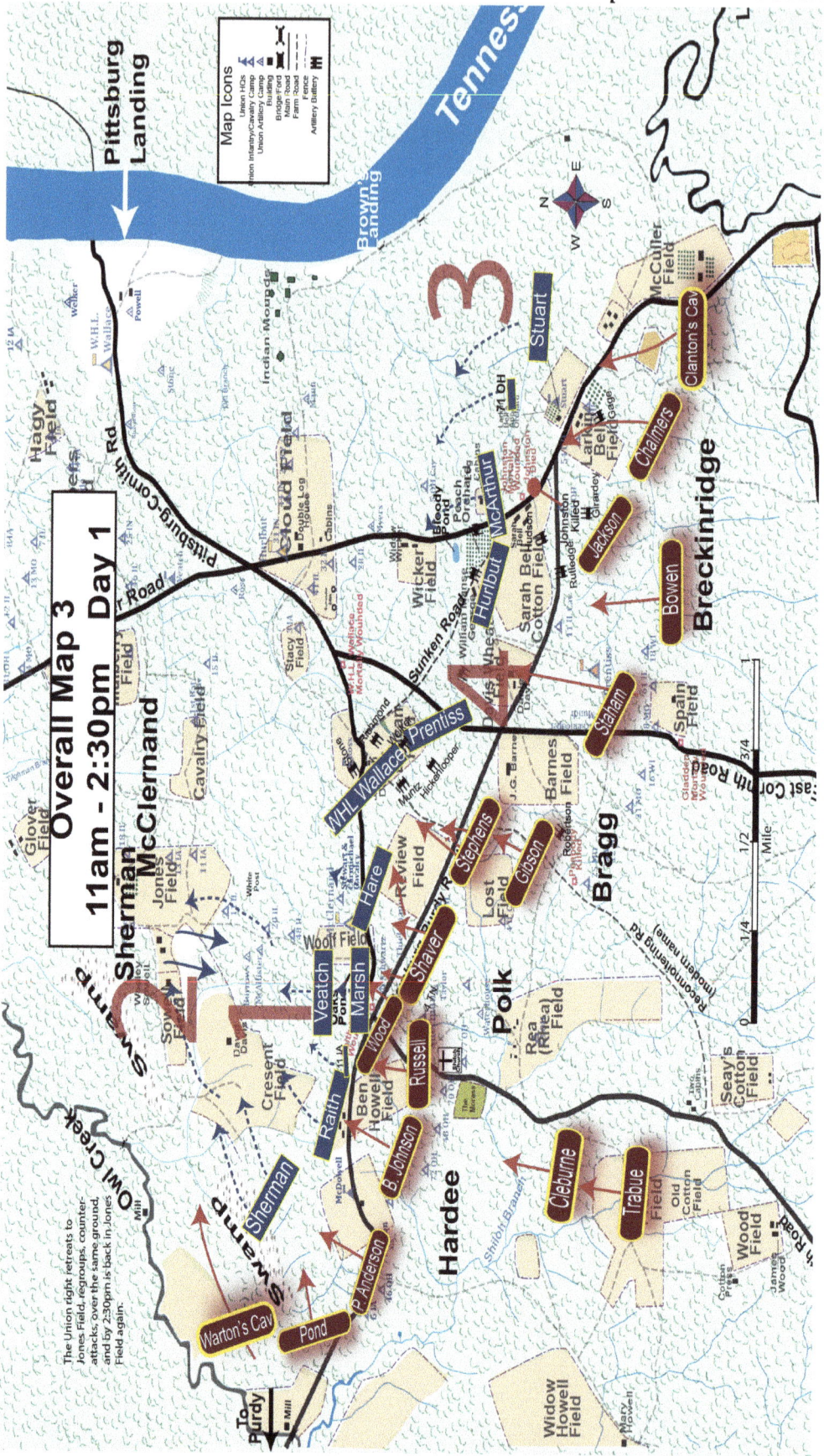

In this same 11am - 2:30pm time frame,

1. The Confederates have broken McClernand's division, pushing back both he and Sherman to Jones Field.
2. But Sherman and McClernand counterattack, driving the Confederates back for a time, before again being driven back to Jones Field.
4. Meanwhile, near the river, the Confederates attacked and drove back Stuart's brigade.
5. In the center of the line, Confederates are attacking the Sunken Road position. (Note that this same map is used in other chapters that pertain to this same time frame).

11 Collapse of the Union Right

10am - 11:30am

After having fallen back to the Hamburg-Purdy Road, Sherman's two exhausted brigades, Buckland's and the remnants of Hildebrand's, stubbornly held their own against fierce Rebel assaults. But farther down the line to the northeast along the Western Corinth Road, McClernand's recently arrived division and its three brigades - Raith's, Marsh's and Hare's - along with Veach's bonus brigade, were soon in big trouble. For one thing, McClernand's battle line had a poor field of fire compared to Sherman's position. A private in Marsh's Illinois brigade explained: "*We could not see them [the Rebels] as they crouched down behind the rising ground, while we were entirely exposed within easy range of their guns... We had to load on our backs and fire on our knees to keep from all being killed, so our fire was not so rapid.*"

Having wrecked Prentiss' division in bloody fighting, Johnston assumed he was on the right flank of the Union line, and so around 9:30am or 10am, he ordered a mishmash of regiments from seven brigades (Smith, Russell, Woods, Shaver, Stewart, Gibson and Stephens) to advance east of Shiloh Church and strike McClernand's division.

Their first target, the Crossroads - the intersection of Hamburg-Purdy and Western Corinth Roads - was in already in chaos, jammed with the 13MO guarding the place, Raith's newly arrived men, and various wagons, frightened horses, panicked fugitives, portions of Buckland's brigade, and fragments of Hildebrand's brigade, all heading to this general vicinity, along with Lt. George Nispel's battery (aka Schwartz's battery) which had its three remaining guns positioned there, including its 70+ horses and cassions. The entire area was more or less under constant fire from various Confederate units.

If that wasn't enough, one of Sherman's artillery batteries, Capt. Frederick Behr's 6IN battery and its 70+ more horses, careened down Hamburg-Purdy Road and rolled into position west of the Crossroads. Behr was immediately shot dead off his horse, which panicked the German cannoneers, who bolted to the rear, abandoning five of the battery's six guns, to the immense disgust of Sherman, who no doubt spouted a few colorful words.

Fight at the Crossroads

Having finally overrun the Shiloh Church sector, Bushrod Johnson's brigade (now under Preston Smith, as Johnson was wounded) now advanced toward the Crossroads. Smith's regiments consisted of the battered Blythe's Mississippi, the 15TN and the 154TN. They were also supported by a single remaining gun of Polk's Tennessee Battery under Sgt. J. J. Pritle.

Coming up behind Smith was Col. Robert Russell and the two of his regiments which happened to be on the east side of Western Corinth Road, the 11LA and 22TN. All these regiments were badly fragmented and tired.

Col. Preston Smith (w)
1823 - 1863

Before his men advanced, Smith called his regiments back to regroup, while he rode back in search of reinforcements. About 200 yards to the rear, he found two regiments of Brig. Gen. Alexander Stewart's brigade - the 13AR and 33TN - minus its commander, who was off hunting for his lost third regiment, the 4TN. Smith ordered or induced these two regiments to follow him across country to also join in the attack on the Crossroads.

Meanwhile, Russell's two regiments came up but, seeing Smith's units apparently withdrawing, Russell also fell back. Witnessing the line to his right retiring, other units on Smith's right (Anderson's brigade) also began to falter. So the whole attack stopped for at least 30 minutes.

11am. Finally, having found his reinforcements and regrouped, Smith ordered his brigade forward, followed by Russell and the rest of the Confederate line.

So now the Confederates crashed into Raith's brigade at the Crossroads. Smith's 154TN and Blythe's regiment led the

Col. Robert M. Russell
1825 - 1893

Page 79

charge, crashing into the right of Raith's brigade and Nispel's three guns, while Russell's 11LA and 22TN attacked Raith's front, chanting *"Bull Run!"* and *"Get up there you Yankee sons a bitches and fight like men!"*

Nispel's battery was taking heavy infantry fire. Maj. Adolph Schwartz, apparently McClernand's chief of artillery, rode up to Raith and requested infantry support. Raith personally led the 17IL and 43IL forward to Nispel's support. In the process, both Schwartz and Raith were immediately shot - Schwartz wounded seriously and Raith mortally.

Raith was badly wounded in his right thigh. His men attempted to carry him off the field but the wound was too painful, and he asked to be laid down to die. They did so, but he didn't die. Instead, the Confederates later found him and placed him in a tent, where he was recovered by the Federals the next day. He was taken to a hospital boat where his leg was amputated, but he died a few days later. His wife having died prior to the war, he left two orphaned children behind.

After Raith was wounded, his 29IL and 49IL fell back, out of ammo, and the 17IL soon followed. The 43IL, failing to receive orders, became surrounded and cut its way out, losing 43 killed, all later buried in the same trench. The 13MO, the orphan regiment guarding the Crossroads, also ran out of ammo, and fell back from the Crossroads, which was now wide open.

Lt. Nispel (aka Maj. Adolph Schwartz Battery) managed to pull out all but one of his guns, rescuing the other three.

Breaking Marsh's Brigade

As Col. Smith's and Russell's brigade rolled through the Crossroads, Brig. Gen. Alexander Stewart's brigade (13AR, 4TN, and 33TN) formed on the east flank of Russell. About this time, S.A.M. Wood's eight small regiments converged from the east, intent on attacking what remained of Marsh's brigade.

Chapter 11 - Collapse of the Union Right

But, in the brush and smoke, the exhausted Confederates were almost as confused as the Yankees. As Stewart's brigade ascended a ravine in the rear of Wood's troops, they assumed Wood's troops were Yankees and opened fire, killing five in the 9AR Btn and a lieutenant in the 8AR, and wounding many more. Wood galloped back to call on Stewart's men to cease fire, but they fired anyway, throwing Wood from his horse and forcing him temporarily to leave the field in a dazed condition. Col. William Patterson took command.

Finally, these two brigades surged across the road and into Review Field (the Federals gave the field its name after using it for that purpose), striking Marsh's brigade.

Here, where the open ground in front allowed an excellent field of fire for the artillery supporting McClernand – Capt. Edward McAllister's Illinois battery of four 24-pounder howitzers. At some point, McAllister's battery was challenged by Thomas J. Sanford's Mississippi Battery, but McAllister's guns soon won the duel, silencing Sanford's guns.

But the Confederates wanted McAllister's deadly guns, and the 4TN and 12TN got the assignment to seize them. Leading the two regiments was hot-tempered Brig. Gen. Thomas C. Hindman of Hardee's Corps. Conspicuous in his white duster, Hindman galloped about in the hail of bullets, deploying his two regiments for the attack while *"whooping like a Comanche, and with his horse on the dead run."* Finally, a shot from one of McAllister's guns smashed directly into the chest of Hindman's horse, bringing the beast to an abrupt halt and hurling the general 10 feet through the air in a spectacular forward somersault. When he slammed to ground he had just enough juice left to stagger to his feet, wave his sword and shout *"Tennesseans, take that battery!"* before collapsing.

His two regiments, now led by Col. Robert Shaver, continued their attack. Thirty-three-year-old Marsh

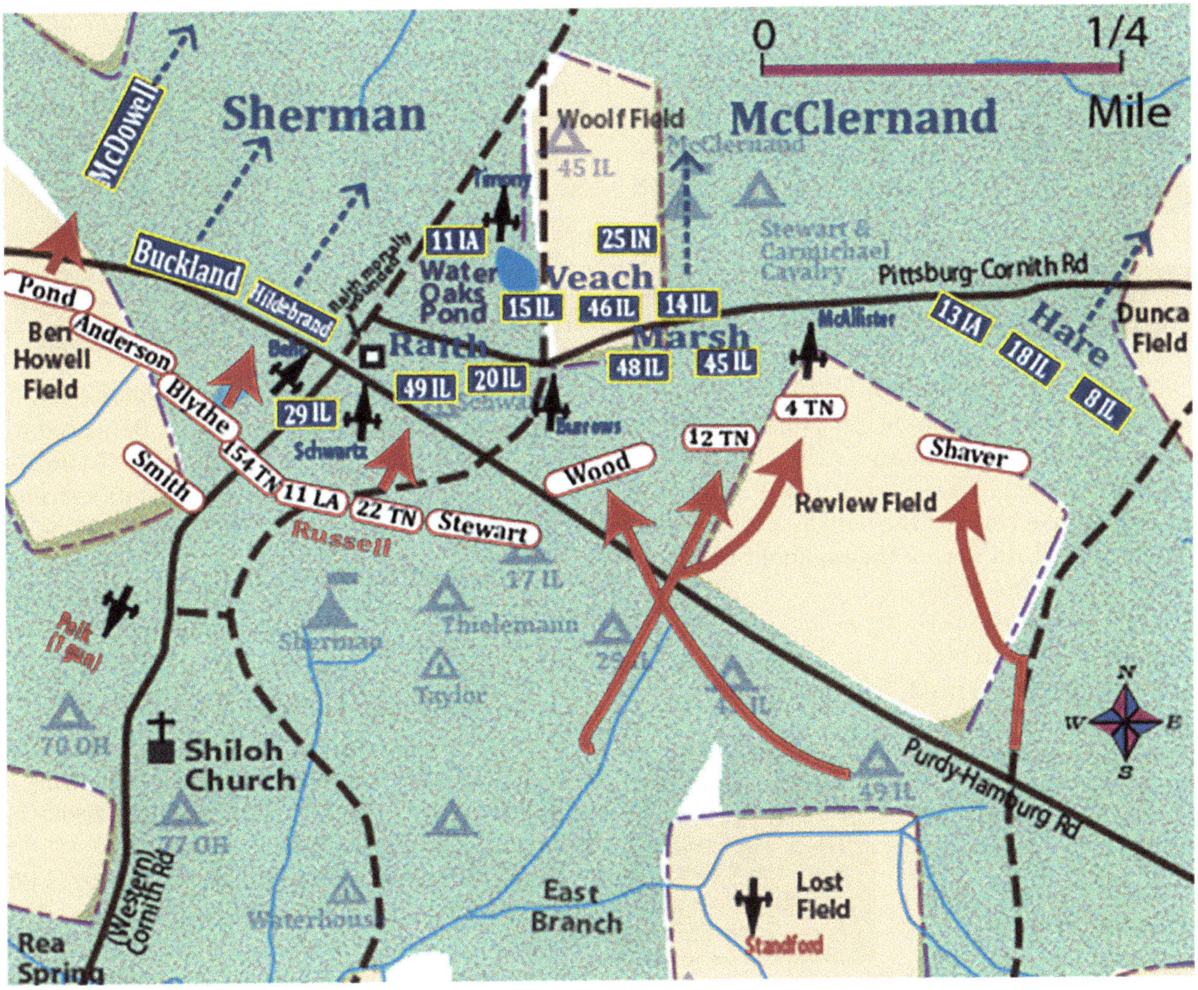

The right side of Grant's line retreats

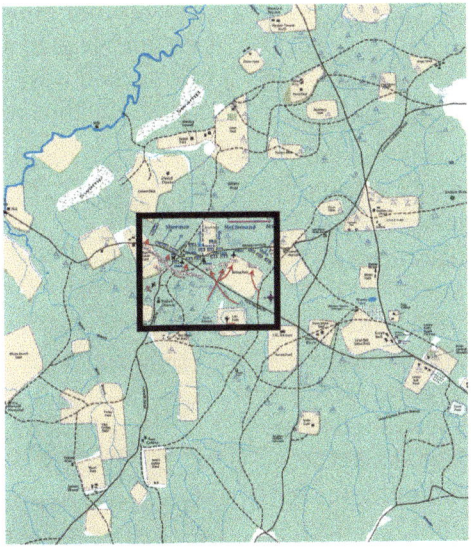

Map's Location on the Battlefield

Chapter 11 - Collapse of the Union Right

Brig. Gen. Thomas C. Hindman Jr. (w) 1828 - 1868

would later confess that Shaver's men advanced *"with a steadiness and precision which I had hardly anticipated."* McAllister's canister induced the 12TN to swerve to its left into the cover of timber, where Confederate S. A. M. Wood's brigade was also attacking toward Marsh's men.

More by luck than design, this brought an overwhelming force against the two defending regiments in that area – the 45IL and 48IL – giving the attackers a three to one numerical advantage. Smoke covered the field as a formation approached the 45th. One of the regiment's officers called for a cease fire, yelling *"Those are our troops!"* The Tennesseans marched to within 30 paces and fired a devastating volley before the Illinoisans realized their mistake. *"Our men fell like autumn leaves,"* recalled one Illinoisan.

The two Union regiments were taking heavy casualties, especially among their officers. The 48IL finally broke, leaving the 45th with no choice but to follow. This left its supporting battery on the far right of

Capt. Edward S. McAllister 1828 - 1900

the line, Lt. Jerome Burrow's 14OH, unprotected. Confederate S. A. M. Wood's brigade charged through Raith's camp toward Lt. Burrow's battery. In a brutal 10 minute fight, the 27TN and 16AL drove off the remainder of Marsh's infantry and captured all six of Burrow's guns.

With Marsh's brigade collapsing, McAllister ordered his battery to retire. McAllister, slightly wounded four times himself, managed to get three of his four guns out. Too many horses had been killed to pull out the fourth gun.

Col. Robert G. Shaver 1831 - 1915

Marsh's brigade was in full retreat, and McClernand's line was cracked. The price the Confederates paid was steep – the 4TN, for instance – left a trail of 31 dead and 160 wounded on the field.

Hare's Brigade Retreats

While Wood and Stewart were dealing with Marsh's brigade, to their right, Shaver's brigade targeted the stern but popular Col. Abraham Hare and his brigade.

But Hare's brigade, seeing the line on their right collapsing, also retreated in confusion, putting up little or no fight. The 13IA, for example, broke after firing only a single volley.

Hare guided his brigade northwest towards Pittsburg Landing, but Marsh and Raith's troops fled directly north through Marsh's camp, not slowing down for another 750 yards until they reached Jones Field – the tent campsite of Hare's brigade.

Veach's Brigade Overwhelmed

Earlier that morning, Sherman had sent an urgent message to 4th Division commander Hurlbut, bivouacked near the river, requesting reinforcements. Hurlbut responded by dispatching one of his three brigades, commanded by Col. James C. Veatch. The colonel and his men reached McClernand's vicinity and formed directly behind Marsh's brigade, more or less in Woolf Field. Veatch's unit arrived at just about the time the Federal line collapsed there. Veach's brigade, lying prone near Pittsburg-Corinth Road, couldn't fire because Marsh's men were frantically streaming back through their lines. Adding to the chaos, Burrow's surviving

Col. Abraham Hare 1811 - 1903

Battle flag of the 4th Tennessee. Delivered to the unit in April 1862 and carried until its surrender in Greensboro, NC on April 26, 1865. The flag is 35.5" X 37". Initially blood red, it's now a faded orange.

horses stampeded into the 14IL, routing the right wing of that regiment.

But finally the brigade rose and unleashed a volley, temporarily halting the attackers. But the Rebels soon returned fire. The 15IL got off between 10-15 volleys. But soon the commander of the regiment, Lt. Col. E. F. W. Ellis, was first wounded, and then killed with a shot to the heart. Second in command, Maj. William Goddard, was already dead. Veach's brigade now broke apart and fled. (After the battle, the bodies of Ellis, Goddard, and a captain were stuffed into a single box and buried).

Veatch's men had fought just long enough to cover McClernand's retreat before falling back in disorder themselves.

Confederates Swarm Into Woolf Field

Col. James C. Veatch
1819 - 1895

With McClernand's line on Western Corinth Road completely destroyed, Confederates swarmed north toward "*a pond of water and mud*" (Water Oaks Pond) and into "*an open field*" (Woolf Field.)

Three regiments of Stewart's brigade – the 5TN, 33TN and 13AR – all under the temporary command of Col. Alexander W. Campbell, crossed the Western Corinth Road in the rear of Wood's brigade. Wood's men had stopped and were firing in a prone position. When Wood's men refused to advance, Campbell ordered his troops to charge over them. Wood's brigade followed in their path.

A Federal watching the Confederate advance described it rather poetically, claiming that, "*Without a waver the long line of glittering steel moved steadily forward, while, overall, the silken folds of the Confederate flag floated gracefully on the morning air.*"

Now, stationed near Water Oaks Pond, only the 11IA and Lt. James P. Timony's Illinois battery of six James rifled-cannons were left to stop the advance. The 11IA and its 750 troops had barely gotten into line before the enemy attacked. Lt. Timony later stated that his men had been deceived by the flags and blue uniforms of the Rebels until they were within 80 yards in his front and 50 yards to his right.

A devastating fire routed the 11IA. With the infantry fleeing, Timony gave the order to limber up his guns, but he was shot 3 times and stunned by the explosion of a shell, and had to be carried from the field. The Confederates engulfed the battery, capturing 4 guns, 5 caissons and a limber, and killing 50 artillery horses.

McClernand and his brigadiers – Marsh and Hare – desperately tried to rally the men, but it was hopeless – the troops were too panicked and the Confederates too close.

11:20am   McClernand's division was in total retreat. In less than an hour, 18 of 25 Federal guns had been captured. McClernand's division lost two colonels, two lieutenant colonels, and five majors. The Confederates had complete possession of the Western Corinth Road.

But to accomplish this, the Confederates had yet again overcommitted strength to their left flank. Time had thus been gained for the Union center and left, and Johnston's clock was ticking. If he didn't destroy Grant's army by sunset, he never would.

The exhausted Confederates here on the Federal right stopped to reorganize, reload, and pillage Federal camps. As they did so, the fighting now shifted eastwards toward the center of the battlefield.

Sherman and McClernand Fall Back and Regroup

McClernand's line was broken, and what was left of Sherman's weary division had no choice but to withdraw. He and his men headed north toward Jones Field, using a country lane (today called "Sherman Road").

As usual, the fleeing Federals got a reprieve when the triumphant Confederates paused after entering Marsh's camps around Woolf Field, partially because by now the Southerners were badly disorganized and partially because they couldn't resist plundering the camp. The inexperienced Confederate officers would not or could not get the men moving again, prolonging the delay.

Actually, Russell's Confederates *did* probe ahead, but got a bloody nose near the south end of Jones Field when it ran into the recently-arrived 15IA and 16IA regiments which Grant had dispatched to reinforce McClernand. (After visiting McClernand earlier, Grant had sent McClernand these two precious regiments, Grant's only reserves).

While the Confederates wasted time ransacking Marsh's camps, Sherman and McClernand back at Jones Field made good use of the lull to regroup their mauled units.

Welcome artillery support arrived in the form of Maj. Ezra Taylor, Sherman's chief of artillery, who had scrounged up nine cannon – Barrett's battery and orphaned guns from other batteries – and deployed them on a rise on the south edge of Jones Field. Taylor's guns were soon in a fierce duel with Capt. Robert Cobb's Kentucky battery at the north end of Woolf Field.

Though the Federals at Jones Field were given a respite to catch their breath, it was clear that this right flank of Grant's army was being pushed back, ever closer to its destruction in the swamps to the north, or to Pittsburg Landing and the river to the east.

On the Line With the 14th Illinois

Lt. Col William Camm's 14IL of Veatch's brigade was one of Hurlbut's regiments sent west to assist Sherman and McClernand. On the way, Camm and his regiment passed a wagon carrying wounded. One soldier's leg was blown off below the knee. "*He stuck the stump out, with the shattered bone almost sticking out into my face,*" Camm said, "*and in a strong voice he cried above the din, 'Give'em hell for that, Colonel!'*

"*The earth was shaking now, and above the cannon and rifle fire we could hear the treble of the rebel yell as the storm came toward us.*" When the Federals reached Review Field, where they used to drill, "*the bullets began to whiz by.*"

Camm handed his wallet to the regimental chaplain, and told him to go to the rear and comfort the wounded. The regiment went into the line south of the Hamburg-Purdy road, facing southwest with a battery of five rifled guns and an old brass howitzer [Burrow's battery]. Camm noticed that one of his color bearers, a boy named Fletcher Ebey, was kneeling, trying to get a look around. Instantly, a bullet through the heart "*laid him down dead, and bleeding on his flag.*" Seconds later, a lieutenant named Opitz was sitting on a stump, stuffing tobacco into his pipe, when a bullet "*struck him in the end of the nose and cut the top of an ear off as it came out.*"

"*I could see the Jonnies running from tree to tree and popping away at us as they came. They had driven everything so far, and seemed to think they could drive us, too. The battery was belching like a volcano, but only seemed to attract the fire of the enemy's guns, and the rush of heavy shot and head-splitting crack of bursting shell all about us were adding to the increasing roar.*"

Chapter 11 - Collapse of the Union Right

Camm heard a Rebel bugle and saw them forming for a charge. Meanwhile a tall Federal artillery sergeant double-shotted the brass cannon.

"*What followed, no man can describe*", Camm said, "*until the Rebels were repulsed. I saw our handsome orderly of company 'G' fall with blood spurting from both temples. Regimental Color Sergeant John Kirkman rolled the body of his dead comrade off the national colors and rose with both flags in his hands, and as he did so a shot passed through the folds of the Stars and Stripes, cutting a gap in the staff and then passing through Kirkman's cap and grazing his head.*"

"*The enemy were checked but were very stubborn, and we murdered each other down at close range,*" Camm wrote. "*Our brigade commander [Col. Veach] rode down the line and I asked him to turn us loose with the bayonet. 'No, no,' he said, 'you'll lose every man!'*

"*My horse was struck behind the saddle and lunged among the men, so I let him go; I tried to get the men to charge but between us [and the Rebels] was a struggling mass of wild and wounded battery horses, many of them harnessed to the dead, and I could not get them started. But I got far enough forward to see a Confederate soldier trying to lead his men into our line. I covered him with my pistol but he was behaving so bravely that I hesitated firing. He pointed me out to a black-bearded soldier on his left,*" Camm continued, "*and as his piece covered me, a quiet and not unpleasant feeling came over me, and I let the point of my saber drop to the ground. I seemed to hear the bullet hiss.*" Camm was hit in the thigh. Just then someone shot the Rebel officer and, moments later, the black-bearded soldier.

At that point there was a lull in the battle, "*but before our muskets could cool,*" Camm said, "*the enemy came on again, and the fight became fiercer than ever.*" A boy named Noble Stout, "*whom the men used to make sport of because of his innocent simplicity,*" staggered up to Camm, crying, "*Oh, Colonel, I'm shot.*" He was gut-shot. Camm led him behind a fallen tree and assumed he would die, though he said a later burial party was never able to find his body.

A man came up with a rifle whose stock had been shot away, saying, "*That is the fourth gun smashed in my hand. What shall I do?*" Camm pointed to a gun on the ground; the man picked it up "*and was soon blazing away.*" Nearby stood another soldier named Hankins, "*blood spurting from his breast at every inspiration,*" said Camm. "*He loaded and fired till a *shot struck him in the chin and went through the neck killing him.*

"Up the road through a rift in the smoke I saw a confederate officer mounted in front of their colors waving a bright sword, leading his men on, but before the smoke hid them again, officer, horse, and colors all went down," blown apart by a battery [Burrow's] of heavy guns in Camm's rear.

Outflanked again, the regiment fell back, with such officers that remained struggling to rally the men. Camm grabbed a color bearer and led him on the run to a ravine in the rear where he began to shout for the men to "*rally on the colors.*" Many did, and in a short time "*the remnant of our regiment was ready for our foes,*" claimed Col. Camm.

It was noon. They had gone into battle at 10:30am.

On the Line With the Dixie Grays

Not far from where the 14IL was engaged but on the opposite side, Shaver's Arkansas brigade was attacking Review Field. One of participants, Pvt. Henry Morton Stanley, of the 6AR, (*the Dixie Grays*) described it.

Having overrun Prentiss' division at about 9am and thinking the battle was "*well nigh over,*" Stanley and his comrades barely had time to loot the Yankee tents when officers began forming the men up for another advance. Soon, Stanley said, "*We came in view of the tops of another mass of white tents and, at almost the same time, we were met with a furious storm of bullets, poured on us from a long line of blue coats, whose attitude of assurance proved that we should have tough work here. After a few seconds we heard the order, 'Lie down men and continue your firing.'*"

Stanley dived behind a large fallen tree where:

"The shells plunged and bounded and flew with screeching hisses over us. I marveled, as I heard the unremitting patter, snip, thud, and hum of bullets, how anyone could live under this raining death. I could hear the bullets beating a merciless tattoo on the outer surface of the log, pinging viciously as they flew off at a tangent to it, and thudding into something or other at the rate of a hundred a second. One here, one there found its way under the log and buried itself in a comrade's body.

"One man raised his chest as if to yawn and jostled me. I turned to him and saw that a bullet had gored his whole face and penetrated into his chest. Another ball struck a man a deadly rap on the head, and he turned on his back and showed his ghastly white face to the sky." Another cursed the enemy and raised his head a little too high, when a bullet skimmed over the top of the log and hit him fairly in the center of his forehead and he fell on his face."

Being cut to pieces by the deadly fire, the 6AR had two choices: attack or retreat, fight or flight. Somehow, the officers and noncoms stood up in the hail of lead, and ordered, *"Forward! Charge!"*

"Just as we bent our bodies for the onset," Stanley recounts, "*a boy's voice cried out, 'Oh stop, please, I've been hurt.'*" It was Stanley's squad mate and good friend, 17-year-old Henry Parker, "*standing on one leg, and dolefully regarding his smashed foot on the other.*" Stanley looked him in the eyes and turned away. "*In another second we were striding impetuously toward the enemy,*" loading and firing.

Just then they got some much welcomed assistance from a Confederate battery which galloped up, dropped trails, and opened on the blue line with shell and canister, slackening the Federal fire.

According to Stanley, big Newton Story, the color bearer, advanced so fast that he was 60 yards out in front of the Dixie Grays before he stopped and looked back with a smile, shouting, "*Why don't you come on boys?*" The regiment raised the Rebel Yell, "*taken up by the thousands,*" according to Stanley, "*and the advance then moved forward at quick-time.*"

The line of Federals seemed "*scornfully unconcerned,*" at first, according to Stanley, but as they took in the "*leaping tide coming at tremendous pace, their front dissolved and they fled in double-quick retreat.*"

Now the Confederate attack crashed through a second camp of white Sibley tents, which represented the far right of McClernand's line – the four Illinois regiments under Col. Julius Raith.

Stanley was exhausted; they had been fighting for five hours. He paused and was immediately hit in the stomach and knocked to the ground, unconscious.

Chapter 11 - Collapse of the Union Right

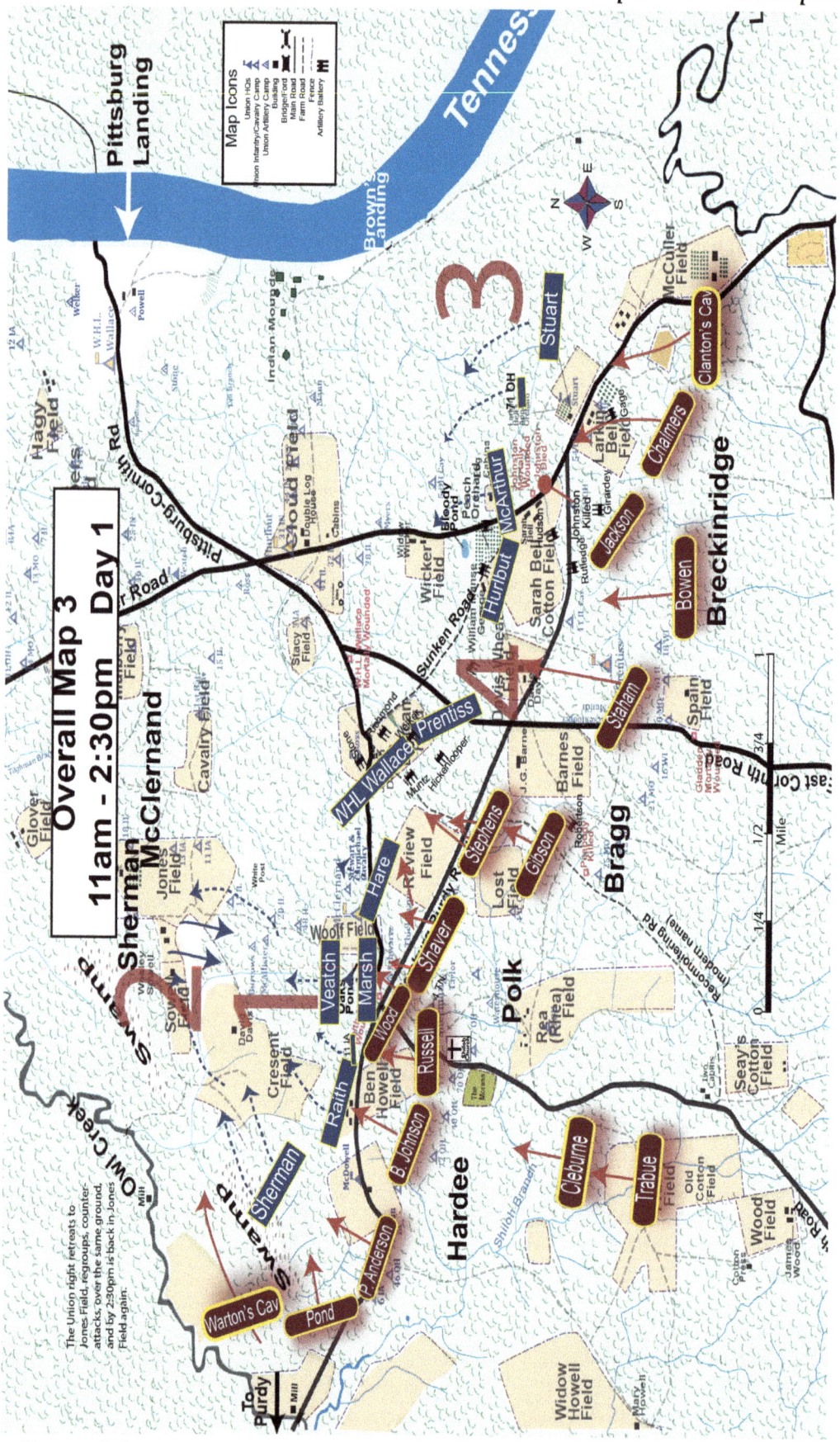

In this same 11am - 2:30pm time frame,
1. The Confederates have broken McClernand's division, pushing back both he and Sherman to Jones Field.
2. But Sherman and McClernand counterattack, driving the Confederates back for a time, before again being driven back to Jones Field.
4. Meanwhile, near the river, the Confederates attacked and drove back Stuart's brigade.
5. In the center of the line, Confederates are attacking the Sunken Road position.
(Note that this same map is used in other chapters that pertain to this same time frame).

Chapter 11 - Collapse of the Union Right

12 Union Counterattack

11:30am - 1pm

Thanks to a Confederate pause to raid the Union camps, by 11:30am Sherman and McClernand, now pushed back to Jones Field, had time to partially reorganize their shattered divisions. Casualties and deserters decimated their force, and many regiments were out of ammunition; but the two generals managed to round up about two thirds of their commands and coax the men back into battle formation.

Col.
John A. McDowell
1825 - 1887

On the bright side, through trial by fire, the Union ranks were now honed down to its toughest soldiers – the ones who didn't run. Also, Sherman's third brigade, commanded by Col. John McDowell (brother of Irvin McDowell who lost the First Battle of Bull Run), was still fresh, having occupied the right of the Union line, which saw little or no action, therefore allowing McDowell's brigade to simply fall back with the rest of the division, unscathed.

Last but not least, Grant had sent over his only reserve - the 15IA and 16IA - to assist McClernand.

The Baptism of the 15IA and 16IA

Sometime between 10 and 11am, McClernand received some much-needed help in the form of an artillery battery and two fresh Iowa regiments – the 15IA and 16IA – gifts from Grant. The two regiments, totalling 1,500 men, were completely green, the former having disembarked only hours earlier.

Lt. Col.
William Dewey
1811 - 1862

After having been hurriedly issued ammunition at the Landing, they were rushed into battle, with Lt. Col. William Dewey of the 15th swearing loudly between gulps of whiskey, *"taking some consolation though the neck of a pint bottle."*

The two regiments marched four abreast to the middle of Jones field, then only occupied by the 70OH. Immediately, the 15IA was ambushed by Rebels of Russell's brigade, which had penetrated into the field and lain in wait in the ditches and the abandoned tents of Marsh's camp. Confederate skirmishers began peppering the Iowans, and the Iowans began firing back.

The 15th's commander, Col. Hugh Reid, rode up and yelled, *"Cease firing: there is not an enemy within two miles of you!"* Instantly, a Confederate bullet hit Reid in neck, knocking him from his horse. Maj. William Belnap rode up and asked the colonel if he was badly hurt. The colonel replied, *"I am killed. Tell my wife I died fighting gloriously."* But within a few minutes, the colonel recovered, and led his men for the rest of the day.

Meanwhile, the Rebels killed two Iowans and wounded several more, rattling the 15th. But somehow the men fumbled into formation and advanced in line of battle with the 16th on the eastern edge of the field and the 15th in the timber to their left. As they advanced they watched with disgust as the 70OH, initially on the right of the 16th, left the field.

Now they were hit with the full brunt of Russell's brigade, including artillery, throwing the two Union regiments into chaos. *"It was every man for himself. We knew nothing about officers or orders. Indeed the companies now became all mixed up and without organization,"* according to one member of the 15IA. The Federals dropped flat on the ground, half rising to shoot. Both regimental commanders fell wounded. The regiments soon fell back to the north edge of Jones Field, having accomplished not much except for suffering 316 casualties.

As already mentioned, about 11:30am, Maj. Ezra Taylor, Sherman's artillery chief, gathered nine guns from McClernand's division and advanced them to a slight ridge on the south end of Jones Field, where they were soon dueling with the six guns of Robert Cobb's Kentucky Battery and another gun from Polk's Tennessee battery. Finally, at about noon, the Federal guns withdrew, having expended their ammunition. But while the Rebel artillery was distracted, Sherman and McClernand began thinking about a counterattack, which says something about the resilience of the Federals - many of them complete amateurs in the business of war - that after being caught totally by surprise and after several hours of being driven back in furious fighting and given just a brief respite, they could be contemplating a counter-attack.

The Federal Counter Attack

With just a bit of time to reorganize, Sherman and McClernand now felt confident enough to launch a counterattack. In what would be the only significant Federal attack of the day, around noon the Federals came roaring back south toward Woolf Field. It wasn't well organized – the battleline was irregular and the units badly mixed, and many units hadn't time to replenish ammunition, or had become separated, or were otherwise just wandering about. So only about half the two divisions' 22 regiments participated in the attack.

Nonetheless the Confederates, who had similar problems, had by now grown accustomed to chasing Yankees, and the plucky counterattack caught them completely off guard. A soldier of the 11IA watched and waited as the Southerners' continued advancing, *"marching right oblique, just in front of us, in double line of battle with their two stands of colors flying."* Once the Rebels were in close range, the Federals rose up and cut loose, throwing the surprised Confederates into confusion. Now McClernand, who was senior to Sherman, ordered a bayonet charge, racing along the line with his staff, yelling *"Forward!"* The Federals charged, with Marsh's brigade on the left, a mix of McClernand's and Sherman's regiments in the center, and McDowell's nearly-fresh brigade on the right in Sowell Field. The counterattack soon developed into two separate battles.

McDowell's men, along with the 13MO, surged forward against parts of Robert Trabue's brigade, which was supported by two artillery batteries - Capt. Edward Byrne's and Capt. Robert Cobb's.

Trabue's men had just reached the line and they frantically deployed in line of battle just before the Federals struck. The two sides settled into a fierce firefight, exchanging volleys for over an hour.

Meanwhile, McClernand's men were having more success against the exhausted brigades of Preston Smith and Robert Russell, knocking the two brigades back through Marsh's camp and then back another half mile to the south side of Woolf Field in such disorder that McClernand's troops overran Cobb's Kentucky Battery and temporarily captured all six guns.

Chapter 12 - Union Counterattack
The Rebel Counter-Counter Attack

But the Confederates soon recovered and launched a counterattack of their own with a motley collection of brigades scraped together from the three main Confederate assault waves – Russell, Stewart and Smith's brigades from Polk's corps; Pond and Anderson's brigades of Bragg's corps; along with Col. Robert Trabue's brigade from Breckinridge's corps. Galloping up to replace Cobb's captured battery, Capt. W. Irving Hodgson's Washington Artillery Battery (a Confederate battery from New Orleans) deployed only about 200 yards from the Union line, blasting canister into McClernand's men, although accurate Union rifle fire soon forced the Southern battery back out of range.

But the Southern numbers were overwhelming. The Rebels swarmed forward into the muddy Water Oaks Pond and then into Woolf Field.

The battle gradually settled into a brutal, toe-to-toe slugging match, with both sides slamming away at each other for over an hour, sometimes fighting hand to hand – which is to say fighting with gun butts and bayonets. Both sides took heavy casualties. (Grant would later write that there were more bodies collected after the battle on this side of the field than any other). Finally, the Confederate brigades of Trabue and Pond stretched farther west than did McDowell's brigade on the far right of the Union line, allowing the Southerners to outflank McDowell's line. McDowell's brigade, virtually untouched until the counterattack, was now a shambles, with nearly a third of its men down. McDowell himself performed quite well, always in the thick of the fighting.

**Col. Robert P. Trabue
1824 - 1863**

Around 1pm, men from Anderson's brigade arrived to support Trabue. So Col. Trabue then ordered his men to fix bayonets and charge. They crashed into the 46OH and broke it. As the Ohioans fled to the rear, Sherman rode up and ordered the 6IA to fall back, and the remainder of the brigade followed. By driving back McDowell, the Confederates now were on McClernand's right flank, forcing McClernand to retreat.

As the Federals grudgingly gave ground, they were pushed back to their starting point at Jones Field

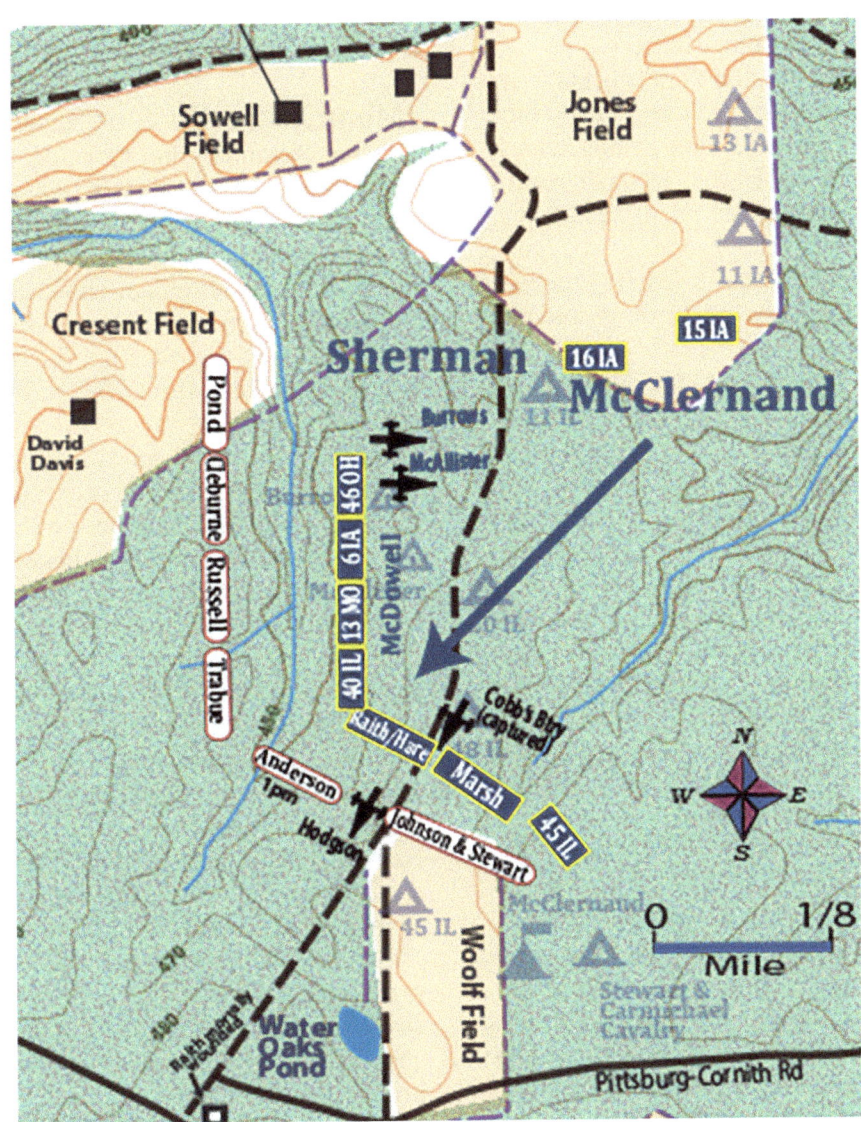

Sherman and McClernand counterattack

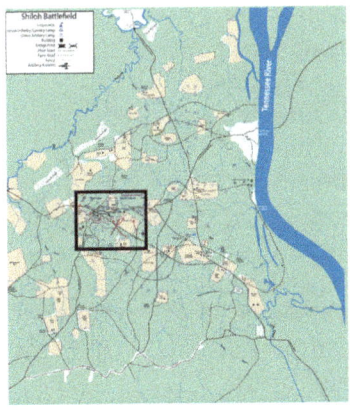

Map's Location on the Battlefield

around 1:30pm. Along the way, the Confederates recovered the six guns of Cobb's battery.

Only Confederate Col. Preston Pond's brigade was supposed to continue pursuing Sherman and McClernand's line through the Yankee camps, where smoldering campfires and clothes in wash buckets told how complete the Yankees' surprise had been. But the pursuit stalled as the troops spent a half-hour rifling the abandoned tents, feasting on bread and butter, not to mention wine, sardines and fruit from a sutler's wagon.

This again bought Sherman and McClernand time to reorganize. Around 2pm, they decided to fall back from Jones Field to the rugged Tilghman Branch ravine, which offered a much better defensive position as Confederate brigadier Pond would discover later in the day.

> As Union artillery pounded Cobb's Kentucky Battery and its supporting infantry, Confederate Kentuckian, Johnny Green, saw three of the four men in the file next to his killed by a single shell. Another shell killed two of Cobb's gunners and tore both hands off a third. Looking at the bloody stumps, the stunned artillerymen gasped, "My Lord, that stops my fighting!"

Now the Southern infantry attack paused, not just for the usual reason – to pillage Union camps – but also to allow ammunition wagons to catch up and to reorganize the jumbled Confederate battleline. Most of these Confederate units now shifted southeast, where a major fight was shaping up in the center of the battleline at the Sunken Road.

Though the Federal counterattack failed, it did drain off Confederate brigades which might otherwise have been used to attack the Federal left, per Johnston's original plan. And besides buying Grant more time to build a defensive line back at Pittsburg Landing, the fight also shattered several Confederate units – leaving Cleburne's brigade completely wrecked, and S. A. M. Wood's brigade with a 62% casualty rate.

Having survived the initial shock and surprise of the Confederate early-morning attack, the Federals everywhere were growing increasingly stubborn. From this point forward, there would be little tactical finesse at Shiloh - if there ever was any - as the battle evolved into a brutal, straight ahead slugging match between two groups of country boys who

Chapter 12 - Union Counterattack

were pretty good shots and who had been raised from birth to hate each other.

Meanwhile, Back at Savannah

Back at Savannah that morning, Nelson and Buell had received Grant's orders to march along the east bank of the river to Pittsburg Landing. The problem was how to do it. Finding a guide wasn't as easy as Grant's message implied. The locals knew the wagon trails winding through the swamps and woods along the east side of the river, but the rain-swollen river had flooded the bottoms, including those wagon trails.

Buell kept hoping Grant would send transports, but none appeared. So he ordered some of Nelson's cavalry to scout the trail on the river's east bank. At around noon, the cavalry returned, having literally ridden some of its horses to death in the process. The scouts reported that the main road was impassable, but there was a higher trail back from the river, though cutting through a marsh, which would allow the passage of infantry, though not artillery or wagons. A local man, "*a hater of Rebels,*" volunteered as a guide.

Buell was itching to get to the Landing. He ordered Nelson to take the land route if no transports arrived. In the meantime, Buell and a few staff boarded a small steamer and headed for the Landing.

At 1pm, Nelson ordered his division to march, prompting a cheer from his troops. At about that same time, Buell arrived at Pittsburg Landing, shocked to see the thousands of stragglers hovering around the river bank.

Following Sherman's order, McDowell withdrew his brigade toward Crescent Field. Lt. Col. Morkoe Cummings, commanding McDowell's old regiment, the 6IA, suddenly about-faced the left wing of his regiment and marched it back to a fence, leaving the remainder of the regiment standing in line in the woods. An irritated McDowell rode back and demanded to know what it meant.
"It means, sir," replied a captain,"that the colonel is drunk."
 McDowell had Cummings arrested and relieved of his sword, placing Capt. John Williams in command.
Cummings was court-martialed and dismissed from the service, after which he returned to his home state of New York. But, somehow, he soon joined the 124NY regiment, again as a lieutenant colonel. The regiment was known as the "Orange Blossoms" because they were from Orange Country.
At Gettysburg in 1863, Cummings was lightly wounded in the leg during the fierce fighting at the Triangular Field next to Devil's Den.
The regiment's commander, Col. Van Horne Ellis was killed, and Cummings assumed command. He was later promoted to full colonel and was seriously wounded in the Battle of the Wilderness, after which he was discharged due to disability.

Lt. Col.
Francis M. Cummings
1822 - 1884

Confederate battery being overrun.

Chapter 12 - Union Counterattack

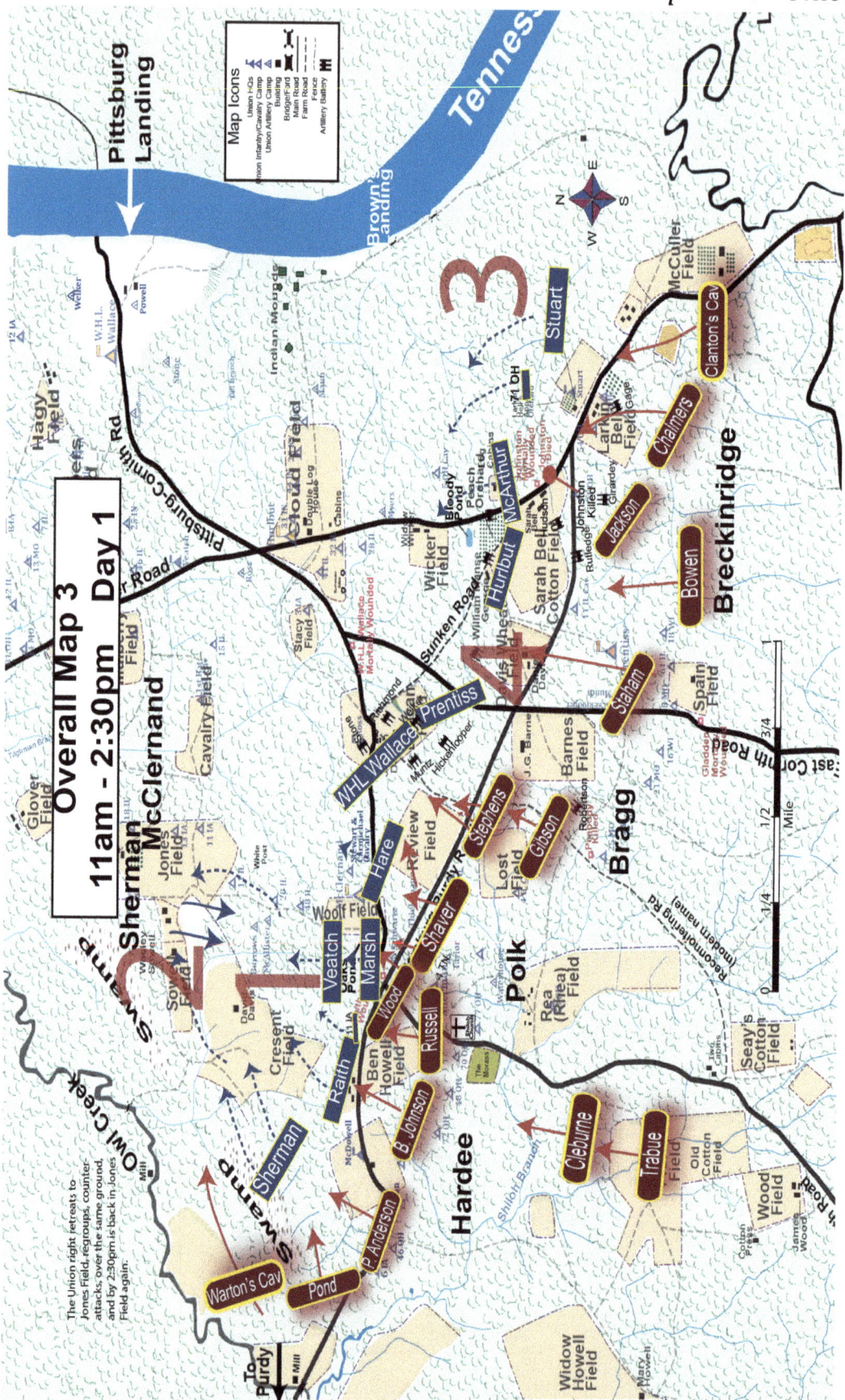

In this same 11am - 2:30pm time frame,

1. The Confederates have broken McClernand's division, pushing back both he and Sherman to Jones Field.
2. But Sherman and McClernand counterattack, driving the Confederates back for a time, before being driven back to Jones Field.
4. Meanwhile, near the river, the Confederates attacked and drove back Stuart's brigade.
5. In the center of the line, Confederates are attacking the Sunken Road position. (Note that this same map is used in other chapters that pertain to this same time frame).

13 Hurlbut Draws a Line

7:30am - 10am

On the morning of the attack, Grant's 4th Division was camped in and around Cloud Field near the Landing. The division was commanded by 47-year-old Brig. Gen. Stephen Hurlbut – a South Carolina-born political appointee, notorious for his drinking binges and shady real estate deals. Col. Isaac Pugh, commanding the 41IL regiment, confided in a letter to his wife on March 22: *"Genl Hurlbut is a drunkard & is drunk all the time when he can get anything to drink on."*

Brig. Gen. Stephen A. Hurlbut 1815 - 1882

"Genl Hurlbut is a drunkard & is drunk all the time when he can get anything to drink on."

Someone circulated a petition throughout the division to request his resignation but nothing came of it.

But on this day at least, drunk or sober, Stephen Hurlbut would earn his pay. He would initiate the Federals' first solid defensive line of battle.

At around 7:30am, over two hours after the first shots, Hurlbut received almost simultaneous urgent requests for help – the first from Sherman on the Union right and a second one from Prentiss on Sherman's left. Both of these officers' inexperienced divisions had taken the brunt of the initial Confederate assault, and they were in serious trouble. Hurlbut immediately dispatched his 2nd Brigade – 2,700 troops under Col. James C. Veatch – to reinforce Sherman. The camps of Hurlbut's two remaining brigades were widely scattered around the Landing, so it took him another half hour to notify and assemble these men, as well as his three artillery batteries and two cavalry battalions – about 4,100 men in all – in preparation for a march to Prentiss' support.

Just after 8am Hurlbut and his men marched off toward the sound of the guns, south down the River Road (aka Savannah-Hamburg Road) through a steady stream of dazed men from Prentiss' division, all heading in the opposite direction. Some of these men were wounded, but most had simply fled the battle; often two or three healthy men would be "assisting" a wounded man. Many of them had thrown away their weapons.

They warned Hurlbut's men, by way of self-justification, "*You' catch hell – we're all cut to pieces – the Rebs are coming!*" Disgusted, one of Hurlbut's captains loudly sneered that if any of his men ran, he'd shoot them. His men cheered, relieved to hear a note of determination in their march toward the inferno. In another case, a hysterical colonel rode up, shouting "*We're whipped! We're all cut to pieces.*" One of Hurlbut's lieutenants grabbed the horse's bridal and drew his revolver, threatening to shoot the colonel if he didn't shut his mouth.

Also, along the way the Federals got their first look at the enemy as they passed a wagon of Rebel prisoners, who defiantly swore the Yankees would get enough of "Dixieland" before the day was over.

By 8:30am, Hurlbut and his reinforcements reached Sarah Bell's cotton field and a peach orchard on the northeastern corner, which we'll now call *The* Peach Orchard. There appears to be no information on Mrs. Sarah Bell herself, except that she was a widow. No doubt she and her late husband would have been amazed at the bloody fighting that would occur in their humble field. But the field was important because its southeast edge fronted the important intersection of Hamburg-Purdy and the River Roads.

Hurlbut Deploys
8:30am-9:30am

At the Peach Orchard, Hurlbut filed his two remaining brigades under Col. Nelson G. Williams, and Brig. Gen. J. G. Lauman onto a country lane leading to a cabin owned by one W. Manse George at the northern edge of the cotton field. This lane was the beginning of what we now call the Sunken Road, famous as a key part of the Union defensive line. But at this point Hurlbut didn't stop at the lane, but instead advanced his men south across Mrs. Bell's field. Reaching the post and rail fence at the field's south edge, Hurlbut faced Williams' men south and Laumen's west, with both units facing timber directly to their front.

He would soon regret this move, as his initial position on the Sunken Road and the Peach Orchard, with their clear field of fire across the cotton field, offered a much better defensive location compared

Page 95

to where he now deployed with his troops facing timber. Also, his new position created a salient – a right angle between his two brigades. Salients were militarily weak because they allowed the enemy to cross-fire into the backs of each defending unit, while the units couldn't support each other with crossfire. He would have been better off maintaining his line along the Sunken Road and deploying a few skirmishers on this south side of the field to give warning of the enemy approach.

In any case, as his artillery rolled up, Hurlbut positioned Lt. Culbert Laing's Michigan battery behind Williams' line, and Lt. Edward Brotzmann's Missouri battery near the intersection of the Hamburg-Purdy and the River Roads. But he soon changed his mind and moved Brotzmann's guns over to the apex of his line between the two brigades. He strung out his cavalry behind the division to serve as a straggler line, which was about the only use for cavalry in Shiloh's forested terrain.

But Hurlbut's third artillery battery, the 13OH, commanded by Capt. John B. Myers, still hadn't arrived. This was odd because of all the units in Hurlbut's division, this battery's camp was the closest to the cotton field, and conveniently adjacent to the River Road.

After the general had sent repeated messengers, the battery finally showed up around 9:30am, over 30 minutes late. Hurlbut ordered the battery to face the timberline behind Laumen's brigade. Myers objected, arguing the battery should be placed farther back on more open ground, but Hurlbut insisted.

More Units Join Hurlbut

Meanwhile, around 8:30, while Hurlbut deployed around Sarah Bell's field, Prentiss and the residue of his battered division, now reduced to about 600 men, began forming on the west flank of Hurlbut's line along this Sunken Road, having no better place to go if they wanted to stay in the fight.

As Prentiss' men filed past Hurlbut's line, one officer described them as "*acting like a flock of sheep, ready to start in any direction.*" The colonel of the 44IN said Prentiss was "*clamoring for he knew not what – the line to be pushed forward to his former position, etc. He was as demoralized as his troops.*"

But Prentiss would soon be reinforced by the 600-man 23MO which had debarked at the Landing a few hours earlier, bringing his strength on this part of the line to a more formidable 1,200 men, and he would hold his position in the center of the Feder-

Chapter 13 - Hurlbut Draws a Line

als' Sunken Road line throughout the afternoon after being visited by Grant and ordered to "*hold at all hazards.*"

And then, on the west side of Prentiss, division commander W. H. L. Wallace's 2nd Division arrived from near the Landing with his three brigades of 5,800 men, and he placed two of them – Col. James Tuttle's and Brig. Gen. Thomas Sweeny's – to the west of Prentiss along the same country lane, the Sunken Road. (Wallace kept his third brigade, McArthur's, in reserve. Wallace's division extended the Sunken Road position all the way west to the Western Corinth Road.

And so, more by accident than design, the Federals were forming a new battle-line along the Sunken Road, all anchored on Hurlbut.

The First "Attack"
9:30 AM to 10 AM

Hurlbut's Federals got their first look at the enemy emerging through the woods south of the Hamburg-Purdy Road. "*His regiments with their red banners were flashing in the morning sun*" according to one 3IA lieutenant.

William's and Laumen's brigades began receiving peppering fire from the surrounding woods. The Federals answered, but with little effect. Soon they also began taking some scattered artillery fire from an unseen battery (probably Capt. Felix Robertson's Alabama battery). The incoming rounds did little harm, with two major exceptions:

First, a shell fragment sliced through Col. Williams' horse, slamming both rider and horse to the ground and paralyzing Williams for weeks, eventually forcing him to resign from the army. The loss of Williams, a classmate of Grant's at West Point before Williams quit because of poor math grades, went unmourned by men and officers of his brigade, who thoroughly hated him because of his harsh discipline. Col. Isaac Pugh of the 41IL now took command of Williams' brigade.

Another casualty of an incoming shell was Myers' battery. Just as Myers was deploying his guns, an incoming shell scored a direct hit on one of his battery caissons. Packed with powder and ammo,

Col. Isaac C. Pugh
1805 - 1874

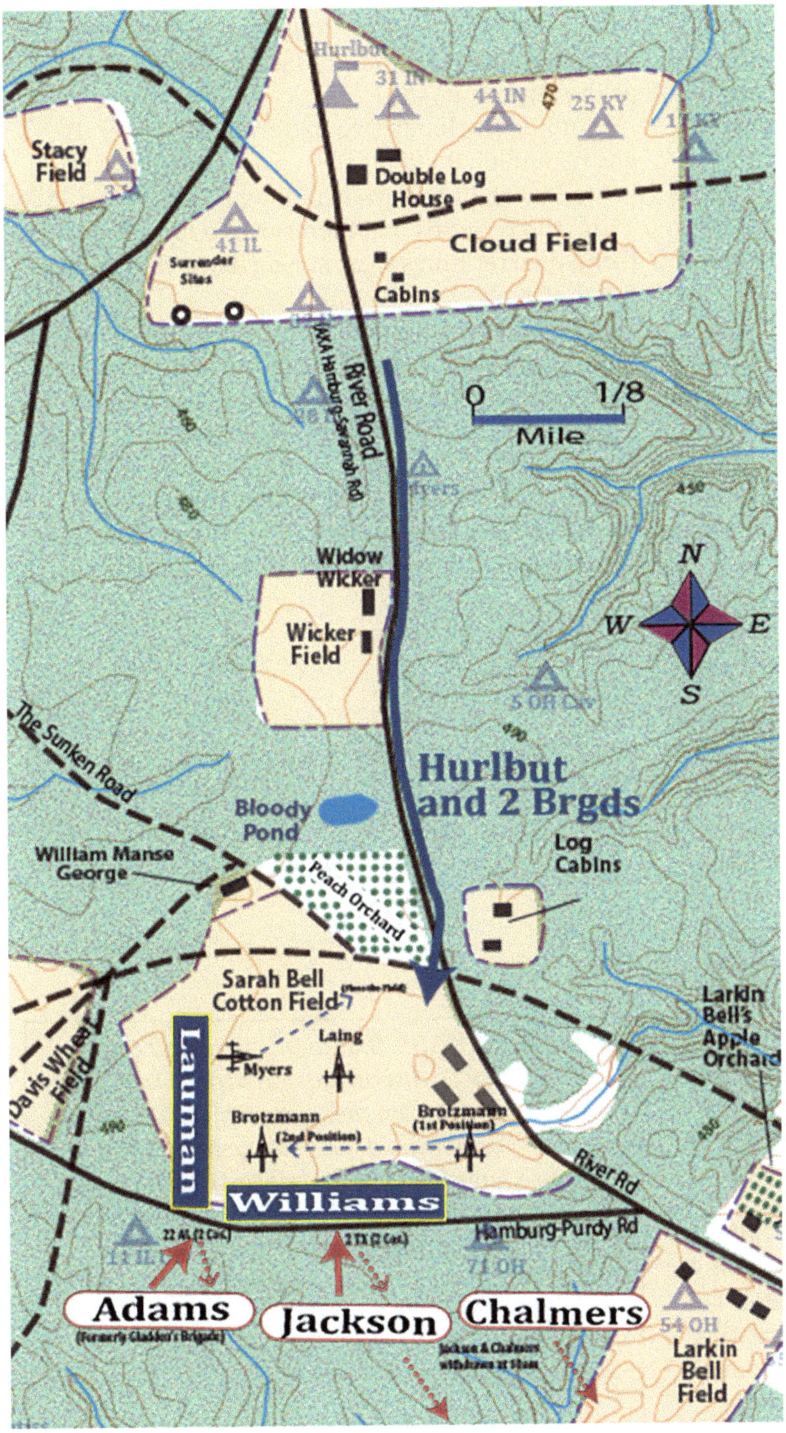

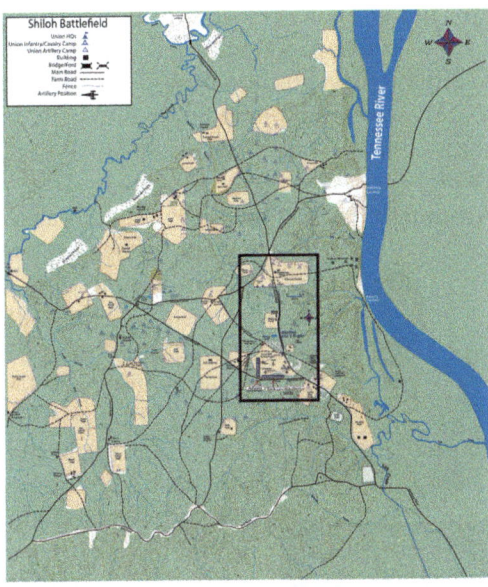

Map's Location on the Battlefield

Hurlbut and his two brigades join the fight at Sarah Bell's cotton field.

Chapter 13 - Hurlbut Draws a Line

the caisson erupted in a tremendous blast, killing one gunner and wounding eight. This was all it took to send Myers and his remaining gun crews flying to the rear, along with at least one out-of-control team of horses, which dragged a gun and caisson along with it. That left five guns on the field with no artillerymen to serve them, so gunners from the other two batteries rushed over to spike the guns and cut the horses from their harnesses. ("Spiking" a cannon renders it inoperable, usually by hammering a metal spike, or sometimes mud, down the vent in the breach.)

Strangely, from the Federals' point of view, the expected Confederate assault didn't happen, at least not yet. As it turned out, the Confederates – men of Wither's Division, exhausted and disorganized by their costly victory at Spain Field – were at the moment more concerned about Hurlbut attacking *them!*

Around 9:30am, it had become increasingly apparent to the Confederates that their battleline was short by perhaps a half mile from stretching all the way to the river. An engineer, Capt. Samuel Lockett, from Hardee's corps, was sent to scout the area. He sent back the alarming news that he'd spotted a full Yankee division near the river – in fact it was only an under-strength brigade, and a frightened one at that. (A division normally includes three brigades). So now, thinking that there was a full enemy division on his right flank, at around 10am Johnston pulled Jackson's and Chalmer's brigades off of the line here in front of Sarah Bell's cotton field, as well as Capt. Charles Gage's and Capt. Isadore Girardey's batteries, and personally deployed them farther east, leaving only Adam's (formerly Gladden's) lone battle-weary brigade of perhaps 1,500 to confront Hurlbut's two fresh brigades of 4,000. Thinking the Rebels were retreating, the Federals cheered and opened fire, whereupon Chalmer's men about-faced and gave the Yanks a parting volley.

But the Confederate pause gave Hurlbut time to reconsider his position. A brief flurry of confusion caused Pugh to withdraw one of his left-flank regiments back to the Peach Orchard at the north end of the cotton field. Thinking about it, Hurlbut decided to move his entire force back to the orchard, which provided a much better defensive position with a clear field of fire across the cotton field.

So now his men quickly took up position behind an old fence along the country lane eventually known as the Sunken Road.

Including Hurlbut's two batteries, the Federals' entire Sunken Road position was eventually supported by eight batteries totaling 33 guns. And so by 11am the Federals had themselves a formidable line, three-quarter miles long, strung along that Sunken Road.

In one of the great might-have-beens of the battle, if the three Confederate brigades had attacked Hurlbut's two brigades in their vulnerable, salient formation, the Southerners would very possibly have charged out of the timber and smashed the Federals here at the cotton field, with nothing to stop them from pushing straight up the River Road (aka Savannah-Hamburg Road) to Pittsburg Landing.

Capt. Samuel H. Locket 1837 - 1891

> *After the battle Hurlbut angrily ordered the 13OH battery be disbanded and urged Capt. Myers be cashiered from the army, which he was. But the governor of Ohio defended Myers and pulled strings to have the captain reinstated. The argument dragged on for years, with even the captain of the Florida battery [Girardey] that had fired the fateful shot chiming in, denouncing Hurlbut and saying his anger was simply a mask to cover his own sluggishness in supporting Prentiss.*

Hurlbut's Division under attack at the Peach Orchard and Sarah Bell's Cotton Field

Looking north from the Confederate position across Sarah Bell's Old Cotton Field. That's the William Manse George's cabin on the opposite side of the field. The Sunken Road runs just behind the cabin. The Peach Orchard is off camera to the right of the cabin.

Chapter 13 - Hurlbut Draws a Line

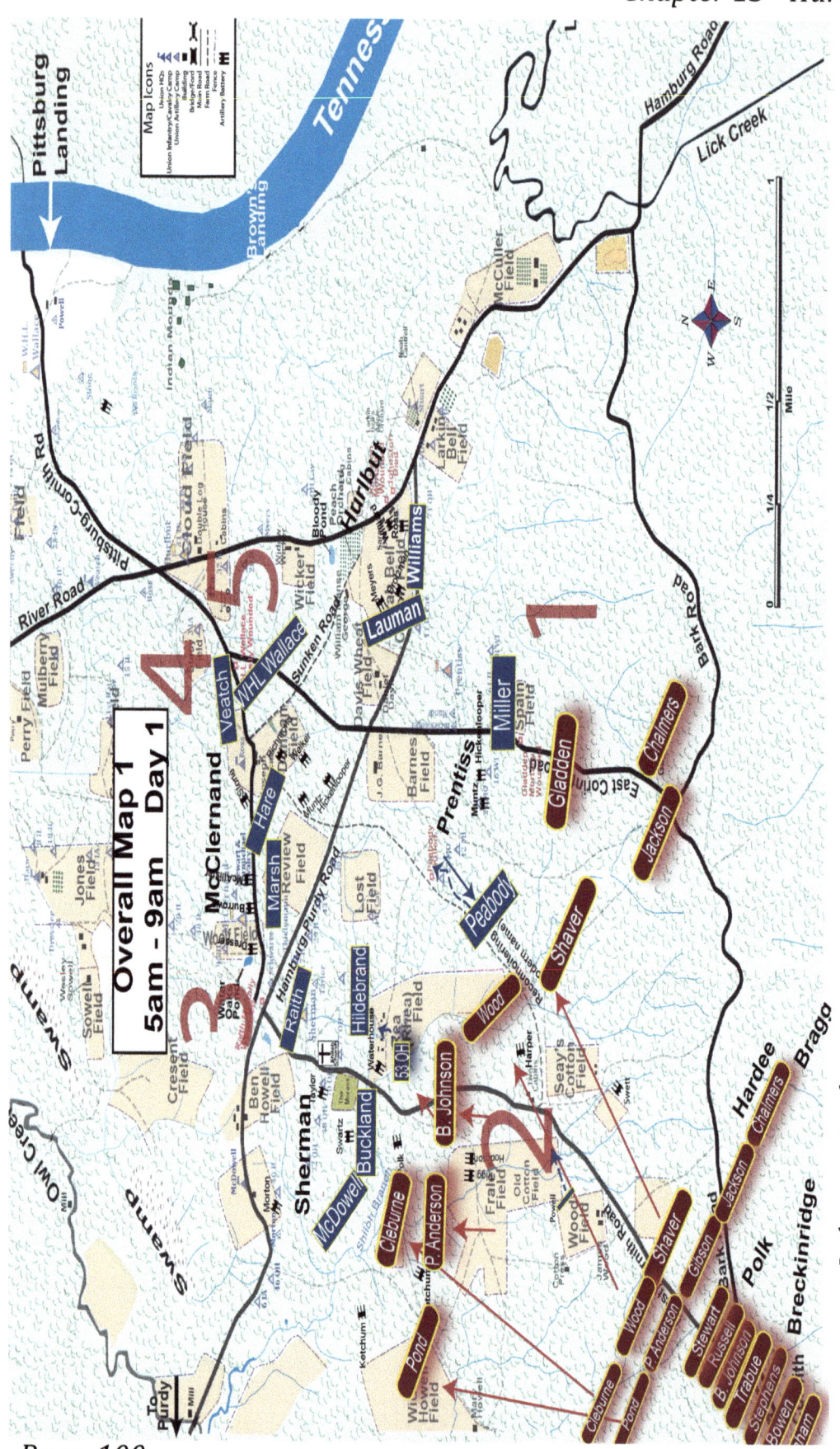

In this same time frame,
1. Confederates were attacking both brigades (Peabody's and Miller') of Prenstiss' division,
2. And attacking both brigades (Buckland and Hildebrand's) of Sherman's division.
3. Farther north, McClernand was moving his brigades toward the sound of battle, and,
4. Hurlbut had sent one of his brigades (Veatch's) to aid McClernand & Sherman, while marching to the Peach Orchard area with his other two brigades, while
5. WHL Wallace was moving his division toward what would be known as the Sunken Road. (Note that this same map will be shown for all chapters in this 5am-9am time frame).

14 The Hornet's Nest

Duncan Field, 10am – 4:30pm

The fight along the center of the Sunken Road – the western portion of it called the "Hornet's Nest" by the Confederates because of the whirring sound of bullets flying about in the brush – is probably the best known aspect of the Shiloh battle, and one of the few scenes of the battle memorialized with a painting.

The Sunken Road was a farm lane used for years by farmers and stage coach drivers as a shortcut connecting the Eastern Corinth Road and the River Road (aka Savannah-Hamburg Road). This scraggly little lane – really just a wagon path – would become known rather grandly as "The Sunken Road," though in fact it wasn't very sunken. Its main attraction to the Federals was that it provided a tangible line to rally upon. It was about three-quarter mile long, intersecting with the Pittsburg-Corinth Road to the west in front of Duncan Field, and with the River Road in the east in front of the Sarah Bell's Cotton Field.

As mentioned in the previous chapter, Gen. Hurlbut initiated the Federals' Sunken Road position at the eastern end of the road, where he was soon joined by the battered remnants of Prentiss' division, and then by W. H. L. Wallace's division. By around noon the Federal line assumed the shape of a bow, with the remnants of Prentiss' division – now reduced to the size of a regiment – bulging out in the center, while Hurlbut's brigades slanted away slightly to the Union left and W. H. L. Wallace's slanting away slightly to the right. About 5,700 Federal infantry and six batteries of 25 guns formed up here because the road was a handy line to rally on.

Wallace's two brigades – commanded by Brig. Gen. Thomas Sweeny and Col. James Tuttle – were mostly veterans of Fort Donelson. They formed along the lane in front of Duncan Field. Tuttle's Iowa regiments, particularly the 2IA and 7IA directly in front of Duncan Field, would see some of the heaviest fighting along the lane.

At the time of the battle, Duncan Field was an old cotton field overgrown with weeds, in some places as high as a man's head. Spiking south into the field on its eastern side, nearly perpendicular from the Sunken Road, was a four or five foot gully and a creek bed, filled with small timber and dense underbrush that hadn't yet leafed out. The gully almost split off the eastern third of the field into a separate field of its own.

A bush-covered rail fence bordered the north edge of Duncan field, giving the defending Federals good camouflage. The Duncan's deserted log cabin and some outbuildings sat on the western side of the field 200 yards in front of the Federal line.

Although there is much discussion as to the depth of the Sunken Road - it was variously described as ranging between 12" and 30", depending no doubt on where one happened to be along the road - the defensive advantage of the road was not the road's meager depth but rather its protective barrier of thick, nearly impenetrable brush between the road and the open Duncan Field beyond. In addition to the undergrowth, the road was covered with hickory and oak trees which had not yet leafed out. This maize of trees and especially the undergrowth served the same military purpose as barbed wire, slowing the Confederate advance but allowing the Federals to see through the brush to shoot at the attackers. We don't know exactly what the brush was, but at least one Confederate of the 4LA described the barrier as *"the thickest undergrowth of blackjack I ever saw."* He claimed that, *"It was almost impossible to walk through."* Apparent-

Brig. Gen.
Thomas W. Sweeny
1820 - 1892

Col.
James M. Tuttle
1823 - 1892

> Tuttle's military career would come to an abrupt end in June 1864 with charges of bribery, profiteering, and collusion that shocked even veteran politicians.
>
> But on this day the slow-talking Iowan, who had no military experience, would give an outstanding battlefield performance.

Page 101

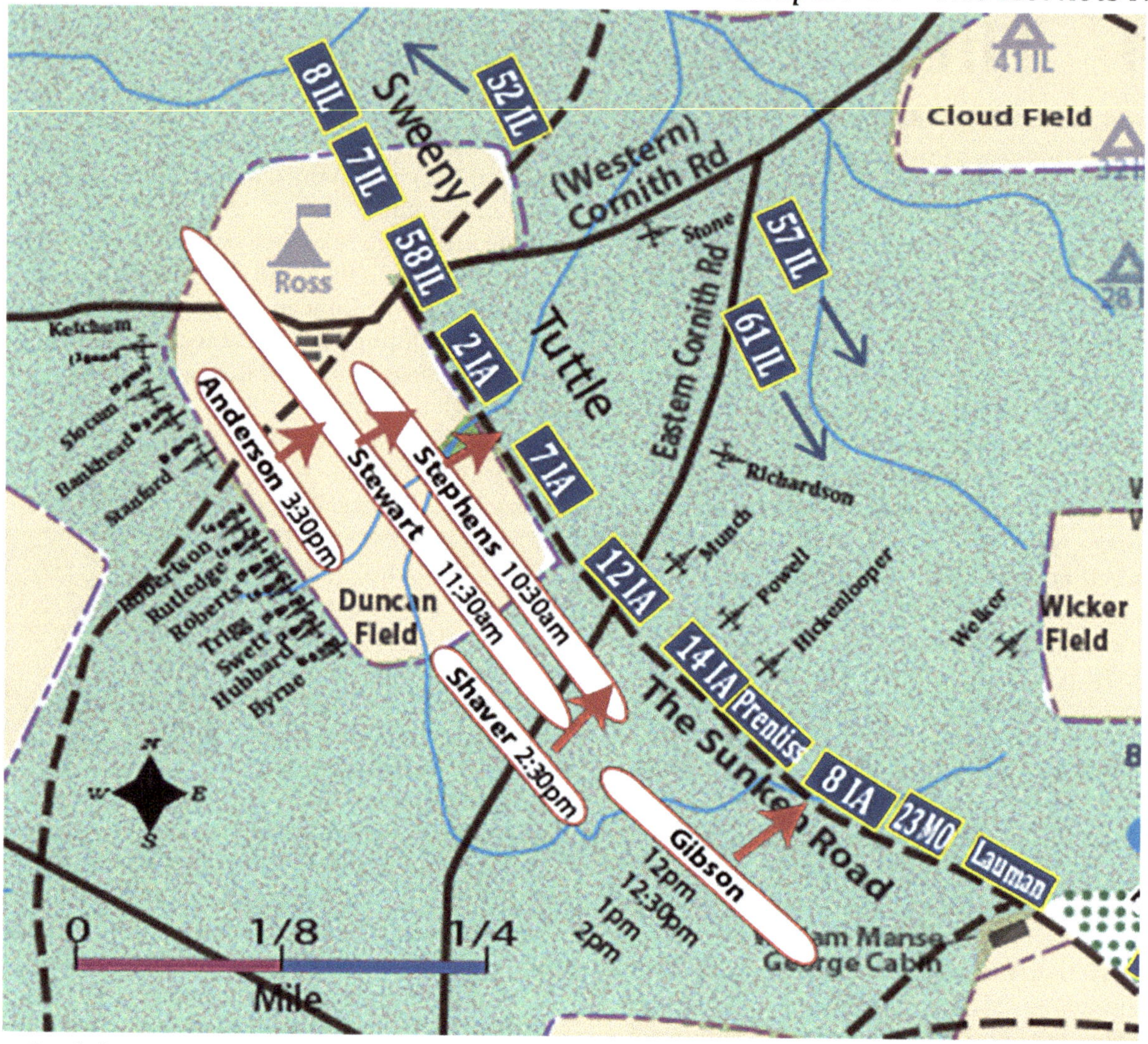

Chapter 14 - The Hornets Nest

Confederates attacked at least eight times across Duncan Field and in the woods to the right of the field, the latter called the "Hornet's Nest."

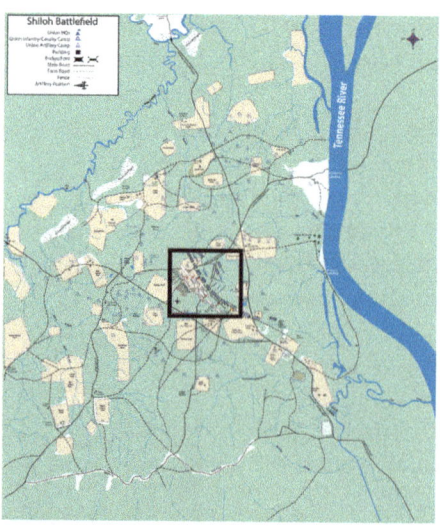

Map's Location on the Battlefield

Blackjack Oak

ly, he was referring to Blackjack Oak, which is basically a very tall and very tough weed, with thick branches all the way to the ground. Whatever the brush was, it, along with the buzzing of Yankee bullets, gave the position its name of the "Hornet's Nest."

There is disagreement as to how many times the Confederates attacked the Sunken Road, and which units were involved. Here, we'll include what seems to be the general consensus as to the which units attacked, and when.

As early as 10am Confederate troops began massing in this vicinity, with Confederate artillery sparring with Federal cannon across the field. But beginning around 10:30am the Confederates began launching assaults against the Sunken Road. Once Sherman and McClernand fell back to Jones Field around 1pm, even more Confederates turned their attention to the Sunken Road line. In all, the Confederates would attack the Sunken Road at least eight times (some historians say nine or ten times), mostly across Duncan Field and the empty pasture(s) to its east – all called the "Hornet's Nest." These attacks do not include the assaults made across Sarah Bell's Cotton Field and the Peach Orchard along the same road, which are discussed in separate chapters.

Confederates Mass In the Center

At around 9:20am, as the battle rolled northward, Beauregard followed and moved his headquarters from the intersection of Pittsburg-Corinth and Bark Roads, to the northern end of Fraley Field near Shiloh Church. He also followed the Napoleonic practice of feeding troops into the areas where the battle was loudest. And right now the noise was growing loudest in the center of the field. One problem was that, by focusing on the center of the field, Beauregard was deviating from Johnston's plan to throw the weight of the attack on the Union far *left*, west near the river. Also, the Federals were weak on their left, but relatively strong in their center, causing no fewer than 10 Confederate brigades to bash against the strongest part of the Union line.

1st Attack 10:30am
Cheatham-Stephen's Brigade

Confederate division commander, Maj. Gen. Benjamin Cheatham – a popular, hard-drinking Tennessee planter-aristocrat who participated in the Gold Rush of 1849 – was the first to encounter the Hornet's Nest as it was just forming around 10am. His division had been ordered by Beauregard to "*ascertain the point where the firing was heaviest and there engage the enemy at once.*"

Marching east from the far left of the Confederate line, Cheatham reached a cotton field [Duncan Field] on the other side of which he "*discovered the enemy in strong force behind a fence and an abandoned road.*" A Yankee battery (Capt. Emil Munch's) blocked the approach. Cheatham's artillery spent nearly an hour trying to knock it out, without success. Finally, Col. Jordan of Beauregard's staff rode up and, on behalf of Beauregard, ordered Cheatham to attack.

Maj. Gen. Benjamin D. Cheatham (w) 1820 - 1886

Cheatham led his 2nd Brigade, Col. William Stephen's – about 1,350 men in three regiments – to make the attack across Duncan Field. But unknown to the Confederates, the Federals had infiltrated that thicket-filled ravine which cut through eastern side of the field, allowing them to fire into the right flank of the attackers.

"*All was silent in front until our ranks were near,*" wrote 6TN Pvt. R. W. Hurdle. Then, when about in the middle of the field, the men came under a "*murderous crossfire,*" both from artillery and infantry to the front and from the ravine to the Confederate right. The 6TN charged against the 14IA, commanded by Col. William Shaw, a Mexican War veteran. To his youthful troops, Shaw seemed a strange old geezer who walked with a gimp and cussed like a sailor. But he was plenty tough.

Shaw ordered his men to lay down and hold their fire; when the Confederates advanced to within 30 paces, the blue line rose up and loosed a devastating volley, "*leaving the dead laying in line of battle as if on dress parade,*" according to a member of the 6TN. "*We began this charge in good spirits,* wrote a captain of the 7KY, "*but when we got well into the field the enemy infantry as well as artillery turned loose on us with terrible effect and our Colonel commanded us out to the right of the timber. ... The balls jumped me on each side and in great profusion during the charge, and after we got into the timber they continued to pass us.*"

Shaw even ordered his Federals to counterattack, but quickly thought better of it and ordered his men back to the road.

In 30 minutes, the 6TN lost 250 men, including 14 officers and the entire 12-man color guard. The regimental flag was shredded beyond recognition. The other two regiments fared little better. Cheatham was shot in the ear. He lost many officers as well as his aide-de-camp, a young boy named John Campbell, who had his head taken off by a cannon ball. Brigade commander Stephens, having risen from his sickbed in Corinth, had his horse shot from under him as he attempted to rally his men at the southern edge of the field; he collapsed from exhaustion. His son William, who served as his aide, was severely wounded.

2nd Attack 11:30am
Stewart's Reinforced Brigade

This second attack, although poorly documented,

was clearly the most formidable assault on the Sunken Road line that day. On Bragg's order, Brig. Gen. Alexander Stewart led a reinforced brigade of approximately 3,600 Confederates – the bulk of 10 regiments – in an attack that stretched from Prentiss' command to the far end of Duncan Field, west of the Western Corinth Road. But the Federals, numbering about 4,300 men and 19 guns in this sector, held their ground, hurling deafening barrages at the attackers. The attack, which lasted about a half hour, failed. Few of the Southern attackers managed to get much more than half way across smoke-covered Duncan field before being driven back by the storm of fire.

3rd Attack 12pm – Gibson's Brigade

After Stewart's failed attack, the Confederate line had become so entangled and intermixed that Polk and Bragg agreed that Polk would command all the troops in the center of the line, while Bragg took the right. Around noon, Bragg assumed command of this right wing and began ordering a series of piecemeal assaults on the Sunken Road. To start, he immediately ordered Col. Randall Gibson to lead his 2,350-man Louisiana brigade in an attack against the section of the line held by Prentiss and Lauman.

Chapter 14 - The Hornets Nest

Gibson was a 31-year-old Yale-educated, New Orleans lawyer and aristocrat. He was already on Bragg's bad side in the early fighting on Barnes Field, where Bragg considered him insufficiently aggressive. Gibson later called for a court of inquiry on the matter.

Gibson's regiments advanced toward Prentiss' and Laumen's position, from left to right, the 4LA, 13LA, 1AR, and 19LA. Like their predecessors, Gibson and his men were walking into a fire storm. When they got within 40-50 yards of the Union line, the Federals opened up with "*a perfect tornado of rifle fire ... in our very faces,*" according to a Louisiana soldier. "*Men fell around us like leaves*," said another. A single artillery blast took out a file of six Zouaves of the 13LA, splattering brain-matter over their captain, Edgar Dubroea. It was mainly this densely wooded sector along the Sunken Road that fronted Prentiss' and Lauman's sectors, that the Confederates began calling *The Hornet's Nest*.

"Men fell around us like leaves."

Two of Gibson's regiments pushed into the thicket, only to be ensnared in the nearly impenetrable tangle of blackjack oak. "*It was almost impossible to walk through it,*" claimed a 4LA soldier. The undergrowth was so dense that soldiers were firing into their own ranks. They tried to push through the tangle with their gun butts and barrels, but command and control was impossible.

Col. B. L. Hodge of the 19LA wrote afterward that, even as his men were being shot down all around him, he couldn't see the Yankees in the thick brush, and "*from the manner of the men looking through the bushes, as if hunting an object for their aim, it was apparent that [his men] were unable to descry the concealed foe, and were only firing at the flash of the enemy's pieces.*" Therefore, Hodge gave the order to cease firing and "*charge bayonets.*" The men plunged another 20 or 30 steps into the thicket but still couldn't see the enemy except for the flashes of their rifles, which were taking a terrific toll on the Rebels. The woods in front of Lauman's Federal position caught fire, roasting many of the wounded who were too crippled to crawl away. Hodge ordered his men to commence firing again, while withdrawing back across the field. The other regiments did the same.

4th Attack 12:30pm
Gibson's Brigade

Gibson rode back to Bragg and requested artillery support, but apparently none was available, and Bragg simply ordered him to renew the attack immediately. At around the same time, one of Breckinridge's battery commanders, Capt. Edward Byrne, approached Bragg and requested permission to move his battery 400 hundred yards to the west, to better fire on the Yankees' flank. Bragg asked why Byrne hadn't sent a lower-grade officer to make such a request. Byrne replied that he felt he could state the case better than a lieutenant. Amazingly, like a parent correcting a child, Bragg ordered him to return to his battery and that, in time, Bragg would send an officer to hear his request. A lieutenant eventually rode to Byrne and took his request, which Bragg granted.

> "Colonel. Allen, I want no faltering now."

Meanwhile, Gibson's men attacked again, but this time they kept a greater distance from the enemy, satisfied to trade gunfire with the Yankees. It was still hell, given that there was plenty of Federal artillery in this area. The Yankees "*mowed us down at every volley,*" according to Pvt. Thomas Robertson of the 4LA. The 4th fired off two or three volleys and then withdrew, but the 19LA and possibly the other two regiments kept fighting for another 30 minutes before withdrawing.

5th Attack 1pm - Gibson's Brigade

As Gibson's exhausted troops came running back after the failed assault, Bragg rode up to Col. Henry Allen, a Harvard-educated attorney commanding the 4LA regiment, and ordered his and the 13LA to ambush the enemy, whom Bragg incorrectly believed to be advancing. "*Serve them as they have served you,*" Bragg cried. Like Gibson, Allen requested artillery support. Bragg admonished him, "*Colonel Allen, I want no faltering now.*" With that, Allen returned to his men, gave them a pep talk,

Col. Henry W. Allen
1820 - 1866

and once again charged into the inferno, again advancing against the Sunken Road from across Davis Wheatfield. The engagement soon degenerated into a long distance, hour-long gun fight. Allen was hit with a bullet that passed through both cheeks, which must have done wonders for his dental work. The commander of the 1AR, Col. James Fagan, leaped from his horse as it was shot dead.

Again the Confederates were driven back, this time breaking into unorganized groups. Many of the men had enough, vowing they would not attack that line again.

A bitter Gibson would later state, "*The brigade was sacrificed by three [actually, four] separate charges, and without the aid of any artillery whatever, although we had it at hand ready to open on the enemy.*"

6th Attack 2pm - Gibson's Brigade

Seeing the troops streaming back across the Davis Wheat Field, Bragg called for Capt. Samuel Lockett – the same man who had earlier passed the incorrect report to Johnston that there was a Union division on the far eastern flank. Bragg ordered Lockett to seize the banner of one of the regiments and lead it forward, stating "*The flag must not go back again.*"

Lockett grabbed the banner of the 4LA just as the color bearer was shot down. A few moments later Col. Allen, blood steaming from the holes in his cheeks, rode up to Lockett and indignantly inquired, "*What are you doing with my colors, Sir?*"

> "Here boys is as good a place as any to die!"

Snatching the flag from Lockett, Allen defiantly rode out in the field and faced the enemy, calling out to his men, "*Forward! Here boys is as good a place as any to die!*" The colonel waved his sword and led his men through the underbrush and dense smoke to within 50 feet of the Federals on the Sunken Road.

Lockett later wrote that "*... brave, shot-up Henry Allen stood out in front of his lines with bullets whistling around him, holding the colors of the regiment he commanded, and defiantly facing the enemy.*" Fortunately for Allen, so much smoke and brush covered the field that he was probably barely visible to the Federals.

The Confederates attacked in two ranks. Here again, the brush was so thick that some of the men in the rear rank were actually firing into their front rank. Eventually, unable to advance further, the attackers simply emptied their rifles into the thick smoke that marked the Federal line.

In the midst of the fight, as a Louisiana soldier rose to advance, a cannon shell snapped off his head. With a blood geyser spurting out of his neck, his comrades watched in amazement as he continued to walk two or three steps before dropping.

The regiment fought for nearly 30 minutes, firing into the smoke with men dropping constantly. Gibson had his second horse shot from under him that day. Finally, the brigade again fell back, leaving 682 dead and wounded on the field.

Gibson's brigade of 2,300 suffered one of the highest Confederate casualty rates of the battle. But Bragg would later write to his wife that Gibson, who led four charges against the Sunken Road, and who would lead more the next day, *"was an arrant coward."*

Col. Allen would survive the battle and go on to be elected governor of Louisiana in 1864.

7th Attack 2:30pm
Shaver's Brigade

Bragg now sent in Shaver's (formerly Hindman's) Arkansas Brigade, which had already fought for five hours in heavy engagements in front of Peabody's camp and in Review Field. With his 6AR detatched by Bragg, what remained of Shaver's 1,500 men of the 2AR, 7AR and the 3rd Confederate Battalion, struck the center of the Sunken Road line in Duncan Field, manned by the 12IA and 14IA and Prentiss' survivors.

Col. Robert G. Shaver
1831 - 1915

Shaver said he advanced *"until my left was in about 50 and my right about 60 yards from their lines when a terrific and murderous fire was poured in on me from their lines and battery. It was impossible to charge through the dense undergrowth,"* Shaver said, *"and I soon discovered my fire was having no effect upon the enemy, so I had nothing left me but to retire or have my men all shot down."*

In the attack, Lt. Col. John A. Dean of the 7AR fell mortally wounded, shot through the neck. As the Confederates withdrew, Capt. Warren C. Jones of the 14IA ran between the lines and spoke briefly to Dean before the Southerner died. Jones crossed the

Chapter 14 - The Hornets Nest

dead man's arms and placed a handkerchief across his face before dashing back to his line.

Not all of Shaver's men retreated, being unable or unwilling to disengage, and some of them maintained a sharp firefight that lasted nearly an hour. But eventually, Shaver's three regiments broke off the attack and were not engaged again that day.

The Federals were taking casualties as well. And supposedly there was an instance where a Federal hid behind a tree. Soon, other Federals hid behind him. Eventually, there was a chain of 30 or 40 men, all hiding behind the same tree as the officers cursed and yelled at them to get back on the firing line.

It Was All a Glittering Lie

One soldier of the 6AR who was not with his comrades in Shaver's attack was Pvt. Henry Morton Stanley. Earlier that morning, in the fighting at Review Field, he had been hit by a bullet to the stomach. Luckily, the bullet hit his belt buckle, knocking the wind out of him but not penetrating. His brigade had continued advancing and was gone by the time Stanley recovered.

He *"struck north in the direction which my regiment had taken, over ground strewn with the bodies and debris of war."*

"The ghastly relics," he said, *"appalled every sense."* He came upon the body of *"a stout English sergeant of a neighboring company ... conspicuous for his good humor, and nicknamed John Bull."* Next to the sergeant was a young lieutenant who *"judging by the gloss on his uniform must have been some father's darling. A clean bullet hole in the center of his forehead had ended his career."*

Moving on, Stanley came upon about 20 dead, *"lying in various postures, each by its own pool of viscous blood, which emitted a peculiar scent, which was new to me then. Beyond these, a still larger group lay, body overlying body. The company opposed to them must*

After the war, Shaver became a leading figure in the Arkansas Ku Klux Klan. Upon being convicted of several murders during Reconstruction, he fled to British Honduras on a steam ship from New Orleans. After Reconstruction ended and the charges were dropped, he returned to Arkansas, spending his later life as sheriff of Howard Country, Arkansas, as well as head of the Confederate Veteran Society in that state.

have shot straight." He never forgot *"those wide open dead eyes," saying later that this "was the first Field of Glory I had ever seen ... and the first time Glory sickened me with its repulsive aspect, and made me suspect it was all a glittering lie."*

Continuing on, Stanley *"moved, horror-stricken, through the fearful shambles where the dead lay as thick as sleepers in Long Park on a bank holiday."* He noticed from the piles of bodies that *"every half mile or so [the Federals] stood and contested the Confederate advance."*

"I overtook my regiment about one o'clock and found that it was engaged in one of these occasional spurts of fury." In fact, he reached his regiment just as it was falling back from its failed attack on the Hornets Nest.

Shaver reported to Bragg on his *"inability to dislodge the enemy, and that his command was very much cut up."* Bragg ordered him to await orders. *"We lay down and availed ourselves of trees, logs and hollows, and annoyed [the Federals'] upstanding ranks,"* Stanley recorded, while *"battery pounded battery, and meanwhile, we hugged our resting places closely."*

8th Attack 3:30pm
Anderson's Brigade

Finally, Patton Anderson's brigade, reinforced with the Crescent Regiment – about 1,300 men in all – advanced once again across Duncan Field, only to meet the same blistering response from the Federals that had broken all the previous attacks. This attack failed, with particularly heavy losses to the 20LA, which had struck the 2IA.

Brig. Gen. James P. Anderson 1822 - 1872

And that ended the major frontal attacks against the Sunken Road line, all of which were futile.

Ruggles' Barrage

Brute, frontal attacks with infantry hadn't budged the Yankee line. After at least eight failed attacks, there was a lull in the fighting as the Confederates once again regrouped. But they were still determined to crack that damn Yankee line if took all summer, and now they began dragging up every piece of artillery they could lay hands on. Brig. Gen. Daniel Ruggles, one of Bragg's division commanders, 51-years-old in poor health and detested by his troops, usually gets credit for organizing this cannonade, although some Confederate accounts contended that it was a group effort by several officers, with Ruggles being just one of the participants, or possibly just a spectator.

In any case, the Southerners decided that they were going to blast that Yankee line to pieces. Eventually they lined up the largest concentration of artillery yet seen on the American continent, somewhere between 53 and 62 guns, hub to hub along the southern edge of Duncan Field.

Shortly after 4pm, these guns, which could fire about three rounds a minute, unleashed a storm of fire on the Federal line, including explosive shells, canister and solid shot. The latter brought down tree limbs on the heads of the defenders. The ground shook and *"the sky lit up in a blaze of unearthly fire."*

Brig. Gen. Daniel Ruggles 1810 - 1897

An officer of the 2IA later wrote:

"I don't know how our regiment escaped. It seemed like a mighty hurricane sweeping everything before it... The great storm of cannonballs made the forest in places fall before its sweep, ... men and horses were dying, and a blaze of unearthly fire lit up the scene. [Yet] at this moment of horror, when our regiment was lying close to the ground to avoid the storm of balls, the little birds were singing in the green trees over our heads!"

The Confederates were also taking incoming shells. W. A. Howard wrote to his wife:

"It was an awful thing to hear no intermission in firing and hear the clatter of small arms and the whizzing Minnie balls and rifle shot and the sing of grape shot, the hum of cannon balls and the roaring of the bomb shell and explosion of same, seeming to be a thousand every minute."

Not only were Federals taking a storm of incoming artillery, but both their flanks were collapsing. It was too much. The Federals on the Sunken Road began withdrawing after six hours of valiant fighting. The massive barrage continued about 20 minutes, until around 4:30pm, by which time the Federals were gone.

Chapter 14 - The Hornets Nest

Some argue that the barrage actually had little to do with the Federal withdrawal from the Sunken Road, since the retreat of McClernand to the west in the early afternoon, and Hurlbut in the east, exposed both flanks on the Sunken Road line and made it inevitable that the Union troops there would have to retreat.

But while the Sunken Road defenders may have been retreating anyway, the cannonade undoubtedly hastened their departure.

As his regiment pulled out of the roadbed, Col. Joseph Woods of the 12IA noted that a "*carpet of paper*" covered the road from bitten-off cartridge wrappings. The brush was chopped to pieces and large trees were so riddled with bullets and shells that veterans visiting the field 30 years later could still see the damage. A soldier of the 7IA wrote that the field was so covered with Rebel dead that it proved possible to walk across them at places without stepping on the ground. In front of the position of Lauman's brigade, which had caught fire, 120 charred bodies were counted, no doubt mostly Confederates, including an estimated 100 wounded who were trapped and burned to death.

The stubborn Union defense of the Sunken Road cost the Confederates precious time and men, and undoubtedly helped make the difference between success and failure of Johnston's grand offensive of the first day.

> *Assuming 53 cannon fired three rounds per minute per cannon, in 20 minutes the math works out to about 3,180 incoming shells – some of which would have been exploding shells and others would have been solid shot (cannon balls) – the latter very effective against troops in timber since the cannon balls knocked down trees and limbs, crushing soldiers below and raining down wooden splinters.*

This is probably the most famous of the few paintings of the Battle of Shiloh; it's by an artist named Thure de Thulstrup, and it shows the Union line on the Sunken Road in the Hornet's Nest.

A modern picture of Duncan Field, standing on the Sunken Road, looking southwest toward the Confederate position. At the time of the battle, this field certainly wasn't in its present, pristine shape. It was said to have weeds in some places that were nearly head high. Also, there were Duncan cabins somewhere on the field.

Chapter 14 - The Hornets Nest

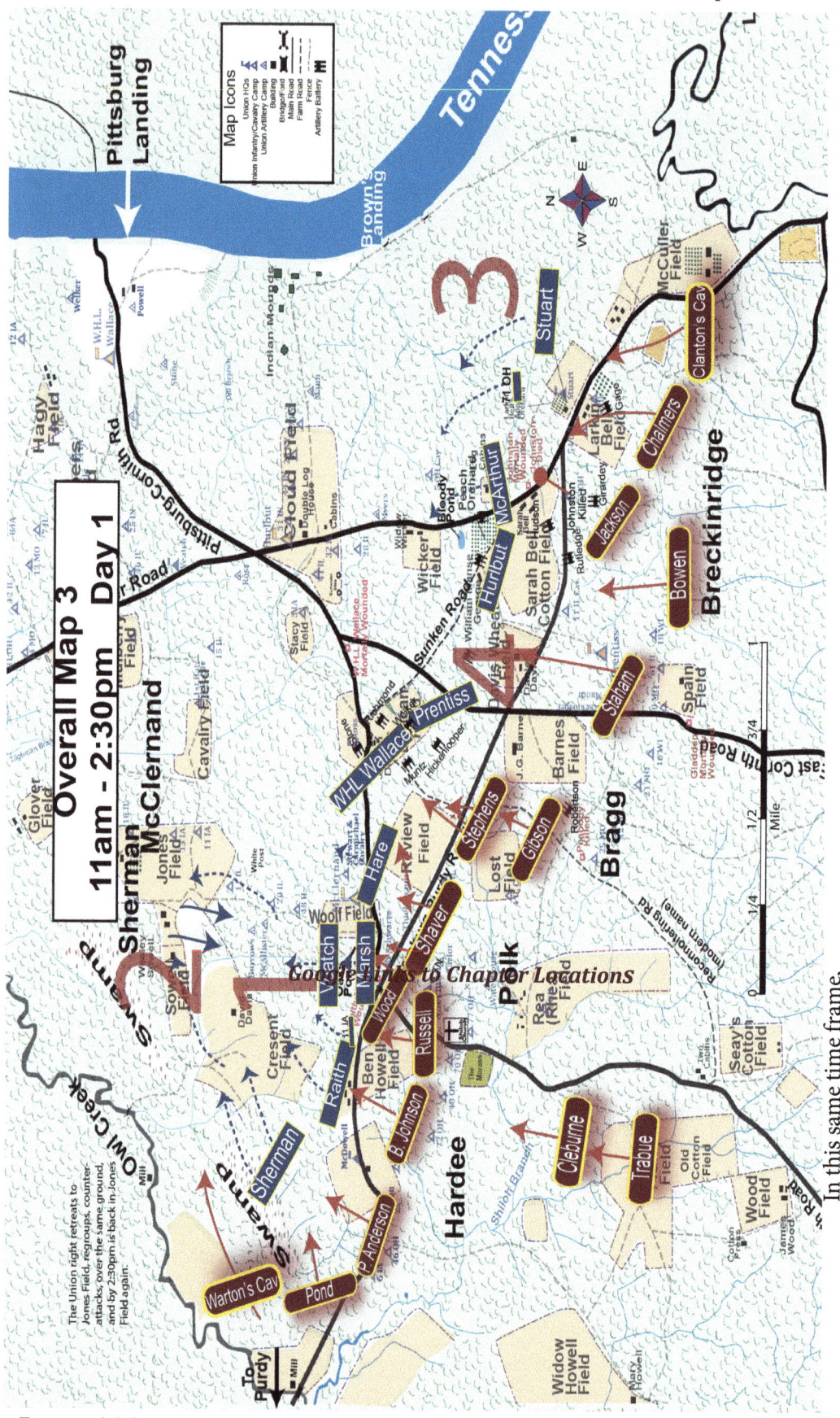

In this same time frame,

1. Confederates were attacking both brigades (Peabody's and Miller') of Prenstiss' division,
2. And attacking both brigades (Buckland and Hildebrand's) of Sherman's division.
3. Farther north, McClernand was moving his brigades toward the sound of battle, and,
4. Hurlbut had sent one of his brigades (Veatch's) to aid McClernand & Sherman, while marching to the Peach Orchard area with his other two brigades, while
5. WHL Wallace was moving his division toward what would be known as the Sunken Road. (Note that this same map will be shown for all chapters in this 5am-9am time frame).

15 Struggle on Union Left

10am to 11am

Hurlbut's morning redeployment started the Union migration to the Sunken Road line, which became the center of the battlefield and the focus of the entire battle by noon of the first day. Hurlbut's two brigades - Pugh's and Lauman's - anchored the east end of that line. Initially, as discussed in a previous chapter, they were placed well south of the road on the south end of Sarah Bell's cotton field, before they eventually fell back to their present position on the north end of that field and the adjoining peach orchard on the northeast corner of that field. This position had its advantages but, unlike the W. H. L. Wallace's and Prentiss' units facing Duncan Field, Hurlbut's men facing Sarah Bell's Field, apparently didn't benefit from a barrier of thick brush to slow Confederate attacks.

In any case, the Federals had cobbled together a fairly organized line in the center of the battlefield. But the Union's far left flank near the river, to the east of Hurlbut's line, was weak. Around 10:30am, to stiffen the eastern flank of the Federal line, Wallace loaned two of his regiments, the 9IL and 11IL, led by Brig. Gen. John A. McArthur, to extend Hurlbut's left flank east of the River Road (aka Savannah-Hamburg Road). Accompanying McArthur was Lt. Peter Wood's (aka Willard's) Chicago battery. Along the way, McArthur accidentally picked up a bonus regiment – the 50IL – which strayed in the woods from its parent brigade and ended up tagging along behind McArthur, who would put it to good use.

All three regiments took up position behind a deeply wooded, 40 foot ravine to the east of Hurlbut's line. Wood's battery set up shop east of the Peach Orchard and slightly in front of McArthur's infantry.

Farther to McArthur's left, next to the river on the critical left flank of the Union line, was the very lonely and nervous brigade commanded by Col. David Stuart. Both he and his men would have been even more nervous had they known that, in theory, they were the bull's eye of Johnston's entire battle plan to sweep the Federal left next to the river.

Stuart's brigade had been placed there days earlier by Sherman to guard the ford at Lick Creek. But Sherman, now on the opposite end of the Federal line, had all he could handle with what was in front of him, and he had no time to give orders to Stuart on the other side of the battlefield.

"Only A Few More Charges"
12:30pm to 2:30pm

Fighting now raged along the Sunken Road to the west in front of Prentiss and Wallace's command. Back here to the east, around 12:30pm the Confederate brigade of Col. Winfield Statham reached the southern edge of Sarah Bell's cotton field and filed into position to the right of Col. William H. Stephens' brigade (now under Col. George Maney), which consisted of the 7KY, 1TN Btn, 6TN and 9TN. Maney's men had earlier suffered severe losses near the Eastern Corinth Road. They now shifted into position facing the southwestern corner of the Sarah Bell's field.

Meanwhile, part of Breckinridge's Reserve Corps, Statham's Confederates took cover under a ridge at the southern end of the cotton field, in the tent camp formerly occupied by the 71OH. (That camp is today hidden by a belt of trees that wasn't there during the battle). From that protected position they initially sparred with Pugh's Federals at a range of about 450 yards. Of Statham's six regiments, only the rightmost of them, the 20TN, got into a serious scrap with the Yankees – elements of McArthur's brigade – and might have gotten into serious trouble had not a regiment from another brigade (probably Jackson's) arrived to shore up its exposed flank.

Perhaps 30 minutes later Gen. Johnston himself led another brigade – commanded by Brig. Gen. John S. Bowen – onto the field and extended the Confederate line eastwards. Bowen's brigade consisted of the 9AR, 10AR, 2nd Confederate, and 1MO.

"Only a few more charges," Johnston assured them, *"and the day is won."* Soon two regiments from Jackson's brigade arrived as well, so that by 1:30 PM the Confederates arrayed 4,000 troops in line of battle, ready to push up the River Road (aka Savannah-Hamburg Road) and drive the Yankees into the river.

Brig. Gen. John S. Bowen (w) 1830 - 1863

Assaults on the Peach Orchard Line
2pm to 2:30pm

At around 2pm, Pugh's brigade in the Peach Orchard watched anxiously as rank upon rank of Confederate troops of Col. Winfield Staham's brigade - the 19TN, 15TN, 22MS, 25TN, 20TN, and 54TN - emerged from the tree line on the south end of the cotton field and advanced with their blood-red battle flags flapping. (In 1862 the tree line was farther back than it is today, beyond the Hamburg-Purdy Road).

Lt. Peter Wood's Federal battery opened fire with canister. Pugh's infantry, lying prone, held their fire until the Confederates got within 200 yards, then stood up with a cheer and unleashed a terrific volley. *"Of the whole Rebel Regiment [fronting the 3rd Iowa], I do not believe more than 200 escaped unharmed,"* according to one Iowan. The Rebels wavered but kept coming. Presently they forced Lt. Edward Brotzman's Union gunners to abandon their guns and flee to the rear. As the Confederates angled toward the abandoned guns and the nearby 41IL, Hurlbut desperately reshuffled his line, sending the 42IL in to support of its fellow Illinois regiment, and extending the 3IA's line to cover the gap thus created. Together, the three regiments managed to repel Statham's Confederates.

But a few minutes later the Southerners rallied and came on again, angling toward Brotzmann's abandoned guns, this time to the west of the cotton field, partially concealed within some timber. Facing them on this sector of the Federal line was Lauman's brigade. Forty-nine year old Jacob Lauman, a veteran of both the battle at Belmont, Missouri and Fort Donelson, was one of Grant's best brigade commanders even though he had no formal military training.

If Johnston had those 15,000 Confederate infantry captured at Fort Donelson, this would have been a perfect time to use them. But now he could only scrape together 1,200 attackers, including Col. William Stephens' (now Maney's) brigade) and the remnants of Gladden's battered brigade, now led by Col. Zachariah C. Deas, its third commander of the day.

Maney and his two regiments – the 19TN and part of the 1TN Btn – had been guarding Greer's Ford on Lick Creek due to Johnston's concern that Buell might land his force there. But by 11am, Maney decided there would be no attack there, and so marched his men to the battle-

Chapter 15 - Struggle on the Union Left

field, leaving only Nathan Forrest and his cavalry to guard the ford, much to Forrest's irritation.

As Maney's small force marched up to assault the Peach Orchard, it was cheered by the wounded. One of the wounded was Col. Mathias Martin of the 23TN, who yelled his support: *"Give'em goss boys! That's right, my brave First Tennessee. Given'em Hail Columbia!"* Somebody asked the heavyset colonel where he was wounded; he yelled back, *"In the arm, in the leg, in the head, in the body, and in another place which I have a delicacy in mentioning."*

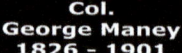

Cheatham ordered Maney to attack Ross's battery (commanded by Lt. Cuthbert W. Laing), with Deas supporting Maney's left flank. The attack commenced at 2:30pm. The Tennesseans drove into the woods west of the Sarah Bell Field. But the assault didn't get far before the Confederates were stopped by a blistering crossfire. They laid down and began a steady but inconclusive gunfight with Lauman's men. The firing was so fierce that eventually the woods again caught fire in front of Lauman's line, again broiling an unknown number of wounded. In the smoke their screams could be heard even through the roaring gunfire. Eventually the Confederate fell back.

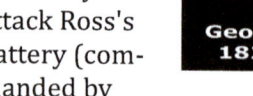

As the Rebels retreated, two battalions of the 5OH Cavalry, which had just arrived on the field, charged

---

Gladden's brigade went through three commanders that day: Gladden, Adams, and Deas.

The second commander, Daniel Adams, had been hit in his right eye at around 11:30am. He was laid in a wagon along with other wounded. On the way back to Corinth, the teamster, thinking Adams was dead, dumped his body along the roadside. But on their retreat the following day, the 10MS found him alive and took him on to Corinth, where he recovered.

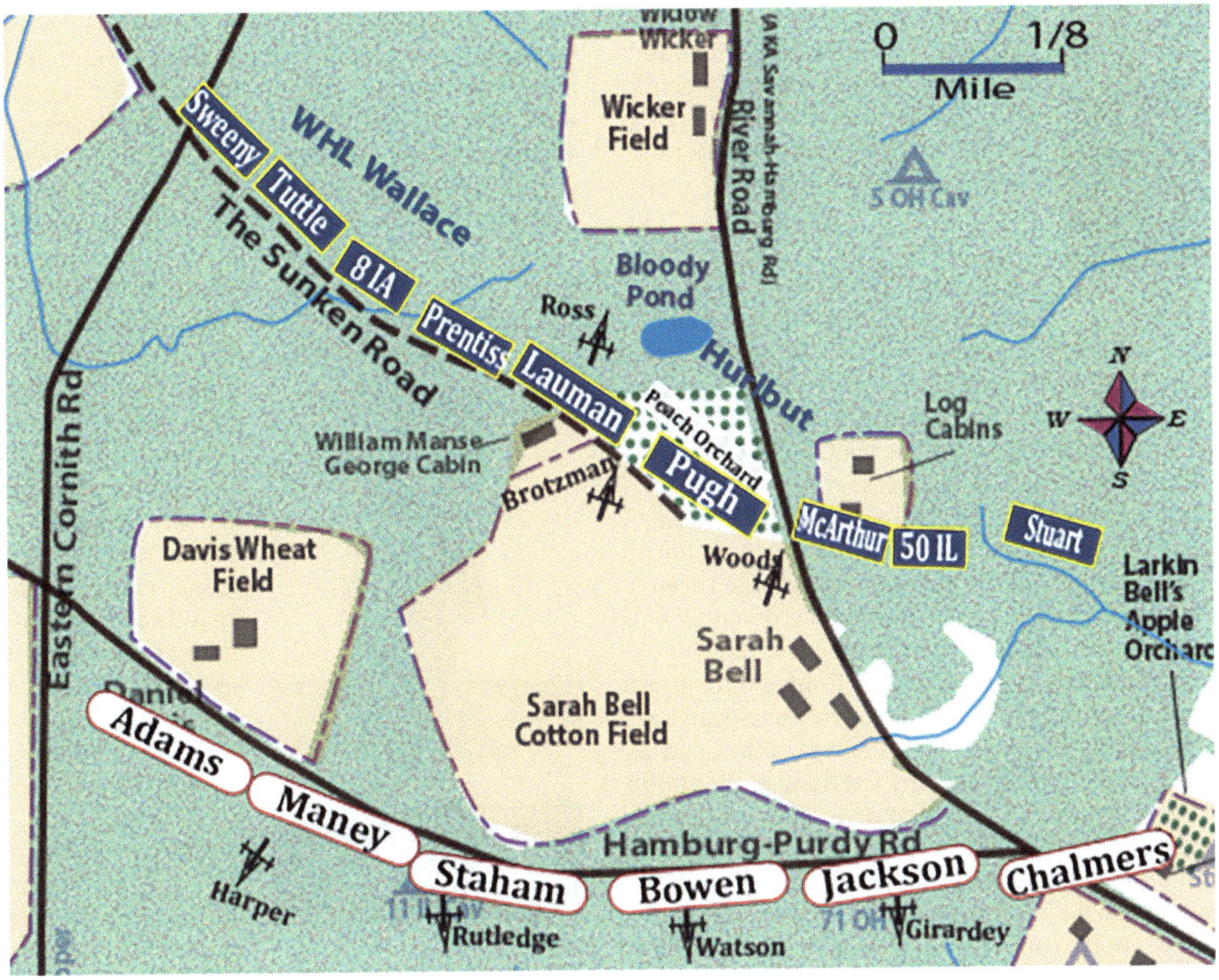

Confederates prepare to assault across Sarah Bell's cotton field

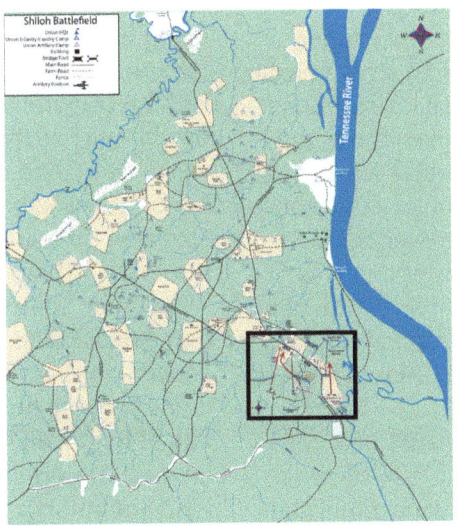

Map's Location on the Battlefield

Col.
Mathis Martin (w)
1812 - 1892

past Ross' guns, chasing the Confederates back to the timber south of the Hamburg-Purdy Road, giving Ross' gunners time to change position. It would be the only Federal cavalry attack of the battle.

Stuart's Stand

While fighting raged along the Sunken Road and in the Peach Orchard, another fight on the Union line was occurring on the Federals' far left flank next to the river.

Several days prior to the battle, before most of the other divisions had arrived at the Landing, Sherman split off one of his four brigades – Col. David Stuart's – and ordered it to set up camp near the river, nearly two miles east of Sherman's main position at Shiloh Church. Stuart's job was to guard the three foot deep ford where the River Road crossed Lick Creek which, because of all the rain, was 80-100 yards wide. As a result, when the Confederate attack began, Stuart and his 2,335 men were separated not only from Sherman, but from the rest of the army as well; by default they were the left flank of the Union line, and pretty much on their own. They were also directly in the path of where Johnston planned to send his 40,000 troops. One thing Johnston didn't know when he made his plans, however, was that there were two or three deep ravines emptying into the river between Stuart and Pittsburg Landing. And these ravines made excellent defensive positions.

David Stuart was "a man with a past." The 46-year-old had once been a Michigan congressman and wealthy Chicago attorney. But he entangled himself in a noisy divorce where, to the horror of proper Chicago society, it came out that he had strayed from the arms of his loving wife, entering a love affair so torrid that it apparently frightened even the buggy horses. When war came, he tried to raise a regiment, but the newspapers raised such an outcry that the governor denied him the honor. However, the U.S. Government desperately needed troops and was less choosy about how it got them, so Stuart quickly got permission to form, not just a regiment, but a brigade. He expected the war would re-launch his public career.

Despite the scandal, or perhaps because of it, Stuart was highly popular with his men.

Hearing the firing early that Sunday morning, and receiving a message that Prentiss was under attack, Stuart deployed his three regiments facing south-

Chapter 15 - Struggle on the Union Left

west. In doing so, he stretched out his line over 600 yards, apparently still trying to keep his far left regiment – the 54OH, a Zouave regiment wearing gaudy red shirts and pantaloons and probably turbans – anchored on the Lick Creek ford, per Sherman's orders. But the deployment was a fiasco. Stuart's line was stretched too far for three regiments to defend; he should have pulled his small force back to a more consolidated position.

Col.
David Stuart (w)
1816 - 1868

Facing him were the two Confederate brigades dispatched by Johnston – Chalmer's and Jackson's – to take on what they had been told was an entire Yankee division (A division usually consists of at least three brigades), but which turned out to be only Stuart's lonely little brigade. But first the Confederates had to pause for ammunition. Resupply was a constant problem for the Confederates during the battle as the rugged ground made it difficult for the ammunition wagons to keep up with the advancing battleline.

Around 11:30am, Brig. Gen. John Jackson, formerly a Georgia lawyer, ordered his brigade to storm through Stuart's abandoned camps and advance north with their left astride the River Road (aka Savannah-Hamburg Road). They also struck the next Federal brigade on the left, McArthur's, but assisted by oblique fire from Hurlbut's division, McArthur was able to fend off the attack on his front for the moment, though with heavy losses.

Jackson then angled toward Larkin Bell Field and the 71OH, Stuart's right-most regiment.

The other Southern brigade, commanded by Brig. Gen. James Chalmers - a 31-year-old Mississippi lawyer who was said to be short, skinny, and belligerent, making him a perfect choice to later become one of Bedford Forrest's best cavalry commanders – headed straight north up McCuller Field toward the 54OH of Stuart's brigade.

Two Confederate batteries, Girardey's and Gage's, quickly deployed on the heights south of Locust

Grove Branch - a creek - and set to work blasting Stuart's formation, and in the process, chasing off four companies of skirmishers from the 55IL stationed along the creek. The gunners now turned their attention to the 71OH, lobbing shells into the Federals.

With the support of this artillery, Jackson's brigade charged the 71st across Larkin Bell Field. The 71st was commanded by rotund, 38-year-old Col. Rodney Mason, who was despised by many of his officers – "*They cannot ask him a civil question without getting a cursing for an answer,*" claimed one lieutenant.

After firing two or three volleys at the Confederates, Mason panicked and allowed, if not led, a disgraceful, headlong race to the rear; the Ohio regiment didn't stop and reform until about 500 yards farther back, without Mason, who kept on running.

So now only the 55IL and 54OH were left to meet the Confederate onslaught. The 71st's bug-out created panic in these two remaining regiments, which began making their own dash for the rear. But they were overtaken by Stuart who, seeing his budding army career dissolving before his eyes, galloped ahead of them, wheeled, and drew himself up to face them. *"Halt, men!"* he cried, *"his voice booming like a trumpet."* He then swung his sword "*like a medieval knight*" and swore oaths at them, calling them cowards, "*whereupon they stopped running and shamefacedly returned to the fight.*"

Meanwhile, on the southeast end of Stuart's line, Chalmer's brigade worked its way through the brush toward the 54OH, which was defending a fence at the north end of an orchard on a slight slope that offered them some protection. But when Chalmer's troops got within 40 yards, the Federals retreated. At some point Stuart was hit in the shoulder. He remained on the field but officially turned over command to the commander of the 55IL, Col. Oscar Malmborg, a Swede, *"... round whose name hung a vague mystery of noble lineage and military glory – the former never verified and the latter scarcely confirmed."* According to the regimental historian, when Malmborg drilled his regiment, "*... the country round about resounded with such orders as: 'Column py fyle,' 'Charge peanuts,' with an occasional exasperated inquiry like: 'What for yu face mit your pack?' – all uttered in ferocious tones and foreign accent.*"

With its sister regiments on its right and left retreating, the 55IL in the middle began feeling lonely. The regiment commander, Malmborg, ordered the men to do a "half wheel left" – a moderately complicated maneuver – attempting to face his attackers with his full battleline. But with artillery shells exploding and the enemy charging, Malmborg's raw troops were unable to perform the maneuver; the regiment's companies were soon colliding into each other, creating panic, and the men began breaking for the rear.

With Stuart's wounding, Malmborg was now in charge of what was left of the brigade. Schooled in European military tactics, he ordered the men of the 55th to form a hollow square, which was an outmoded defensive tactic used against cavalry charges. But the maneuver perplexed the Confederates, who "*had never seen a hollow square, or even heard of it.*" They were extremely wary of it, warning each other that it was a damn Yankee trick. They suspected the Federals had a hidden battery somewhere behind the formation, "*or perhaps something more mysterious and dreadful.*"

When the Federal formation, bristling with bayonets poking out on all sides like a porcupine, remained ominously still, the Confederates ap-

Brig. Gen. John K. Jackson
1828 - 1866

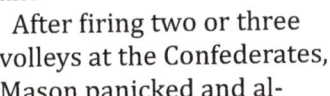

Brig. Gen. James R. Chalmers
1831 - 1898

Col. Rodney Mason
1824 - 1893

> After the battle, Mason went to Grant with tears in his eyes, claiming extenuating circumstances and pleading for a second chance. Grant agreed. But four months later, while commanding an outpost in Clarksville, Tennessee, Mason surrendered half of the 72OH and some other troops to a band of Rebel partisans. Humiliated and disgraced, he was cashiered from the army.

Chapter 15 - Struggle on the Union Left

Col. Oscar Malmborg
1820 - 1880

proached it like it was a rattlesnake. Malmborg then ordered the square to withdraw a hundred yards or so back. The Rebels troops halted again to discuss this, while their apoplectic officers yelled, cursed and cajoled them forward. Finally they advanced. But again, like some kind of weird ballet, the mysterious formation daintily scampered backwards another hundred or so yards, bayonets still spiking out in every direction.

But now Malmborg ran out of room, finding himself at the brink of an huge ravine 100 or so feet deep. He ordered his troops to disburse and take up position on the opposite side of the ravine, which turned out to be a wonderful defensive position.

So now, secure in a protected position, the raw troops – about 500 of the 55IL and 300 of the 54OH – held their position in furious fighting for about an hour until Chalmer's left flank began to curl around the Federal right. Stuart, now back in command, ordered a withdrawal across yet another ravine just behind them. The Federals managed it, but at the cost of 200 more casualties. A Union captain described it: *"Almost instantly the ground [we had] left was occupied by swarms of exultant and yelling rebels, who now, without danger to themselves, poured a shower of bullets down upon and among the fugitives."* A major in the 9MS agreed, stating after the war, *"We were right on top of you. It was like shooting into a flock of sheep."* In addition, Confederate cannon spewed canister at the retreating Federals.

But once in their new position on the opposite lip of a second ravine, the Federals again checked the Confederate assault in more horrific fighting. *"Only the excitement of battle could sustain a man in the midst of such carnage,"* wrote Union Lt. Elijah Lawrence. *"As man after man was shot down or mutilated, a feeling of perfect horror came over me at times, and I berated the powers that placed us in such a position and left us alone to our fate. Can it be wondered at when forty-three out of sixty-four of my own company were killed or wounded in that short time?"*

The fight raged for another hour, until 3pm, when Stuart's men were down to their last bullets and Confederates had pushed to within 20 feet of their line. At the last moment, the Federal gunboat *Tyler* steamed near the bank and began lobbing eight-inch shells into Chalmer's line. The boat couldn't lower its guns enough to kill any Confederates, but it could scare them. The blasts caused the Rebels to take cover, giving just enough time for what remained of Stuart's brigade to flee back through the woods to Pittsburg Landing.

In two hours of fighting as furious as any Federal unit experienced that day, the raw Federals had held out against a combined Confederate force three or four times their size on the critical left flank of the Union line. Had they not done so, the path to Pittsburg Landing was wide open. In fact, Stuart's brigade, even after the bug-out of the 71OH, suffered the second highest casualty rate of Sherman's four brigades.

Once Stuart retreated, it's unclear why Chalmers and Jackson didn't just keep driving all the way to Pittsburg Landing. Instead, both brigades shifted left and joined the fighting against McArthur's unit. It may simply be that the terrain next to the river was extremely rough, so that the two Confederate commanders instinctively followed the River Road, which headed left (northwest).

At any rate, the Federal left flank was collapsing.

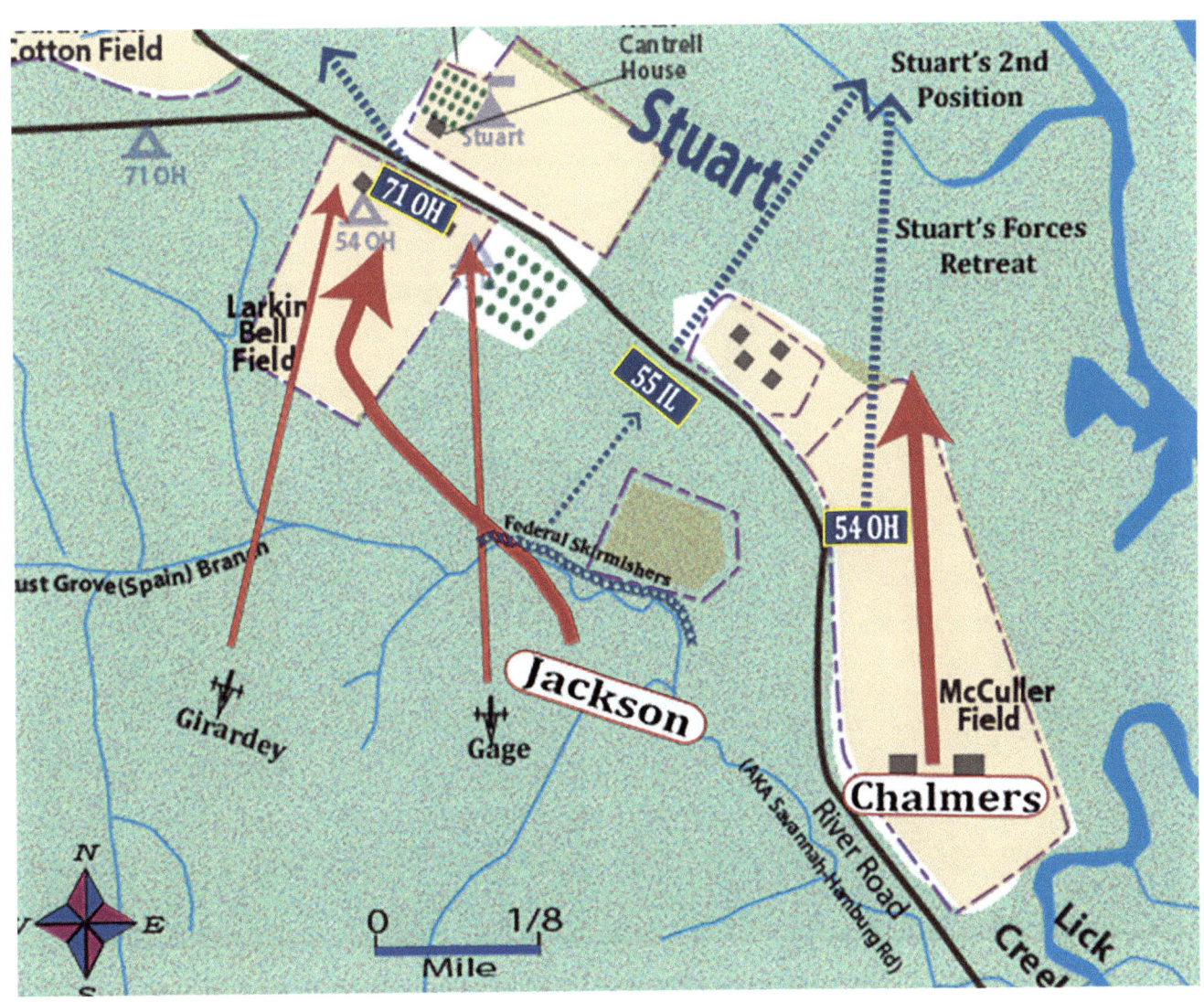

Confederates Jackson and Chalmers break Stuart's line on the left flank of the Union line

Chapter 15 - Struggle on the Union Left

> The Federals weren't the only ones with problems with raw troops performing complex maneuvers under fire. Chalmer's 52TN crossed the Spain (Locust Grove) Branch Bridge in the early stages of the attack on the 54OH. Upon reaching the other side, the Tennesseans were ordered to lie down and allow the rear rank to fire over them. Then they were told to fall back across the stream to clear a field of fire for Gage's artillery. Apparently mistaking the order as a retreat, the green regiment broke and fled. Chalmers frantically tried to rally the unit but only succeeded in corralling a couple of the companies. Disgusted, he attached the two companies to a different regiment and refused to allow the 52nd back into the fight, which apparently suited the 52TN just fine.

Officers and NCOs of Capt Arthur Rutledge's Tennessee Battery, which supported the Confederate attack on the Peach Orchard.

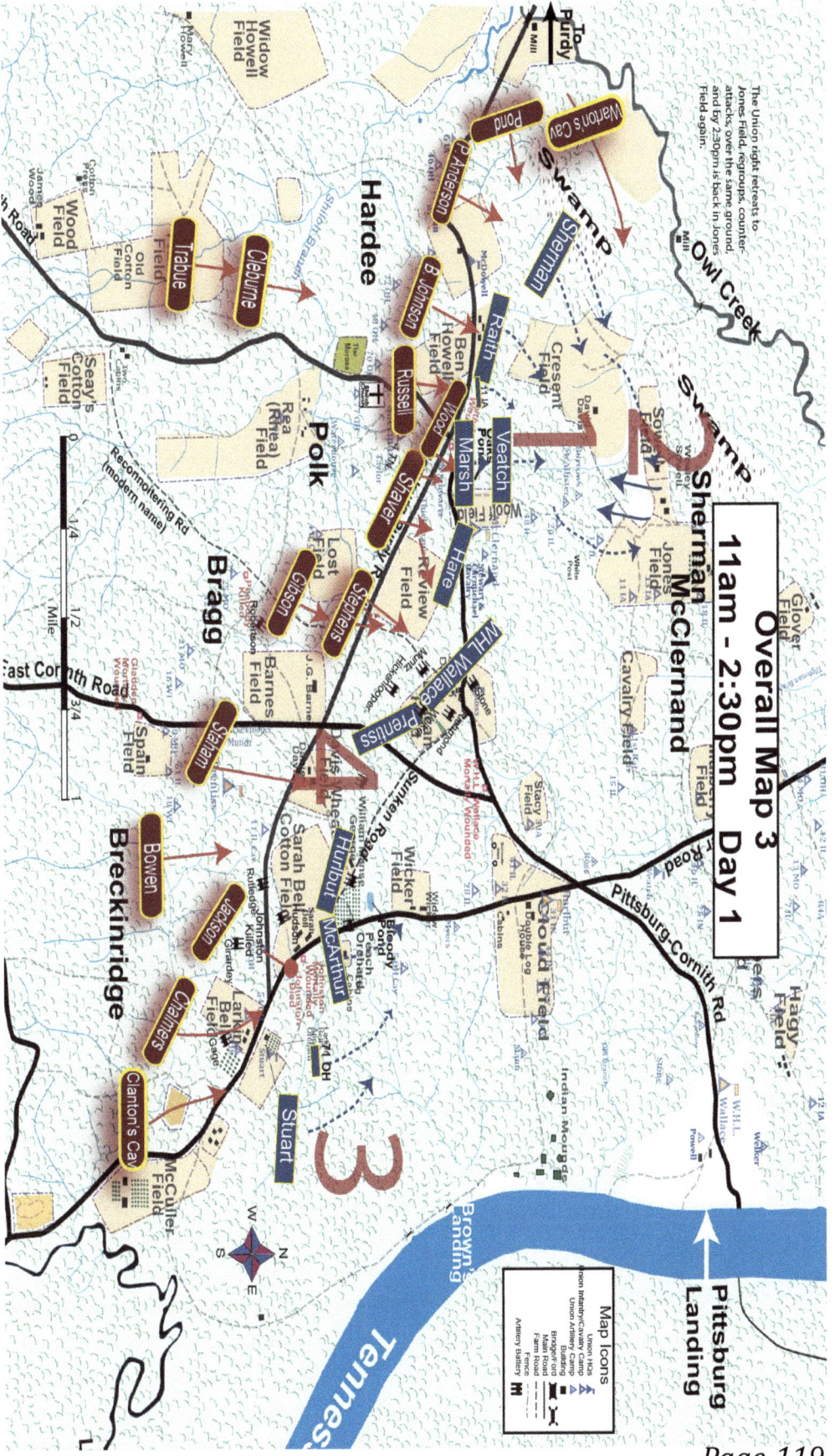

In this same time frame,
1. Confederates were attacking both brigades (Peabody's and Miller') of Prenstiss' division,
2. And attacking both brigades (Buckland and Hildebrand's) of Sherman's division.
3. Farther north, McClernand was moving his brigades toward the sound of battle, and,
4. Hurlbut had sent one of his brigades (Veatch's) to aid McClernand & Sherman, while marching to the Peach Orchard area with his other two brigades, while
5. WHL Wallace was moving his division toward what would be known as the Sunken Road. (Note that this same map will be shown for all chapters in this 5am-9am time frame).

Chapter 15 - Struggle on the Union Left

16 Johnston Cracks the Union Line

The western side of the Federals' Sunken Road line – the side facing Duncan Field – was repelling attack after attack until finally it would be blasted out of the position with cannon around 4:30pm. Meanwhile, the eastern end of the Union line on the Sunken Road, which was held by Hurlbut's division and Brig. Gen. John McArthur's small unit, were locked in their own separate battles. A tall, fierce Scotsman, McArthur would grow into one of the best Federal generals in the west. That morning, his small brigade of two Illinois regiments – *The Highland Brigade* – decked out in Scottish tams, marched toward the battle past the what would be known as the "Bloody Pond," with drums beating and bagpipes squalling, while fifes tweeted *The Joy Bird* and other tunes. Around 10:30am, W. H. L. Wallace ordered McArthur and two of his regiments - the 9IL and 12IL - to extend the Federal line eastward, becoming the left flank of Hurlbut's line. Along the way, McArthur picked up the 50IL, which had gotten lost and simply tagged along with McArthur.

Brig. Gen. John McArthur (w) 1826 - 1906

In all, McArthur had about 1,200 men. With Stuart's brigade next to the river now having retreated, there was nothing on McArthur's left but air. So, his unit now constituted the extreme left flank of the Union line.

On the march to their position, it must have been hard for McArthur's men not to be shaken, as so many fugitives flooded past that McArthur's men could barely maintain formation. They invited the stragglers to join them, and about 50 did, their names dutifully recorded by McArthur's officers.

Johnston Concentrates His Attack
2pm to 4pm

Bragg's piecemeal attacks on the Hornets Nest hadn't worked. So Johnston organized a concerted attack that he hoped would do the job. Four Confederate brigades – Stephens, Staham (Maney), Bowen, and Jackson – were lined up to push the Yankees into the swamps or river and complete the victory. Johnston personally placed the brigades in line himself – on the Confederate right, in front of the Peach Orchard and Sarah Bell's field, where there was good fighting ground, on the east end of the Sunken Road, away from the terrible Hornets Nest.

Part of Breckinridge's reserve corps, consisting of Col. Winfield Staham's and Brig. Gen. John Bowen's brigades, was concentrated in front of the Peach Orchard and Sarah Bell's field. As the only Confederate corps commander with no military background, Breckinridge, described by one officer as "*the finest looking man on the field that day, in his shiny jacket of new Kentucky jeans [a butternut uniform],*" was anxious to prove himself. But Johnston was on the scene and very much in charge.

It was around 2pm. After four hours of fighting, the Federal right had been broken and Sherman and McClernand had been pushed back but not destroyed, while on the Federal left, Stuart was making his last stand before being routed. Only the Federal center refused to budge.

Johnston ordered Breckinridge and his two brigades to break the Union line at the Peach Orchard.

To support the attack, two Confederate batteries - Capt. Alfred Hudson's and Lt. Col. Daniel Beltzhoover's - galloped up and deployed on the south side of Locust Grove Branch

Bowen's brigade would step off first. Under Johnston's personal supervision, Bowen arranged his brigade in a double line with the 1MO and the 2nd Confederate regiment in front, and with the 9AR and in the rear. Jackson's brigade, on Bowen's right, would also join Bowen's attack.

The Confederates charged out of the woods and surged across the eastern side of Sarah Bell's field and to the right of the Peach Orchard. The bulk of the attack hit McArthur's already-battered brigade, consisting of the 9IL, 12IL and 50IL on the east side of the River Road, and Pugh's left-flank regiments, of the 41IL and 28IL on the west side of the road.

The Federals here were supported directly by the Lt. Peter P. Wood's (aka Willard's) Illinois battery

Chapter 16 - Johnston Cracks the Union Line

of four 6 pounders and two 12 pounders. But they could also count on help from Hurlbut's two batteries stationed on the Sunken Road line.

As they crossed the open field, Bowen's green troops, armed with ancient flintlock muskets, where hammered by infantry and artillery fire. As they got closer to McArthur's line, the Federal artillery switched to canister.

The Arkansans' regiments began falling apart. The men stopped advancing and, upon reaching a slight ravine, instead took cover and simply returned fire. Breckinridge and Bowen, with their respective staffs, rode up and down the south side of the ravine, urging the men forward, but with little success.

Finally, Johnston rode up, still holding his tin cup. He rode down the line, clinking the cup on the men's bayonets, saying, "*Men of Arkansas, you who boast of using cold steel, don't waste your ammunition, ... come and show us what you can do with the bayonet.*"

With this encouragement, Bowen's men surged across the ravine, charging straight into McArthur's line, and forcing the Federal brigade back.

Trouble in Staham's Brigade

Staham's brigade was supposed to be attacking to the left of Bowen, directly across Sarah Bell field. As Statham's men deployed, they marched over areas where the battle had swept past earlier that day. One member of the 11MS was Pvt. Augustus Harvey Mecklin, who described what he saw as they were marched to Spain Field, where they were told to rest:

> "*Here and there we saw the bodies of dead men – friends and foes lying together – some torn to mincemeat by cannonballs. Some still writhing in the agonies of death. The cannon seemed to be carrying on this contest wholly among themselves. Though at some distance from us. Some of the balls reached us and while we were halted one struck a tree nearly a foot through & splitting it asunder tore a poor fellow who was behind it into a thousand pieces.*
>
> "*The sky was clear but for the horrible monster death ... on all sides lay the dead and dying. Before us were the rifle pits dug by the Yankees, behind them lay the camp. While resting here, Gen. Beauregard, as I suppose, came charging by [in fact, it was Gen. Johnston and his staff, banners flying]. Our men greeted him with a deafening cheer. We were not allowed to rest long.*"

Statham ordered his brigade to attack. The problem was that, to get at the Federals, Staham's men had to cross an exposed ridge, descend a slope, and then ascend another slope into the Peach Orchard – in total about 100 yards – while being "*raked by this deadly ambuscade*." Tennessee Gov. Harris called the fire "*the heaviest as any I saw in the war.*"

No sooner had the men marched over the brow of a hill when Federal Col. Pugh's 32IL and 41IL – nearly a thousand rifles – blasted the lead of the Rebel column. According to Pvt. Mecklin, who was farther back in the column, "*We were saluted by a violent volley from the enemy. For the first time in my life I heard the whistle of bullets.*" The head of the column broke and headed for the rear. Mecklin's company took cover in the former camp of the 71OH. Now his company engaged in a long range shooting contest with Pugh's Yankees. According to Mecklin:

> "*We took shelter behind the tents and some wagons & a pile of corn & returned the fire of the enemy with spirit. Soon men were falling on all sides. Two in Co. E just in front of me fell dead shot through the brain. I fired until my gun got so foul that I could not get my ball down.*"

He picked up a gun from a wounded comrade and fired until it too became hopelessly fouled with powder.

But others began drifting off individually or in units down the slope and out of close range.

Most notably, the 45TN fell back to the fence along the Hamburg-Purdy Road near the bottom of the hill. An aide reported to Breckinridge that, "*Squads of men would leave the ranks, run up to the fence, fire, and fall back into place; but the regiment would not advance.*" The mortified Staham tried his best to get the regiment moving; Breckinridge also tried. But the Tennesseeans absolutely refused to go back up that terrible slope.

Col. Hodge, Breckinridge's adjutant, stated, "*The crisis of the contest had come; there were no more reserves, and General Breckinridge determined to charge.*"

But the 45TN wouldn't budge. It was inconceivable! A Tennessee regiment wouldn't fight on Tennessee soil? Not knowing what else to do, Breckinridge rode over to Johnston to report that he had a regiment that wouldn't fight.

Johnston had been watching from a knoll and had seen Staham's column faltering. He remarked to Tennessee Gov. Isham Harris – who was in exile since Buell had occupied Nashville, and who was now serving as Johnston's aide – "*Those fellows are*

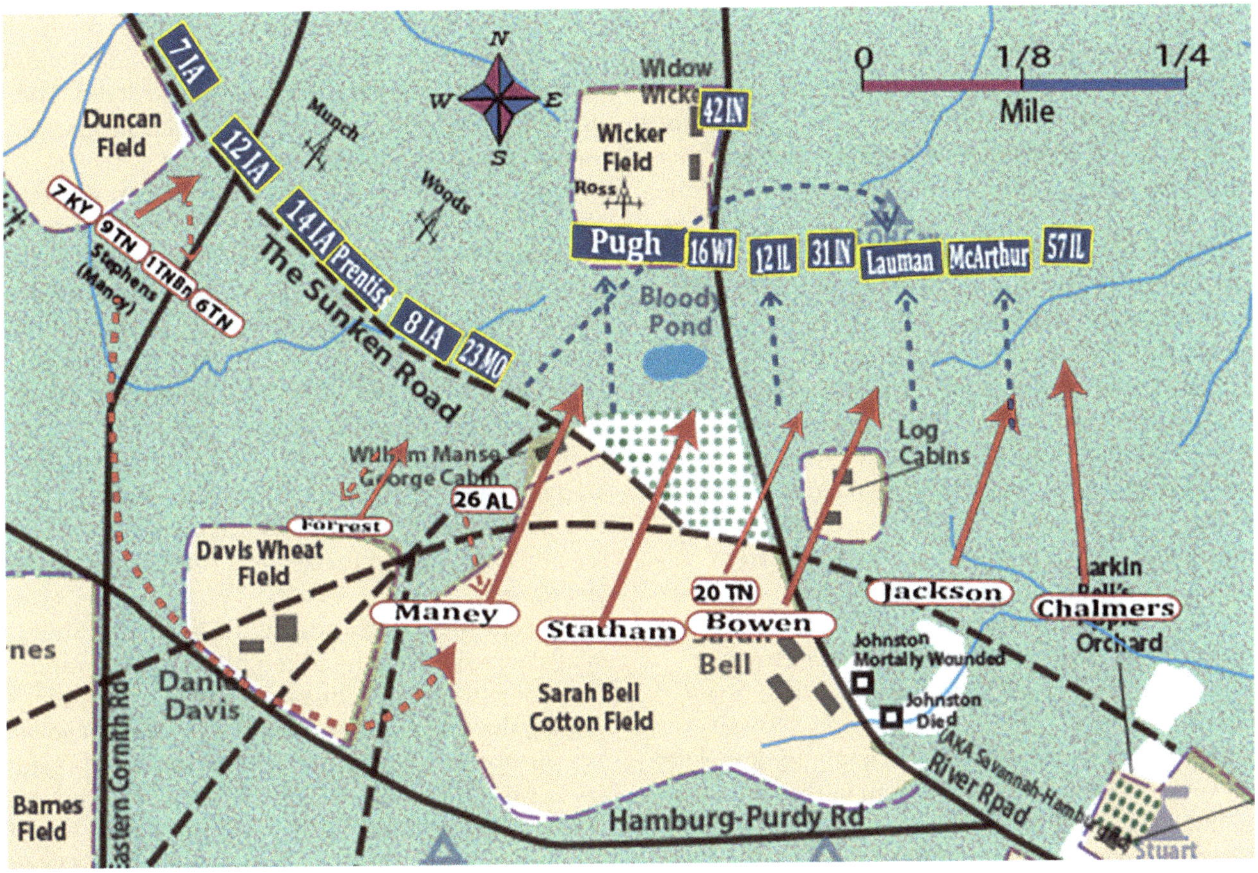

The Confederates break the Federal line on the Sunken Road

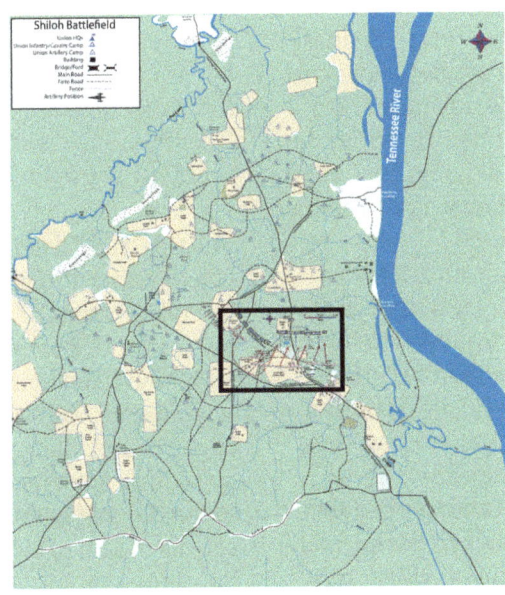

Map's Location on the Battlefield

Chapter 16 - Johnston Cracks the Union Line

making a stubborn stand here; I'll have to put the bayonet to them."

Now up rode Breckinridge, reporting that he had a Tennessee regiment that wouldn't fight. Cowardice was contagious and couldn't be tolerated. But before Johnston could respond, Gov. Harris spoke up, "*General Breckinridge, show me that regiment.*" Breckinridge looked to Johnston, who said, "*Let the governor go to them.*" Harris, his Tennessee pride on the line, rode off toward the front and with some difficulty put the regiment in line of battle on the hill, but after some delay the line continued to waver.

Johnston had no sooner ordered all the brigades to prepare to charge when Breckinridge rode up again, "in a highly emotional state," saying he "feared he could not get his brigade [Statham's] to make the charge." This was very serious.

Johnston replied calmly, "*Then I will help you.*"

Galloping over to Staham's brigade, he made a similar speech as he had made to Bowen's men: *"Men, they are stubborn; we must use the bayonet."* He reached the center of the line and cried, *"I will lead you!"*

Staham's troops answered with a mighty Rebel yell and surged forward. Leading them in the center of the line was Johnston, the highest ranking western officer in the Confederate army; on the left was Breckinridge, former Vice President of the United States; and on the right, pistol in hand, was Isham Harris, Confederate governor of Tennessee.

The battleline rolled forward up the slope. Johnston at one point was 40 paces in front of the line. As it reached the crest a thousand or more Federal rifles opened on them, along with artillery spraying canister. The Confederate line now advanced into the murderous fire at the double quick, leaving the field behind strewn with dead and dying, until they reached the Peach Orchard and charged the Yankees with bayonets.

One of those Federals meeting this attack was a 16-year-old Musician Fourth Class (ie a drummer boy), John Cockerill, who wasn't supposed to be a combatant. He had initially been a member of the 70OH under Sherman on the Federal far right. His father, Col. Joseph Cockerill, commanded that regiment. But when that regiment broke apart in the chaos, young John joined the mob and headed for the Landing. At some point, a soldier from that regiment told him that his father had been killed. Now an orphan in more ways than one, John happened upon the Highland brigade of Gen. McArthur, wearing their cocky Scottish tams, their regimental bands playing and flags flying. Cockerill thought them "*the handsomest body of troops I ever saw.*" A lieutenant invited him to join them, which Cockerill did. The lieutenant dutifully jotted down Cockerill's name and regiment in his notebook.

With Cockerill in their ranks, the Scots marched toward the sound of battle as its band struck up *Hail Columbia*. They were ordered to support an artillery battery, a job infantrymen hated because it attracted counter-battery fire. Now, they hugged the ground as cannons roared all around them. "*Everything looked weird and unnatural,*" Cockerill recalled, "*The very leaves on the trees seemed greener than I have ever seen leaves, and larger. The wounded and butchered men who came up out of the blue smoke in front of us, and were dragged or sent hobbling to the rear, seemed like bleeding messengers come to tell the fate awaiting us.*"

Brig. Gen. McArthur rode by, his hand, like Sherman's, wrapped in a handkerchief from a wound. Now Johnston's battleline appeared through the smoke; the Rebels stopped to fire a volley. "*The bullets shrieked over our heads and in our ranks,*" said Cockerill, "*soon the dry leaves were on fire, and the smoke added to the general obscurity. At this moment the young lieutenant [the one who had invited Cockerill to join them] who was gallantly waving his sword at the front, was struck by a bullet and fell instantly dead, almost at my feet. I shuddered at the thought – dead and unknown.*" Cockerill kept shooting until he was out of ammunition; then the Rebels charged bayonets. "*I saw the gray dirty uniforms of the enemy. I heard their fierce yells. I saw their flags flapping in the grimy atmosphere. That was a sight I have never forgotten. I can see the tiger ferocity in those faces yet; I can see them in my dreams.*"

Hurlbut's Line Breaks

Meanwhile, Pugh's brigade of Hurlbut's division, directly in front of the Peach Orchard, was struck by the better part of three Confederate brigades – Maney's (formerly Stephens'), Statham's, and Bowen's, all well supported by artillery. Pugh's men began falling back. Hurlbut desperately reorganized by pulling back his whole line, reshuffling his units to bolster Pugh and forming a new line across the southern end of Wicker Field, facing the Bloody Pond.

But on the left flank of Hurlbut's line, McArthur's regiments were being overwhelmed and flanked by

"I saw the gray dirty uniforms of the enemy. I heard their fierce yells. I saw their flags flapping in the grimy atmosphere .... I can see the tiger ferocity in those faces yet; I can see them in my dreams."

fierce attacks hurled at them by Jackson's, Chalmer's and part of Bowen's brigades. Also, the Federals were running low on ammunition.

And, since the collapse of Stuart's brigade around 2:15pm, Statham's brigade was now freed up to join the attack on McArthur. The Rebels swarmed around the left flank of the 50IL, which earlier had mistakenly attached itself to McArthur's brigade. The 50th broke, exposing the left of the 12IL, which fell back, exposing the left of the 9IL, which fell back. So now McArthur's small force, under attack from parts of four Confederate brigades, began falling back, either due to pressure or simply to stay abreast of Hurlbut's line. McArthur sent Hurlbut a message, warning that the left flank was breaking.

Hurlbut, frantically trying to hold together the collapsing left flank, sent the 9IL back to replenish its ammunition. McArthur's other two regiments, the 12IL and 50IL, fell back 50 paces and kept fighting, holding on by their fingernails. Now Hurlbut pulled out Lauman's 1,000-man brigade and the 57IL on the right of his line, and sent them to the left end of his line to plug the gap between himself and McArthur, even though doing so would expose his own right flank – Pugh's brigade. Hurlbut also called on W. H. L. Wallace for help; Wallace sent McArthur two more regiments. By 2:30pm, with all the reinforcements, the Federal left flank had somewhat stabilized, though it was still under attack and very shaky.

But now, by 3pm, Hurlbut's *right* flank – Pugh's brigade – was in trouble, with its own right flank exposed and some regiments running out of ammunition. Hurlbut ordered Pugh out of the Peach Orchard, to establish a new line in southern Wicker Field, backed by Willard's and Ross' batteries and a section [two guns] of Richardson's 1MO battery on loan from Tuttle's brigade.

But Chalmer's Confederate brigade, having dispatched Stuart's brigade, eventually swarmed around the east side McArthur's line, continuing to force the Federals back and exposing Hurlbut's left flank. By around 4pm, it was clear that the Federal left flank had collapsed. Hurlbut ordered a withdrawal to Pittsburg Landing. His two brigades and McArthur's men retreated in fairly good order – making a running fight back toward the Landing, though they weren't sure what they were going to do once they got there.

Fortunately, as we shall see, Grant had been busy at the Landing, preparing for this moment by building what is now known, and probably was then known, as *Grant's Last Line*. Once behind this final line, the Federals had nowhere else to retreat, except to plunge into the Tennessee River or flee into the swamps north of Pittsburg Landing.

In any case, the left flank of the Federal line on the Sunken Road was shattered beyond repair. The remainder of the Federals on that road would now have to retreat as well.

Johnson's charge marked the beginning of the collapse of the entire Sunken Road line and the Hornet's Nest.

Johnston was ecstatic; the battle was won! His aide, Maj. Edward Munford, wrote, "*We sat on our horses, side by side, watching [Chalmers'] brigade as it swept over a ridge and, as the colors dipped out of sight, the general said to me, 'That checkmates them ...' He laughed and said, 'Yes sir, that mates them.'*"

My God! My God! Is It So?
2:30pm

Johnston had joined, and in fact led, Staham's Confederate brigade during its 2:30pm assault. In the process his horse, Fire-Eater, had been shot a number of times, and Johnston had been nicked three times. But thinking the attack was succeeding, the general rode to the south end of Sarah Bell's field where Gov. Harris encountered him, sitting on his horse alone. Occasional bullets still snapped around them, fired by small bands of Yankee survivors, "*who delivered volley after volley as they sullenly retreated.*" Johnston paid them no mind. He showed off his polished riding boot with its sole flapping open, ripped from toe to heel by a bullet, remarking cheerfully, "*Governor, they came very near putting me hors de combat in that charge!*" Concerned, Harris asked Johnston if he was wounded. The general assured him he wasn't, and sent Harris off to deliver a message to Staham to "*silence that Yankee battery.*" The governor later recalled that he had "*never in his life seen Johnston looking more bright, joyous and happy.*"

Two staff officers now joined Johnston – Capts. Lee Wickham and Theodore O'Hara. Wickham thought he heard a thud as a bullet stuck Johnston's horse.

Chapter 16 - Johnston Cracks the Union Line

Then he noticed blood dripping from the heel of Johnston's boot. *"General, you're wounded, and we had better go down under the hill, where we won't be exposed to the bullets."* Johnson replied, *"No; Hardee's fire is very heavy. We'll go where the firing is heaviest."* As Johnston turned, O'Hara exclaimed, *"General, your horse is wounded!"* "Yes," said Johnston, *"and his master too."*

After delivering the message to Staham about 200 yards away, Harris returned and was giving Johnston a brief report when he saw the general swaying in his saddle. Harris and other aides held Johnston on his horse. *"General, are you wounded?,"* asked the governor. *"Yes, and I fear seriously,"* Johnston admitted. He was right. The bullet had cut an artery behind his right knee; he was rapidly bleeding to death.

(Johnston may not have even been aware he was hit until he became weak from loss of blood. A quarter century earlier, he had been wounded in his right hip in a duel which damaged the sciatic nerve. Ever since then he had always had numbness to heat, pain and cold in that leg.)

Harris dispatched one of Johnston's captains to find a surgeon and then led the general on his horse into a ravine about 40 yards away; on the way, Johnston slumped and dropped his reins. Harris caught the general and eased him to the ground. He was clearly dying but the party could find no wound, other than *"a profuse amount of blood"* running onto the ground from the general's knee-high right boot, but they assumed that the general's wound had to be something more serious than that. Harris raised the general's head and tried to pour some brandy down his throat, but it just dribbled from his lips. His brother-in-law, Col. William Preston, arrived and propped the general's head in his lap, asking repeatedly, *"Johnston, do you know me?"* But the general died without saying a word. Preston called out, *"My God! My God! Is it so?"*

Johnston's death at the high tide of the battle, when Confederates were sweeping the field, was devastating. Everyone was crying, Preston most of all. *"Pardon me, gentlemen,"* he sobbed, *"but you all know how I loved him."* Then, back to business, he removed his notebook from his pocket and scrawled a message to Beauregard:

"Ravine, 2:30pm General Johnston has fallen, mortally wounded, after a victorious attack on the left of the enemy. It now devolves on you to complete the victory."

"Ravine, 2:30pm General Johnston has fallen, mortally wounded, after a victorious attack on the left of the enemy. It now devolves on you to complete the victory."

Johnston's body was wrapped in a blanket and removed from the field without ceremony to keep his death a secret from the troops. But word gradually spread.

It would later turn out that he had been hit four times – twice by bullets or shell fragments to the body that failed to penetrate, once in the sole of his boot, and the fatal shot which clipped his right popliteal artery, which lies behind the knee, causing him to bleed to death in about 15 minutes.

After Johnston's death, command devolved to Beauregard on the opposite, western end of the line, near Shiloh Church. By now he had moved to "Headquarters No. 3," which was a clump of trees at the bloody, corpse-strewn Crossroads. Beauregard received the stunning news from Harris at around 3pm. He said nothing for a moment, hiding any emotion on bad news as military commanders must, and then replied, *"Well, Governor, everything else is progressing well, is it not?"*

Col. William Preston
1816 - 1887

Gov. Isham G. Harris
1818 - 1897

Without Johnston's commanding presence, there was a critical hour-long lull in the fighting on the Confederate right at this time. Not a complete lull, of course – there was still plenty of shooting – but no advances. Beauregard would later be heavily criticized for allowing the loss of this precious hour, just as the Yankee line was cracking. But Beauregard was in no physical condition to be galloping over to the right flank, let alone leading charges – he remained

Modern photo of ravine where Johnston died. The view faces east.

Painting of Johnston's Death. National Park Service

Chapter 16 - Johnston Cracks the Union Line

seriously ill with his throat condition and could barely speak. Surgeons had taken his pulse earlier in the day and found it to be 100 (normal pulse rate for men is between 60-100 beats per minute). They thought he should be confined to his ambulance.

In any case, as army commander, it was not his job to be leading charges. In fact, he [and not a few others] later condemned Johnston for leading charges from the front, *"behaving like a division or corps commander, instead of commanding an army."*

Actually, *Breckinridge* was the corps commander and senior man on the scene. If anyone should have immediately taken command and led further attacks, it probably should have been him. He knew what Johnston wanted. But the troops on his line were exhausted and dangerously low on ammunition, and it took time for wagons to bring up more.

Meanwhile, the battle in the center of the line continued unabated. But now, by 4pm, the sun was beginning to sink. And though the Confederates didn't know it, Buell's 18,000 troops and Lew Wallace's missing 7,300 troops were fast approaching Pittsburg Landing.

Did Johnston's Death Change the Course of the Battle?

The jury is out, and will forever be, on what kind of leader Johnston might have become had he lived. He certainly had charisma, and after Shiloh no one could doubt his willingness to fight. True, like almost every officer on both sides at this early stage of the war, Johnston made serious mistakes, but probably no more than did Grant and Sherman, who went on to become the top generals in the their army. They lived long enough to learn from their mistakes, and Johnston might have as well. But probably an unbiased view would be that Johnston was better suited for a corps or division command where he was out in the field leading his men by example; he seemed overwhelmed when it came to making strategic decisions on a broad scale.

The jury will also forever be out on the question of whether the Confederates would have won the battle had Johnston remained in command. In another of those might-have-beens, many Southerners contend then and now that Johnston's death cost them the battle.

But that's a stretch.

Johnston died at 2:30pm. The fight wasn't over by then. Hurlbut and McArthur will still fighting delaying actions. If the Confederate drive failed to reach Pittsburg Landing by 4pm, most likely it never would. By then Grant's Last Line was ready. Packed with artillery, including siege guns and supporting naval gunboats, and the retreating troops rapidly gathering on the Last Line were now concentrated and motivated by fighting with their backs to the wall, or at least to the river.

The Confederate units, on the other hand, were scattered, low on ammunition, and exhausted. They also assumed the battle was won, allowing them to relax and mop up what remained of Grant's army at their leisure the next day. They didn't know Buell's troops would begin arriving before dark. (However, Beauregard and Johnston must have known through their spies that Lew Wallace's division of 7,300 men would soon be joining the fight, although maybe they assumed that Wallace's troops were already engaged.)

It took the exhausted Confederates six hours to break the Sunken Road Line, and they only did so by eventually curling around its flanks. By contrast, Grant's Last Line *had* no flanks – with one end protected by the river and the other end by the swamp. Very likely his line could have held on for three hours – until nightfall and/or until Buell's and/or Lew Wallace's troops arrived.

Johnston himself died happy, thinking he had won the battle. But likely the battle was lost, with its unheard of casualties and that fact, combined with the losses of Forts Henry, Donelson, Columbus, and Nashville, made it very possible his head would have rolled. Ironically, his death allowed him to die a hero, while the blame for the loss was dumped on Beauregard.

After his death, Johnston was criticized for having put so much energy in smashing the heavily defended Peach Orchard position, rather than striking farther east, where there were fewer Federals – namely McArthur and Stuart's battered brigades. But the Peach Orchard was critical to Johnston because it commanded the River Road (aka Savannah-Hamburg Road), which was the fastest route to Pittsburg Landing. Though Johnston initially planned to focus on the east side of this road next to the river, once he was on location he could plainly see the deep, swampy ravines at right angles to the river – three or four of them – blocking the Confederates' route to Pittsburg Landing. Had Johnston attempted to go off road and attack through these jungle-like ravines, his troops would have had an extremely tough fight.

Contemporary illustration of the Bloody Pond, looking west. There was much fighting around this pond as the two sides surged back and forth. Both sides drank here even though the water was tinged pink with blood.

Modern view of the Bloody Pond.

> After their successful attack through the Peach Orchard, Staham's exhausted troops collapsed, parched with thirst. Near by was a large pond around which *"the dead of the enemy lay thickly, & down in the bottom of the pool of clear blue water there was a dead man in one edge of it,"* according to Confederate Augustus Mecklin. *"Our boys rushed to the water and with their cups drank deeply. If the water had been mixed with blood it [was] all the same."*
>
> The water hole, later known as Bloody Pond, was used by both sides to drink, wash wounds, or just soak – sometimes both sides used the pond at the same time with an unspoken agreement not to shoot.

Chapter 16 - Johnston Cracks the Union Line

From the opposite banks of these deep ravines even a small Union force could, and did, put up a stout defense, as Stuart's men had demonstrated.

The South's "missed opportunity" occurred that morning, due to Johnston's understandable but fatal decision to shift forces (Jackson and Chalmers brigades) to attack Stuart – based on false information that there was a Union division lurking there to threaten his right flank. Ideally he should have continued his attack straight ahead, against Hurlbut's poorly-deployed and under-strength division at the south end of Sarah Bell's Cotton Field.

> *Earlier that morning Johnston had sent his own surgeon, Dr. D. W. Yandell, to treat wounded Federal prisoners of the 18WI. When the doctor protested that his duty was to stay with the commanding general, Johnston said, "No, those men were our enemies but are our prisoners now, and deserve our protection." The decision to dispense with his doctor proved fatal.*

Overall Map 4
2:30pm - 4:30pm Day 1

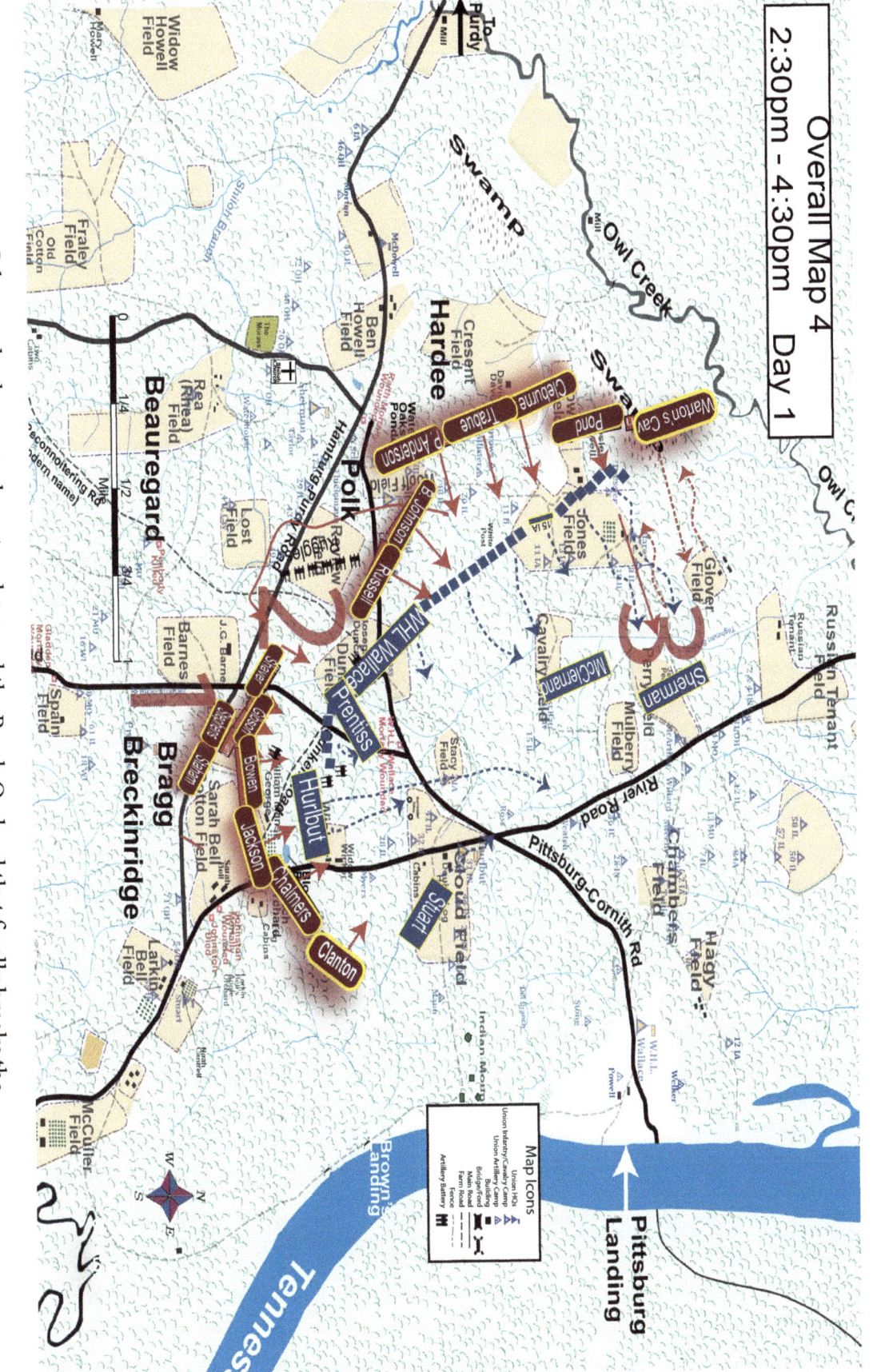

1. Johnston leads an attack centered around the Peach Orchard that finally breaks the Union line at the Sunken Road.
2. Meanwhile, Confederates are shelling the Sunken Road line.
3. On the Union right, Sherman and McClernand fall back from Jones Field to a much better defensive position at Locust Grove Branch, eventually forming the right flank of what would be called "Grant's Last Line."

Chapter 16 - Johnston Cracks the Union Line

17 Surrender at Hell's Hollow

4pm – 5:45pm

By 4pm both flanks of the Federal line on the Sunken Road were collapsing. The first to give way was Hurlbut's division on the Union left, which was under attack by three Confederate brigades – Chalmers', Jackson's and Bowen's. Hurlbut ordered a withdrawal back to Pittsburg Landing.

It was also clear to W. H. L. Wallace on the Union right that his division's position at the Sunken Road was untenable. Sweeney's brigade on the right flank was faltering because McClernand's division on the right had retreated. Meanwhile, on the opposite side of Duncan Field, the Confederates were lining up enough cannon to pulverize anything that stood in their way.

Wallace ordered a withdrawal up Pittsburg-Corinth Road, but in the process of standing up in his stirrups to take a look back, a bullet slammed through his head, smashing him to the ground face-first. His brother-in-law, Cyrus Dickey, and three other soldiers tried to carry the general to the rear. But Confederates were swarming the vacated Sunken Road position, trapping any lingering Yankees. The three helpers dropped Wallace and ran. Dickey couldn't carry Wallace by himself; thinking him dead anyway, he left the general on the side of the road near some ammo crates so he wouldn't be trampled.

At least some of Wallace's troops withdrew in fairly good order, making a fighting retreat. Around 4:15pm, for example, the 2IA and 7IA retreated through the southwest side of Cloud Field – today known as *Hell's Hollow*. There they encountered Confederates in Stacy Field blocking their path. The two Iowa regiments formed a battleline, drove the Confederates off, and broke through to Pittsburg Landing.

By 4:45pm eleven of Wallace's fifteen regiments and his division artillery had escaped the Sunken Road position. One of the regiments that didn't make it was the 58IL, which had manned the far right flank of the Union line on the Sunken Road, and at one point had even briefly charged out on Duncan field to seize some farm buildings. But when the regiment's 300 survivors attempted to retreat through Hell's Hollow they found their path hopelessly blocked by Confederates surging in and around them. It was the same story for the 8IA and 23MO. The 14IA, also trapped, laid down its weapons in the abandoned camp of the 41IL. A triumphant Confederate cavalryman dragged the Iowans' regimental flag back and forth in a mud puddle.

But Prentiss, still commanding about 1,200 men – including only about 600 of his original division – still believed he could hold out. When his brigadier, Col. Madison Miller advised Prentiss that the new line couldn't hold, the general insisted that Lew Wallace's division would soon arrive and he would sleep in his own tent that night. He sent a courier requesting reinforcements and, according to what he wrote seven months later, even contemplated a charge.

But by 5:45pm Prentiss and all the units still within Hell's Hollow – some 2,200 men – had surrendered. Prentiss yielded his sword to the 9MS's Col. William Rankin of Chalmer's brigade, who would himself be killed the next day.

In Hindsight

Once Sherman's and McClernand's divisions were driven back from their positions in Woolf Field, and McArthur's brigade was pushed back east of the Peach Orchard, the collapse of the Sunken Road position was inevitable. The Confederate tide began to flow around both the left and right flanks of the defenders. For example, Trabue's Kentucky brigade, which had been fighting McClernand's division in Woolf Field, shifted southeastward and eventually took a position clear up on the north end of Cloud Field, blocking the Union retreat up River Road. Other Confederate units made similar deployments.

Nevertheless, the six hours during which Wallace's division, along with Hurlbut's and the remnants of Prentiss', stalled the Confederate advance were

Brig. Gen. William H. L. Wallace (mw) 1821 - 1862

Chapter 17 - Surrender At Hells Hollow

> While raiding the Yankee camps, Sgt. Henry Cowling of the 5KY of Trabue's Confederate brigade discovered a true prize – a big hunk of Ohio cheese. Unwilling to relinquish such a feast, and with no other way to carry it, he stuck it on the end of his bayonet. Not long after, the 5KY formed up to attack. The commander, Col. Thomas Hunt, rode down the battle line for a last minute inspection, during which he spotted Cowling's bayonet – it being the only one with cheese on it.
>
> The colonel *"almost took Sgt. Cowling's head off and made him throw the cheese away."*

probably decisive in saving Grant's army. Prentiss had diligently followed Grant's order to hold at all costs, but Grant never fully appreciated it. His memoirs criticized Prentiss in a backhanded way for having allowed himself and 2,200 men to be captured.

We Meet in Heaven

Contrary to the belief of his brother-in-law, W. H. L. Wallace hadn't died on the field, though he was horribly wounded – a musket ball had hit him above and behind the left ear, passing through his skull and out his left eye. Like hundreds and probably thousands of wounded soldiers, he lay on the battlefield in the pouring rain throughout the night of April 6-7. Around 10am the following day, when Union troops retook the ground, they found Wallace, still clinging to life.

Early on the morning of the 6th, Wallace's 29-year-old wife, Ann, had arrived by steamboat at Pittsburg Landing to pay her husband a surprise visit, and also her father, a colonel, along with both her brothers who were officers, and two of her husband's brothers, as well as a number of other distant relatives, all in Grant's army.

The outbreak of the battle prevented her from entering the camps, and her planned happy reunion turned into a horror of tending the wounded brought aboard her steamboat. That evening she received the news of her husband's death, his body left on the field. *"God gave me strength,"* she later recalled, and she went on tending the wounded throughout the night.

But the next day she was overjoyed when her beloved Will was brought in from the field, terribly wounded but conscious and able to recognize her voice and speak to her. Taken to Cherry Mansion in Savannah, Grant's pre-battle headquarters, the tenacious Wallace lingered for days, frequently conversing with his wife. Hope rose that he might actually recover. But on April 10th an infection set in and he sank rapidly. His last words were to his wife, *"We meet in heaven."*

Sherman and McClernand Also Driven Back

Meanwhile, back on the western end of the battlefield, Sherman and McClernand formed strong defensive positions on the eastern edge of a deep ravine at Tilghman Branch. At around 4pm, just about the time the Confederates began bombarding the Sunken Road, Ketchum's Alabama battery, soon joined by the Washington Artillery, began pounding the Union battery defending the Tilghman position – Capt. Edward Bouton's Illinois battery. In a brutal duel, dubbed by the Chicago press as "*The Great Artillery Duel*", Bouton held his position for about an hour, despite having one gun knocked out.

Ann Wallace

Now Hardee sent a courier, Lt. Col. Samuel Ferguson, with an order for Col. Preston Pond to assault the Yankee position on the opposite side of the ravine of Tilghman Branch. Pond, with his command down to about 1,000 men, protested. *"Go back and tell the General I fear he does not know the great strength of the enemy and the weakness of my command."* Ferguson rode off but returned shortly with the same order. *"Very well, sir. I will obey the order, but do so under protest,"* declared Pond, who then ordered the 18LA to attack, solo. For some reason, Pond sent in only this one regiment, holding his two others back - the Orleans Guard Battalion and the 16LA.

The 18th's commander, Col. Alfred Mouton, also protested,*"You will make me sacrifice all my men to no avail."* But realizing it was no use arguing, Mouton called out, *"Forward, the 18th! Follow me!"* His 500 men scaled the ravine and formed a line in the southwestern corner of Mulberry Field, then ad-

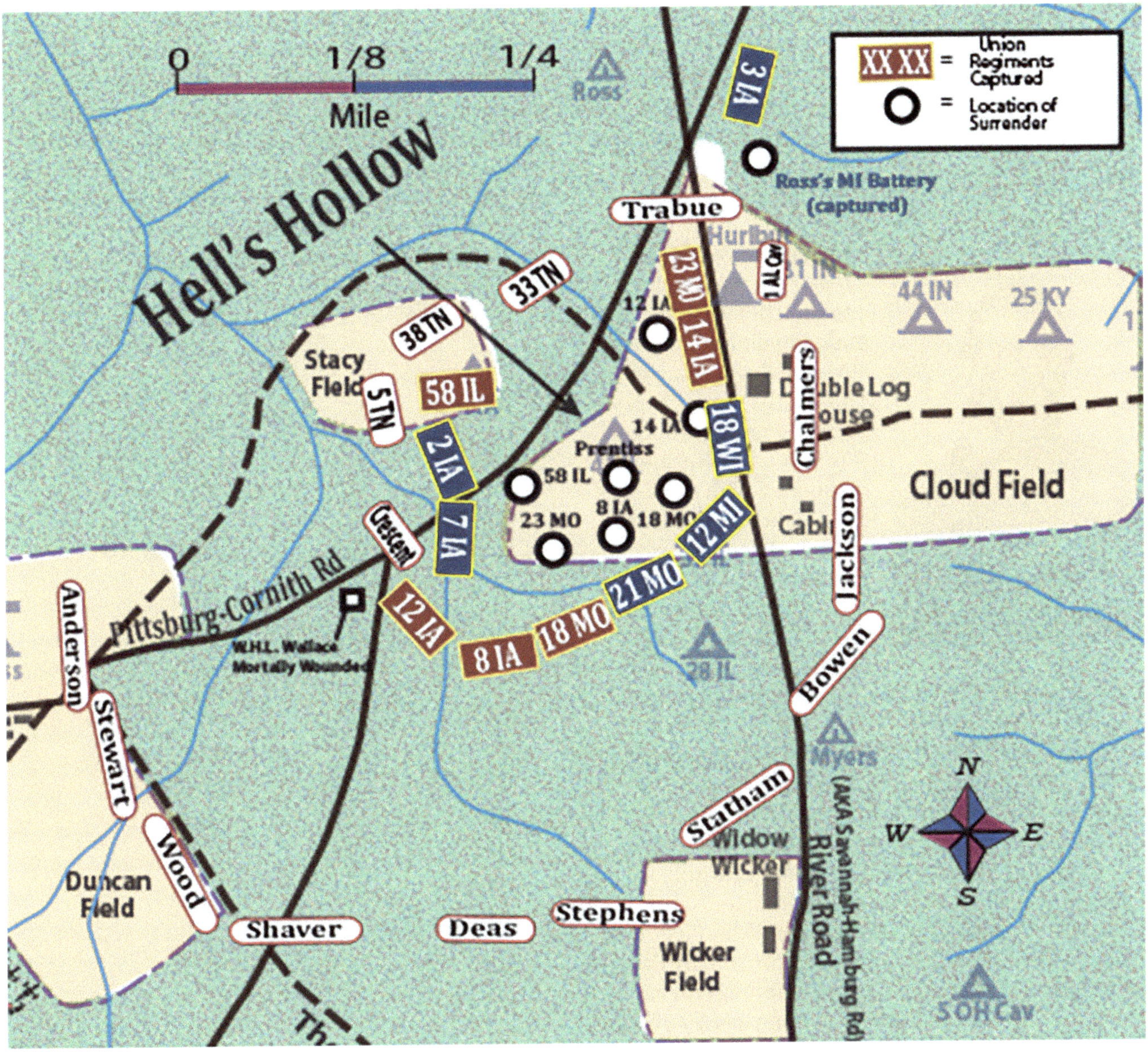

Union regiments surrounded and captured in Cloud Field

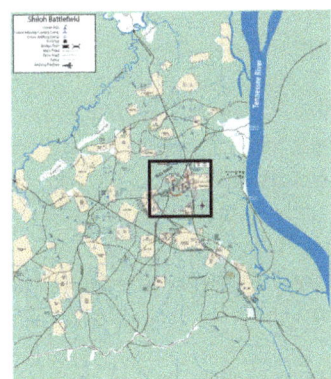

Map's Location on the Battlefield

Chapter 17 - Surrender At Hells Hollow

vanced southeast in line of battle. It was slaughter. A solder of that regiment described it: "*Before we had gone 50 yards, the battery [McAllister's] opened upon us. Our company was next to the flag of our regiment, and the bullets rang out about our ears like bees swarming. Once I looked behind me to see Col. Mouton's horse falling from under him.*" After a few minutes, the 18th retreated, leaving 207 dead and maimed on the field – 41% of the regiment.

Col. Preston Pond Jr. 1823 - 1864

As the 18th limped back, Pond now shouted, *"Orleans Guard, charge!"* The Guards' major, Col. Leon Querouze, ordered, *"Fix bayonets.*" His men responded with a cheer as they clicked their blades in place. Then they scaled the ravine and advanced through the survivors of the 18LA. Pvt. Edmond Livaudais of the Orleans Guard described it: "*It was truly horrendous, as we ascended the hill [ravine] to see on all sides those unfortunate men of the Eighteenth coming down bathed in their blood; some had been wounded in their face, others, in the body, arm, etc. They fled through our ranks, asking for water and help.*" Then the Federals opened up. The Guard penetrated to within 40 paces of the Union line, forcing McAllister's guns back. But the storm of lead was merciless. Five color bearers were shot down in succession; finally Capt. Alfred Roman saved the flag by wrapping it around his body. The Guards fell back, having lost 90 of their 150 men.

(Although Pond vehemently protested the order to make the bloody attacks on the Federal line, his men blamed him for the slaughter. After the battle, an election was held and the brigade voted him out as brigade commander.)

Simultaneously with Pond's attack, Hardee launched Col. John Wharton's Texas Rangers in a dismounted attack on Cavalry Field, which was easily repulsed. But Hardee also ordered the 5TN, 23TN and 24TN to strike McClernand's exposed left flank, where there was a 450 yard gap, bisected by Tilghman Branch, between McClernand's left and the crumbling Sunken Road line.

The Tennesseans struck the 15IL and 46IL, which were already jittery, being inundated with fugitives and wagons retreating from the Sunken Road sector. The two Illinois regiments broke and the chaos rippled down McClernand's line, turning a retreat into a rout. McClernand's shattered division, what remained of it, fled southeast. Sherman's division had no choice but to follow, and by 5pm, the two commanders had cobbled together another new line – their fourth or fifth of the day – at the River Road (aka Hamburg-Savannah Road), forming the western flank of what would become Grant's Last Line.

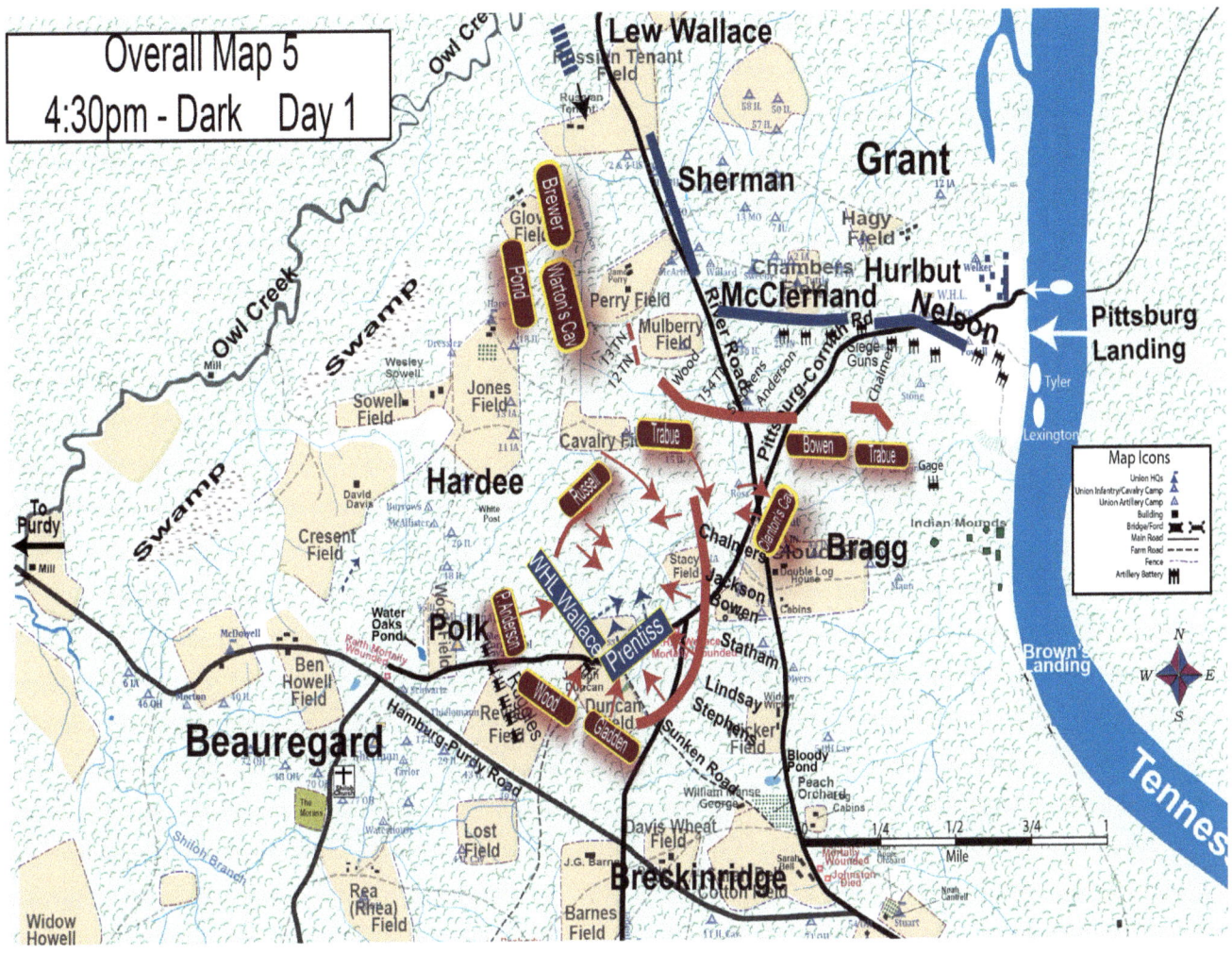

Confederates close in on the southwestern side of Cloud Field, known as Hell's Hollow, capturing 2,200 Federals. Meanwhile, the remainder of the Federal army retreats to Grant's Last Line at Pittsburg Landing. Confederates make a half-hearted attempt to break this last line, but soon fall back for the night.

Confederate Pvt. Jessie W. Wyatt, 12TN, found a small pocket Bible on the field that belonged to Federal Pvt. Samuel Lytle of the 11IA. The Iowan greatly regretted the loss, as it was a keepsake from his father.

Two years later, on May 17, 1864, a private with the 73IL, C. W. Keeley, picked off a Confederate sharpshooter near Adairsville, Georgia. Pvt. Jessie Wyatt was his target. Rifling through the dead Confederate's haversack, Keeley found the bible with Lytle's address still in it. Some years after the war, Keeley sent it back to Lytle.

Chapter 17 - Surrender At Hells Hollow

18   Grant's Last Line

5 PM – 6:30 PM

By 4:30pm, what remained of all three wings of Grant's army – left, right and center – had been pushed back to the muddy road leading from Pittsburg Landing.

In the west, Grant's right wing under Sherman and McClernand had made a fighting retreat from Shiloh Branch, then back to the Crossroads, then back to Jones Field, then back to Tilghman Branch. There they made another stand against Pond's Confederate brigade before finally falling back to the River Road (aka Savannah-Hamburg Road) and the Snake Creek Bridge, where they patched together a shaky line only a half mile west of the Landing. But, by holding the road and bridge, they at least had secured the approach route for Lew Wallace's division, if it *ever* arrived.

And that was the good news. Grant's left wing was completely shattered, as was his center, where 2,200 of his men had been trapped and forced to surrender, with the survivors fleeing back to the Landing in varying degrees of disorder. The Landing itself was in bedlam, crammed with 5,000 to 15,000 stragglers – up to a quarter or a third of Grant's army – including many officers, who had simply thrown away their weapons and quit the fight. No one, including Grant, could rally them. They simply sat or wandered aimlessly, looking for opportunities to run even further. The transports, now crammed with wounded, cut their cables and dropped anchor in the middle of the river so as to avoid being swamped with fugitives. But periodically some of the panicked soldiers would drown trying to swim out to the boats. Many tried to float across the river on logs.

W. H. L. Wallace's wife, Ann, who was tending wounded on the transport *Minnehaha*, stated that a one point she was in the pilot house when a hysterical Union officer, one of the stragglers, somehow got aboard. He raced to the pilot house, pulled a revolver, and threatened to kill the pilot if he didn't take the officer's men aboard. The pilot stalled, pretending to obey, "*giving the frenzied man time to come to his senses*" and put his pistol down.

Musician 4th Class John Cockerill, who wandered all over the battlefield that day before retreating with McArthur's brigade back to Pittsburgh Landing, stood on the bluff above the Landing and observed the pandemonium.

"*Below lay thirty transports, at least,*" he recalled, "*all being loaded with the wounded, and all around me were baggage wagons, mule teams, disabled artillery teams and thousands of panic-stricken men. Some of the stragglers were being forced to carry sandbags up to fortify batteries of heavy siege guns.*"

Cockerill also noted that the log cabin on the bluff was "*turned into a temporary field hospital where hundreds of wounded men, brought down in wagons and ambulances, were being unloaded, and where their arms and legs were cut off and thrown out to form gory, ghastly heaps.*"

Surgery on the boats was more convenient. A nurse aboard a hospital ship – a Sister of Charity nun – described it: The deck of the hospital was "*looking like a slaughterhouse, with the doctors tossing overboard arms and legs to a watery grave.*"

Another witness, Pvt. Robert Fleming, was wounded and loaded on one of the boats. Men with stretchers were kept busy, he said, carrying the wounded onto the boats, and also "*carrying men off the boats as quickly as they succumbed to their wounds, and laying them in a row on a level ledge about halfway up the bank.*" Fleming also noted that one of the men being carried to the dead line "*attempted to raise his head. Two Sisters of Charity nuns who were on the boat quickly went to his aid, and brought him back aboard.*"

Yes, it was a mess, But on the front line, the remainder of the army continued to fight stubbornly hour after hour, resisting Confederate onslaughts and buying Grant time. Grant had two big aces up his sleeve. One ace was reinforcements: Lew Wallace's division of 7,300 fresh troops out there, *somewhere*, which should have arrived hours ago. Also, Buell's reinforcements were expected within the hour. The other ace was that nightfall was approaching – Civil War armies rarely fought at night due to command and control problems. So time was on Grant's side. All he had to do was hold out another 90 minutes, after which reinforcements would surely arrive or, if nothing else, at least he was guaranteed that darkness would arrive.

But Grant wasn't just waiting on reinforcements. He had spent much of the afternoon building a final

Chapter 18 - Grant's Last Line

defense line here at Pittsburg Landing, and a formidable line it was – the most imposing defense the Confederates would encounter that day.

Early that afternoon, Grant ordered Col. Joseph Webster, sort of his unofficial Chief of Staff, to collect every cannon he could lay hands on, and stack them hub to hub facing the oncoming enemy. Webster, a former artilleryman, went to work with a vengeance, collecting the guns of two uncommitted batteries, plus the surviving guns from batteries that had fallen back to the Landing. He even dragged the army's big siege guns, intended for later use at Corinth, up on this line. One or more of the just-arrived batteries had been issued their cannons, but had not yet been issued horses and other implements. So, Webster had the men drag the guns into position by hand. The cannoneers had never fired their guns and so, once the Confederates attacked, Webster would give the gunners on-the-job training during the battle as to how to load, aim and fire their guns.

Col. Joseph D. Webster
1811 - 1876

By 6pm, Grant's Last Line bristled with cannon, including 10 of them in two batteries deployed on a ridge jutting out from the river, allowing some of them to fire straight up the hollow of Dill Branch Ravine – the most likely point of assault – which was on a high bluff, almost a fortress, from which the Federals could fire down on attacking Confederates.

And two timberclad gunboats – the *USS Tyler* and *USS Lexington* – old friends of Grant, having accompanied him since the Belmont, Missouri raid - bolstered Grant's firepower with their eight inch cannon. Far larger than even the army's big siege guns, these naval guns could throw shells "*bigger than a hog.*" (In fact, the gunboats were of limited help in the close-in fighting around Dill Branch because they couldn't lower the elevation of their guns enough, but the attackers didn't know that, and the guns' enormous blasts certainly *sounded* dangerous.)

Also manning the line were an estimated 18,000 Federal infantry - probably about equal to Beauregard's remaining army - made up of retreating units of Grant's five divisions who still had some fight in them.

Grant appeared at the Landing about 4:30pm. He pleaded with the mass of stragglers to return to ranks, calling to them that "*Buell's army would soon be on the field, and he [Grant] did not want to see his men disgraced.*" They ignored him. Grant then ordered a squadron of cavalry to drive the mob away from the river's edge. The troopers drew their sabers, divided up at each end of Landing, and drove toward each other, temporarily pushing the mob from the water's edge and back up the embankment. But by 5pm the mob had returned.

Strange Riders Appear

About this time - between 5pm and 5:30pm - skulkers at the Landing spotted two riders observing them from a cornfield on the opposite bank, one of them carrying a white flag with a red square in it. The jumpy spectators concluded it was Texas cavalry. But the rider was signaling them. About 15 minutes later Col. Jacob Ammen's brigade, of Brig. Gen. William "Bull" Nelson's division, emerged from the woods. It was the van of Buell's army, which had endured a brutal 8-10 mile march from Savannah, down the east bank of the river, "*through country presenting nothing but interminable swamps and pathless bottom lands with rank overgrowths of jungle.*"

Just prior to Nelson's order to begin the march in Savannah, a soldier of the 4KY asked the local guide about the trail; the man answered, "*Wal, stranger, I've been going and coming through that thar swamp far years and it is nighly hell!*"

And indeed it was. The first three miles of the march weren't too bad. But then the trail turned sharply west, heading closer to the river and heavily timbered, muddy bottom land. Some lagoons were crudely bridged, but there was basically no road, in places barely a rut, "*dank and unwholesome,*" and impeded by fallen trees, shallow, scummy ponds, with "*slippery mire shoetop deep.*" All the while they could hear the growing roar of a fierce battle awaiting them. One Federal on this march, Lt. Ambrose Bierce, who would later become a noted author of the era, stated that the men arrived breathless, footsore, and faint from hunger. "*It had been a terrible race; some regiments had lost a third of their number from fatigue, the men dropping from the ranks as if shot, and left to recover or die at their leisure.*"

Now Nelson, Ammen and their exhausted men stared in amazement and rage at the chaotic spectacle on the opposite side of the river. Thirty or more transports packed with wounded were parked in mid-river. Two or three transports hugged the

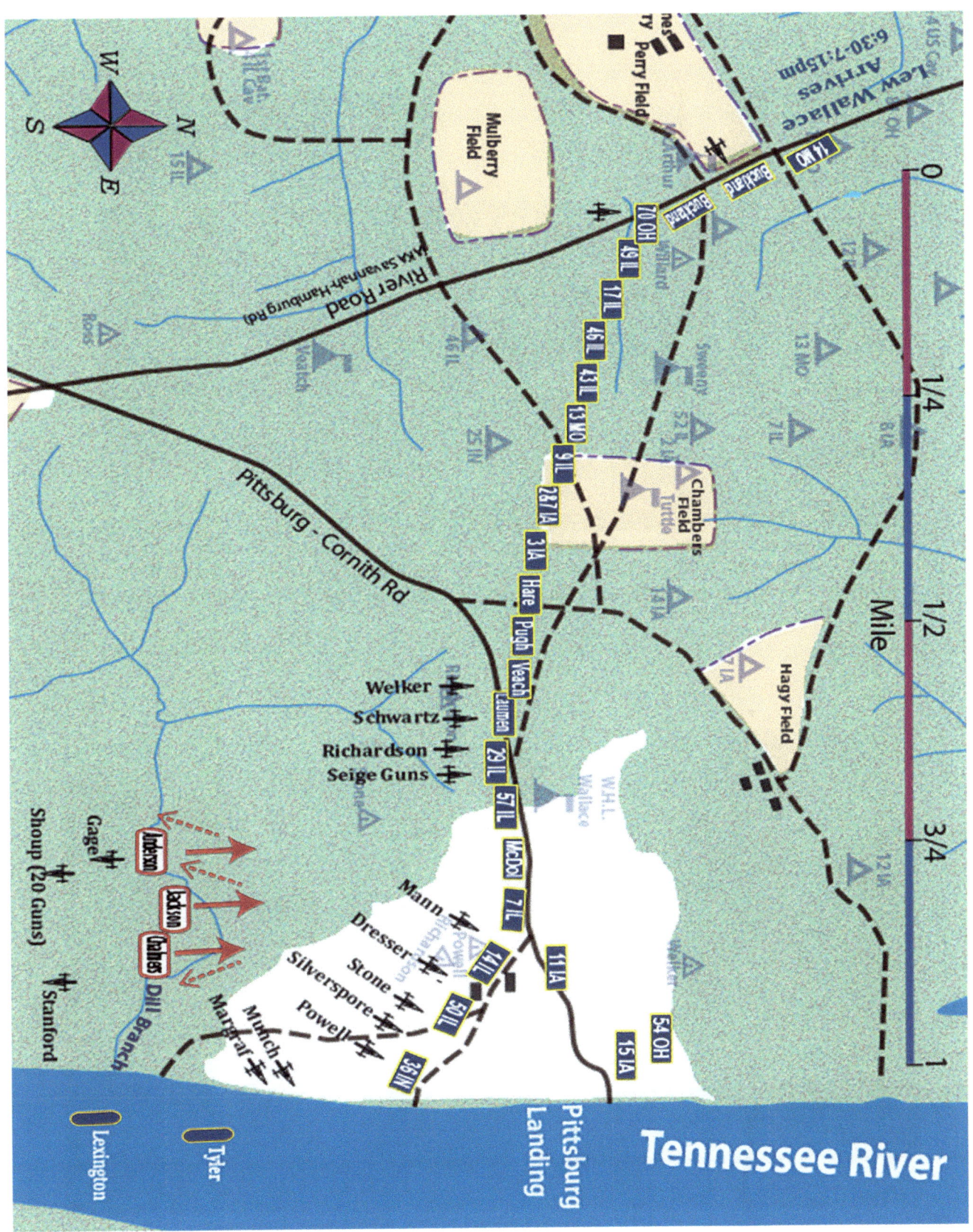

Grant's Last Line, facing south

Chapter 18 - Grant's Last Line

A battery of five 24-pounder siege guns set up along "Grant's Last Line" by Grant's Chief of Staff, Col. Joseph D. Webster. The photo was taken a couple of days after the battle. A 24-pounder was about twice the size and weight of what would become one of the standard field guns of the war, the 12-pounder Napoleon.

Modern view of Grant's Last Line, looking east toward the Tennessee River, about 300 yards away. The guns are pointing south toward Dill Creek, the direction of the last Confederate attack of the day.

shoreline on the north end of the landing. But what particularly stunned Buell's men was the panorama of 5000, 10,000 or 15,000 soldiers milling around the opposite river bank, pleading for Ammen's 550 men to save them. Having just slogged through miles of jungle to reach the battle, the sight enraged Ammen's troops. "*I blush to describe it,*" wrote a 6OH soldier. "*The entire bank of the river, for a mile up and down, was crowded with cowardly poltroons who were crowding down to be out of harm's way.*"

Lt. Bierce described the scene:

"*The air was full of thunder and the earth was trembling beneath [our] feet. Below us ran the river, vexed with plunging shells and obscured in spots by blue sheets of low-lying smoke. In the distance, the battle was burning brightly enough; a thousand lights kindled and expired every second. Through the smoke, the branches of the trees showed black; sudden flames burst out, here and there, singly and in dozens, fleeting streaks of fire crossed over to us, followed by the musical humming of the fragments as they struck the ground on every side, making us wince, but doing little harm.*

There were deep shaking explosions and smart shocks, and faint, desultory cheers could be heard from the battlefield. Occasionally, against the glare behind the trees, could be seen moving black figures, distinct, but no larger than a thumb; they seemed to be like the figures of demons in old allegorical prints of hell."

Lt. Ambrose G. Bierce
1842 - 1914

Nelson ordered his pioneers to cut a road to the river bank. No transports were immediately handy, so he commandeered a sutler boat to transport the first load of men across, which consisted of three companies – about 200 men – of the 36IN of Ammen's brigade, plus Nelson and eight mounted officers. They crowded aboard and ferried across. Along the way, the Hoosiers begged to shoot the stragglers floating on logs. Nelson reluctantly declined. The captain stopped the boat just short of the Landing for fear he'd crush stragglers in the water. Nelson erupted and ordered him to push into the Landing – if a few cowards were mushed, all the better. Now the gangplank slammed down, and the first company splashed ashore, bayonets extended. At the top of the gangplank, flanked by mounted officers, stood the giant black stallion, *Ned*. And astride Ned was the 330-pound Bull Nelson, his hat tastefully adorned with a tall black ostrich feather.

Now the mounted officers rode down the gangplank and formed the troops into two lines, bayonets extended. Nelson rode to the front and bellowed, "*Gentlemen, draw your sabers and trample these sons a bitches into the mud! Charge!*" Like Moses parting the sea, Nelson and his troops drove through the mob. One of Nelson's aides, Lt. Horace Fisher, recalled that they "*cut through the mob of runaways, who tumbled over each other in abject terror.*" As the troopers jabbed at the skulkers, the Bull roared: "*Damn your souls, if you won't fight, get out of the way, and let men come here who will.*" He then ordered his men to shout "*Buell!, Buell!, Buell!*" and beat time on a tree with his saber.

Somewhere in the midst of the insanity, a small drummer boy among the stragglers pounded furiously on his drum, possibly to welcome the reinforcements, or possibly because he didn't know what else to do. Drummer boys averaged pretty tough in Grant's army. A Lt. Crocker of the 55IL remembered that "*the belligerent little drummers nearly all preferred to fight and were found along the line, gun in hand, as fierce as fighting cocks, with no notion of shirking.*"

Also blocking the way was a chaplain who ran about shouting: '*Rally, men, rally, and we may yet be saved. Oh rally! For God and your country's sake, rally! Rally! Oh! Rally round the flag of your country!*" It was all too much for Ammen, who exploded, "*Shut up, you God damned old fool, or I'll break you head! Get out of the way!*"

Though loaded with wounded, soon all the steamers at the Landing began crossing the river, back and forth, ferrying across Buell's troops and horses. Weary surgeons on the upper, hurricane, decks tended the wounded, while Buell's men were crammed below decks. When the steamers ferried Buell's men to the Landing, the boats had to keep a slight distance from the shore to keep from being swamped by hysterical stragglers.

Ambrose Bierce described it:

"*Whenever a steamboat would land, this abominable mob had to be kept off her by bayonets; when*

Chapter 18 - Grant's Last Line

she pulled away they sprang upon her, and were pushed by scores into the water, where they were suffered to drown one another in their own way. The men disembarking insulted them, struck them. In return they expressed their unholy delight in the certainty of our destruction by the enemy."

Sometime about now, a steamer arrived – the *Fort Wayne* – carrying pontoons. An officer requested the boat's captain to land so that the pontoons could be used as boats to ferry the Army of Ohio across. But Grant's adjutant, Capt. John Rawlins, worried that stragglers would use the pontoons to flee. He threatened to burn the boat if she docked.

Col. Jacob Ammen
1807 - 1894

But now another boat – the *Rocket* – arrived, towing two ammunition barges. In this case, Rawlins ordered the boat to dock. As the crates were being unloaded a shell exploded nearby, prompting the captain to give orders to cast off. Rawlins stepped aboard and threatened to shoot every man aboard if any departure was attempted.

Once he was up on the Landing, Lt. Horace Fisher of Nelson's staff, described the scene:

"As we sat on our horses we saw the flotsam and jetsam of Gen. Grant's army drift by in flight toward The Landing. We saw double-decked ambulances galloping wildly with well men on the front seats prodding the horses with bayonets and swords, the ghastly load of wounded men inside shrieking in agony as the ambulances collided with each other or with trees in their flight. Shells were shrieking through the air and trees were breaking and casting their branches upon the ground. Nor were the bullets less vicious as they ripped around us. In a word, it was pandemonium broken loose."

Grant seemed to be the only person on the field – Union or Confederate – who was still optimistic about the Federals' situation. From his original 40,000 man army, excluding Lew Wallace's missing 7,300 men, Grant was down to about 18,000 men of his own and 550 from Buell, along with, depending on which account you believe, 25, 41 or 60 cannon, plus two gunboats off-shore.

But Grant had his defensive line – his "Last Line" – with its back to the river and the swamps, stretching about a mile with Sherman and McClernand on the far right, Buell's fresh troops on the left, and a hodgepodge of battered units in between. He directed Nelson to form his men atop the bluff, even as more stragglers raced through their ranks. Between Nelson's troops and the log cabin on the bluff, Grant, Buell and Nelson held a conference. At some point Capt. Irving Carson, one of Grant's cavalry scouts, rode up to make a report. He dismounted and was holding his horse's bridle *"when a six pound shot carried away all of Carson's head, bespattering Grant's clothing with blood."* Lt. Fisher, who was present, wrote later, *"I heard a thud and some dark object whizzed over my shoulder. It was Captain Carson's head."*

Grant simply carried on. He asked Nelson for a liaison, and Nelson gave him Lt. Fisher. As Fisher and Grant rode down the line, *"I could see no organized force to resist any serious attack,"* said Fisher. As the Rebel brigades loomed on the opposite ridge and he and Grant stopped to watch the attack, Fisher *"decided that within a short time all of us would have been captured."* Then, he wrote years later, *"I heard [Grant] say something. I rode forward, saluted, and waited for his order. He paid no attention. His eyes were fixed to the front. Again I heard him mutter something without turning, and I saw that he was talking to himself: 'Not whipped yet by a damned sight,'"* Grant muttered.

"I heard a thud and some dark object whizzed over my shoulder. It was Captain Carson's head."

Later that evening, Grant's engineering officer, James McPherson, returned from reviewing the army's condition and reported to Grant that fully one third of the army was out of action and the remainder was *"much dispirited."* Grant simply nodded. Receiving no further reply, McPherson asked, *"Well, General Grant, under this condition of affairs, what do you propose to do, Sir? Shall I make preparations for a retreat?"*

Surprised at the question, Grant replied, *"Retreat? No! I propose to attack at daylight and whip them."*

Dill Creek

Fronting Grant's troops near the river – the most obvious point of attack – was the formidable barrier called Dill Creek or Dill Branch. "Creek" is a misnomer; at least near the river it wasn't so much a creek as a deep, dense, jungle-like ravine, 60-90 feet high on both sides, where water flowed in and out, eroding the ravine ever deeper as the river rose and fell. The ravine's sides were steep – probably 60 degrees or more. The bottom of the ravine, about 50 feet wide near the river, was a soggy marsh for a half mile inland, and with all the recent rain it currently held about three feet of water near the river. Even a half mile upstream, away from the river, the ravine was difficult to cross. Grant's troops formed along the north side of this ravine, as well as on a spur that jutted out 200 feet towards the river on the far left of the Union line, where two Federal batteries of 10 cannon aimed down the length of the ravine. And anchored right behind them were the two gunboats with their massive eight inch guns.

Federal skirmishers carefully worked their way over to the south side of the ravine, so as to give early warning of an attack.

The Day's Last Attack

Several hundred yards to the south, only Braxton Bragg still seemed to be driving the attack; neither Breckinridge nor Polk joined this final assault. Even after the Federal retreat and the surrender in Cloud Field, it took some precious time for the Confederates to reach Grant's Last Line because pockets of retreating Federals continued to stop and resist along the way, requiring time to clear them out.

Bragg gathered about 30 cannon and 4,000-5,000 troops, mainly from Chalmer's and Jackson's brigades and a few remnants of Anderson's, and ordered them to attack this last line, promising the exhausted troops, *One more charge my men, and we shall capture them all!"*

The attack would be across Dill Creek, less than a quarter mile south of Pittsburg Landing. Because of all the rain, the river was 16 feet higher than normal, causing it to deeply flood the ravine. This not only greatly hindered any Confederate assault, but also allowed the two Federal gunboats to sail right up to the edge of the ravine and fire at point blank range. Though, as mentioned, their big guns couldn't be lowered enough to fire directly into the bottom of the ravine, just the sound of the their blasts was terrifying.

Chalmer's brigade, which had been fighting since 8 or 9am, anchored the Confederate right, next to the river, and next to the gunboats.

Lt. Col. Camm of the 14IL had just escaped capture at the Hornets Nest. He watched from the north side of the ravine as the Confederates massed for their attack.

"Again the battle was opened afresh, but for a time nothing was used but cannon; the sun looked like a ball of fire as it went out of sight, and the clouds of powder smoke hastened the gloaming. The scene was grand but fearful and the thunder terrific. We cold see red flashes of our own and the enemy's guns, and shells burst all about us. A mounted man had his buttocks cut off and the horse's back broken. I saw one cannon shot that seemed to jump out of the ground. It cut the top out of a bush my hungry horse was biting at, brushed my body and mangled a soldier sitting on a log a hundred feet or so behind me. One could not help wondering how any living thing could escape wounds or death.

"The Confederates attacked from the southwest, the worst point they could have chosen, for it forced them to cross a hollow that opened into the river [Dill Branch], and exposed them to the fire of the gun boats Tyler and Connestoga [actually the Lexington]. The large-bore guns aboard the boats had been double-shotted with canister."

"The execution was dreadful," said one Confederate who watched the attack. *"The cannon fire from the vessels was continuous."*

Things weren't going any better on the Confederate left, farther inland, where Jackson's and Anderson's brigades were attacking. Grant had placed the bulk of his artillery here, the center of his line, including his heavy siege guns. Rebel Capt. Gage's Alabama battery rolled up to support the attack, but no sooner had it opened on the Yankee line when it was pounded with so much counter-battery fire from those siege guns that it was forced to pull back.

Many of Jackson's and Anderson's men were out of ammunition but, as it was dusk, they were instructed to charge with bayonets alone. As soon as the Confederates clambered up the north crest of the ravine they were slaughtered by Federal rifles and those siege guns, which were now double-shotted with canister, easily breaking the attack.

Somehow, the Confederate officers managed to get their men to charge twice more. Those attacks were probably half-hearted, and they quickly fizzled, with more losses. By now the bottom of the ravine was filled with dead and wounded, many of the latter drowning in the bloody water. Finally, the men

Chapter 18 - Grant's Last Line

refused to charge again unless they received more support.

Compared to the Confederate losses, Ammen, by contrast, whose Federals manned the deepest part of the ravine near the river, lost only one man. The attacks were over in about 20 minutes. It was around 6pm. The sun set at 6:25pm.

In fact, Bragg and his division commander, Jones Withers, were still looking around for more troops to add to their force in preparation for a larger assault. But then Withers said "*to my astonishment, a large portion of the command to my left was observed to move rapidly [away] from the fire of the enemy.*" Withers immediately ordered his adjutant to "*go and arrest the commanding officers, and place the troops in position for charging the batteries.*"

But just then a courier arrived from Beauregard, who was well to the rear near Shiloh Church. Beauregard's message ordered the attack halted and to pull the troops back, stating that "*Victory was sufficiently complete.*" Bragg supposedly muttered, "*My God, when is victory ever sufficiently complete?!*" He later claimed he was tempted to disregard the order, but other units were already withdrawing, and there wasn't time to reverse their movements and make another assault before nightfall. "*My God, my God,*" he cried, "*It's too late!*" In his official report, he stated that he was in the midst of "*a movement commenced with every prospect of success.*" However, he spent the night with Beauregard in Sherman's old tent, and apparently didn't mention this at the time. Nor did he express any anger about the order in his letter a couple of days later to his wife, with whom he was usually quite candid. One of his own staff officers, Col. David Urquhart, admitted that by the time the order arrived "*our troops at the front were a thin line of exhausted men who were making no further headway and who were glad to receive orders to fall back.*"

But Beauregard's order would forever be controversial, becoming known in the South as *The Lost Opportunity*, though one wonders how many of those making that claim were among those who had the opportunity to make a bayonet charge into Grant's double-loaded siege cannon.

Beauregard's headquarters was near the Crossroads, two miles from where Bragg's attack was taking place. He had just assumed army command three hours earlier, and he wasn't in the best physical shape to be riding about the battlefield. So he relied on his aides, who were reporting that the roads were clogged with Confederate stragglers; companies, regiments and brigades were scattered everywhere; and a large percentage of the troops were wandering about, plundering Yankee camps. Also, he could hear the tremendous cannonading by the Yankee gunboats, as well as the siege cannon, and he must have believed his troops were catching hell near the river. He wanted time to reorganize his exhausted army.

"My God, when is victory ever sufficiently complete?!"

(We know a lot about the Federal stragglers hanging around the Landing. What we don't know is how many Confederates simply left the battle and headed back down the roads to Corinth).

Weirdly, visitors to Beauregard's tent found the army commander tending a large bird on his lap. It apparently was a pheasant with a broken wing, picked up by a soldier who donated it to the general for a meal. But Beauregard pitied the shell-shocked creature, and ordered a box altered to make a cage which he brought back to Corinth with him after the battle.

In any case, the commander had just received a wonderful piece of intelligence. A courier from Corinth brought a telegram from Rebel general Ben Helm in north Alabama, stating that his cavalry scouts had spotted Buell's army marching south toward Decatur, Alabama, rather than west toward Pittsburg Landing! This left Beauregard with the impression that he had whole next day to finish off Grant's army before Buell arrived. Unfortunately for the Confederates, the intelligence was false – only one division of Buell's army was marching toward Decatur Alabama; the others were heading toward Pittsburg Landing, and in fact were already arriving.

Also, Beauregard may have been influenced by Federal Gen. Prentiss, the captured division commander, who met with Beauregard and who shared a tent that night with some of Beauregard's aides. Exactly what the chatty Prentiss said is a matter of dispute. He later claimed that he slyly misled Beauregard by stating that Buell's army was at least 48 hours away. However, after the war, some of Beauregard's aides stated that Prentiss bragged that Buell would be on the field by daylight. If he said that, the Confederates didn't believe him.

Believing that Buell was far away, Beauregard dictated a telegram while the battle at Pittsburg Landing was still roaring, informing Davis of the

Five months after the battle, "Bull" Nelson dismissed one of his subordinates, Brig. Gen. Jefferson C. Davis, a Union regular army officer with a face like a hound dog. An angry Davis confronted Nelson in a Nashville hotel lobby. An argument started. Eventually, Davis picked up a hotel registration card from the lobby desk, wadded it up, and threw it in Nelson's face. The massive Nelson back-handed Davis across the face. Davis departed but returned minutes later with a borrowed gun and shot Nelson dead. Some, who no doubt disliked Nelson, considered it justifiable homicide; but others, including Buell, believed Davis should be court martialed. But somehow, possibly because of the shortage of senior officers, or maybe because Nelson was a navy man, Davis was never prosecuted. But though he performed well throughout the rest of the war under Sherman, he never received a full promotion to a higher rank.

Brig. Gen.
Jefferson C. Davis
1828 - 1879

Modern photo looking west into Dill Branch Ravine. The Tennessee River is about 50 feet behind the camera.

death of Johnston, as well as rashly claiming the "*complete victory*" of the Confederate arms that day. The enemy had been thoroughly beaten, he said, and *"the remnant of his army driven in utter disorder to the immediate vicinity of Pittsburg and we remained undisputed masters of his ... [camps]."*

And so, due to his confidence of victory the next day, and due to the exhaustion and disorder of his army and looming darkness, he gave the order for all commanders to call off their attacks and withdraw to the shelter of the Yankee camps.

Nightfall

At last, at 6:25pm, blessed darkness arrived, shielding Grant's line from more attacks until daybreak. Later, needing to catch some sleep, Grant returned to one of the shacks that had served as his headquarters at the top of the bluff, but now it was packed with wounded and filled with the stench of medicine and blood and the moans of the wounded. Preferring to sit out in the pouring rain rather than stay in that building, Grant hobbled out – he was still on crutches – to a big tree that was some protection against the rain. (He had a cabin on the nearby steamer, the *Tigress*, docked a few yards away. Why didn't he spend the night there? Probably because he didn't want it reported that he was sleeping comfortably in the boat's cabin while his men were in the rain.)

Around midnight Sherman, his arm in a sling, went looking for Grant, assuming the next step was "*to put the river between us and the enemy and recuperate.*" He found Grant alone in the pouring rain propped against his tree, his collar up, his hat pulled down, and a cigar poking out his mouth, Sherman later said he was "*moved by some wise and sudden instinct*" not to talk about retreat. Instead, he said, "Well, Grant, we've had the devil's own day, haven't we?"

Grant replied, "*Yep. Lick'em tomorrow though.*"

Could the Confederates Have Won on that First Day?

Beauregard's decision to halt the attack is yet another of the great what-ifs of the battle. What if he had continued attacking? Could he have broken Grant's line and destroyed his army before Union reinforcements arrived? Probably not. Grant's line consisted of at least 41 cannon, naval gun support, and 18,000 Federal infantry well situated behind the steep Dill Creek Ravine, with their flanks solidly protected by the river and the swamps. This position was far stronger than the Federal position on the Sunken Road line, which had taken the better part of the day for the Confederates to crack, and then only be attacking its flanks.

Especially with Buell's fresh troops beginning to trickle in, boosting morale, it's extremely unlikely that the Confederates, exhausted, hungry, and badly disorganized after a day's fighting, could break the Union line in the 30 minutes or less of remaining full-daylight.

In fact, an argument could be made that once Grant was firmly settled in his defensive position, behind a 40' ravine and hub-to-hub cannon, with the imminent arrival of 7,300 fresh troops of Lew Wallace's division, and with a ready supply of food and ammunition delivered by Savannah transports protected by gunboats, the exhausted and starving Confederates couldn't have broken Grant's line even if Buell didn't arrive for another month.

"Lick'em tomorrow, though."

But you'll never convince die-hard Confederate supporters of that! Nor could you convince Buell and his troops, who firmly believed that their 550 men (suffering one casualty) saved Grant's army on that first evening.

Checking the Confederate Advance on the Evening of the First Day at Dill Branch.

Chapter 18 - Grant's Last Line

Union gunboats, the Tyler and Lexington, bombard Confederate positions. Mariners Museum; Newport News; VA

USS Tyler moored at a river bank on laundry day.

Modern photo of a naval gun used by the Tyler and Lexington. They were much larger than even Grant's siege artillery.

USS Lexington

Chapter 18 - Grant's Last Line

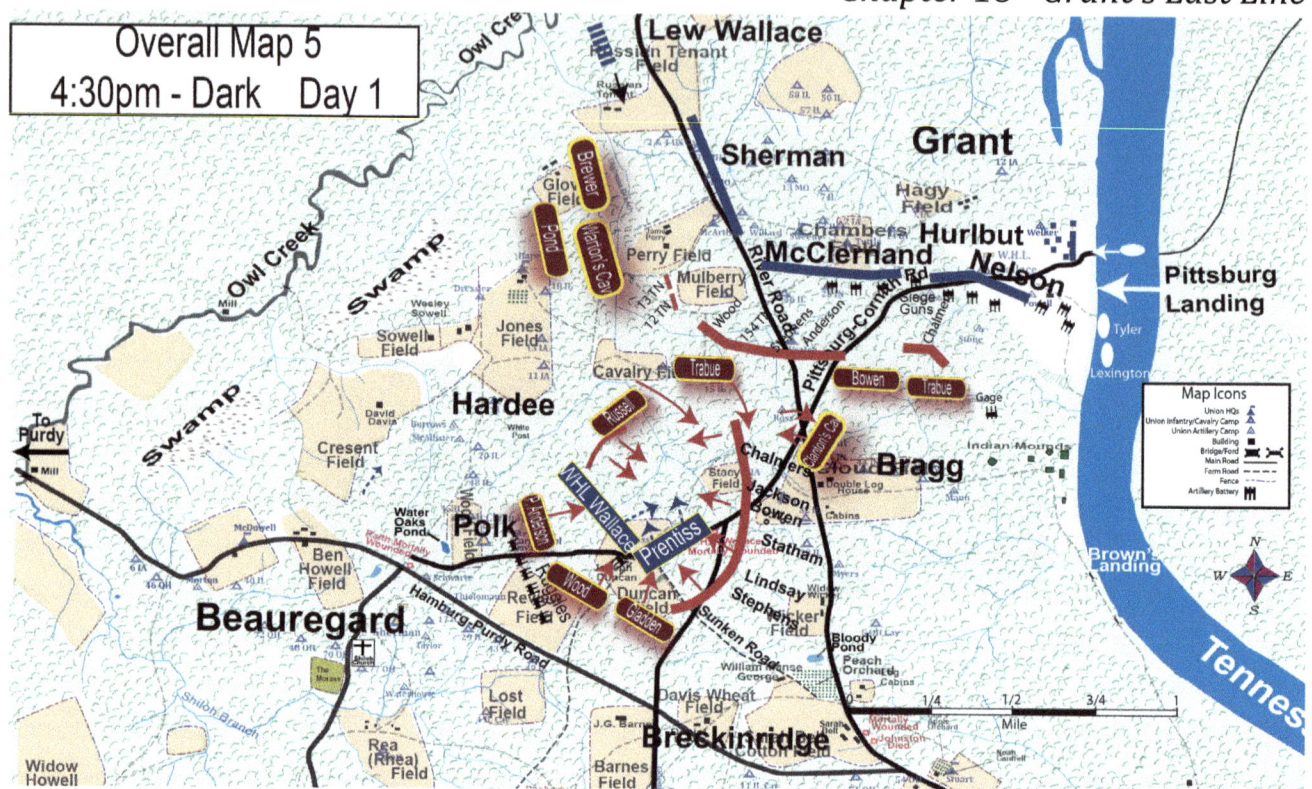

Confederates close in on the southwestern side of Cloud Field, known as Hell's Hollow, capturing 2,200 Federals. Meanwhile, the remainder of the Federal army retreats to Grant's Last Line at Pittsburg Landing. Confederates make a half-hearted attempt to break this last line, but soon fall back for the night.

19   Lew Wallace Finally Arrives

12 NOON – 7:15 PM

By noon that first day, as the fighting raged at Shiloh, with the Federal line teetering on the brink of collapse and being pushed back ever closer to the Landing, Grant kept looking north, anxiously awaiting Lew Wallace's 3rd Division of 7,300 men. Wallace was deployed near Crumps Landing, just five or six miles north of Pittsburg Landing by the shortest route, which was the River Road (aka Savannah-Hamburg Road). But, unknown to Grant, Wallace hadn't taken the shortest route, and he would spend the next 40 years of his life explaining why it took him almost eight hours to cover the six miles to Pittsburg Landing, at a time when Grant so desperately needed him.

The heart of the problem was that most of Wallace's division wasn't actually located at Crumps Landing. His division was initially posted there, but Grant suspected that Crumps Landing would be the most likely target for a Southern attack, and in the event of such an attack, Wallace expected that nearest assistance would come from Sherman's division to the south, up a road called the Shunpike. The careful Wallace had his pioneers restore, corduroy and re-bridge the Shunpike Road for rapid movement, and Wallace personally inspected the entire route all the way to Sherman's camp during the last week of March. He never considered using the River Road, which led to W. H. L. Wallace's division, not Sherman's, and which wasn't in as good a condition as the Shunpike, now refurbished for Sherman's speedy arrival.

Sherman's division was the farthest inland (west) from Pittsburg Landing. So, to put himself within easy reach by Sherman, Wallace left only one of his brigades, commanded by Col. Morgan Smith, at Crumps Landing. He moved the second one, commanded by Col. John Thayer, two and a half miles inland (west) to a village named Stoney Lonesome.

And then he sent the third one, commanded by Col. John Whittlesey, five miles west to another small village, Adamsville, along the same road. This was done with Grant's knowledge and approval.

But on the morning of April 6th, the Confederates struck Grant's main army at Pittsburg Landing instead of Wallace's isolated division at Crumps Landing. Hearing the firing, Wallace alerted his troops and concentrated them near his center brigade at Stony Lonesome, two and a half miles inland from Crump's Landing, which was the reasonable thing to do, but quite wrong as it turned out. He was simply following his original plan to use the Shunpike, except in reverse – instead of Sherman reinforcing him using that road, Wallace would now reinforce Sherman via the same road. He was still at Crumps Landing about 8:30am when Grant's boat steamed up from Savannah, heading to Pittsburg Landing. Grant briefly halted his vessel to confer with Wallace. The commander wasn't yet sure what was happening at Pittsburg Landing, but in a shouted conversation between boats, he ordered Wallace to have his division to be ready to march, and await orders. Wallace had to quiet his disappointed staff. They were anxious to march *now*!

Upon reaching Pittsburg Landing, Grant soon realized his army was fighting for its life, and he directed his adjutant general, Capt. John Rawlins, to order Wallace's 3rd Division to come quickly. Rawlins, a close personal friend of Grant's, was sort of the general's PR man whose unofficial duty was to make sure Grant stayed sober. (Sherman, for one, was unimpressed with Rawlins as a staff officer.)

Rawlins in turn repeated the Grant's command to another staff officer, Capt. A. S. Baxter, who was assigned to relay the message to Wallace. To avoid mistakes, Capt. Baxter requested the message in

Page 153

Chapter 19 - Lew Wallace Finally Arrives

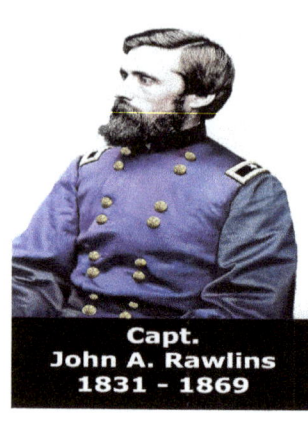

Capt. John A. Rawlins
1831 - 1869

writing. Rawlins hastily scrawled a message and handed it to the captain. Baxter then boarded a steamboat and sailed north to Crumps Landing, reaching Wallace at around 11:30am or slightly earlier. The written message was handed to Capt. Frederick Knefler, Wallace's adjutant, who tucked it under his sword belt but later lost it. Exactly what it said has always been a matter of heated dispute, creating a controversy that ultimately ended Lew Wallace's military career.

Rawlins claimed the order he wrote directed Wallace to march on the road "*nearest the river*"– the River Road and "*form a line of battle at a right angle with the river and be governed by circumstances.*" But Wallace swore that the message didn't specify a route.

Grant, back at Pittsburg Landing, had no idea Wallace would do anything but haul his troops down to Pittsburg Landing as fast as possible using the shortest route, the River Road. The arrival of Wallace's 7,300 fresh troops would have made all the difference in the current struggle.

For whatever reason – whether deliberately disobeying orders as to which road to use or because he thought he was free to make his own choice – Wallace chose to march his division via the Shunpike, the better road and the one roughly in the center of his three brigades at Stoney Lonesome. His intent was to arrive at the northwest side of Sherman's camps, north of Shiloh Church, and hopefully strike the left flank of the Confederate army, winning the battle and perhaps the war. Grant always suspected this desire for glory caused Wallace to deliberately disobey his order.

(Between the possibilities that (a) Wallace deliberately disobeyed the order or (b) the message didn't specific a route, there is a third possibility - Wallace was so sure he would be using the Shunpike, and so anxious to get into the battle, that he may have not bothered to fully read the hand-scrawled note, and simply assumed it would say to use the Shunpike. We'll never know!)

Using the wrong road was one problem. But another problem was that Wallace just never seemed to appreciate the urgency of the situation. When the initial courier, Capt. Baxter, arrived at 11:30am, Wallace inquired about the progress of the battle. Baxter responded that the Rebels were being repulsed. (It should be remembered that when Grant encountered Buell at Pittsburg Landing around mid-day, he informed Buell that "*all looks well*.") So, based on the courier's optimistic view, Wallace was under the impression that the battle was being won, and his main purpose was to march down the Shunpike and strike the enemy a devastating blow on his left flank.

Grant expected Wallace to be on the battlefield shortly after noon, but it was noon before Wallace even put his troops on the march after allowing them a full half-hour for lunch.

Meanwhile, back at the Landing, at around 11am - two or more hours after he had sent Capt. Baxter with orders for Wallace to march to Pittsburg Landing immediately, Grant "*expressed considerable solicitude*" that Wallace had not yet arrived. He sent an aide galloping over to the Federal right to see if he could spot any sign of Wallace, remarking that it could not *possibly* be many minutes before he arrived.

Shortly after noon, Capt. William Rowley, one of Grant's aides and a friend and neighbor of Grant's prior to the war, said "*A cavalry officer rode up and reported to General Grant, stating that General Wallace had positively refused to come up unless he received written orders.*" Grant lost his famous calm. He ordered Rowley to personally ride to Wallace and "*tell him to come up at once*," and that "*if he should require a written order of you, you will give him one*." And he told Rowley to be sure he had writing materials in his haversack and "*see that you don't spare the horse flesh.*"

Rowley and the aforementioned cavalry captain galloped north toward Crumps Landing along the River Road, increasingly concerned as they saw no sign of Wallace along the way. After six miles, they reached Wallace's camp at Crumps Landing, but no one was there except a lone baggage wagon which was just then moving off. The teamster told Rowley that the division had marched southwest down the Purdy Road, which was a side road that led to the Shunpike Road. So the two riders now raced down the Purdy Road. But a mile or so later, they came across signs that the division had veered off down the Shunpike. After galloping another four or five miles, they finally reached the tail end of Wallace's division, which was stretched out over two miles.

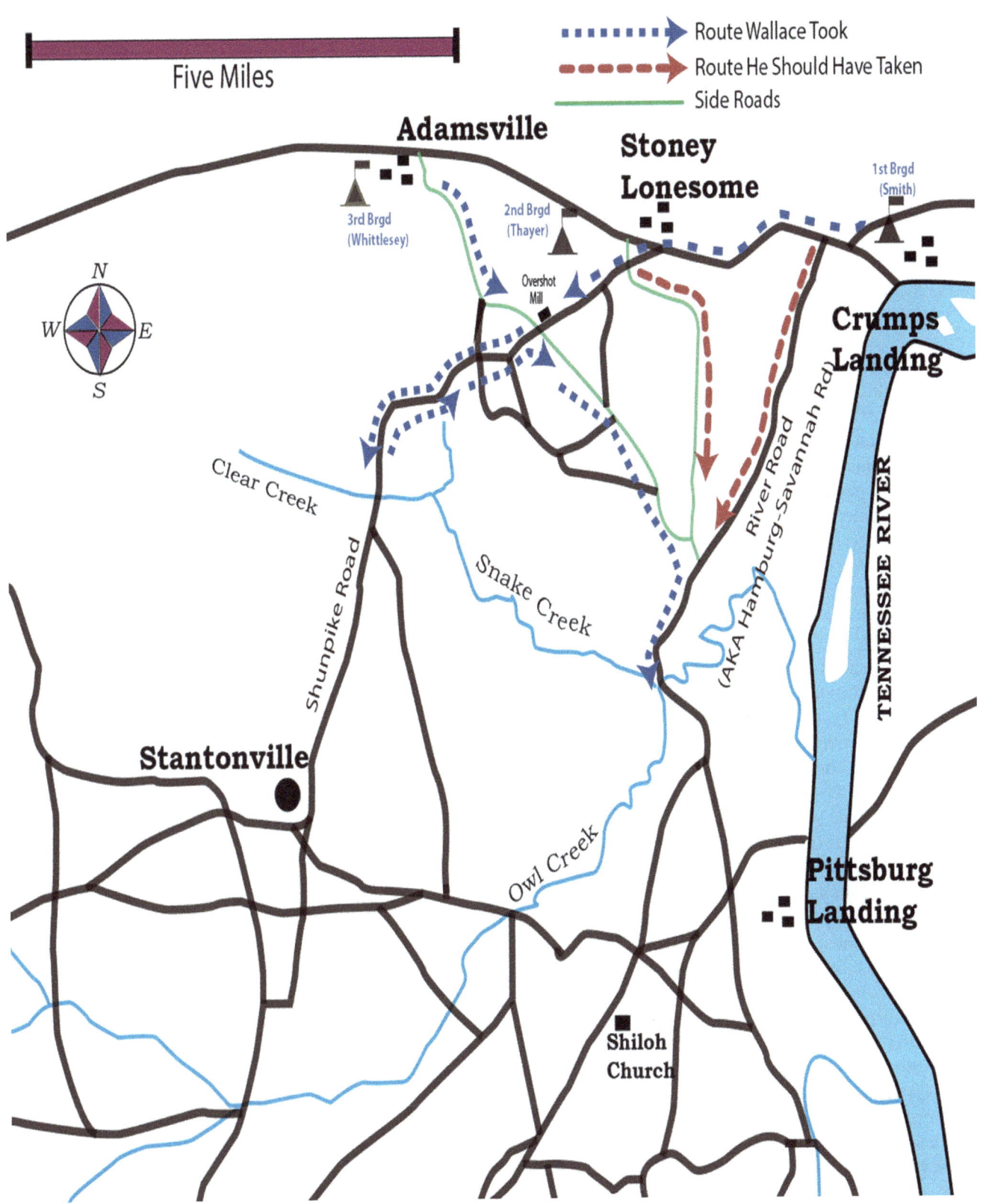

Wallace marches down the wrong road, Shunpike Road, and then has to countermarch back down the River Road

"They were at rest, sitting on each side of the road," Rowley later wrote, "*some with their arms stacked in the middle of the road. When I reached the head of the column I found General Wallace sitting upon his horse, surrounded by his staff, some of whom were dismounted and holding their horses by their bridles.*"

When Rowley told Wallace it had been reported to Grant that he refused to march without written orders, Wallace "*seemed quite indignant, saying it was a 'damned lie!' In proof of which he said, 'Here you find me on the road.'*" Rowley replied it was indeed a road, but not the road to Pittsburg Landing, and in fact Wallace was now considerably farther away from the battlefield than he had been at his original camp. Wallace responded that this was the road his cavalry had led him down, "*and the only road he knew anything about,*" and that it led around Snake and Owl Creeks to Sherman's camps.

Rowley quietly stepped aside with Wallace and whispered: "*My God! Don't you know Sherman has been driven back? Why, the whole army is within a half-mile of the river, and it's a question if we are not all going to be driven into it!*" Wallace then asked if Grant's order was peremptory. "*Yes!*" declared the exasperated Rowley, "*He wants you at Pittsburg Landing – and he wants you there like hell!*"

At just this time, Wallace's own cavalry scouts rode up, confirming that if the division continued on its present course it would encounter the enemy's line.

So now Wallace would have to counter-march, using a short-cut trail that led from the Shunpike to the River Road. It was now 2pm. But rather than simply about-facing his division, he insisted on turning the brigades in order from the lead brigade, so as to keep his best brigade, Col. Smith's, at the head of the column. But doing so wasted even more precious time while Smith's unit doubled back along the entire length of the column so as to remain in the lead of the division.

Now more of Grant's staff officers arrived, increasingly frantic. All failed to impress upon Wallace the urgency of the situation. Once turned around, Wallace's troops made a respectable two and a half miles per hour, but he nearly drove Grant's staff officers to distraction with the frequency and length of the division's rest halts, and also at his reluctance to leave his artillery behind or otherwise sacrifice marching order for speed. He was too much of a

"Grant wants you at Pittsburg Landing, and he wants you there like hell!"

Chapter 19 - Lew Wallace Finally Arrives

perfectionist. Capt. Rowley even considered placing the general under arrest. But he didn't, and in the end Wallace's division was useless in the first day's fighting.

Finally, after dark (6:25pm), and after the Confederate assaults had ended for the day, at around 6:30pm and possibly as late as 7:15pm, Lew Wallace's division reached the Russian Tenant Field, joining Grant's army to the right of Sherman along the River Road (aka Hamburg-Savannah Road), seven hours after Grant had expected him to cover six miles.

Grant never forgave Wallace and, with Halleck's approval, he cashiered him soon after the battle. Wallace spent years appealing to every authority he could in hopes of reviving his tarnished military career, arguing that he had acted properly at Shiloh. And after the war he would continue arguing for decades. But Grant remained unmoved, and maintained for the rest of his life that Wallace had failed him in Grant's hour of need, although he did relent slightly in his memoirs, written just before his death in the 1880s, by stating that it was possible the message didn't specify the River Road.

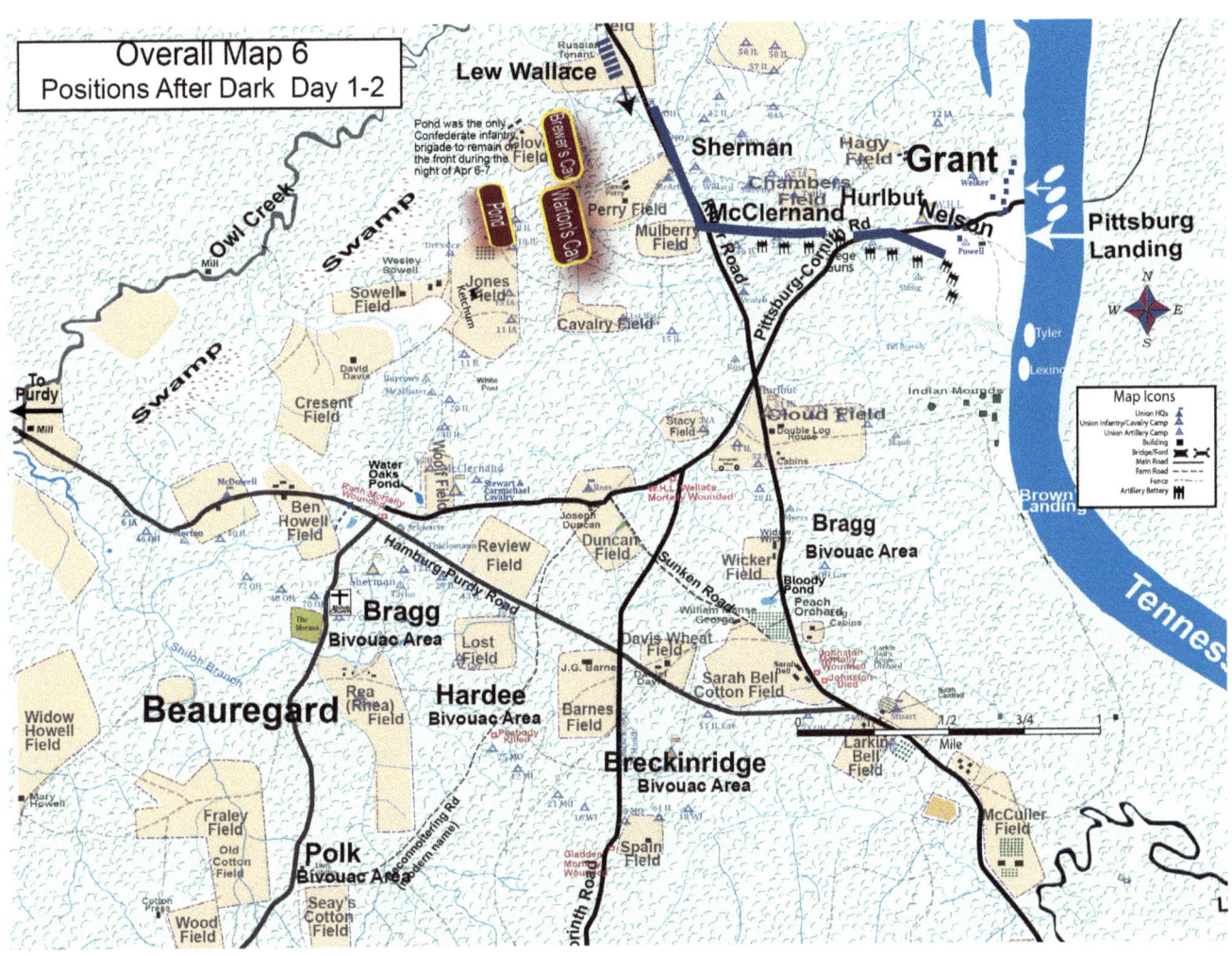

The Confederates fall back for the night, bivouacking in the abandoned Federal camps. Meanwhile, fresh Union troops disembark at Pittsburg Landing throughout the night.

Chapter 19 - Lew Wallace Finally Arrives

> *In theory, if an infantryman fires three rounds a minute, that puts about 6,000 bullets in the air per minute from a single brigade (assuming 500 men per regiment in four regiments). And there were 33 brigades at Shiloh on the first day, excluding Lew Wallace's three brigades. On the second day, with the arrival of Wallace and Buell's troops, there were 47 brigades on the field.*
>
> *As Grant and Rawlins were riding around during the day to visit the divisions on the firing line, they were accompanied by Capt. Douglas A. Putnam, a paymaster, who was serving as one of Grant's aides for the day. Riding with Rawlins behind the general as they approached the fighting, Putnam heard a steady patter on the surrounding leaves and asked how could it be raining under a clear sky.*
>
> *"Those are bullets, Douglas," Rawlins informed him.*

20 Buell Advances

DAY TWO OF THE BATTLE
5am - 10am   April 7

Throughout the night of April 6th - 7th, troops of Buell's Army of Ohio poured in after being ferried from the east side of the river, or steaming south ten miles from Savannah.

By 9pm, Cols. William Hazen's and Sanders Bruce's brigades of Nelson's division crossed the river and, with the use of torches, deployed to the right of Ammen's brigade. Hazen watched as a *"continuous stream of men, a rod [five and a half yards] or more in breadth,"* marched up the bluff.

Between 9pm and 11pm, another of Buell's divisions – Brig. Gen. Thomas Crittenden's two brigades – arrived from Savannah via river transports. By daybreak, Buell had 13,000 troops on the field, with another 4,000 arriving shortly, which combined with the 7,300 of Lew Wallace, gave Grant nearly 25,000 fresh troops, which was more men than Beauregard had left in his entire army, considering casualties and stragglers.

As we know, many of Grant's troops and nearly all of Beauregard's troops except Bragg's, were completely green, many having only been in the army a matter of days. By contrast, although Buell's troops hadn't seen combat, they had been in the army long enough to have fully adapted to army life and receive training, and they were eager for a fight. Among other things, they had just spent three weeks marching down from Nashville, and before that, they had spent weeks marching to Tennessee from central Kentucky.

But when Buell's reinforcements tramped down the steamers' gangplanks they entered the surreal world of Pittsburg Landing. Milling around the Landing were the beaten and frightened stragglers – variously estimated at between 5,000 and 15,000 by the evening of the first day – filled with horrifying tales about the Rebels. When asked their regiment number, some of the stragglers unashamedly answered, *"the 1448th Skedattlers."* Wounded and moaning men were everywhere, as was the stench of blood and cordite. In the darkness, nervous officers barked orders to form up the new arrivals and march them to the battle-line, conveniently located just a 100 or so yards from the Landing.

Along with the rest of the Union army, the new arrivals were in for a rough night. From about 10pm to 3am the sky unloaded sheets of rain, accompanied by massive peals of lighting and thunder. The rain was so heavy and the water so high that many or most of the troops couldn't lie down. They could only stand and stare out into the blackness toward their unseen foe. When the rain occasionally paused, they could hear piteous cries of the wounded out there, somewhere. One of Lew Wallace's soldiers of the 20OH stated the problem: *"To lie on the ground was an impossibility, for the water was flowing in torrents. There were no logs or stones on which to sit, and all that weary night I stood or walked about in the pitiless rain, soaked through and through. The moans of the wounded could be heard in the distance, but none dared to try and help them."*

Maj. Gen.
Don Carlos Buell
1818 - 1898

Meanwhile, troops and artillery continued to arrive and unload onto the Landing throughout the night. 70OH drummer boy John Cockerill stated:

"Every now and then an artillery piece would get stuck in the mud, and then a grand turmoil of half an hour followed, during which time every man found in the neighborhood was impressed to aid in relieving the embargoed gun. The whipping of the horses and the cursing of the drivers were often mixed with the soul-shattering gunboat blasts. There never was a night so long, so hideous, or so utterly uncomfortable."

If anyone did manage to drift off to sleep he would be jolted awake every 15 minutes by the blast from one of gunboat's massive eight inch cannons. The *USS Tyler* and the *Lexington* dropped rounds intermittently throughout the night into suspected Rebel positions, just to hassle the enemy and hopefully kill a few. (Four Confederate soldiers were found the next day, stone dead but with no obvious wounds, seated around an oilcloth they had spread inside a

> *Sixteen-year-old John Cockerill indeed had a rough night after wandering the battlefield throughout the day and being told his father, commander of the 70OH, was dead. But he did get a good piece of news a day or so later - he and his father found each other, both of them alive and well.*

Sibley tent to play cards. A burned-out candle sat atop a bayonet stuck in the ground. "*Each had three cards in his hand,*" said one of the soldiers who found them, "*and four cards lay in the middle of the blanket.*" Apparently they were all instantly killed just by the concussion from a nearby hit.)

Beauregard ordered his troops to fall back for the night into the abandoned Federal campsites. Though under the unpleasant harassing fire from the Union gunboats, most of the Confederates enjoyed their driest, best-fed night of the campaign, sleeping in tents and eating rations courtesy of the U.S. Government, though they did grumble that their accommodations leaked due to numerous bullet holes.

And the cannon fire didn't deter the plundering. Believing that the battle was essentially over, hundreds of soldiers roamed around with lighted candles looking for booty or to discover the fate of comrades. A Louisiana surgeon, surely with exaggeration, estimated that by midnight nearly half the army was on the road to Corinth, "*loaded with belts, sashes, swords, officer's uniforms, Yankee letters, daguerreotypes of Yankee sweethearts ... [Some were] prostrate with Cincinnati whiskey – some enlivened with Philadelphia claret.*"

But more than plunder was on the roads headed to Corinth. One soldier noted at least 200 wagons, each filled with eight to twelve wounded, leaving the battlefield between 8am and 4pm. "*The groans and piteous shrieks of the wounded were heart-rending in the extreme,*" according to one infantryman.

Over on the Confederate left on the west of the line, around dusk, Pond's brigade heard a commotion from the direction of the Landing – the cheering of a large number of men. Believing that the battle was won and that their comrades had achieved yet another success, Pond's men joined in the cheering. But after things quieted down, the men heard a band playing *Hail Columbia* – a Yankee tune.

Early the next morning, the Confederates received their only reinforcements of the battle – 600 raw recruits of the 47TN, armed with shotguns, squirrel rifles, and six bayonets. They had marched from

Chapter 20 - Buell Advances

their place of recruitment in Trenton, Tennessee, having been issued two crackers per day per man since April 2nd. They reached the blood-drenched battlefield around 8am on April 7th, where they were directed to Prentiss' surrender site at Hell's Hollow. There they were issued captured Yankee percussion muskets or whatever weapons were collected from the casualties, and assigned to Preston Smith's brigade. They must have been stunned at the carnage and no doubt wondered what they had gotten themselves into.

Buell Finds Grant

On the previous morning, the first day of the battle, Buell and his staff rode ahead of the troops and, after a grueling ride, reached Savannah before daybreak. He made his way over to meet Grant at his headquarters, and it didn't improve his mood when he discovered that Grant had already sailed for Pittsburg Landing.

The two finally connected around 1pm that day at the Landing. According to an account Buell wrote after Grant's death, he found Grant and some of his staff "*on his boat, in the ladies' cabin.*" According to Buell, Grant "*held out his sword to call my attention to an indentation which he said the scabbard had received from a shot.*" Buell was supremely unimpressed. According to Rawlins, Grant's adjutant, when Buell inquired, "*What preparations have you made for retreating?,*" Grant responded, "*I have not yet despaired of whipping them, General,*" and he told Buell that he expected the arrival of Lew Wallace's 7,300 fresh troops at any moment, which would allow him to regain the momentum.

The two generals – the scruffy Grant, a reputed drunk, and the stern, icy Buell – were already on bad terms because of the incident in Nashville when Grant captured the city with Buell's men. And it was not lost on either of them that Buell's army was in considerably better shape than Grant's. Buell was appalled by what he saw – Grant hobbling around on crutches, with half his army a mob of deserters sitting in plain view, *right **there** in front of him on the Landing!* Buell suggested turning the gunboat cannons on them, but Grant prudently declined; one can only imagine what the newspapers would say about that! At one point Sherman worried that Buell might even refuse to land his army. "*He seemed to mistrust us,*" Sherman said in a massive understatement, "*and did not like the looks of things.*"

Buell's Troops Debarking at Pittsburg Landing Sunday Night.
Contemporary illustration.

Though Grant was technically senior by several weeks, under the circumstances he apparently couldn't summon the nerve to give Buell orders, and their attack the next day was only loosely discussed and coordinated, resulting in nothing more than a tacit understanding that Buell's army would attack on the left, and Grant would attack on the right.

Later that day, Buell, still in a foul mood, toured the Landing. Col. Hugh Reed of the 44IN of Grant's army rode up and asked if Buell knew where he could obtain ammunition. Buell snapped, "*No sir, nor do I believe you want ammunition, sir.*" The surprised Reed demanded his name. "*It makes no difference sir, but I am General Buell.*" The colonel whipped his horse around and rode away, but Buell raced after him, demanding to know *his* name. "*My answer was as fierce and insulting as I could make it in my anger,*" Reed later said.

Restarting the War

The fighting on day two, April 7th, would be the inverse of the fighting on the previous day. On the first day, the Confederates spent the day pushing the Federals back to their starting point at the Landing. On the second day, the Federals would spend the day pushing the Confederates back to *their* initial starting point.

Around 5am, an hour before daylight, Bull Nelson's division – Cols. Jacob Ammen's, Sanders Bruce's, and William Hazen's brigades – restarted the war when they gingerly advanced southwest toward the Dill Branch Ravine. They tripped over many a corpse in the spooky blackness. "*The ground was strewn with dead bodies, some wounded, some with their legs shot off, some almost tore to pieces, groaning in the greatest agony,*" according to a Union private. The nervous Federals advanced toward the unseen foe who had done all this terrible damage, lurking out there somewhere in the darkness, waiting to give the new arrivals the same reception. Col. Ammen ("Old Jakey"), riding in front of his brigade, chanted: "*Now, boys, keep cool. Give' em the best you got,*" which probably made the troops even more nervous.

With constant halts to redress ranks in the dense timber, it took Nelson's wary men until 8am just to reach Cloud Field. By that time, Brig. Gen. Thomas Crittenden's division of Buell's army had joined up on Nelson's right. And to the right of Crittenden was Brig. Gen. Alexander McCook's division, also from Buell's army.

Chapter 20 - Buell Advances

As the lines advanced, Lt. Ambrose Bierce noticed that every single tree still standing was a mass of bullet holes "*from the root to a height of ten to twenty feet one could not have laid a hand [on the trunk] without covering several punctures.*"

Now, boys, keep cool. Give'em the best you got."

Musician John Cockrell noted that one the most piteous sights, "*were the poor wounded horses, their heads drooping, their eyes glassy and gummy, waiting for the slow coming of death. No painter ever did justice to a battlefield such as this, I am sure.*"

Hazen's brigade first struck opposition about halfway across Cloud Field, near Hurlbut's old camp headquarters. Confederate skirmishers fired off some quick shots and raced back toward their lines. Hazen's men kept advancing for another thirty minutes, almost to Wicker Field, when they hit solid resistance. Confederate infantry and artillery opened on them. This being their first time under artillery fire, the men on Nelson's right flank wavered.

Friendly cannon are great confidence-boosters for nervous infantry, but Nelson's artillery was still back in Savannah, so Buell loaned him Capt. John Mendenhall's Battery from Crittenden's division. Soon Mendenhall's teams rolled up and unlimbered on the west side of the River Road. Then Capt. William R. Terrill's battery of smooth-bore Napoleons also raced up and deployed across from Mendenhall on the east side of the road. Both batteries came under accurate fire from a Confederate battery hidden somewhere near W. Manse George's cabin near the Peach Orchard to the southwest. The Federals couldn't see the battery, only its gun smoke rising above the trees after each discharge. Then another Confederate battery to the west

Brig. Gen. Thomas L. Crittenden 1819 - 1993

Federal Brig. Gen. Thomas Crittenden's older brother was Confederate Brig. Gen. George Crittenden, the general who was relieved of command for drunkenness and replaced by Breckinridge. Had the older brother not been replaced, the two brother-generals would have been directly facing each other at Shiloh.

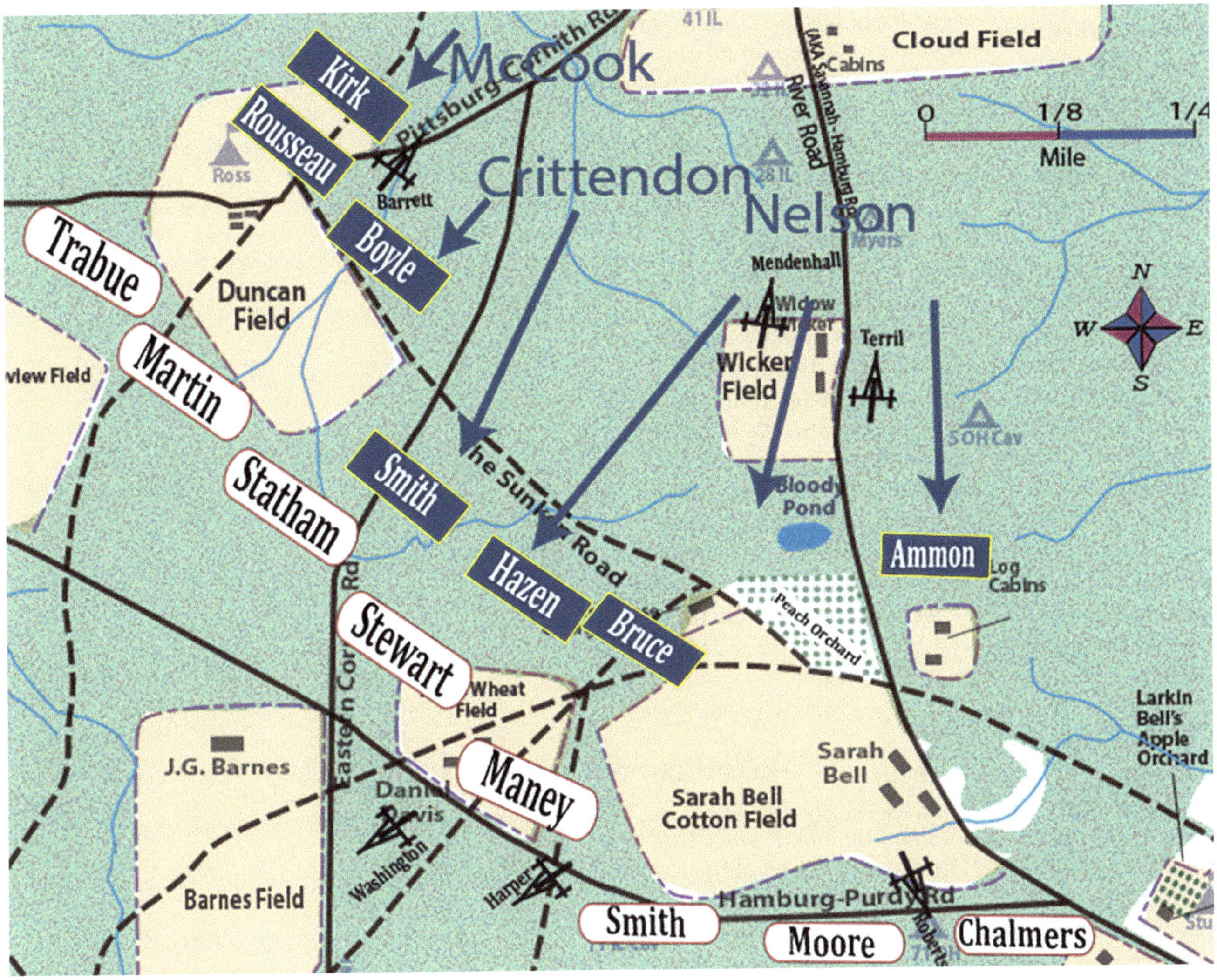

Buell's army counterattacks on the morning of the second day.

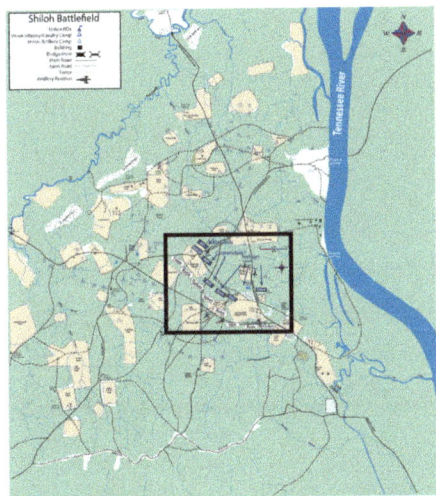

Map's Location on the Battlefield

"No painter ever did justice to a battlefield such as this, I am sure."

began lobbing shells into them, forcing both Mendenhall and Terrell to re-face their guns so as to return fire. Finally, after a spirited half-hour fight, which included Federal infantry advancing and sniping at the Rebel guns, the Confederate batteries withdrew.

Nelson's division now swept past Bloody Pond. Emerging from the timber, Bruce's brigade fronted the Peach Orchard, while Ammen's deployed east of the River Road, along the deep ravine that had proven such a handy barricade for Stuart's brigade the day before. Hazen's brigade, on Bruce's right, reached the Sunken Road. All of these areas – scenes of bitter fighting the day before – would have been a carpet of dead and wounded. And now the Federals saw the main Confederate line, arrayed from the Larkin Bell Field in the east to the Eastern Corinth Road in the west.

Nelson halted to assess the situation.

Aftermath

Even from their rocking chairs in the 1880s, Grant and Buell were still arguing about the effect of Buell's arrival on the Shiloh battle. Buell swore that the arrival of his army late that afternoon of the first day saved Grant's army from disaster. Grant disagreed, pointing out that only a couple of Buell's regiments were deployed on the battleline by nightfall, though he did concede that the arrival of even a few of Buell's troops was *"probably"* a morale-booster for his men.

Overall Map 7
5am - 10am Day 2

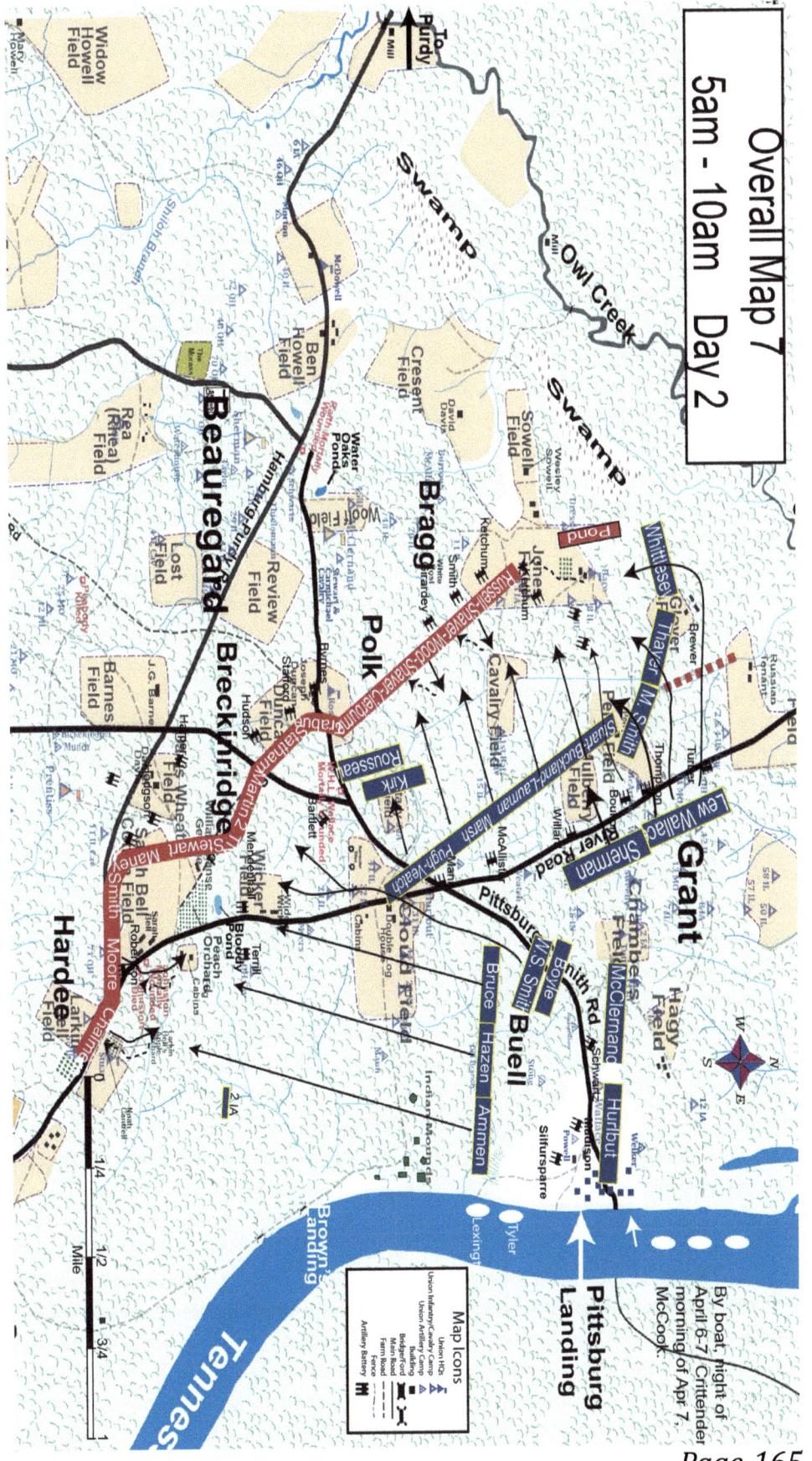

Early on the second day, Monday, Buell and Grant advance, with Buell on the left flank and Grant on the right. Buell encounters heavy resistance in the area of the Sunken Road and Sarah Bell's cotton field, but slowly drives the Confederates back.

21 Confederate Counterattacks

DAY TWO OF THE BATTLE

Bloody Fighting In Davis Wheatfield
10am to 11am, April 7

With the surrender of thousands of Federals late in the afternoon of the first day's fighting – Sunday, the 6th – most Southerners assumed the battle was all but over. Also, a message reached Beauregard the previous evening reporting that Buell's army had diverted to some other destination, and so Grant's Army was expected to be ripe for plucking the next morning, even with including the arrival of Grant's long-lost 3rd Division commanded by Lew Wallace. (Beauregard's scouts kept him well appraised of Wallace's progress, or lack of same, to the battlefield).

Forrest's Reconnaissance

So the Confederates got a nasty surprise around mid-morning of the second day when they realized Grant had been heavily reinforced.

But someone had tried to warn them.

All during the first day, the fierce Col. Nathan Bedford Forrest had been itching to get his cavalry into the battle. But in the densely wooded terrain, there really wasn't much for cavalry to do but guard roads and bridges. But late in the morning, as fighting raged around the Peach Orchard, Forrest chafed at his order to guard the crossing at Lick Creek on the southeast of the battlefield, against any attempt by the Federals to land by transport there. Finally, Forrest could stand it no longer, and called to his men, "*Boys, you hear that shooting? And here we are guarding a damn creek! Let's go and help them!,*" and away they went.

Upon reaching the battle, Forrest and his men ended up at the worst place possible for cavalry – the Hornets Nest, which as we know was fronted by nearly impenetrable thicket and brush. Forrest requested permission from the nearest commander, Ben Cheatham, to allow Forrest to attack. Cheatham declined, saying it was an infantry fight and no place for cavalry. Forrest declared, "*Then I'll charge under my own orders!*" And so he did, leading his men in a column of fours toward the Sunken Road. The Federals opened with massed artillery and infantry fire while Forrest and his men and horses plunged into the dense thicket of the Hornets Nest. Three riders and four horses immediately dropped. In no time, horses and riders were entangled in a nightmare of vines and thorns while the Federals peppered them, thoroughly convincing Forrest that this fight was indeed no place for cavalry. He and his men retreated back to the Confederate far right near some ancient Indian mounds by the river, where they licked their wounds.

But during the night, Forrest decided to do some reconnaissance, a traditional cavalry job, even though in this case his men would recon on foot. In the pouring rain which covered any sounds, Forrest ordered a Lt. Sheridan and his squadron of a dozen men armed with pistols and knives to slip on overcoats of dead Yankees and slither into the cold, pitch-black waters of the Dill Ravine swamp and then slide through the Union lines to observe Pittsburg Landing. In what must have been an interesting excursion, the spies made it, there and back, and reported seeing Yankee soldiers by the thousands unloading from transports. But the good news was, according to Lt. Sheridan, there was so much disorder at the Landing that a surprise night attack might devastate the Yankees.

That's all Forrest needed to hear. He decided the only way to win the battle was to launch an immediate night attack. He tramped around the ghastly battlefield in the rainy blackness, stepping over bodies, first waking up Chalmers, who told him that only a corps commander or Beauregard could make a decision like that, but Chalmers didn't know where they were. So Forrest went looking for a corps commander. He found Hardee and told him that if the army didn't make a night attack, "*[We] will be whipped like hell before ten o'clock tomorrow.*" Hardee told him that only Beauregard could make that decision, but

Col. Nathan Bedford Forrest (w)
1821 - 1877

he didn't know where Beauregard was. So Forrest continued wandering through the rain. But he never found the commander, and nothing was done with his information.

It turned out that Beauregard and Bragg were sharing Sherman's old tent near Shiloh Church, nearly two miles from the river, not that there was the slightest possibility that Beauregard could have organized an attack at that hour in the pouring rain. What he might have done though, was order his men to immediately construct defensive fortifications, which would have made a major difference in the second day's fighting.

Daybreak: Beauregard Organizes a New Battleline

When he awoke on the morning of the second day, Beauregard probably half assumed that the Yankees would have evacuated across the river during the night. It's unclear when he was informed of Forrest's shocking report. In any case, now aware of changed situation, the commander and his generals spent the early hours of April 7 organizing a coherent battleline. On the eastern side of the battlefield, five exhausted and decimated infantry brigades and four artillery batteries manned a line commanded by Hardee and Breckinridge. The two divided their command, with Hardee commanding Confederate forces from the southwest end of Sarah Bell's Cotton Field to the river, and Breckinridge taking responsibility from the western edge of the cotton field to the Eastern Corinth Road.

Around 9am, Beauregard gave Hardee the order *"to charge the enemy in conjunction with General Breckinridge."* In fact the two generals' assaults were uncoordinated since they had no time to consult prior to the attacks.

Hardee's men launched their assault from the Davis Wheatfield, angling toward the Bloody Pond, striking Hazen's and Bruce's brigades and threatening to overrun Mendenhall's battery in the process.

Among those meeting Hardee's attack was Federal Lt. Bierce. "*I can't describe it – the forest seemed all at once to flame up and disappear with a crash like that of a great wave upon the beach,*" he said. There was "*the sickening 'spat' of lead against flesh, and a dozen of my brave fellows tumbled over like ten pins. Some struggled to their feet, only to go down again. Those who stood, fired into the smoking brush and retired. We had expected, at most, a line of skirmishers.*" Instead, he continued, "*what we found was line*

Chapter 21 - Confederate Counterattacks

of battle, holding its fire till it could count our teeth."

Desperate to hold his line, Hazen personally led the Federal 6KY in a bayonet charge. Mendenhall's sweating gunners blasted the onrushing Rebels with case shot (air-bursts) and canister. Finally, the combination of canister and infantry broke the Confederate attack. "*They run!,"* cried some of Bruce's men, and the cheer went up and down the Union line.

The Confederates fell back and formed a new battle line along the Hamburg-Purdy Road, centered approximately at the Davis Wheatfield. Some of the fiercest fighting of the second day occurred around this field and the area to the immediate east.

Col. William B. Hazen 1830 - 1887

One can only admire the tenacity of the Confederates, who were completely untrained and exhausted from the previous day's fighting, and yet they were not only able to halt Buell's fresh and trained troops, but even drive them back.

By 10:30am, having fought off Hardee's spoiler attack, Nelson's division advanced across Sarah Bell's Cotton Field, the scene of so much carnage the day before. At the south end of the field, the Federals came under a storm of fire from Confederate infantry deployed just south of Hamburg-Purdy Road, as well as enfilading fire from Davis Wheatfield to the west where the Washington (New Orleans) Artillery and McClung's Tennessee battery were posted. Ammen's and Bruce's brigades were badly cut up.

Lt. Bierce described what he saw when his brigade reoccupied the Hornets Nest, which had caught fire the day before in the savage fighting:

> "Death had put his sickle into this thicket, and fire had gleaned the field. Here lay bodies, half buried in ashes; their clothing was half burnt away – their hair and beard entirely. Some were swollen to double-girth, others shriveled to manikins."

Furious SeeSaw Fighting

Seeing the Yankees wavering, Hardee, nicked in his arm and his uniform shredded by several bullets, decided to counterattack using Col. John Moore's brigade. But the attack got only as far as the W. Manse George cabin before Hazen's brigade drove the Southerners back once again. Now Hazen, along

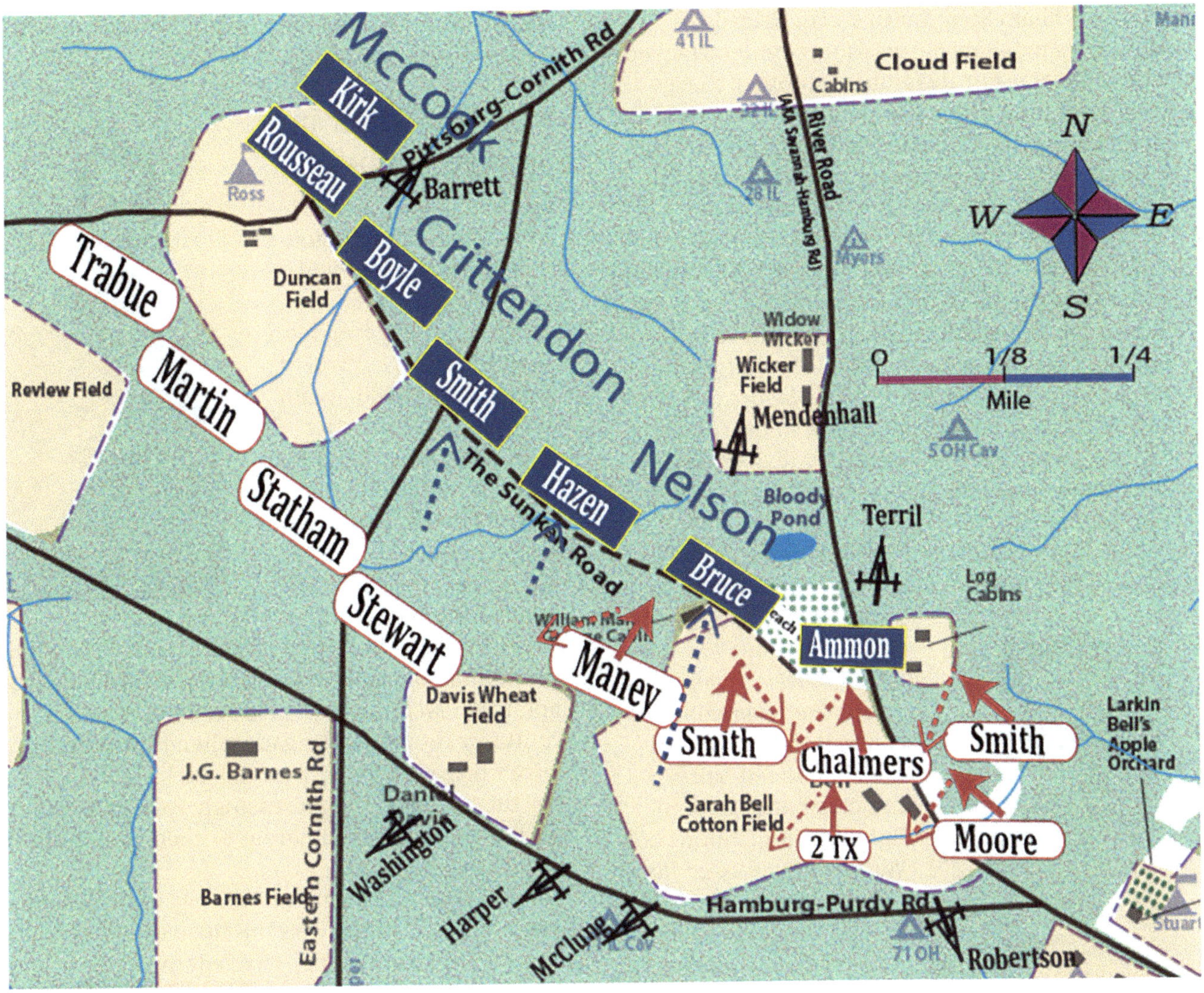

Confederates counter-attack Buell's force on the second day.

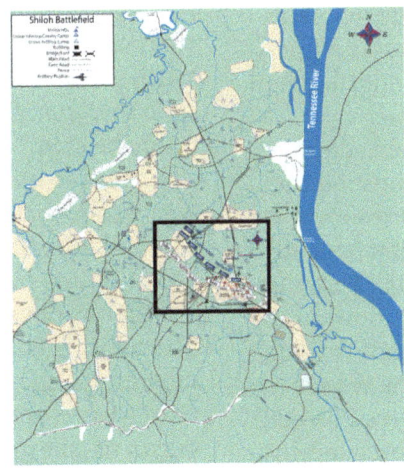

Map's Location on the Battlefield

with Col. William Sooy Smith's 11th Brigade of Crittenden's neighboring division, counterattacked the counterattackers, leading yet another charge across Sarah Bell's blood-soaked field. This time the Federals drove the Confederate infantry back from the Hamburg-Purdy Road and surged toward the Confederates' Washington Artillery battery.

The New Orleans gunners pumped some 60 rounds of canister into the onrushing Yankees, slowing but not checking them. The gunners decided it was time to leave. According to Louisiana cannoneer, John Pugh, the decision was a bit late: *"The balls [bullets] were falling around us like hail, and before we could get ready three horses at my piece and the same at two others were killed, our sergeant was killed, and Lieut. Slocomb wounded, and we had to run, leaving these three pieces on the field."*

A Washington artillery officer galloped up to the 19LA and the Crescent Regiment, both in reserve south of the road. *"For God's sake, boys, hurry up or our battery is gone!"* he cried. The two regiments charged the Yankees at the abandoned battery. In fierce hand-to-hand fighting, 6KY (Union) Col. W. C. Whitaker used his saber to cleave the skull of at least one young Rebel who tried to yank him off his horse. In the confusion and smoke, Union Sooy Smith's men unleashed a volley into Hazen's Union brigade, creating even more chaos. The Federals finally gave up and fell back, but not before spiking the three guns – jamming their fuse ports with mud and rendering them temporarily useless.

Col. John C. Moore
1824 - 1910

But the issue was far from settled. The Federals now regrouped, counterattacked, and pushed the Louisianans back well past the Hamburg-Purdy Road. Then the Confederate 1MO, hidden beneath the brow of a hill, rose up and blasted the Federals, sending *them* reeling. With the Yankees now on the run, the Crescent Regiment charged again, driving the blue soldiers back through the Davis Wheat Field and into the underbrush; once there, the Federals about-faced and ambushed the Confederates, now forcing *them* to withdraw. But Hazen's brigade was shattered in this crazy, see-saw battle, having

Chapter 21 - Confederate Counterattacks

suffered more than half the loss of Nelson's entire division during the battle.

More Slaughter in Sarah Bells Cotton Field

Brig. Gen. William Sooy Smith
1830 - 1916

While the fighting raged in the Davis Wheat Field, just to the east, Union Col. Bruce's Kentucky brigade fought to regain control of the Sarah Bell Field. Again it was a bloody, see-saw battle. The Union 13KY lost a third of its men on this same field where so much blood had been spilled the day before. The Union 2KY regained the woods between the Sarah Bell Field and the Davis Wheatfield, overrunning one gun in the process – probably from Capt. Hugh McClung's Tennessee Battery. Bruce eventually retired his brigade when Hazen's and Smith's brigades to the west fell back.

For the moment, the increasingly weary Confederates had managed, just barely, to check Bull Nelson's tough, fresh division.

Somewhere in this chaotic fighting, future explorer Henry Morton Stanley and the Dixie Grays advanced across an open area when the Federals opened fire. There being *"no convenient tree or stump,"* Stanley spotted a shallow depression ahead and raced toward it. He dived into it and began firing, *"becoming so absorbed with some blue figures in front of me"* when, *"to my speechless amazement I found my companions had retreated!"*

As he rose from his hollow, Stanley heard, *"Down with that gun, Secesh, or I'll drill a hole through you!"* Then, he said, *"two men sprang at my collar and marched me into the ranks of the terrible Yankees. I was a prisoner!"*

Meanwhile, Beauregard would spend much of the day shuffling regiments from one part of the field to another as desperate commanders called for help. The fighting continued like this throughout the morning with small, fierce attacks, but the Confederates were exhausted and outnumbered, and they began to give ground as the men sensed they were losing; by now most of them knew the Federals had been reinforced and that Johnston was dead. They fought on like cornered animals, still dangerous, making the Yankees pay for every foot of ground. But numb with exhaustion and shell-shock, they were losing hope and growing weaker as the day progressed.

"We Don't Give a Damn!"

Just prior to Hardee's counterattack around 11:30am, Confederate Moore's troops were warned that Col. John Martin's brigade (Breckinridge's Corps) was somewhere to their front and under no circumstances should they fire on it. The 2TX, the left wing of Moore's brigade, had the hard part – advancing out of the underbrush and into the open of Sarah Bell field, west of the River Road.

According to one of the Texans, *"The silence was oppressive. I do not remember that on our way across the open space, a command was given or a word spoken."*

Some 200 yards ahead, on the northern edge of the field, a large unit of troops appeared out of the smoke. The Texans were cautioned not to fire – that must be Martin's brigade. The Texans kept advancing. Suddenly, the mysterious unit unleashed a terrific volley, decimating the Texan ranks. *"Our line seemed actually to wither and curl up,"* according to one Texan. When one Confederate raised his rifle to fire back, an officer threatened to blow his head off, still insisting those were friendlies in front.

The Texans had enough of *this*! They fled the field, and no amount of threats or pleas could coax them back in ranks. Hardee sent word that he would call them *"a pack of cowards"*; the Texans sent his courier back with their reply: *"We don't give a damn if you do!"*

> *Stanley ended up in the dreaded Camp Douglas prison camp in Chicago, where the dead were carted off daily. He talked himself out of the place by agreeing to join the U.S. Navy, from which he promptly deserted and escaped to his native Wales.*

> *"The silence was oppressive. I do not remember that on our way across the open space, a command was given or a word spoken."*

> **Description of Sarah Bell's Cotton Field on the 2nd day.**
>
> *"...all the wretched debris of battle still littered the spongy earth as far as one could see, in every direction. Dead horses were everywhere...ammunition wagons standing desolate behind four or six sprawling mules. Men? There were men enough; all dead..."*
> 1st Lt. Ambrose Bierce
> Co. C, 9IN

Chapter 21 - Confederate Counterattacks

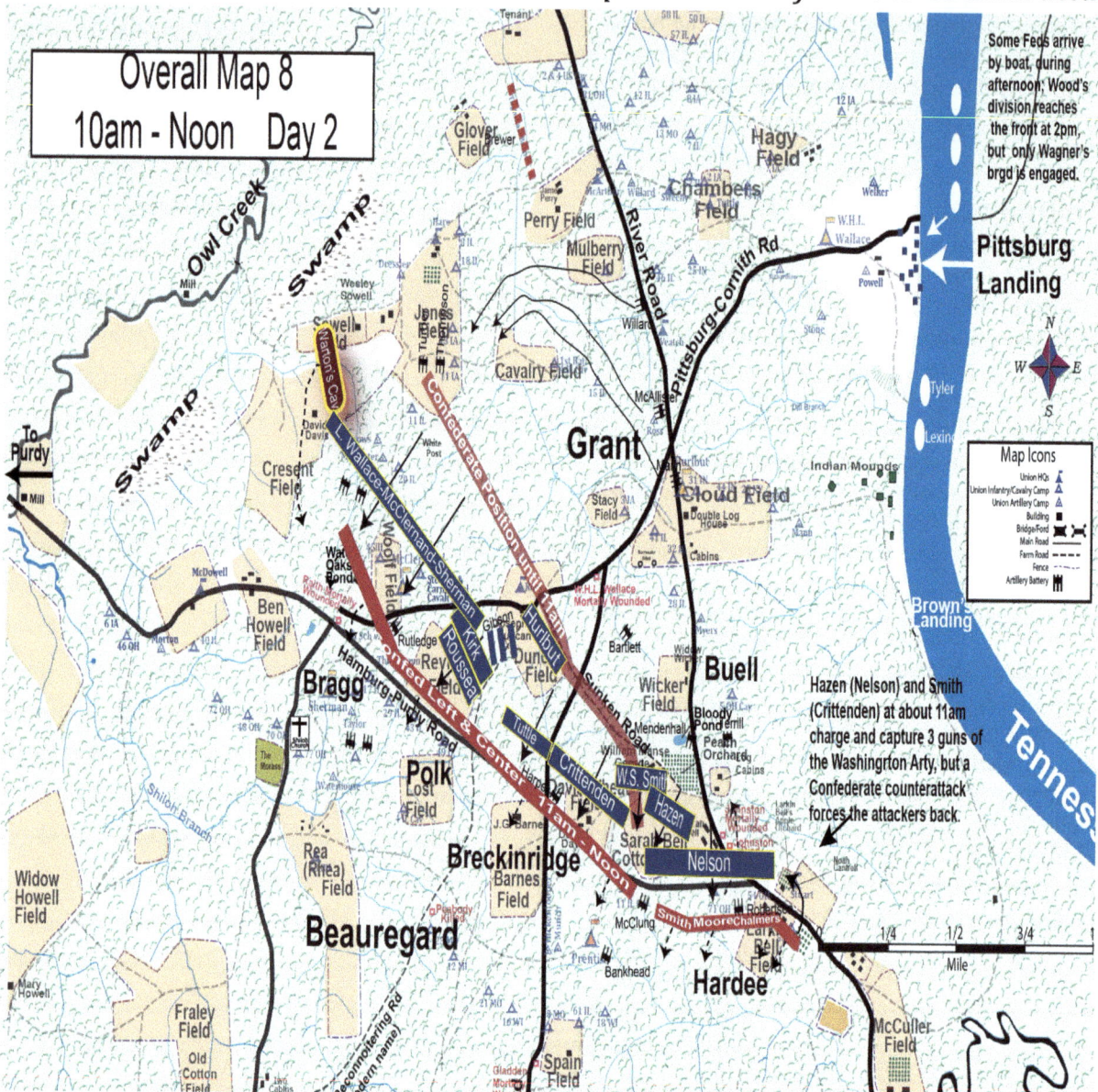

The Confederates continue to resist fiercely as the Federals relentlessly drive them back. But in the process, the Confederates make one or more counterattacks, especially in Buell's sector.

22   Grant Attacks

DAY TWO OF THE BATTLE

Tilghman Branch
6:30am – 9am, April 7

Early on the morning of April 7th, Grant ordered Lew Wallace to advance to the west, crossing the gorge of Tilghman Branch. Waiting on the high bluff on the opposite side of the branch was Confederate Capt. William Ketchum's Alabama Battery, supported by Col. Preston Pond's brigade, newly deployed into line along the top of the bluffs. Pond's unit, by accident, was the most advanced Confederate infantry that morning; somehow he hadn't gotten the word to pull back to the Yankee tents the previous evening.

Col. Preston Pond Jr.
1823 - 1864

Wallace, probably wisely, elected not to immediately send his infantry across Tilghman Branch and up its 50-60 feet ravine. First, he wanted to soften up the Rebel position, particularly its artillery. He called up Lt. Charles Thurber's and Capt. N. S. Thompson's batteries for the job. The two Federal gun crews engaged in a 30 minute duel with Ketchum's gunners before one of the Federals' shots dismounted one of Ketchum's guns, causing Pond to withdraw both the battery and his infantry back to the south end of Jones Field.

So now Wallace's troops crossed the ravine of Tilghman Branch with no losses and scaled the bluffs on the far side. Wallace had managed his advance over the ravine well, except for one thing – it was slow; a consistent problem with him.

Retaking Jones Field
9am – 12 noon

Having seized the bluffs on the west side of Tilghman Branch, Wallace faced virtually no opposition, with his men on the left flank of the Confederate army, exactly where he had hoped to be on the previous day. Using the swamps along the Owl Creek bottoms to shield his own right flank, he initially decided to wheel his division left, from the west to the southwest, and attack the exposed Confederate

Modern photo of Tilghman Branch, looking north.

left flank. He had overwhelming numbers in this sector, giving him a perfect opportunity to destroy the Confederate army. Had he attacked immediately, Lew Wallace would today probably be famous as the Union hero of Shiloh.

But again he halted his advance; this time because Sherman's division hadn't yet caught up to support Wallace's left flank. And he continued to remain stationary in the face of even more temptation – Confederate Gen. Ruggles unwisely ordered Pond's brigade to another part of the field, leaving only scattered Confederate units to resist any Federal advance.

Detecting Pond's departure, Thurber's Federal artillery shelled the marching column. This in turn drew counter fire from a Confederate battery at the south end of the field, creating *"a fine artillery duel,"* according to Wallace. Taking advantage of the uneven terrain, Wallace ordered his men into the woods and lower ground, sheltering his troops from the barrage. A Capt. Emmons, for one, appreciated it, writing of *"the skill of our commander in taking advantage of the hills and causing us to lie down, shells and cannonballs flying close overheads."*

Then Louisiana and Arkansas infantry from Gibson's brigade, and even Confederate cavalry, got the order to attack Thurber's battery. As Gibson's men prepared to charge, a soldier in the 4LA discovered a fife on the ground. Having been a fifer in the Regular Army during the Mexican War, the soldier picked up the instrument and began playing *Dixie*. Both sides listened as the shrill notes drifted over the still battlefield. Then Beauregard rode down the line shouting, *"The day is ours! One more charge and we have the victory!"* With a storm of cheers, the weary Southern farm boys surged forward, as they had countless times in the last two days.

They succeeded in getting among Thurber's guns in hand to hand fighting, and for some moments the blue cannoneers defended their guns by swinging hammers, axes, and ramrods, while the screaming gray infantry surged in with gun butts and bayonets. Finally Union infantry from Morgan Smith's brigade arrived and drove off the attackers, rescuing the cannon.

Sherman's division now lined up on Wallace's left. Sherman's men may have been recruits yesterday, but they were veterans today – at least those who survived Sunday and remained in ranks and today they formed a determined, though short and ragged, line of battle.

Chapter 22 - Grant Attacks

Finally convinced that his left flank was safe, Wallace renewed his advance, continuing to wheel his three brigades left in echelon. Smith's and Thayer's brigades, both out in the open field at the same time, apparently made quite an impressive sight with their neat formation and fluttering flags; at least they impressed the Confederates on the other side of Jones Field, who quickly withdrew.

Meanwhile, just to the east, Sherman's and McClernand's decimated divisions also advanced across Jones Field, where they were soon checked in the timber south of the field by three decimated Confederate brigades under Brig. Gen. Ruggles. The Federals halted and reformed their line before continuing their advance around 10:30am.

Oddly, the word of Buell's arrival during the night hadn't reached Lew Wallace's troops. But just as the Federal advance began, word reached them that Buell's army had landed. The news was electrifying. According to one of Wallace's troopers: *"Then we advanced yelling like we were wild ... And they [Rebels] ran – not retiring in good order, but they ran for their lives."*

Ruggles' exhausted men fell back toward Woolf Field.

Increasingly desperate to stop the Union tide, Bragg ordered what remained of Cleburne's brigade, less than 800 men, to counterattack. Cleburne protested that his left flank would be completely in the air. The courier returned with Bragg's command to proceed with the charge. Cleburne did, but his attack was soon broken.

Now Anderson's brigade surged forward to try to blunt the Federal drive. The first Yankee regiment they encountered was the 53OH, formerly commanded by Col. Jesse Appler, who had fled the field on the morning of the first day. Though the 53rd was one of Sherman's regiments, today it was attached to McClernand. When Anderson's men opened fire, the Buckeyes immediately raced for the rear – running had now become a habit with the 53OH.

McClernand, disgusted at their *"disgraceful and cowardly"* action, ordered the regiment from the field, which was fine with the 53OH.

With his three brigades, McClernand quickly broke Anderson's attack and pressed the Federal advance toward The Crossroads.

The Texas Rangers Try to Help

By 9am, Pond's Confederate infantry had been pushed back toward the Hamburg-Purdy Road, leav-

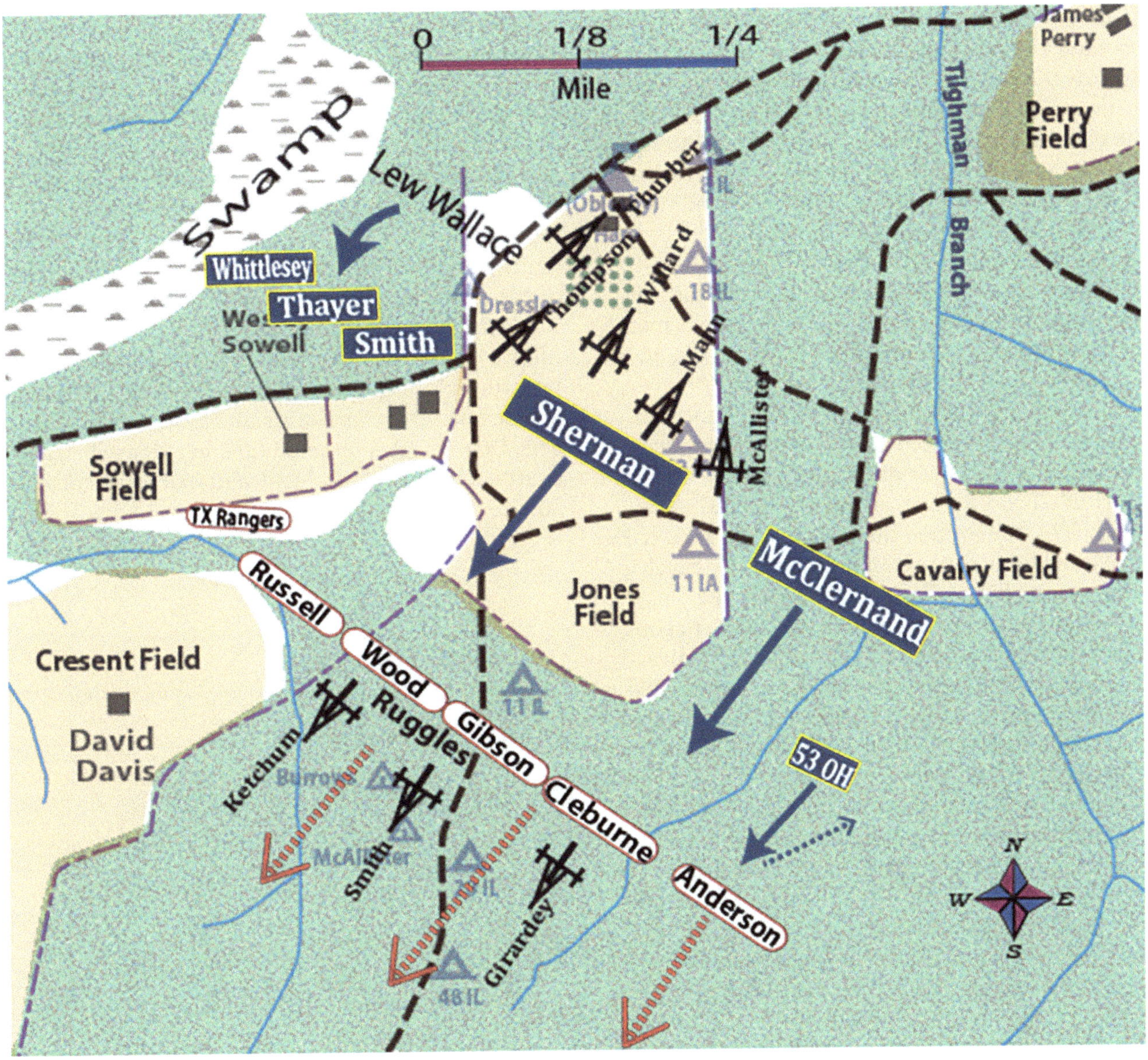

Grant's men retake the ground lost the previous day, constantly pushing the Confederates back step by step.

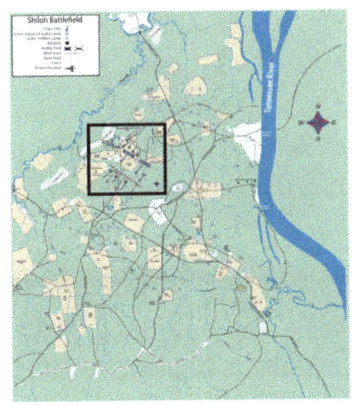

Map's Location on the Battlefield

Chapter 22 - Grant Attacks

ing Ketchum's battery and the Texas Ranger cavalry to conduct a rear-guard action.

By now the Confederate army was flailing wildly like an exhausted boxer, determined to remain on its feet and still swinging, but hopelessly over-matched, Lew Wallace's fresh Union division finished clearing out the southern edge of Jones Field, and then continued its left wheel into another field to the west, Sowell Field, until the battle line faced south. Col. Thayer's brigade had ended up on the far right flank of the Union line since Col. Whittlesey's men had not been able to keep up in the wheel due to the rough ground on that far end of the line.

Still engaging retreating Confederate infantry to his front, Thayer noticed a band of Rebel cavalry attempting to pass his right flank. This was Col. John Wharton's Texas Ranger regiment, ordered by Beauregard to ride around the Yankee flank and strike the Union line in the rear in one of the few cavalry actions of the battle. To avoid being flanked, Thayer ordered his right flank regiment, the 23IN, to shift its battle line 100 yards farther to the right, directly blocking the path of the Texas horseman. The Texans, riding in single file due to the terrain, were now themselves flanked because the Federals could fire straight down their line.

Wharton and his troopers in the lead opened fire with their fast-shooting carbines, hoping the rest of the troopers behind them would have time to catch up and spread out in a battle line before they were shot to pieces. But it was no use. Wharton's horse was shot from under him, and many of his troops were toppled from their saddles. Desperate, Wharton pulled his men back and ordered them to dismount, hoping to form a proper skirmish line on foot. But in a cavalry vs. infantry slugging match, the Texans were soon getting the worst of it. Mercifully, orders came from Beauregard to fall back and cover the retirement of other Confederate forces on the left.

As Wharton later described it, *"I was sacrificing the lives of my men, fighting 30 men against at least a regiment, [which had] the advantage of position, and with no prospect but that the men would all be killed as they came into view, as they could only advance in single file."*

After a brief pause to again regroup and allow Whittlesey's brigade to catch up, Wallace's division pressed on. At around this same time, Confederate Brig. Gen. Ruggles directed Gibson's weary brigade to attack toward Jones Field, and that attack also failed.

Col. Morgan L. Smith
1822 - 1874

Col. John M. Thayer
1820 - 1906

Col. Charles Whittlesey
1808 - 1886

Wallace's brigade commanders - Smith, Thayer and Whittlesey

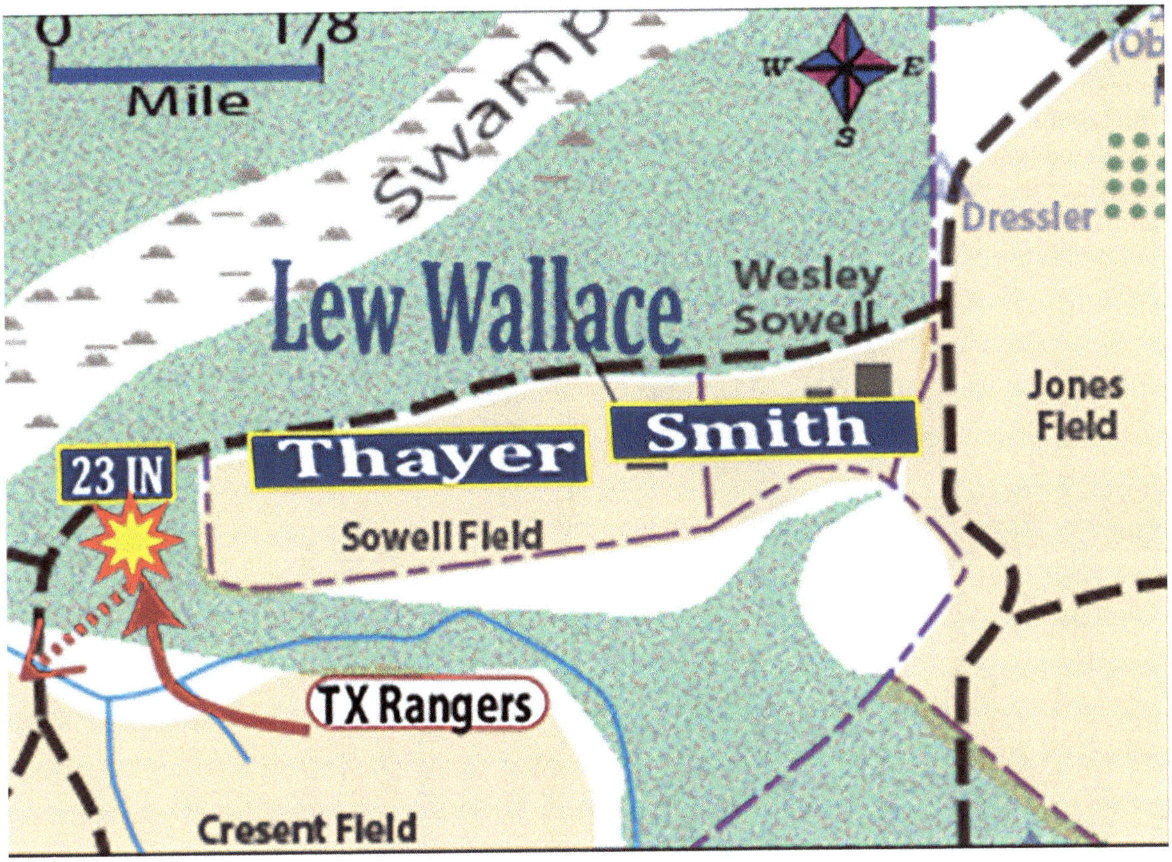

The Federals block a cavalry attack by the Texas Rangers

Col. John A. Wharton (w)
1828 - 1865

Wharton, a former Texas attorney, would survive the war only to be shot dead during a quarrel in a Houston hotel in April 1865. The shooter was Col. George W. Baylor, an aide to Albert Sidney Johnston.

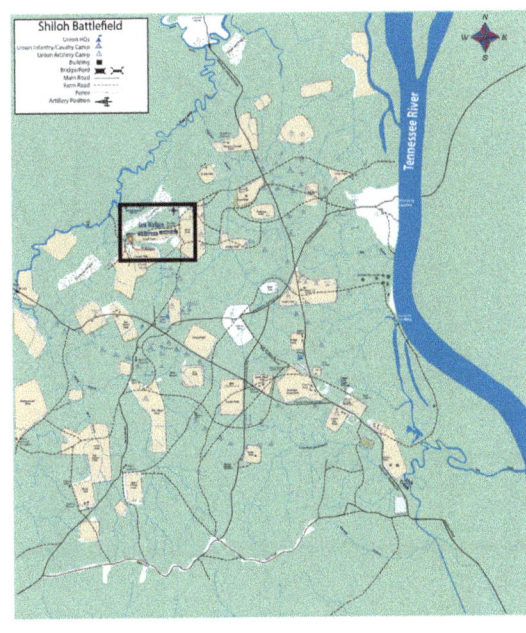

Map's Location on the Battlefield

Chapter 22 - Grant Attacks

In Hindsight

Lew Wallace commanded a fresh and well rested division, his men had full ammo pouches and they outnumbered Confederate Pond's brigade five to one. Grant expected Wallace and his fresh troops to strike like a tiger. But Wallace advanced timidly both at Tilghman Branch and at later at Jones Field. This disappointed Grant, who was already extremely unhappy with Wallace's tardy arrival on the field the evening before.

Grant would soon relieve Wallace.

Wallace's concern about his men's welfare did pay off with a low casualty rate. Of the 7,337 men in his division, there were only 491 casualties (6.7% - very low by Civil War standards). But a more aggressive advance earlier in the day might have won the entire battle.

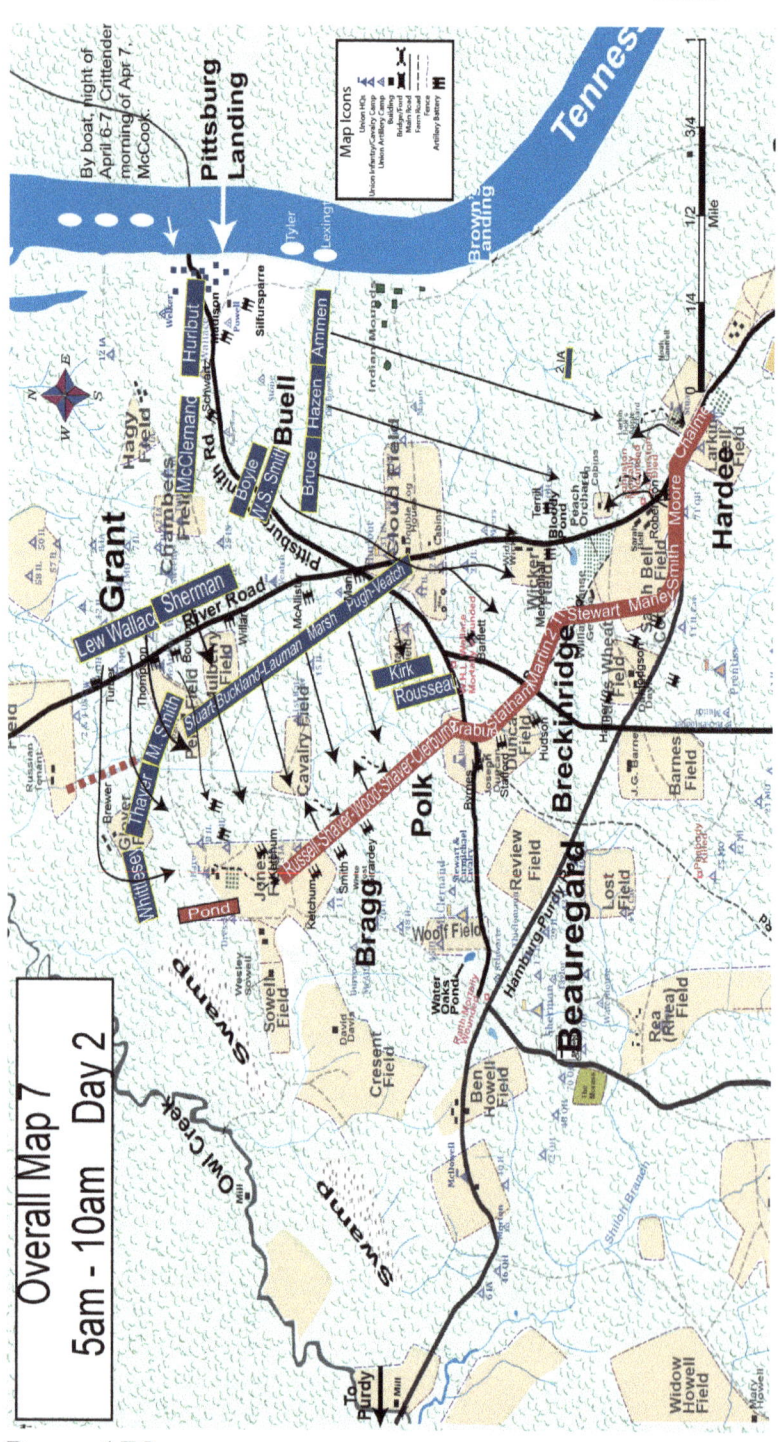

Grant's army presses the Confederates on the Federal right, relying especially on Lew Wallace's 7300 fresh troops. However, Wallace moves slowly, possibly losing an opportunity to crush the Confederates' weak left flank. Nonetheless, the Confederates are being pushed back and approaching exhaustion.

23 Final Attacks & Withdrawal

DAY TWO OF THE BATTLE

12pm - 2pm, April 7

While Grant's Army of Tennessee in Jones and Sowell fields battled its way closer to The Crossroads, with McClernand and Sherman approaching from the north and Lew Wallace from the northwest, elements of Buell's Army of the Ohio slugged its way southwestward from Pittsburg Landing, linking up with Grant's line.

The Confederate left in the west was being overwhelmed; Bragg desperately tried to stitch together a defense line he hoped would halt the Federal advance at least temporarily. Ironically, help came from Lew Wallace. Having repulsed the minor cavalry attack by the Texas Rangers, and finally advancing after Sherman's arrival on his left flank, Wallace now grew concerned that if he pursued the enemy farther in the current direction (southeast) his men would become entangled with Sherman's neighboring division. So he again halted his division and began the time-consuming process of wheeling his line back to the right in order to scoot some distance west before turning south and continuing the attack.

Bragg was the main beneficiary of this maneuver since it gave him time to reform his lines. That done, he put up a stiff fight not only against Grant's columns, but also against Buell's troops advancing from the northeast.

But the exhausted Confederates were coming to believe that damn Yankees just sprouted out of the ground like mushrooms.

Responding to an urgent order from Bragg, Maj. Gen. Cheatham rushed five regiments past Shiloh Church, formed a line of battle, and advanced to the Crossroads, where they were joined by Wood's brigade, now down to less than 650 men. At Bragg's order, the Confederates stepped off their counterattack. Wood, at the head of his men, plunged straight across the waste-deep water of Water Oaks Pond – the same pond Confederates fought their way across the day before. Cheatham meanwhile rode back and forth in front of his line, waving a battle flag and encouraging his men. In some of the heaviest fighting of the second day, the attack then continued on across Woolf Field, pushing Sherman's and McClernand's division back 300 yards.

Brig. Gen. Sterling M. Wood (w) 1823 - 1891

Though Bragg's counterattack had driven Sherman's and McClernand's divisions back, it also exposed the Confederate's left flank to Wallace, who was now once again in a position to destroy the Confederate army. Instead, he went over to the defensive and even momentarily considered retreating. The Confederates attacked him but couldn't drive him back – particularly due to his right flank regiment, the 11IN, which fought fiercely to hold its position.

Now, still more fresh Federal troops joined the battle; McCook's division of Buell's army, with Brig. Gen. Lovell Rousseau's brigade in the lead, marched up Corinth Road and struck the right flank of Bragg's line in Woolf Field. Once again fierce fighting erupted, with the two sides surging back and forth across the ground with charge and counter-charge. Sherman declared that the firing was *"the severest musketry fire I've ever heard."*

> *"[It was] the severest musketry I have ever heard."*

To support the Confederate line, Capt. Arthur Rutledge's Tennessee Battery raced up and dropped trails just east of The Crossroads, firing into the Yankee positions for a half hour.

At one point a desperate Beauregard galloped up to the 18LA and Orleans Guards Battalion (now combined as one unit) and seized the colors of the latter. The flagstaff holding the banner was a hollowed relic of Fort Sumter, and had been sent by Beauregard to New Orleans earlier in the war. He now personally led the Louisianans to the left of Bragg's line, shouting "*Charge them, charge them*

Maj. Gen. Benjamin D. Cheatham (w) 1820 - 1886

Page 179

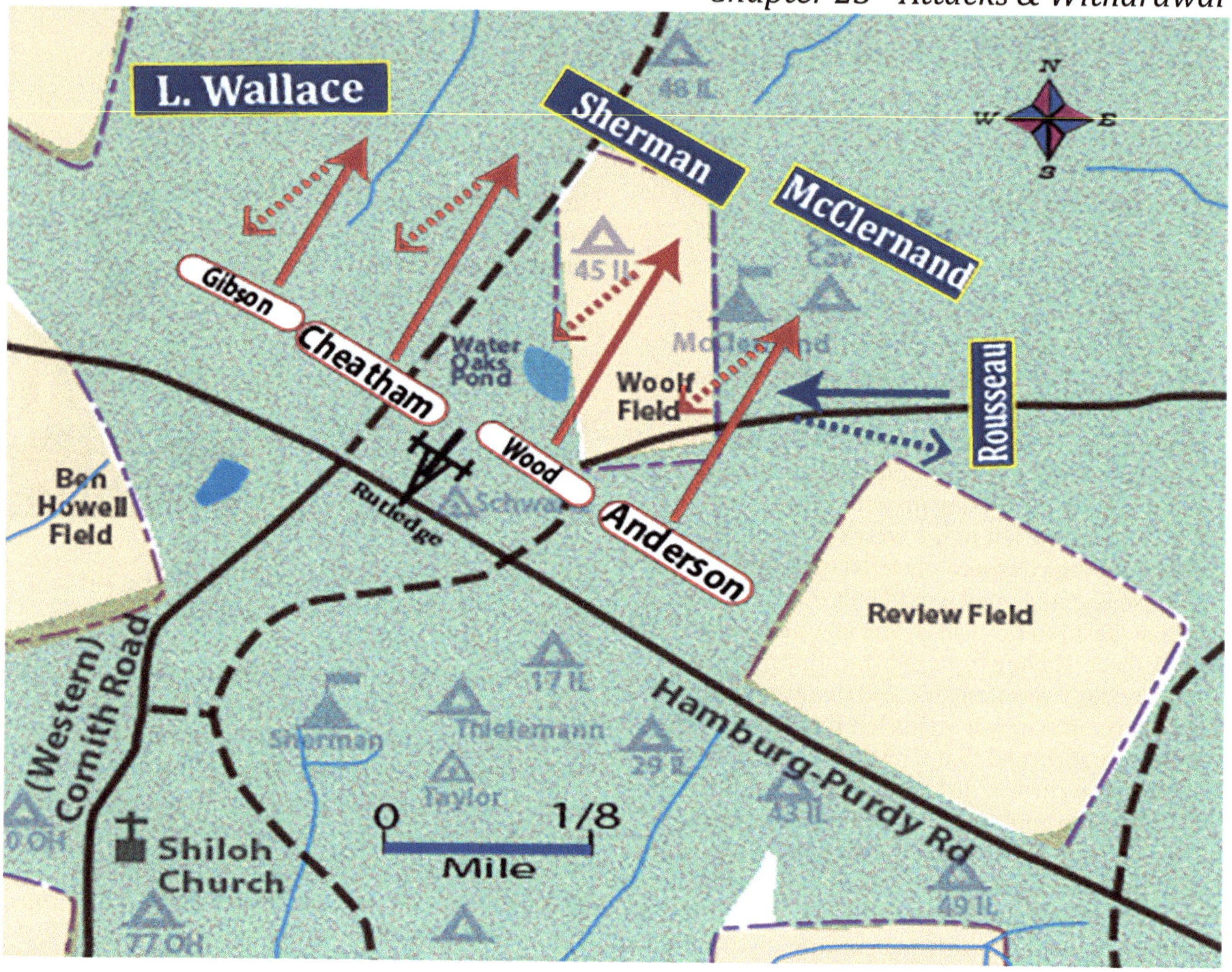

Chapter 23 - Attacks & Withdrawal

The last, desperate Confederate assaults

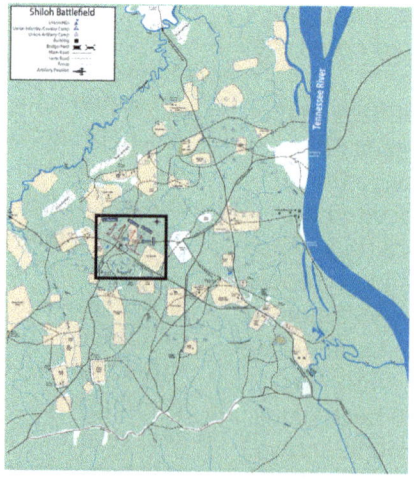

Map's Location on the Battlefield

my braves!" A private pleaded with the general not to expose himself to the enemy's fire. Beauregard's blood was up and he snapped: *"Never mind my good fellow, you do your duty and I'll do mine."* The private replied that it was his duty to die and not to general's. The army commander smiled and moved to the rear. But then Beauregard, who doctors thought should be in bed, returned to the church and led two Tennessee regiments into position, although he was too frail to carry their heavy battle flags.

But gradually the Confederates were pushed back to the Hamburg-Purdy Road. The fighting now rippled east into the southern edge of Review Field. Reduced to plugging holes in a cracking dam, the Confederates rushed troops into Review Field, including the 20TN and remnants of other regiments - the 7KY under. Col. Charles Wickliffe and the 20LA under August Reichard. They were met on the opposite side of the road by the fresh Union regiments of Colonels William Gibson's and George Wagner's brigades of Buell's army. Confederate Wickliffe, a West Pointer and Mexican War veteran, was mortally wounded with a shot to the head. Slowly, very slowly, the Southerners gave ground to the inexorable Federal advance, until by 2:00pm the Yankees held the Hamburg-Purdy Road.

Retreat
2pm - 5pm

By early afternoon the Confederates were clearly being overwhelmed. Though they refused to quit, fighting for every foot of ground, the disorganized and exhausted men were nearing a complete collapse. Col. Thomas Jordan, the officer who had drawn up the initial battle plan, now asked Beauregard, *"General, do you not think our troops are in the condition of a lump of sugar, thoroughly soaked with water, but yet preserving its original shape, though ready to dissolve?"* Beauregard sadly agreed, stating that he intended to give the withdrawal order in a few minutes.

At 3pm, the retreat commenced. *"It was sad beyond measure ..."* Bragg later wrote to his wife. The retreat was orderly, aided by a feeble Federal pursuit and covered by a Rebel rear-guard of about 2,000 infantry of Wood's and Trabue's brigades, along with 12 to 15 guns. At one point, to keep the Yankees at bay, the Southerners even launched a quick counterattack, allowing Beauregard and the rest of his army to depart through Rea Field – the same field where they began their attack the day before – a thousand years ago, before they'd seen the elephant. After all their hard fighting, not an inch of ground had changed hands.

"It was sad beyond measure."

The cavalry tried to set fire to the Yankee tents, but many were so rain-soaked that they didn't catch fire. Much of the captured artillery and other valuable loot had to be left since there weren't enough horses available. But Beauregard did find room for the 34 Federal flags – national, state and regimental – taken from the Yankees during the battle.

By 5pm, the Confederates were gone.

Grant Doesn't Follow

If there was a "lost opportunity" at Shiloh, it was probably Grant's failure to aggressively pursue the beaten Rebel army after the battle, as it slipped and slid through the mud over two jam-packed roads back to Corinth. Had he done so, the Civil War in the west might have ended then and there. But the Federal army did little to hinder the Confederates' departure. Grant later claimed he didn't feel he had the authority to order Buell's fresher troops to pursue the retreating enemy, while Buell stated that Grant was the senior commander and he gave no order to pursue. The truth probably is that everyone in the Union army, probably most of all Grant, had more than enough of the Confederate army for the moment – much like McClellan after Antietam, and Meade after Gettysburg. Sherman said as much; when asked years later why there was no pursuit of the Rebels, he said,

"I assure you, my dear fellow, we had had quite enough of their society for two whole days, and were only too glad to be rid of them on any terms."

And so the Battle of Shiloh was over.

The battle was the Confederacy's best chance to break the string of Union victories that had begun with Forts Henry and Donelson the preceding February. If the Confederates had those 15,000 troops lost at Fort Donelson, and/or had they attacked one or two days sooner, they might have won. They fought valiantly and nearly pulled it off. But not quite.

Close, but no cigar.

Postscript: The Battle of Fallen Timbers
April 8th

Actually, there *was* a minor, but mean, scrap the day after the battle, on April 8th, notably mainly for

Chapter 23 - Attacks & Withdrawal

The Confederates in withdrawal

the ferocity of one man who would remain a thorn in the side of the Union army, and especially in Sherman's side, for the rest of the war. That man was Nathan Bedford Forrest – a former Memphis slave trader.

Tuesday morning Forrest and 350 cavalry – consisting of about 150 of his own men, plus some Texas Rangers and a few other horsemen – were patrolling the Ridge Road, guarding the Confederate rear from any pursuing Yankees. Meanwhile, to make sure the Confederates were indeed retreating, and not merely reforming for another attack, Grant ordered Sherman to scout the roads south of the Landing.

So down the road came Sherman with a heavy force of two infantry brigades and the 4IL Cavalry regiment. Along the way he found many Rebel hospital tents containing hundreds of wounded, dying, and dead from both sides. Sherman arrested the Rebel surgeons but then paroled them on the condition that they continue treating the wounded and then turn themselves in to the Federals as prisoners.

Presently, the Federals spotted some Southern horsemen in a muddy cotton field bordered by a clearing of fallen timber – trees cut down by farmers – several hundred yards wide.

Col.
Nathan Bedford Forrest (w)
1821 - 1877

Sherman sent forward two companies of the 77OH as skirmishers, followed by the remainder of the decimated regiment – about 240 men in all – to scout the roads south of the Landing. The skirmishers proceeded to push back the small group of Rebel troopers, who fought dismounted and slowly retreated. But it was a trap. Forrest, who could see that the Yankees were having trouble maneuvering through the fallen timber and a small creek, ordered the bulk of his force to charge.

Suddenly "*a fierce yell filled the air,*" according to a 77OH lieutenant, and hundreds of Rebel horsemen – Forrest's troopers plus Texas Rangers – armed with shotguns, pistols and sabers, thundered over a ridge straight at the Yankee skirmish line. The Federal skirmishers took off on a dead run back to their main line. And right behind the skirmish line, the screen of Federal cavalrymen also broke and fled back toward the main line. But the surprised Federal infantrymen on the main line fired their weapons prematurely; they then tried to make a stand with a double line of fixed bayonets. But the Confederates, with Forrest in the lead, smashed through their ranks, shooting, slashing and cutting down Federals. Sherman admitted that he and his staff were put on the run, "*through the mud, with pistols already emptied, closely followed by Forrest and his men.*"

"Suddenly a fierce yell filled the air."

With a loss of no more than 20 of his men, Forrest had killed 15, wounded 25 and captured 53 Yankees. (Forrest grumbled that he wished the Yankee prisoner hadn't surrendered, so he could have killed them all).

Sherman began reforming his line and called up his second brigade. Forrest, either out of excitement or because his horse bolted, depending on who tells the story, charged on his own, crashing into the waiting line of blue infantry. Shouting "*Kill him! Knock him off that horse!,*" Federals tripped over each other to get at the rider, who slashed at them right and left with his saber. Finally one Federal shot Forrest at point-blank range, the ball lodging against his left hip next to the spinal column, numbing one of his legs and leaving it dangling. Forrest spurred his horse and escaped in the woods to the south. According a biography written in 1906, Forrest yanked a Yankee soldier up on the saddle behind him to cover his escape. But that seems unlikely, given Forrest's fresh wound, and given that he only had two hands, one of which was clasping his saber and probably the other holding his reins or a pistol. Also, Forrest himself never mentioned it.

Sherman, who probably witnessed the action, would in the coming years have plenty of reasons to wish his men had killed Forrest that day. The two implacable foes shared many traits, including genius and possibly a touch of madness.

But anyway it was clear that the Confederate cavalry was just a rear guard, protecting the withdrawal

Chapter 23 - Attacks & Withdrawal

of the army, and so Sherman withdrew. Even though he had just received a bloody nose in this scrap, he returned to the main battlefield to the thunderous cheers of the troops. Despite their stormy beginning, Sherman and the volunteer troops had now bonded. He would soon be calling them "*his boys*," and they would be calling him "*Uncle Billy*." It was the beginning of one of the Civil War's great love stories.

Amazingly, though painfully wounded, Forrest would be back in the saddle within two months. He was probably the last casualty of the battle of Shiloh.

Forrest buffs may be disappointed to hear that the story about him grabbing a Yankee for protection as he escaped probably didn't happen. On the other hand, one story that apparently IS true is that he was leading a charge 1864 when his horse was shot in the neck, hitting the artery.

Forrest plugged the hole with his finger and kept on charging.

After driving off the Yankees, he got off the horse and pulled out his finger, and the horse keeled over dead.

During the war Forrest would drive Sherman into towering rages by attacking his long and vulnerable supply line, and he was undoubtedly a major catalyst behind Sherman's daring decision to cut his supply lines in Atlanta and let his men eat their way through Georgia – gutting the Confederacy.

But a decade or so after the Civil War, war with Spain appeared imminent. By now Sherman was Commander of the Army and Forrest was nearly destitute, living in a log cabin in Tennessee. Hoping for employment, Forrest wrote Sherman requesting a position in the army. With regret, Sherman replied a week later that even if the war should happen, it probably would be naval war, and so cavalry probably wouldn't be needed.

But Sherman sent a letter to the War Department with a note stating that "he regarded Forrest as one of the most extraordinary men developed by our Civil War and were it left to me in event of a war requiring cavalry I would unhesitatingly accept his services and give him a prominent place. I believe now he would fight against our national enemies as vehemently as he did against us, and that is saying enough."

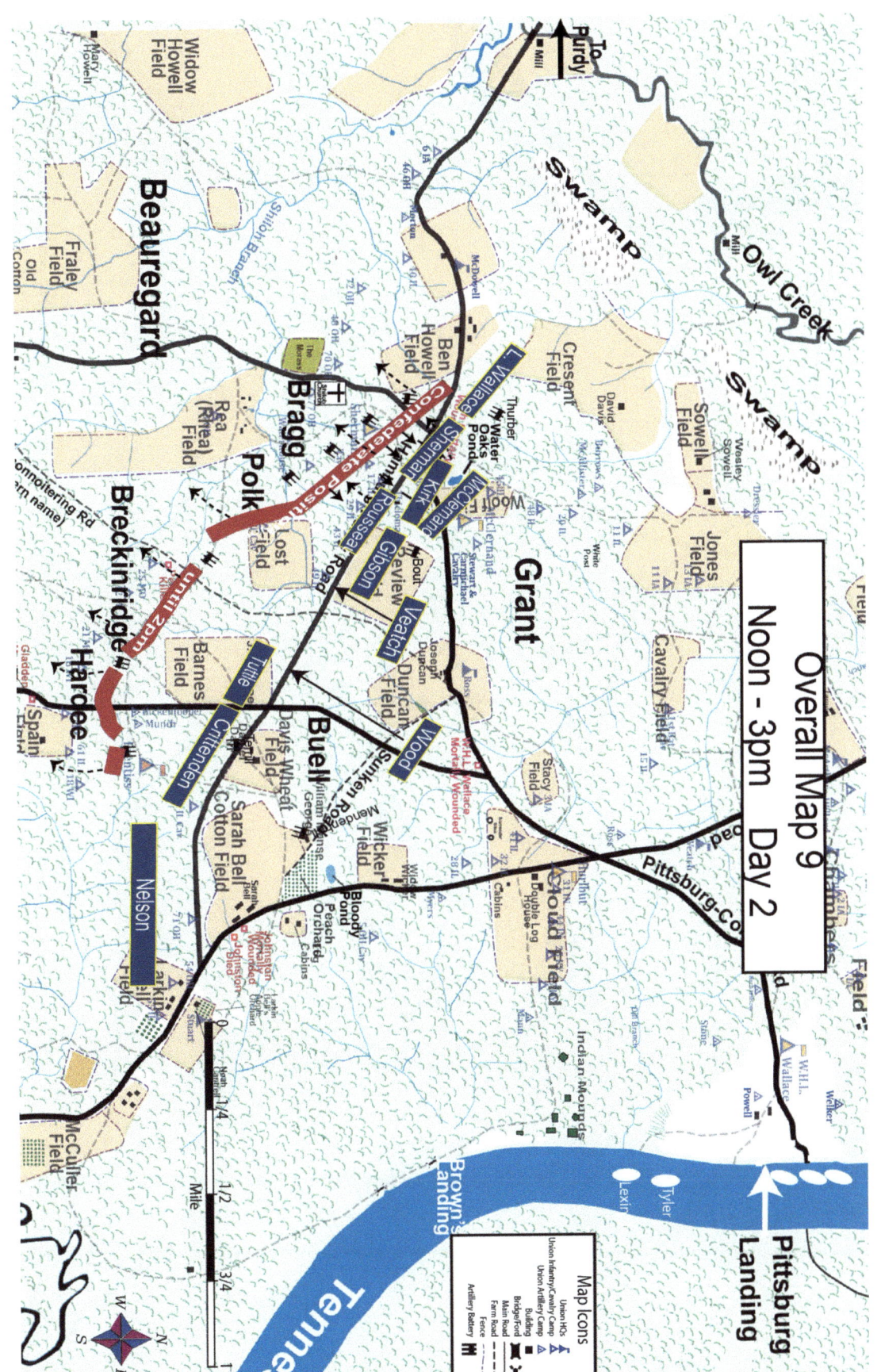

By about 3pm, the Confederate line is approaching total collapse, and Beauregard orders a retreat.

Overall Map 9
Noon – 3pm   Day 2

Chapter 23 - Attacks & Withdrawal

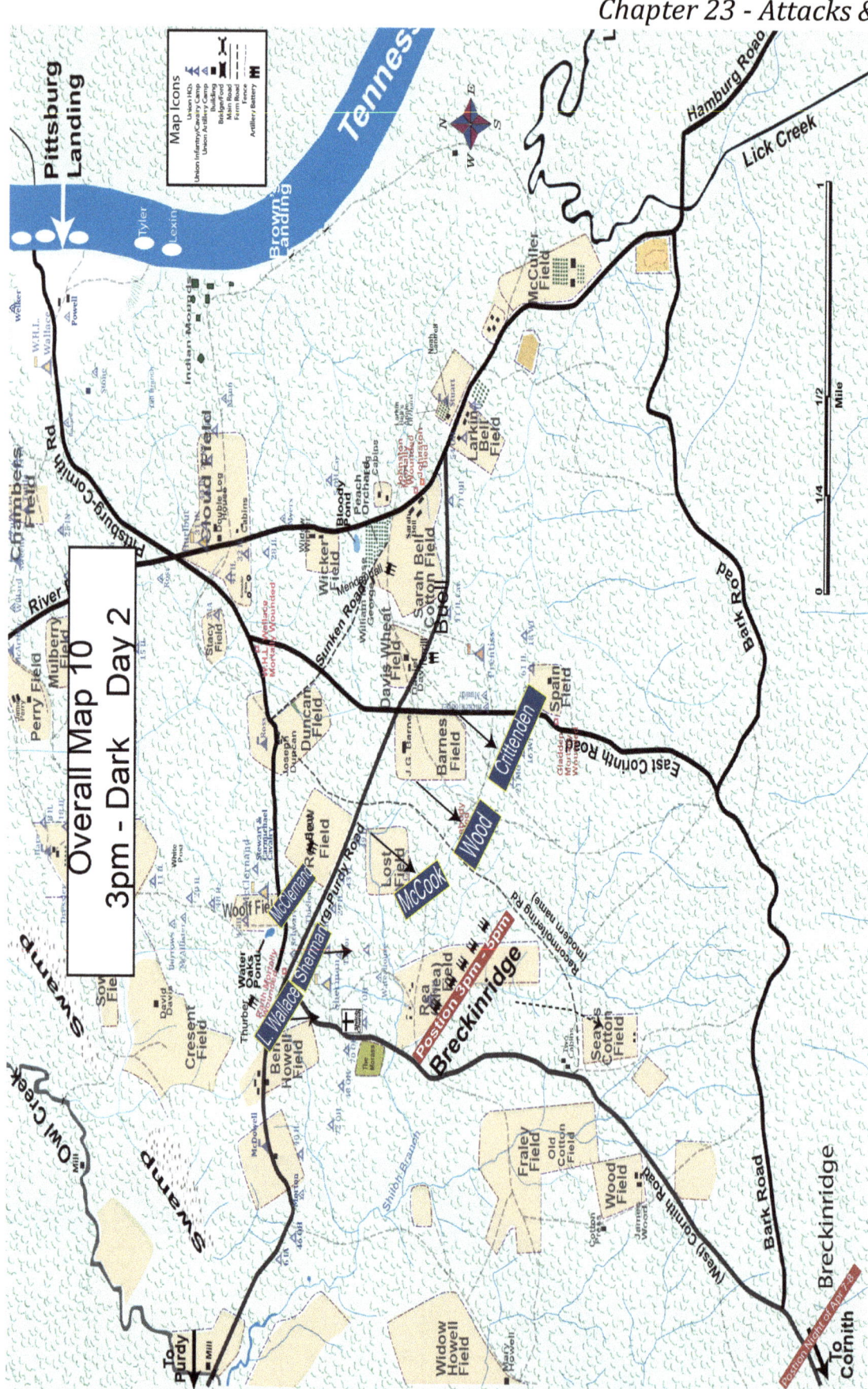

As the Confederates retreat, units from Breckinridge's corps form a rear guard and even make brief counter attacks. But by dark, the Confederates are gone.

24 Aftermath

The Battlefield

The departed Confederates left in their wake a man-made disaster the likes of which had never been seen on the American continent, and rarely seen since. The exhausted Union army, almost in shock, had to immediately contend with thousands of rotting and mangled corpses of men and horses, and nearly 10,000 wounded, and all of them threatened to spread disease. Besides the swarms of fat flies gorging on carrion, plus the overwhelming stench which would last for days, if not weeks, the field was littered with the debris of battle – wrecked wagons and tents, artillery pieces, and discarded weapons. Food was scarce to nonexistent. Grant's men had no food or personal effects because their tents had been raided. Buell's men had no food or personal effects because they had left everything back at Savannah in their haste to reach Pittsburg Landing.

The Federals were dealing with 8,400 wounded Union soldiers and 1,000 wounded Confederates. The main hospital was the small log cabin on the bluff at the Landing, located approximately where the U.S. flag stands at the modern National Cemetery. Incredibly, for the first couple of days, often only one surgeon was available due to fatigue. There were few standing tents; so the vast majority of the wounded had to lay out in the rain for two days. There was not even straw for bedding, so they lay on the ground. And once the wounded were finally evacuated to transports, their ordeal wasn't over. According to William Swan of the 3IA, who was among the wounded taken aboard a transport, "*... nearly every spot upon which a man could lie was occupied – on boxes, and under tables; the floor of the cabin was covered. No surgeons attended the wounded, and from Sunday night to Wednesday morning the patients had no water – hundreds begged for water.*"

Gen. McClernand found his tent perforated with 27 bullet holes, declaring that, "*Within a radius of 200 yards of my headquarters tent, the ground was literally covered with dead.*" A wounded Rebel had staggered inside McClernand's tent, dying with his head resting on the general's desk.

"Within a radius of 200 yards of my headquarters tent the ground was literally covered with dead."

The dead horses were gathered into huge mounds, doused with kerosene, and burned. The sickening smell of burning flesh wafted over the battlefield for days. By Thursday most of the dead soldiers on both sides were buried, though for decades thereafter bones would be discovered throughout the timber and brush.

The Union dead were buried in trenches. It was only after the war that their bodies were re-interred into what is now the National Cemetery overlooking the Tennessee River.

The Park Service today identifies five Confederate mass-grave locations, but there were almost certainly more. It's also very likely that many exhausted and hungry Union privates, who hadn't joined the army to dig graves for their enemies, simply pitched many Rebel body parts into the fires along with the horses, or dumped them into the many deep, brush-covered ravines. According to one Union soldier, "*The Rebels were buried with as little concern as I would bury a dog.*" Nine-year-old Confederate sympathizer, Elsie Duncan, agreed: "*The Yankees did not bury the Confederate dead. They threw them into the gullies and ravines and covered them with leaves and left them for the hogs to root up and eat up. This I know to be the truth. I could not understand anyone to be so heartless to leave a human being unburied even if they were a rebel - they were dead.*"

On April 8th, a Confederate officer was halted four miles from Michie's Farm, bearing a message from Beauregard to Grant, requesting permission to send details through the lines to bury the Confederate dead. Grant wrote back: "*Owing to the warmth of the weather I deemed it advisable to have all the dead of both parties buried immediately. Heavy details were made for this purpose, and it is accomplished.*"

But despite Grant's assurances, it took until Friday and possibly Saturday, four or five days after the battle, before the last of the wounded would be located on the field and removed to a field hospital. And for the wounded laying out in the woods, wild hogs were a serious threat. Droves of hogs could be heard wandering about, devouring dead and wounded men alike, their sounds "*unmistakable, quarreling over their carnival feast.*"

Chapter 24 - Aftermath

And the field hospitals – houses, barns and tents woefully inadequate in the best of circumstances – were overwhelmed with thousands of Union and Confederate wounded. The surgeons worked 20 hour days, much of that time spent sawing off limbs (Doctors back then were called "surgeons" or "sawbones" for good reason. Their primary tool was a small saw that looked like a modern hacksaw, and was used in exactly the same manner). And once a young soldier lost a limb, his future was grim – there not being much demand for one-legged, or even one-armed, farmers.

It would be a week after the battle before the army could deliver adequate provisions by steamer to Pittsburg Landing. When the steamers did arrive, as many as 40 boats lined up two or three deep at the Landing. Scores of sacks of corn were scattered over the muddy bank to create better footing.

Back at the Cherry Mansion in Savannah, the man who had led the Federals to Pittsburg Landing, Maj. Gen. C. F. Smith, lingered on until finally dying of his infection on April 25th. His name is barely known today, but had he lived, he might have been one of the most important generals of the Civil War.

Grant's Problems

The first news reports in the North announced a great victory at Shiloh. Lincoln proclaimed a day of celebration. One paper even printed an illustration of Grant on horseback, waving his sword and leading a charge.

But days later, a reporter named Whitlaw Reid of the *Cincinnati Gazette* didn't hold back. (Some believe he actually witnessed the battle by slipping aboard Grant's boat while it was stopped at Crumps Landing, but that seems far-fetched).

He told the real story, albeit slightly exaggerated, in shocking detail, about the blundering, stupidity and cowardice – especially the failure to fortify and reconnoiter – that resulted in a battle that not only was "*not a great victory for the Union, but a near disaster.*" He also discussed the embarrassing scene of thousands of stragglers hugging the river bank at the Landing.

In Reid's article, only Buell emerged as a hero, causing Sherman to suspect that it was Buell who furnished Reid with much of the information for the story. Reid's story wasn't the first to report the true facts of the battle, but it was the story that stunned the North.

Furthermore, many "stragglers" who fled the battle were the first on the transports back north and, once safely in taverns at the various river towns, for the price of a beer they were more than happy to tell any reporter how fouled up the whole operation was. So even wilder stories began to circulate, such as Union soldiers were bayonetted in their tents.

Grant at first denied being surprised and insisting he had been attacked by 70,000 Confederates, stating, "*If the enemy had sent us word when and where they were to attack us, we could not have been better prepared,*" though he soon dropped these ridiculous lies. But neither Grant nor Sherman ever frankly admitted that they were surprised by the Confederate attack.

In truth, despite all Grant's mistakes, Shiloh was indeed a great victory that solidified the Union's hold on both the Tennessee Valley and the Upper Mississippi Valley. And another Confederate stronghold, Island No. 10, fell to the Federals the day after Shiloh. Memphis fell soon after that, and Union gunboats would soon be sailing all the way down to Vicksburg, Mississippi. But at the moment, all those benefits were eclipsed by the terrible casualty list and the stories of how close the Federals came to defeat.

Grant's head was definitely on the chopping block; even his troops knew he had grossly underestimated the threat of a Confederate attack. And the Northern public was stunned at the butcher's bill. The casualties in the two-day battle exceeded the combined casualties of all of America's previous wars. Grant was criticized for being caught by surprise without fortifications, which was true, and for being drunk during the battle, which was not true. Grant's fall from grace after Shiloh was as fast as Johnston's after Fort Donelson. Now, instead of being hailed as

---

In his memoirs Buell would write about Grant and his army's situation:

"*An army comprising 70 regiments of infantry, 20 batteries of artillery, and a sufficiency of cavalry, lay for two weeks and more in isolated camps, with a river at its rear and a hostile army claimed to be superior in numbers 20 miles distant in its front, while the commander made his headquarters and passed his nights 9 miles away on the opposite side of the river. It had no line or order of battle, no defensive works of any sort, no outposts, properly speaking, to give warning, or check the advance of an enemy, and no recognized head during the absence of the regular commander.*"

Dead horses burned on the battlefield near the Peach Orchard.   Library of Congress

Shiloh Field Hospital

Chapter 24 - Aftermath

the hero of Fort Donelson, Grant was being castigated in the media and in the halls of Congress as a fool and a drunk.

Halleck, arriving at the Landing four days after the battle, was more than happy to take up one of his major projects – neutralizing Grant and removing a potential rival. Halleck himself was behind much of the criticism of Grant; he wrote a letter to a fellow general in Washington, describing Grant as "*little more than a common gambler and drunk.*"

Taking personal command of Grant's and Buell's armies, Halleck also summoned the army of Maj. Gen. John Pope, which had just seized Island Number 10 and New Madrid on the Mississippi River the day after the Shiloh battle ended. With his consolidated army now numbering almost 125,000 men, Halleck planned to assault Corinth. But rather than leaving Grant in command of the largest component in this new force, the Army of Tennessee, Halleck turned the command over to Maj. Gen. George Thomas, and instead named Grant to the meaningless post of second-in-command.

Grant had at least one stout defender – Sherman. Amazingly, by some miracle, Sherman escaped media criticism himself; in fact, he was pronounced a hero and promoted to major general! He used his new clout to spew out letters to important politicians, denouncing those who criticized Grant and soon returned to his favorite subject – those dirty newspapers. "*When a man is too lazy to work, & too cowardly to steal, he becomes an editor & manufactures public opinion.*" His brother John, the U.S. Senator from Ohio, advised him to shut up, but he wouldn't.

Grant considered resigning, and history gives Sherman credit for talking him out of it, though some feel Grant had already changed his mind by the time Sherman talked to him. Whatever they discussed, it probably had a lot to do with Grant eventually choosing Sherman as western commander when Grant was sent east.

Actually, Grant *did* have one other friend – Abraham Lincoln. When it was clear that Grant had made major mistakes at Shiloh, and when the appalling casualty list was known, and when everyone in the country was yelling for Grant's head, and when Lincoln was being heavily criticized for not sacking him, a good friend of Lincoln's, A. K. McClure, visited the President in the Old Cabinet Room and spent two hours detailing every reason why

"I can't spare this man; he fights."

Grant should be fired. The weary President, his feet propped up by the fire on the high marble mantel, said little. But finally, staring at the fireplace, he spoke with finality: "*I can't spare this man; he fights.*"

Grant would keep his job.

Retreat to Corinth

No matter how miserable the Federals were back at Pittsburg Landing, their problems paled in comparison to those of the Confederates, for their return march to Corinth was a true horror. First of all, the Southerners had no choice but to use the same two muddy roads used in their march to Shiloh – Monterey Road and Ridge Road. The roads, already badly churned during the Confederate advance, were now quagmires. Monterey Road was by far the worst. "*I am not exaggerating when I inform you that all the way the mud was knee deep, and we were obliged to wade several streams which were waist deep,*" Pvt. Thomas Robertson wrote his mother. The usually hard-bitten Bragg sounded almost hysterical when he notified Beauregard on April 8th, "*Troops utterly disorganized and demoralized. Road almost impassable ... Our artillery is being left all along the road by its officers; indeed, I find but few officers with their men... The whole road presents a scene of rout.*" At around 2pm the following day, Bragg dismounted 200 cavalry to use their horses to haul artillery. Fatigue parties were put to work in repairing the muddy road. Bragg later stated that if the Federals had pursued, the entire rear of the Confederate army would have been destroyed.

According to a sergeant of the 17LA, "*The trip back to Corinth used me up worse than the battle as we were gone five days and slept about ten hours during that time. We ate nothing almost, traveled very hard, and it rained on us every night.*"

It rained not only every night of the march but every night for 10 days after the battle. It also turned cold, and the rain became hail.

According to a 47TN private, "*We have been without anything to eat but two crackers per day since Sunday morning & traveled in water & mud waist deep all day.*" An artilleryman of Ketchum's battery said, "*The men looked as if they did not have life enough left in them to move ... Completely saturated with rain, and .. standing in mud ankle deep all night.*"

The wounded suffered the most. "*Some of them as they jostled along over the rough road in spring-*

less wagons gave most pitiful groans, which made me forget I was hurt," recalled one passenger. About 300 wounded died in the retreat and were dumped along the road. Some of the more seriously wounded were left to die in homes along the way. Only those who couldn't walk were allowed to ride in the wagons, leaving the walking wounded with mangled arms and gouged eyes to trudge 22 miles through the mud.

Throughout the battle, wagons had been continuously carting wounded back to Corinth, their constant arrival shocking the town residents. And now the town was flooded with the mass of torn and broken bodies that arrived with the main army.

When the men finally stumbled into Corinth, their ordeal wasn't over. The surgeons now got busy with their saws. "*The Railroad platform is almost covered with coffins and wounded soldiers – every train brings some anxious parents looking after their sons,"* wrote one soldier. Another soldier from Louisiana, walking past a church filled with wounded, noticed a ghastly sight, casually sitting out back – a large box "*filled with feet and arms & hands. It was so full that horrible & bloody feet protruded out of the top."*

Corinth was now a gigantic hellhole of misery, with wounded jammed for days in churches, schools, and homes. Running out of space, hundreds were simply laid out on porches, sidewalks and railroad platforms. The sweet smell of gangrene was everywhere. Not surprisingly, many of the men died of pneumonia – a killer at that time – especially given the soldiers' weakened condition. Eventually the wounded would be shipped out to hospitals throughout Mississippi and Tennessee.

Morale was a rock bottom. "*The camp, once so gay, so joyous, now lay under the pall of death. Everywhere prevailed a mournful silence,"* according to one of the Orleans Guardsmen. "*Everyone was hushed in sadness."*

As one Southern writer later said, the South never smiled again after Shiloh.

> **"The camp, once so gay, so joyous, now lay under the pall of death. Everywhere prevailed a mournful silence. Everyone was hushed in sadness."**

> **"Every train brings some anxious parent looking after their sons."**

The Corinth Campaign
April 8 - May 30, 1862

Halleck, who had never commanded a Boy Scout troop in the field, now commanded 125,000 men in three armies. He began his Corinth campaign by grandly announcing to Washington that he would "*leave here tomorrow morning and our army will be before Corinth by tomorrow night.*" That didn't quite happen. Halleck's 22 mile advance on Corinth has been almost universally described as "*glacial.*" It took him three weeks just to begin rolling his massive army southward, after which it creeped along, averaging two thirds of a mile per day for the next month. Determined not to be caught by a surprise like Grant, Halleck ordered his troops to elaborately entrench along an eight mile front every night, much like the Roman army. He had his engineers corduroy and bridge the roads, and made sure the wooded roads intersected between his armies' camps for mutual support. Obviously, his cavalry scouts where hyper-vigilant to any possible enemy approach, but there was no enemy on the road except in Corinth and in Halleck's mind.

At first Halleck estimated that Beauregard had 75,000 troops; but the estimates grew each day until it reached 200,000. In fact, even with the arrival of Gen. Earl Van Dorn's 15,000 men from Arkansas, Beauregard could muster no more than 52,000 fit for duty, due to losses at Shiloh plus the outbreak of disease at Corinth.

Halleck's snail's pace practically begged the Confederates to take back the initiative. But doing so required a daring commander, which Beauregard was not. In any case, he was in poor health, and he did have serious military issues – including being badly outnumbered and facing serious supply and transportation problems.

On May 29, with the town about to be surrounded, Beauregard realized he could no longer hold Corinth. Overnight he carried out a masterful evacuation, complete with ordering his troops to cheer when the trains chugged into Corinth (It was actually just one locomotive that ran day and night on different tracks), along with military bands, bugles, and drums, giving the Yankees the impression that massive reinforcements were arriving – when in fact they were departing. He sent out "deserters" to wander into the Federal camps, telling tales

Page 191

of new Confederate regiments arriving from other locations. And he set up logs to look like massive siege guns defending the Rebel fortifications, much as he had done in Virginia to fool McClellan.

It worked splendidly. Federal Gen. John Pope reported to Halleck, "*The enemy is reinforcing heavily, by trains, in my front and on my left. The cars are running constantly and the cheering is immense every time they unload in front of me. I have no doubt, from all appearances, that I shall be attacked in heavy force at daylight.*"

Meanwhile, Beauregard and his army slipped away and took up a new position in Tupelo, Mississippi, two day's march south of Corinth.

The next morning Halleck's troops warily crept into Corinth, only to find it deserted. There was practically nothing to indicate that the Confederate army had ever been there, except no doubt, the graves.

But the Union had finally seized the vital railroad junction. And within weeks the Federal army would march west a hundred miles and seize Memphis on the Mississippi River.

Halleck's slow pace and his failure to snare any part of the Confederate Army disappointed Lincoln, but at least Halleck had captured Corinth, which compared favorably to George McClellan's humiliating defeat by Robert E. Lee at the gates of Richmond, and the string of losses in the east prior to that. And so Lincoln chose to replace the difficult, erratic McClellan with "Old Brains" Halleck, as the new General in Chief of all Union armies. The promotion had two benefits: first, it put Halleck and his hemorrhoids permanently behind a desk, for which he was far better suited than a field command, and being sent to Washington was, for a bureaucrat, like being summoned to paradise. From his new post Halleck could fuss with files and papers to his heart's content, parsing words, and slipping in sly innuendos. Eventually, he would succeed in making himself despised by nearly every general in the United States Army. Lincoln would eventually say that he was "*nothing but a first rate clerk.*"

The second benefit was that he was out of Grant's hair.

Halleck's Confederate opponent had more serious political problems. Beauregard pitched his withdrawal from Corinth in glorious terms, suggesting that it amounted to a great victory. And in fact, it *was* a brilliant withdrawal. But Jefferson Davis was unimpressed. He, like many Southerners to this day, was convinced that Beauregard halted the Shiloh attack prematurely with victory in his grasp after Davis' old West Point friend, Johnston, was killed. A couple of weeks after arriving in Tupelo, Beauregard took an unauthorized sick leave. Davis quickly and permanently replaced him with Bragg.

The Civil War in the west would drag on for years. Many soldiers who faced each other for the first time at Shiloh would meet again and again at Stones River, Perryville, Champions Hill, Vicksburg, Chickamauga, and more. But the growing Union war machine, led by the relentless Grant and Sherman, would slowly, inexorably, grind down Southern resistance. And the South would never again have as great a chance of complete victory in the West, and come as close to achieving it, as it had in the terrible woods and fields around Shiloh Church in April of 1862.

There were 2 main methods used to amputate large limbs during the War: Flap and Circular Amputations. In the field the Flap Method was more widely used where time was a factor. With this method the bone was dissected and flaps of deep muscle and skin were used to close the operation. When implementing the flap method it was imperative to cut the bone away a few inches above the place where the flaps were brought together.

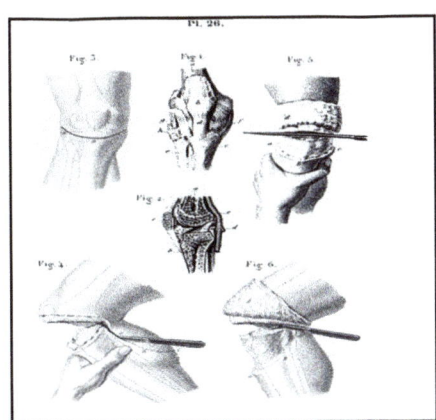 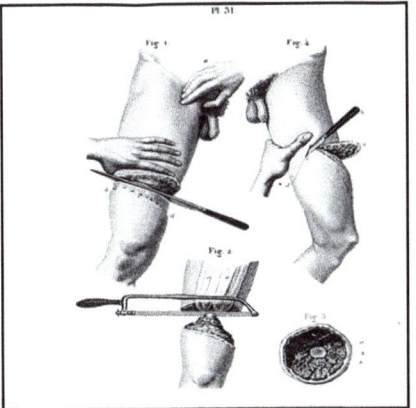

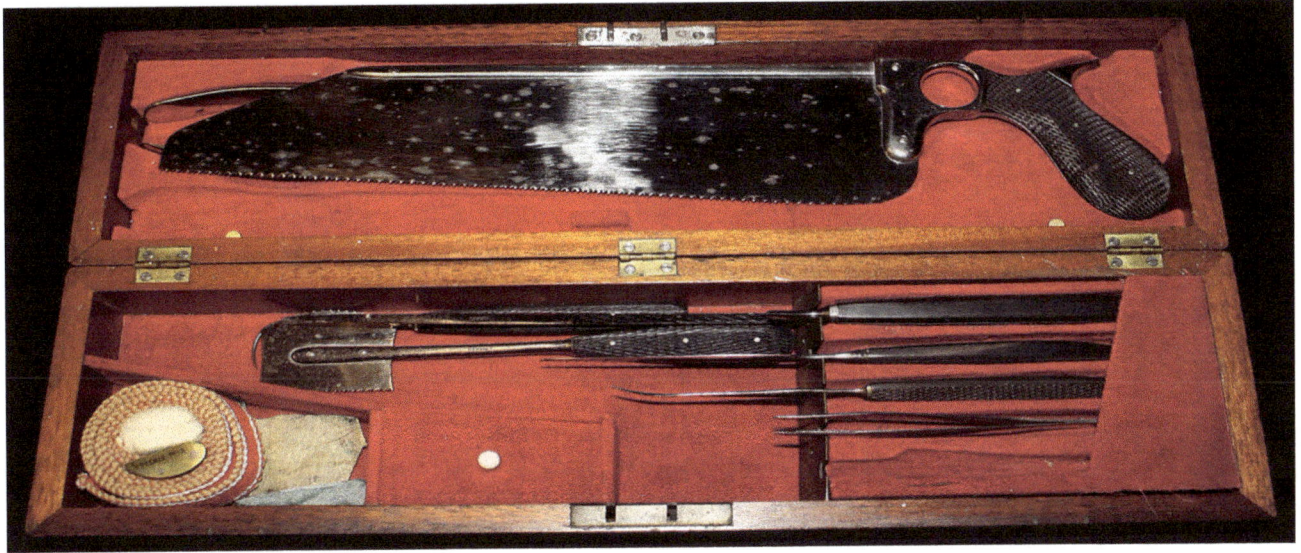

Civil War Surgeon's Kit

Chapter 24 - Aftermath

Modern Photo of Shiloh National Cemetery

Appendix A - Order of Battle
Army of Tennessee - Order of Battle
Maj. Gen. U. S. Grant, Commanding   44,894 soldiers
k = Killed   w = Wounded   mw = Mortally Wounded   d = Disabled   c = Captured

1st Division
Maj. Gen. John A. McClernand

1st Brigade
Col. Abraham M. Hare (w)
Col. Marcellus M. Crocker

8IL
Capt. James M. Ashmore (w)
Capt. William H. Harvey (k)
Capt. Robert H. Sturgess

18IL
Maj. Samuel Eaton (w)
Capt. Daniel H. Brush (w)
Capt. William J. Dillion (k)
Capt. Jabez J. Anderson

11IA
Lt. Col. William Hall (w)

13IA
Col. Marcellus M Crocker

2nd Brigade
Col. C. Carroll Marsh

11IL
Lt. Col. T. E. G. Ransom (w)
Maj. Garrett Nevins (w)
Capt. Lloyd D. Waddell
Maj. Garrett Nevins

20IL
Lt. Col. Evan Richards (w)

45IA Col. John E. Smith

48IA
Col. Isham N. Hayniea
Maj. Manning Mayfield

3rd Brigade
Col. Julius Raith (mw)
Lt. Col. Enos P. Wood

17IL
Lt. Col. Enos P. Wood
Maj. Francis M. Smith

29IL
Lt. Col. Charles M. Ferrell

43IL
Lt. Col. Adolph Endelmann

49IL
Lt. Col. Phineas Pease (w)

Artillery
Dresser's Btry D, 2 IL Arty
Capt. James P. Timony

McAllister's Btry D, 1 IL Arty
Capt. Edward McAllister (w)

Schwartz's Btry E, 2 IL Arty
Lt. George L. Nispel

Burrows' Btry, 14 OH Arty
Capt. Jerome B. Burrows (w)

Cavalry
1st Bn, 4 IL Cavalry
Lt. Col. William McCullough

Carmichael's Co. IL Cavalry
Capt. Eagleton Carmichael

Stewart's Co. IL Cavalry
Lt. Ezra King

2nd Division
Brig. Gen. W. H. L. Wallace (mw)
Col. James M. Tuggle

1st Brigade
Col. James M. Tuggle

2IA
Lt. Col. James Baker

7IA
Lt. Col. James C Parrott

12IA
Col. Joseph J. Woods (w & c)

14IA
Col. Wm. T. Shaw (c)

2nd Brigade
Brig. Gen. John McArthur (w)

9 L
Col. August Mersy

12IL
Lt. Col. Augustus L. Chetlain

13MO
Col. Crafts J. Wright

14MO
Col. B. S. Compton

81OH
Col. Thomas Morton

3rd Brigade
Col. Thomas W. Sweeny (w)
Col. Silas D. Baldwin

8IA
Col. James L. Geddes (w & C)

7IL Maj. Richard Rowett

50IL
Col. Moses M. Bane (w)

52IL
Maj. Henry Stark
Capt. Edwin A. Bowen

57IL
Col. Silas D. Baldwin
Capt. Gustav A. Busse

58IL
Col. Wm. F. Lynch (c)

Artillery
Willard's Btry A 1 IL Arty
Lt. Peter P. Wood

Richardson's Btry D, 1 MO Arty
Capt. Henry Richardson

Welker's Btry H, 1 MO Arty
Capt. Frederick Welker

Stone's Btry K, 1 MO Arty
Capt. George H. Stone

Cavalry
Co. A, 2 IL Cavalry
Capt. John R. Hotaling

Co. B, 2 IL Cavalry
Capt. Thomas J. Larison

Co. C, 2 US Cavalry
Lt. James Powell

Co. I, 4 US Cavalry
Lt. James Powell

Army of Tennessee - Order of Battle (page 2)

k = Killed   w = Wounded   mw = Mortally Wounded   d = Disabled   c = Captured

3rd Division
Maj. Gen. Lewis Wallace

1st Brigade
Col. Morgan L. Smith

11IN
Col. George F. McGinnis

24IN
Col. Alvin P. Hovey

8MO
Lt. Col. James Peckham

2nd Brigade
Col. John M. Thayer

23IN
Col. William L. Sanderson

1NE
Lt. Col. William D. McCord

58OH
Col. Valentine Bausenwein

68OH
Col. Samuel H. Steadman
(Not engaged at Shiloh - remained at Crump's Landing)

3rd Brigade
Col. Charles Whittlesey

20OH
Lt. Col. Manning F. Force

56OH
Col. Peter Kinney
(Not engaged at Shiloh - remained at Crump's Landing)

76OH
Col. Charles R. Woods

78OH
Col. Mortimer D. Leggett

Artillery
Thompson's Btry, 9 IN Arty
Lt. George R. Brown

Buel's Btry I, 1 MO Arty
Lt. Charles H. Thurber

Cavalry
3 Bn, 11IL Cavalry
Maj. James F. Johnson
(not engaged at Shiloh - remained at Crump's Landing)

3 Bn, 5 OH Cavalry
Maj. Charles S. Hayes
(not engaged at Shiloh - remained at Crump's Landing)

4th Division
Brig. Stephen A. Hurlbut

1st Brigade
Col. Nelson G. Williams (w)
Col. Isaac C. Pugh

28IL
Col. Amory K. Johnson

32IL
Col. John Logan (w)

41IL
Col. Isaac C. Pugh
Lt. Col. Ansel Tupper (k)
Maj. John Warner
Capt. John N. Nale

3IA
Maj. William M. Stone (c)
Lt. George W. Crosley

2nd Brigade
Col. James C. Veatch

14IL
Col. Cyrus Hall

15IL
Lt. Col. Edward F. W. Ellis (k)
Capt. Louis D. Kelly
Lt. Col. William Cam

46IL
Col. John A. Davis (w)
Lt. Col. John J. Jones

25IN
Lt. Col. William H. Morgan (w)
Maj. John W. Foster

3rd Brigade
Brig. Gen. Jacob G. Laumen

31IN
Col. Charles Cruft (w)
Lt. Col. John Osborn

44IN
Col. Hugh B. Reed

17KY
Col. John H. McHenry, Jr

25KY
Lt. Col. Benjamin H. Bristow
Maj. William B. Wall (w)
Capt. B. T. Underwood
Col. John H. McHenry

Artillery

Ross's Btry, 2 MI Arty
Lt. Cuthbert W. Laing

Mann's Btry C, 1 Mo Arty
Lt. Edward Brotzmann

Myer's Btry, 13 OH Arty
Capt. John B. Myers

Cavalry

1st & 2nd Bn 5 OH Cav
Col. William H. H. Taylor

Army of Tennessee - Order of Battle (page 3)

k = Killed   w = Wounded   mw = Mortally Wounded   d = Disabled   c = Captured

5th Division
Brig. Gen. William T. Sherman (w)

1st Brigade
Col. John A. McDowell (d)

40IL
Col. Stephan G. Hicks (w)

6IA
Capt. John Williams (w)
Capt. Madison M. Walden

46OH
Col. Thomas Worthington

2nd Brigade
Col. David Stuart (w)
Lt. Col. Oscar Malmborg
Col. T. Kilby Smith

55IL
Lt. Col. Oscar Malmborg

54OH
Col. T. Kilby Smith
Lt. Col. James A. Farden

71OH
Col. Rodney Mason

3rd Brigade
Col. Jesse Hildebrand

53OH
Col. Jesse J. Appler
Lt. Col. Robert A. Fulton

57OH
Lt. Col. Americus V. Rice

77OH
Lt. Col. Willis De Hass
Maj. Benjamin D. Fearing

4th Brigade
Col. Ralph P. Buckland

48OH
Col. Peter J. Sullivan (w)
Lt. Col. Job R. Parker

70OH
Col. Joseph R. Cockerill

72OH
Lt. Col. Herman Canfield (k)
Col. Ralph P. Buckland

Artillery
Maj. Ezra Taylor, Chief of Arty

Taylor's Btry B, 1 IL Arty
Capt. Samuel E. Barrett

Waterhouse's Btry E, 1 IL Arty
Capt. Allen C. Waterhouse (w)
Lt. Abial R. Abbott (w)
Lt. John A. Fitch

Morton's Btry, 6 IN Arty
Capt. Frederick Behr (k)

Cavalry
2nd & 3rd Bns, 4 IL Cav
Col. T. Lyle Dickey

Thielemann's Two Cav Cos.
Capt. Christian Thielemann

6th Division
Brig. Gen. Benjamin M. Prentiss (c)

1st Brigade
Col. Everett Peabody (k)

12MI
Col. Francis Quinn

21MO
Col. David Moore (w)
Lt. Col. H. M. Woodyard

25MO
Lt. Col. Robert T. Van Horn

16WI
Col. Benjamin Allen (w)

2nd Brigade
Col. Madison Miller (c)

61IL
Col. Jacob Fry

18MO
Lt. Col. Isaac V. Pratt (c)

18WI
Col. James S. Alban (k)

Not Brigaded

15IA
Col. Hugh T. Reid (w)

16IA
Col. Alexander Chambers (w)
Lt. Col. Addison H. Sanders

(the 15 and 16 IA were on the west side of the field in an independent command)

23MO
Col. Jacob T. Tindall (k)
Lt. Col. Quin Morton (c)

(23 MO arrived on field about 9am on Apr 6th)

Artillery
Hickenlooper's Btry, 5 OH Arty
Capt. Andrew Hickenlooper

Munch's Btry, 1 MN Arty
Capt. Emil Munch (w)
Lt. William Pfaender

Cavalry

1st & 2nd Bns, 11 IL Cav
Col. Robert G. Ingersoll

Appendix A - Order of Battle

Army of Ohio - Order of Battle
Maj. Gen. Don Carlos Buell, Commanding
17,918 soldiers
k = Killed   w = Wounded   mw = Mortally Wounded   d = Disabled   c = Captured

2nd Division **Brig. Gen.** **Alexander McD. McCook**	4th Division **Brig. Gen.** **William Nelson**	5th Division **Brig. Gen.** **Thomas L. Crittenden**	6th Division **Brig. Gen.** **Thomas J. Wood** (Division arrived on field 2pm April 7th)
4th Brigade Brig. Gen. Lovell H. Rousseau 6IN Col. Thomas T. Crittenden 5KY Col. Harvey M. Buckley 1OH Col. Benjamin F. Smith 1st Bn, 15US Capt. Peter T. Swain, Maj. J. H. King 1st Bn, 16US Capt. Edwin Townsend, Maj. J. H. King 1st Bn, 19US Maj. Stephen D. Carpenter, Maj. J. H. King **5th Brigade** Col. Edward N. Kirk (w) 34IL Maj. Charles N. Levanway (k) Capt. Hiram W. Bristol 29IN Lt. Col. David M. Dunn 30IN Col. Sion S. Bass (mw) Lt. Col. Joseph B. Dodge 77PA Col. Frederick S. Stumbaugh **6th Brigade** Col. William H. Gibson 32IN Col. August Willich 39IN Col. Thomas J. Harrison 15OH Maj. William Wallace 49OH Lt. Col. Albert M. Blackman	**10th Brigade** Col. Jacob Ammen 36IN Col. William Grose 6OH Lt. Col. Nicholas L. Anderson 24OH Lt. Col. Frederick C. Jones **19th Brigade** Col. William B. Hazen 9IN Col. Gideon C. Moody 6KY Col. Walter C. Whitaker 41OH Lt. Col. George S. Mygatt **22nd Brigade** Col. Sanders D. Bruce 1KY Col. David A. Enyart 2KY Col. Thomas D. Sedgewick 20KY Lt. Col. Charles S. Hanson **Artillery** Terrill's Btry H, 5 US Arty Capt. William R. Terrill	**11th Brigade** Brig. Gen. Jeremiah T. Boyle 9KY Col. Benjamin C. Grider 13KY Col. Edward H. Hobson 19OH Col. Samuel Beatty 59OH Col. James P. Fyffe **14th Brigade** Col. William Sooy Smith 11KY Col. Pierce B. Hawkins 26KY Lt. Col. Cicero Maxwell 13OH Lt. Col. Joseph G. Hawkins **Artillery** Bartlett's Btry G, 1 OH Arty Capt. Joseph Bartlett Mendenhall's batteries H & M, 4 US Arty Capt. John Mendenhall	**15th Brigade** Col. Milo S. Hascall 17 IN Col. John T. Wilder 58 IN Col. Henry M. Carr 3 KY Col. Thomas Bramlette 26 OH Col. Edward P. Fyffe **20th Brigade** Brig. Gen. James A. Garfield 13MI Col. Michael Shoemaker 64OH Col. John Ferguson 65OH Col. Charles G. Harker **21st Brigade** Col. George D. Wagner 15IN Lt. Col. Gustavus A. Wood 40IN Col. John W. Blake 57IN Col. Cyrus C. Hines 24KY Col. Lewis B. Grigsby

Army of Mississippi - Order of Battle
Gen. Albert Sidney Johnston (k), Gen. P. G. T. Beauregard, Commanding
40,335 soldiers
k = Killed   w = Wounded   mw = Mortally Wounded   d = Disabled   c = Captured

I Corps
Maj. Gen. Leonidas Polk

1st Division
Brig. Gen. Alexander P. Stewart
Brig. Gen. Charles Clark (w)

1st Brigade
Col. Robert M. Russell

11 LA
  Col. Samuel F. Marks (w)
  Lt. Col. Robert H. Barrow

12 TN
  Lt. Col. Tyree H. Bell
  Maj. Robert P. Caldwell

13 TN
  Col. Alfred J. Vaughan Jr.

22 TN
  Col. Thomas J. Freeman (w)

Bankhead's TN Btry
  Capt. Smith P. Bankhead

2nd Brigade
Brig. Gen. A. P. Stewart

13 AR
  Lt. Col. A.D. Grayson (k)
  Maj. James A. McNeely (w)
  Col. James C. Tappan

4 TN
  Col. Lt. Col. A.D. Grayson (k)
  Maj. James A. McNeely (w)

5 TN
  Lt. Col. Calvin D. Venable

33 TN
  Col. Alexander W. Campbell (w)

Stanford's MS Btry
  Capt. Thomas J. Stanford

2nd Division
Maj. Gen. Benjamin F. Cheatham (w)

1st Brigade
Brig. Gen. Bushrod R. Johnson (w)
Col. Preston Smith (w)

Blythe's MS Bn
  Col. A. K. Blythe (k)
  Lt. Col. David L. Herron (k)
  Maj. James Moore

2 TN
  Col. J. Knox Walker 15 TN

154 TN (Senior)
  Col. Preston Smith (w)
  Lt. Col. Marcus C. Wright (w)

Polk's TN Btry
  Capt. Marshall T. Polk (w)

2nd Brigade
Col. William H. Stephens
Col. George Maney

7 KY
  Col. Charles Wickliffe (mw)
  Lt. Col. William D. Lannom

1 TN Bn
  Col. George Maney
  Maj. Hume R. Field

6 TN
  Lt. Col. Timothy P. Jones

9 TN
  Col. Henry L. Douglass

Smith's MS Btry
  Capt. Melancthon Smith

II Corps
Maj. Gen. Braxton Bragg

1st Division
Brig. Gen. Daniel Ruggles

1st Brigade
Col. Randall L. Gibson

1 AR   Col. James F. Fagan

4 LA   Col. Henry W. Allen (w)
       Lt. Col. Samuel E. Hunter

13 LA
  Maj. Anatole P. Avengno (mw)
  Capt. Stephen O'Leary (w)
  Capt. Edgar M. Dubroca

19 LA
  Col. Benjamin L. Hodge
  Lt. Col. James M. Hollingsworth

Bains's MS Battery Capt. S. C. Bain

2nd Brigade
Brig. Gen. Patton Anderson

1 FL Bn
  Maj. Thaddeus A. McDonell (w)
  Capt. W. G. Poole
  Capt. W. Capers Bird

17 LA   Lt. Col. Charles Jones (w)

20 LA   Col. August Reichard

1 MS Cavalry
  Col. Andrew J. Lindsay

Conf Guards Bn
  Maj. Franklin H. Clack

9 TX   Col. Wright A. Stanley

Washington (LA) Artillery
  Capt. W. Irving Hodgson

3rd Brigade
Col. Preston Pond

16 LA   Maj. Daniel Gober

18 LA
  Col. Alfred Mouton (w)
  Lt. Col. Alfred Roman

(LA) Crescent Reg
  Col. Marshall J. Smith

(LA) Orleans Guard Bn
  Maj. Leon Querouze (w)

38 TN   Col. Robert F. Looney

Ketchum's AL Arty
  Capt. Wm Ketchum

2nd Division
Brig. Gen. Jones M. Withers

1st Brigade
Brig. Gen. Adley H. Gladden (mw)
Col. Daniel Adams (w)
Col. Zach C. Deas

21 AL Lt. Col. Stewart W. Cayce
       Maj. Frederick Stewart

22 AL   Col. Zach C. Deas
        Lt. Col. John C. Marrast

25 AL   Col. John Q. Loomis (w)
        Maj. George D. Johnston

26 AL Lt. Col. John G. Coltart (w)
       Lt. Col. William D. Chadick

1 LA   Col. Daniel W. Adams
        Maj. Fred H. Farrar, Jr

Robertson's AL Battery
  Capt. Felix H. Robertson

2nd Brigade
Brig. Gen. James R. Chalmers

5 MS   Col. Albert E. Fant
7 MS   Lt. Col. Hamilton Mayson
9 MS   Lt. Col. Wm A. Rankin (mw)
10 MS   Col. Robert A. Smith
52 TN   Col. Benjamin J. Lea

Gage's AL Battery
  Capt. Charles P. Gage

3rd Brigade
Brig. Gen. John K. Jackson

17 AL   Lt. Col. Robert C. Fariss
18 AL   Col. Eli S. Shorter
19 AL   Col. Joseph Wheeler
2 TX   Col. John C. Moore
        Lt. Col. William P. Rogers
        Maj. Hal G. Runnels

Girardey's GA Battery
  Capt. Isadore P. Girardey

Clanton's AL Cav
  Col. J. H. Clanton (w)

Appendix A - Order of Battle

Army of Mississippi - Order of Battle (page 2)

k = Killed   w = Wounded   mw = Mortally Wounded   d = Disabled   c = Captured

III Corps
Maj. Gen. William J. Hardee

1st Brigade
Brig. Gen. Thomas C. Hindman (w)
Col. R. G. Shaver (d)

2 AR
Col. Daniel C. Govan
Maj. Reuben F. Harvey

6 AR Col. Alexander T. Hawthorn

7 AR
Lt. Col. John M. Dean (k)
Maj. James T. Martin

3rd Confederate
Col. John S. Marmaduek

Miller's TN Battery
Capt. William Miller

Swett's MS Battery
Capt. Charles Swett

2nd Brigade
Brig. Gen. Patrick R. Cleburne

15 AR
Lt. Col. Archibald K. Patton (k)

6 MS
Col. John J. Thornton (w)
Lt. Col. W. A. Harper

2 TN
Col. William B. Bate (w)
Lt. Col. David L. Goodall

5 (35th) TN
Col. Benjamin J. Hill

23 TN
Lt. Col. James F. Neill (w)
Maj. Robert Cantrell

24 TN
Lt. Col. Thomas H. Peebles

Soup's AR Battalion
Trigg's (Austin) AR Btry
Capt. John T. Trigg

Calvert (Helena) AR Btry
Capt. J. H. Calvert

Hubbard's AR Btry
Capt. George. T. Hubbard

3rd Brigade
Brig. Gen. Sterling A.M. Wood(d)
Col. William K. Patterson

16 AL
Lt. Col. John W. Harris

8 AR
Col. William K. Patterson

9 (14th) AR Bn
Maj. John H. Kelly

3 MS Bn
Maj. Aaron B. Hardcastle

27 TN
Col. Christopher H. Williams (k)
Maj. Samuel T. Love (k)

44 TN
Col. Coleman A. McDaniel

55 TN
Col. James L. McKoin

Harper's MS Battery
Capt. William L. Harper (w)
Lt. Putnam Darden

Georgia Dragoons
Capt. Isaac W. Avery

Reserve Corps
Brig. Gen. John C. Breckinridge

1st Brigade
Col. Robert P. Trabue

4 AL Bn Maj. James M. Clifton

31 AL
Lt. Col. Montgomery Gilbreath

3 KY
Lt. Col. Benjamin Anderson (w)

4 KY Lt. Col. Andrew R. Hynes (w)

5 KY Lt. Col. Thomas H. Hunt

6 KY Col. Joseph H. Lewis

TN BN
Lt. Col. James M. Crews

Byrne's (Cobb's) KY Btry
Capt. Robert Cobb

Byrne's MS Btry
Capt. Edward P. Byrne

Morgan's Squadron KY Cav
Col. John H. Morgan

2nd Brigade
Brig. Gen. John S. Bowen (w)

9 AR
Col. Isaac L. Dunlop

10 AR
Col. Thomas H. Merrick

1 MO
Col. Lucius L. Rich

2nd Confederate
Col. John D. Martin
Maj. Thomas H. Mangum

Hudson's MS Btry
Capt. Alfred Hudson

Watson's LA Btry
Capt. Allen A. Burlsey

Thompson's Co. KY Cavalry
Capt. Phil B. Thompson

3rd Brigade
Col. Winfield S. Statham

15 MS
Maj. William F. Brantley (w)
Capt. Lamkin S. Terry

22 MS
Col. Frank Schaller (w)
Lt. Col. Charles S. Nelms (mw)
Maj. James S. Prestidge

19 TN
Col. David H. Cummings (w)
Lt. Col. Francis M. Walker

20 TN
Col. Joel A. Battle (w & c)
Maj. Patrick Duffy

28 TN Col. John P Murrary

45 TN Lt. Col. Ephraim F. Lytle

Rutledge's TN Btry
Capt. Arthur M. Rutledge

Forrest's Reg TN Cavalry
Col. Nathan B. Forrest (w)

Unattached
Wharton's TX Reg Cavalry
Col. John A. Wharton (w)

Wirt Adams MS Reg Cav
Col. Wirt Adams

McClung's TN Battery
Capt. Hugh L. W. McClung

Roberts AR Battery
Capt. Franklin Roberts

Appendix C - Army Organization

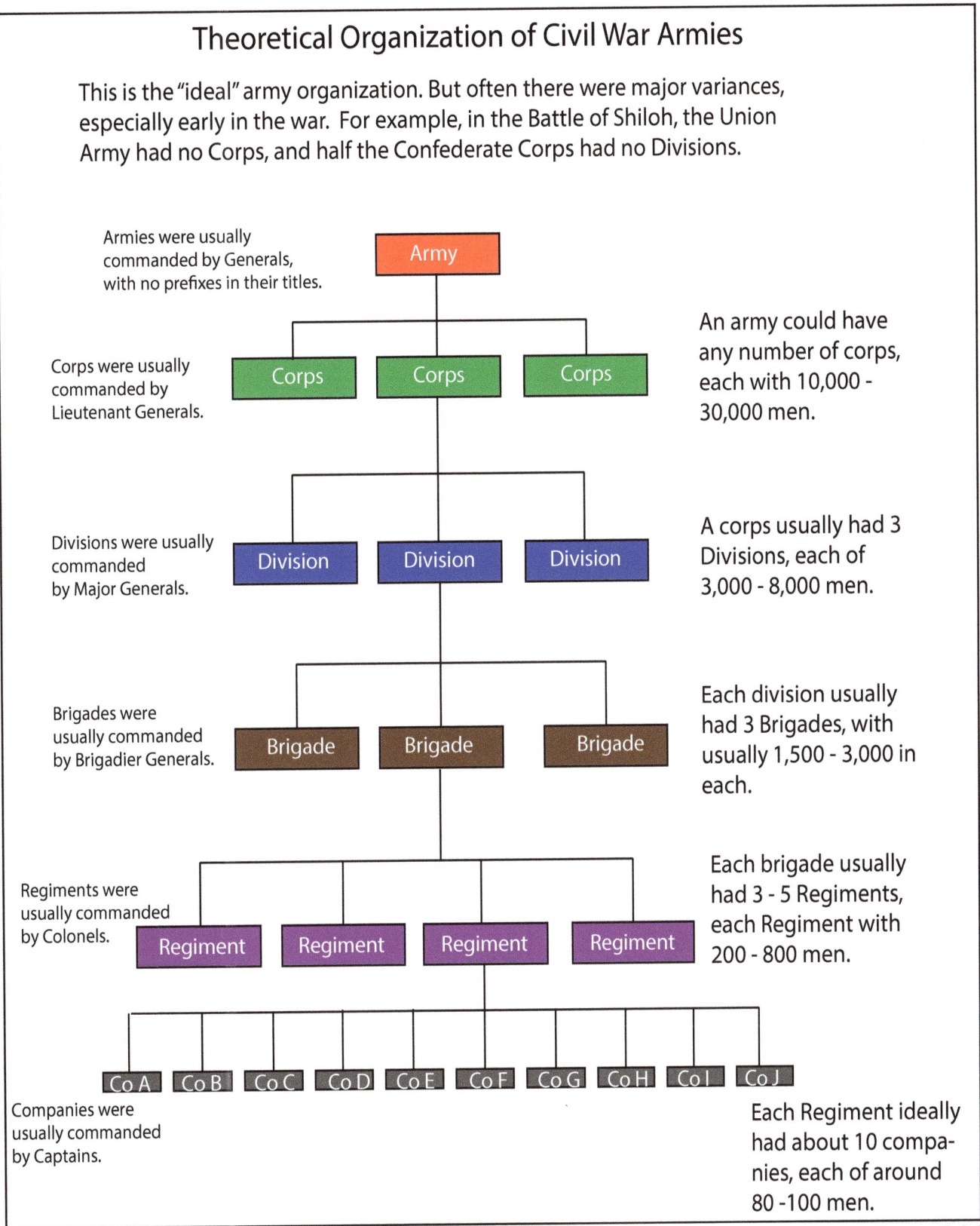

Appendix C - Army Organization

References

Not being quite old enough to have participated in the battle personally - though some might disagree - all of my knowledge of the battle comes from previous histories. Compared to other Civil War battles I've written about - specifically, Gettysburg and Antietam - there really aren't many books on the Shiloh battle. But the books I've found most enlightening are listed here. If I had bothered to reference all the facts in this book, it would be filled with footnotes, of which probably 50% of them would come from the below books.

But the other 50% of the footnotes would come from Wikipedia, The American Battlefield Trust, the Shiloh National Park, and countless lectures and documentaries on YouTube, along with bits and pieces of information I've picked up from God-knows-where in seven decades of off-and-on reading about and studying the Civil War.

BATTLES AND LEADERS OF THE CIVIL WAR: THE STRUGGLE INTENSIFIES/VOL 1 (1883)

This book series of four volumes was written in 1883 and is still one of the best historical references of the Civil War for my money. It is long out of print but you can buy it used, and for very little cost. The series covers the entire Civil War, not just Shiloh, of which there is only a 26 page section. Most of the drawings used in my book came from this series, although I modified many or most of them, as well as colorized them.

SHILOH (1997) LARRY J. DANIEL

One of the definitive modern works on the battle. I used this book constantly in my own research. He goes into much more detail, sometimes too much detail, about the battle, compared to most of the other books on the subject. His maps are hard to follow, but given that they were created using 1997 technology, they're not bad.

SHILOH AND THE WESTERN CAMPAIGN OF 1862 (2007) O. EDWARD CUNNINGHAM

Contains a detailed discussion of the Shiloh battle, as well as the events and policies leading up to it. For the serious student, this book makes a good companion to Daniel's book, mentioned above. It's sort of a compromise between the heavily detailed books such as Daniels' book, and the books with too much fluff, such as Groom's.

SHILOH: A BATTLEFIELD GUIDE (2006) MARK GRIMSLEY AND STEVEN E. WOODWORTH

This book is intended only to be a tour guide. It therefore heavily summarizes the events of the battle. But I found it to be a good starting point in figuring out exactly what, where and when things happened on the battlefield.

SHILOH, 1862 (2012) WINSTON GROOM

This book is light on the actual events of the battle. Mostly, it focuses on background stories of some of the participants, and some of the stories seem to drift too far off the subject of the battle. As a writer mainly focused on the tactics and maneuvers during the battle, I didn't find this book to be of much help. Nonetheless, it's a good fit for readers who enjoy personal interest stories.

SHILOH (2012) BLUE & GRAY MAGAZINE - SESQUICENTENNIAL EDITION

This is a single magazine edition, not a book, but all on the subject of Shiloh. Written or at least edited by the Shiloh Park's historian, Stacy Allen. Very good maps, and in color, although at a higher level than where I targeted most of my maps and discussion. Overall, a very helpful guide in my research. The magazine is defunct, but you can probably buy this edition on eBay or someplace like eBay.

References

Index

Symbols

1st Division 19, 73
2nd Division 16, 19, 96
3rd Division 19, 153–158, 167
4th Division 16, 19, 83
5th Division 15, 16, 19, 62–66, 73
6th Division 19, 33, 37, 73

A

Adairsville, GA 137
Adams, Brig. Gen. Daniel W. 50, 52, 98, 112
Adams, Pvt. David 77
Alabama
  26AL 43
Alcatraz Island 13
Allen, Col. Ben 43
Allen, Col. Henry W. 105
Ammen, Col. Jacob 45, 140–152, 159–166, 170
Anderson, Brig. Gen. James P. 61, 63, 64, 68–72, 90, 107, 146, 174
Antietam 181
Appler, Col. Jesse R. 55–66, 71, 174
Arkansas
  1AR 104
  2AR 106
  2nd Confederate Regiment 112, 121
  6AR 44, 85, 106
  7AR 106
  8AR 80
  9AR 80, 112, 121
  10AR 112, 121
  13AR 65, 79, 80, 83
  15AR 67–72
Army of Mississippi 25
Army of Tennessee 11, 12, 26, 190
Army of the Ohio 11, 12, 26, 144, 159–166, 179
Atlanta, GA 4, 5, 12

B

Bankhead, Capt. Smith P. 68
Bark Road 34, 103
Barnes Field 104
Barrett, Capt. Samuel E. 61, 64, 68, 70, 71, 84
Bate, Col. William B. 68
Bate, Humphrey 68
Battle of Mill Springs 13
Battle of Pea Ridge 13
Baxter, Capt. A. S. 154

Baylor, Col. George W. 177
Beauregard, Gen. Pierre G.T. 14, 25–32, 34, 71, 103, 128, 146, 148, 159, 160, 167–172, 174, 176, 181–186, 187, 192
Behr, Capt. Frederick 79
Bell, Mrs. Sarah 95
Belmont, MO 3, 112, 140
Belnap, Maj. William 89
Beltzhoover, Lt. Col. Daniel 121
Ben Howell Field 76
Ben-Hur 9, 19
Bierce, Lt. Ambrose 12, 143, 162, 168
Blackjack Oak 103, 104
Blaisdell, T. M. 60
Bloody Pond, The 125, 129, 164, 168
Blythe, Col A. K. 64
Bouton, Capt. Edward 134
Bowen, Brig. Gen. John S. 111, 121–132, 133
Bowling Green, KY 7, 13
Bowman, Maj. Samuel 56
Bragg, Maj. Gen. Braxton 14, 25–32, 33, 47, 61, 63, 64, 71, 90, 104–110, 121, 146, 168, 179–186, 190
Breckinridge, Brig. Gen. John C. 25–32, 33, 90, 105, 121–132, 145, 168, 171
Breckinridge's Reserve Corps 111
Brig. Gen. William Nelson 11
Brinton, Dr. John H. 9
British Enfield 18
Brotzmann, Lt. Edward 96, 112
Brown, John 1
Bruce, Col. Sanders D. 159–166, 168, 170
Buckland, Col. Ralph P. 55, 67–72, 73, 79
Buckner, Brig. Gen. Simon Bolivar 8–14
Buell, Maj. Gen. Don Carlos 2–14, 16–17, 26, 38, 45, 92, 112, 124, 128, 139–152, 154, 159–166, 167–172, 174, 179, 181, 187, 77
Bull Run, First Battle of 14, , 89
Burrow, Capt. Jerome B. 76, 82
Byrne, Capt. Edward P. 105

C

Cairo, IL 1, 3, 11, 18, 21, 37
Cameron, Simon 20
Camm, Lt. Col. William 84, 85, 145
Campbell, Col. Alexander W. 83
Canister 49
Carondelet, USS 8
Carson, Capt. Irving 144
Cavalry Field 136
Chalmers, Brig. Gen. James R. 47, 49, 50, 52, 98,

Index

114–120, 125, 126, 130, 133, 145, 167
Charleston, SC 53
Chattanooga, TN 6
Cheatham, Maj. Gen. Benjamin 103, 104, 114, 167, 179
Cherry Mansion, The 18, 19, 38, 45, 134, 188
Cherry, Mrs. 38
Chickamauga 192
Cincinnati Gazette 188
Cincinnati Sanitary Commission 23
Clark, Brig. Gen. Charles 63
Clarksville, TN 115
Cleburne, Brig. Gen. Patrick R. 56, 58, 61, 65, 67–72, 92, 174
Cloud Field 95, 133, 134, 135, 137, 152, 162
Cobb, Capt. Robert 84, 89, 90, 92
Cockerill, Col. Joseph 124
Cockrell, Pvt. John 124–132, 139, 162
Columbia, TN 45
Columbus, KY 10, 11, 13, 14, 26, 45
Comanches 13
Connestoga, USS 146
Corinth, MS 12–14, 15, 21, 22, 25–32, 55, 112, 160, 190–194
Corinth Road 34, 53, 55, 96, 179
Cottonclads 4, 5
Cowling, Sgt. Henry 134
Crescent Field 73, 76, 93
Crescent Regiment 27, 170
Crittenden, Brig. Gen. Thomas L. 159, 164, 170
Crittenden, Maj. Gen. George B. 13, 25, 26
Crocker, Lt. 144
Crockett, Maj. LeRoy 31
Crossroads, The 71, 73, 74, 76, 79–88, 128, 139, 176, 179
Crumps Landing 15–17, 18, 38, 53, 153–158
Cumberland River 3–14, 15
Cumberland Valley 6
Cummings, Lt. Col. Morkoe 93

D

Davis, Brig. Gen. Jefferson C. 147
Davis, President Jefferson 1–14, 26, 27, 148, 192
Davis Wheatfield 105, 167, 168, 170
Dawes, Lt. Ephraim 56–66, 71
Dean, Lt. Col. John A. 106
Deas, Col. Zachariah C. 112–120
Decatur, AL 148
Department of Mississippi 2–14
Department of Missouri 15
Dewey, Lt. Col. William 89
Dickey, Cyrus 133
Dill Branch Ravine 140–152, 162
Dill Creek 140–152
Dill Creek Ravine 148, 167

Dixie Grays, The 44, 85, 171
Dixon, Lt. George E. 53
Dorn, Brig. Gen. Earl Van 13, 192
Douglas, Stephen A. 26
Dover, TN 6
Dubroea, Capt. Edgar 104
Duck River 18, 45
Duncan, Elsie 65, 187
Duncan Field 53, 74, 101–110, 121, 133

E

Eastern Corinth Road 47, 101, 111, 164, 168
Eastport, Mississippi 16
Ebey, Pvt. Fletcher 84
Ellis, Lt. Col. E. F. W. 83
Embly, Pvt. Edgar 47
Emmons, Capt. 174
Enfield Rifle 27
Evans, Pvt. Samuel 68

F

Fagan, Col. James 105
Fallen Timbers, The Battle of 183
Fearing, Maj. B. D. 60
Ferguson, Lt. Col. Samuel 134
Fighting Bishop, The 26
Fire Eater 34
Fisher, Lt. Horace C. 143, 144
Fleming, Pvt. Robert 139
Florence, AL 6, 10, 12
Florida
   1FL Btn 63
Floyd, Maj. Gen. John B. 8, 10
Foote, Flag Officer Andrew H. 4–14, 5–14
Forrest, Col. Nathan Bedford 8, 167, 183–186
Fort Donelson 6–14, 15, 19, 21, 28, 45, 76, 112, 183, 190
Fort Henry 7–14, 15, 21, 28, 45, 183
Fort Sumter 10, 14
Fort Wayne, USS 144
Fraley Field 33–36, 37, 55, 103
Fraley, James 34
Fremont, Gen. John C. 2, 4, 5

G

Gage, Capt. Charles P. 49, 98, 115, 146
Gettysburg 181
Gibson, Col. Randall L. 65, 104, 105, 106, 174, 176, 181
Girardey, Capt. Isadore P. 98, 115
Gladden, Col. Adley H. 47–54, 98, 112
Goddard, Maj. William 83
Gold Rush, The 3, 103
Grant, Maj. Gen. Ulysses S. 2–14, 26, 37, 90, 96, 105,

128, 134, 139-152, 153-158, 164, 173-178, 179, 187-188
Grant's Last Line 125, 130, 136, 139-152
Greer's Ford 112
Gulf of Mexico 4, 5

H

Halleck, Maj. Gen. Henry W. 2-14, 15-17, 156, 190, 191
Hamburg-Savannah Road 136, 156
Hardcastle, Maj. Earon B. 34
Hardee, Maj. Gen. William J. 8, 25-32, 33, 34, 49, 71, 72, 82, 98, 126, 134, 136, 168-172
Hardee's Tactics 26
Hardin County 15
Hare, Col. Abraham M. 76, 83-88
Harris, Gov. Isham G. 124-132
Harris, Maj. J. T. 68
Hazen, Col. William B. 159-166, 168-172
Helena, AR 67
Hell's Hollow 133-134, 137, 152
Helm, Gen. Ben 148
Henricle, Lt. Jack 62
Herron, Lt. Col. D.L. 64
Hickenlooper, Capt. Andrew 47, 51
Hildebrand, Col. Jesse 55-66, 70, 73, 79
Hill, Col. Benjamin 68
Hindman, Brig. Gen. Thomas C. 59, 61, 67, 82, 106
H. L. Hunley, CSA 53
Hodge, Col. B. L. 104, 124
Hodgson, Capt. W. Irving 63, 90
Holiday, Sgt. Thomas 56
Hornets Nest, The 101-110, 121, 145, 167
Howard Country, AR 106
Howard, W. A. 107
Hudson, Capt. Alfred 121
Hunt, Col. Thomas 134
Hurdle, Pvt. R. W. 103
Hurlbut, Brig. Gen. Stephen A. 15, 16, 52, 83, 95-100, 101, 108, 111-120, 121-132, 133, 164
Huston, Felix 13

I

Illinois
  4IL Cavalry 56, 60, 64, 183
  9IL 111, 121, 122, 125
  11IL 111
  11IL Calvary 51
  12IL 121, 122, 125
  14IL 84, 85, 145
  15IL 83, 136
  17IL 80
  28IL 122
  29IL 80
  32IL 122
  41IL 95, 96, 112, 122, 133
  42IL 112
  43IL 74, 80
  44IN 96
  45IL 82
  46IL 136
  48IL 82
  49IL 74, 80
  50IL 111, 122, 125
  52IL 21
  55IL 115, 116, 144
  57IL 125
  58IL 133-134
  61IL 47, 49
  73IL 137
Indiana
  6IN 198
  9IN 198
  11IN 196
  15IN 198
  17IN 198
  23IN 176, 196
  24IN 196
  25IN 196
  29IN 198
  30IN 198
  31IN 196
  32IN 198
  36IN 143, 198
  39IN 198
  40IN 198
  44IN 162, 196
  57IN 198
  58IN 198
Iowa
  2IA 101, 107, 133
  3IA 112, 187
  6IA 90, 92
  7IA 101, 108, 133
  8IA 133-134
  11IA 83, 90, 137
  12IA 106, 108, 133-134
  13IA 83
  14IA 103, 106
  15IA 52, 84, 89
  16IA 52, 84, 89
ironclads 4, 5, 7, 8
Island No. 10 6, 188, 190

J

Jackson, Brig. Gen. John K. 47, 52, 98, 121-132, 133, 145, 146

Index

Jefferson Mounted Rifles, The 34
Johnson, Brig. Gen. Bushrod R. 64, 90
Johnston, Gen. Albert Sidney 12–14, 18, 22, 25–32, 33, 41, 43, 52, 71, 92, 103, 108, 111, 121–132, 148, 177, 190, 77
Johnston, Gen. Joseph 26
John Warner, USS 38
Jones, Captain Wells S. 58
Jones, Capt. Warren C. 106
Jones Field 74, 83, 84, 89, 90, 103, 139, 173–178, 176, 178, 179
Jordan, Col. Thomas 27, 103, 181

K

Keeley, C. W. 137
Kentucky
  2KY (Union) 170
  4KY (Union) 140
  5KY (CSA) 134
  6KY (Union) 170
  7KY (CSA) 103, 111
  13KY (Union) 170
Kentucky Jeans 27
Kentucky Shield, The 2
Ketchum, Capt. William 134, 173, 176, 191
Kirkman, Sgt. John 84
Knefler, Capt. Frederick 154
Ku Klux Klan 106

L

Laing, Lt. Culbert W. 96, 114
Larkin Bell Field 115, 164
Lauman, Brig. Gen. J. G. 104, 105, 111–120, 125
Lawrence, Lt. Elijah 116
Lee, Gen. Robert E. 192
Lexington, MO 41
Lexington, USS 5, 8, 15, 140–152, 146, 150, 4
Lick Creek 16, 49, 73, 114, 167
Lincoln, President Abraham 1–14, 26, 74, 190, 192
Lincoln, Willie 11
Livaudais, Pvt. Edmond 136
Livingstone, Dr. David 44
Lockett, Capt. Samuel 98, 105, 106
Locust Grove Branch 49, 115. *See* Spain Branch
Longstreet, James 3
Lost Field 74
Louisiana
  1LA 50, 105
  4LA 65, 101, 104, 105, 106, 174
  11LA 63, 80
  13LA 104, 105
  16LA 31, 136
  17LA 63, 191
  18LA 136, 181
  19LA 104, 105, 170
  20LA 68, 107
  Crescent Regiment, The 107, 170
Louisiana State University 20, 21
Lytle, Pvt. Samuel 137

M

Malmborg, Col. Oscar 115, 116
Maney, Col. George , 111, 112, 114–120, 77
Marsh, Col. C. Carroll 76, 79, 80–88, 90
Martin, Col. John D. 171
Martin, Col. Mathias 112
Mason, Col. Rodney 115
McAllister, Capt. Edward 76, 82–88, 136
McArthur, Brig. Gen. John A. 96, 111–120, 121, 124, 130, 133, 139, 164
McBride, Pvt. George W. 47, 50, 51
McClellan, Gen. George B. 7, 11, 181, 192
McClernand, Maj. Gen. John A. 18, 5, 9, 12, 19, 21, 22, 56, 73–78, 60, 73–73, 89–94, 89–89, 103, 108, 121, 133, 134, 139, 144, 174, 176, 4
McClung, Capt. Hugh L. W. 168, 170
McClure, A. K. 190
McCook, Brig. Gen. Alexander McD. 162, 179
McCuller Field 115
McDowell, Col. John A. 71, 73, 76, 89–94
McDowell, Gen. Irvin 89, 90
McInerney, Pvt. John 62
McPherson, Col. James 5, 22, 53, 4, 76
Meade, Gen. George 181
Mecklin, Pvt. Augustus Harvey 122, 129
Memphis & Charleston RR 12
Memphis, TN 64, 188
Mendenhall, Capt. John 164, 168
Methodist Episcopal Church 22
Mexican War, The 2, 3, 20, 25, 37, 74, 103
Michie's Farm 187
Michigan
  12MI 33, 37, 41
  15MI 47, 50
Miller, Col. Madison 33, 41, 47–54, 133
Mill Springs, KY 25
Minnehaha, USS 139
Mississippi
  3MS Btn 34
  6MS 56, 58, 67
  7MS 50
  9MS 50, 116, 133
  10MS 50
  11MS 122
  22MS 112
  Blythe's Mississippi Regiment 64, 79, 80
Mississippi River, The 1–14, 190

Mississippi Valley, The 2, 12, 20
Missouri
  1MO (CSA) 112, 121, 170
  13MO 76, 79, 80, 90
  18MO 47
  21MO 33, 37, 41
  23MO 52, 96, 133–134
  25MO 33, 37, 41, 43
Mobile, AL 14, 53
Mobile & Ohio RR 12, 14
Monterey Road 28, 190, 191
Moore, Col. David 33, 37–40, 43
Moore, Col. John C. 170, 171
Morass, The 71, 72
Mouton, Col. Alfred 136
Mulberry Field 136
Munch, Capt. Emil 47, 103
Munford, Maj. Edward 126
Muscle Shoals, AL 12, 13
Myers, Capt. John B. 96–100

N

Napoleon 27, 28, 71
Nashville, TN 6, 10, 11, 12, 14, 45, 124, 162
National Cemetery 187
Nelson, Brig. Gen. William 11, 38, 44, 53, 92, 140–152, 159–166, 171
New Madrid, MO 6, 190
New Orleans, LA 6, 11, 90, 104
Nispel, Lt. George 79, 80
Nixon, Lt. Liberty I. 43

O

O'Hara, Capt. Theodore 126
Ohio
  5OH Cavalry 114
  6OH 143
  13OH Battery 96, 98
  14OH Battery 82
  20OH 159
  46OH 90
  48OH 67
  53OH 55–66, 67, 76, 174
  54OH 114, 115, 116
  57OH 55–66, 76
  70OH 67, 89, 124
  71OH 111, 115, 117, 122
  72OH 31, 67–72, 115
  77OH 55, 76, 183
Ohio River, The 1, 3, 6
Old Cabinet Room 190
Old Reliable. *See* Hardee, Maj. Gen. William J.
Opitz, Lt. 84

Orleans Guards Battalion 59, 136, 181, 191
Owl Creek 16, 27, 156, 173

P

Paducah, KY 3, 6, 45
Parker, Pvt. Henry 87
Pathfinder, The 2
Patterson, Col. William 80
Peabody, Col. Everett 33–36, 37–40, 41–46, 47, 55
Peach Orchard, The 95–100, 111, 122, 125, 129, 130, 133, 164, 167
Peeples, Col. Thomas H. 68
Pensacola, FL 14
Pillow, Maj. Gen. Gideon 3, 8, 10
Pittsburg-Corinth Road 15, 55, 79, 83, 103, 104, 133
Pittsburg Landing 15–24
Polk, Capt. Marshall T. 64, 79, 89
Polk, Maj. Gen. Leonidas 2–14, 25–32, 33, 45, 61, 68, 90, 104, 145
Pond, Col. Preston Jr. 73, 90, 92, 134, 139, 160, 173, 176
Pope, Maj. Gen. John 12, 16, 190, 192
Powell, Maj. James E. 33–36, 37, 38, 43
Prentiss, Brig. Gen. Benjamin M. 19, 33, 37–40, 41–46, 47–54, 55, 73, 79, 85, 95, 104, 133–134, 148, 76
Preston, Col. William 126
Princeton University 26
Pritle, Sgt. J. J. 79
Pugh, Col. Isaac C. 95, 96, 111–120, 122–132
Pugh, John 170
Purdy-Hamburg Road 41, 52, 71, 73, 74, 79, 95, 96, 112, 122, 168, 170, 176, 181
Purdy Road 156
Putnam, Capt. Douglas A. 76, 158

Q

Querouze, Col. Leon 136

R

Raith, Col. Julius 74, 79–88
Rankin, Col. William 133
Rawlins, Capt. John A. 53, 153, 154, 76
Rea Field 55–66, 67, 181
Rea Springs 58
Reconnaissance Road 33
Reed, Col. Hugh 162
Reichard, Col. August 181
Reid, Col. Hugh T. 52, 89
Reid, Whitlaw 188
Review Field 76, 80, 106, 181
Rhea Field. *See* Rea Field
Rice, Lt. Col. A. V. 59
Richmond, VA 12, 13, 14, 25, 192

Index

Ridge Road 28, 190
River Road, The 52, 95, 96, 98, 111, 112, 114, 115, 117, 154–158
Robertson, Capt. Felix 49, 96
Robertson, Pvt. Thomas 105, 190
Roberts, Pvt. John 68
Roman, Capt. Alfred 136
Ross' Battery 114, 125
Rousseau, Brig. Gen. Lovell H. 179
Rowley, Capt. William R. 53, 154
Ruggles, Brig. Gen. Daniel 68, 107–110, 174, 176
Russell, Col. Robert M. 63, 64, 79, 80–88, 89, 90
Russian Tenant Field 156
Rutledge, Capt. Arthur M. 118, 179

S

Sanford, Thomas J. 80
San Francisco Bay 13
Sarah Bell Cotton Field 52, 95–100, 101–110, 111, 114–120, 130, 168, 170
Savannah-Hamburg Road 95, 98, 101, 111, 112, 130, 134, 139, 164, 171
Savannah, TN 11–14, 15–17, 31, 38, 44, 92, 134, 140, 149, 153, 159, 188
Schwartz, Maj. Adolph 70, 80
Schwartz's battery 79
Scott, Gen. Winfield 13, 20
Seay Field 33, 34, 37, 43
Seay, Lewis 33
Sharps Rifles 64
Shaver, Col. Robert.G. 41, 82–88, 106
Shaver's Brigade 44
Shaw, Col. William 103
Sheridan, Lt. 167
Sherman, Brig. Gen. William T. 15–17, 18–24, 32, 33, 41, 55–66, 70–72, 73–78, 79–88, 89–94, 95, 103, 121, 128, 133, 134, 139, 144, 148, 153–158, 162, 174–178, 179–186, 190
Sherman Road 84
Sherman, Senator John 20
Shiloh Branch 56, 58, 59, 62, 63, 67–72, 139
Shiloh Church 21, 22, 55, 58, 60, 63, 64, 67–72, 79, 103, 114, 128, 146, 154, 168, 179, 193
Shiloh Creek 63
Shoup, Maj. Frances 58, 63, 68, 70
Shunpike, The 153–158
Sibley, Capt. Henry Hopkins 43
Sibley Tent 43, 87, 160
Sisters of Charity 139
Slocomb, Lt. 170
Smith, Brig. Gen. Charles. F. 45
Smith, Col. Morgan L. 153, 156, 174, 176
Smith, Col. Preston 64, 79, 80–88
Smith, Col. William Sooy 170
Smith, Maj. Gen. Charles F. 9, 10, 12, 15, 16, 19, 188
Smith, Robert 68
Snake Creek 16, 27, 156
Snake Creek Bridge 139
Southern Methodist Episcopal Church 22
Southgate, Lt. 45
Sowell Field 90, 179
Spain Branch. See also Locust Grove Branch
Spain Field 33, 47, 51, 98, 122
Special Order Number Eight 28
Springfield, US 18
Stacy Field 133
Stanley, Pvt. Henry Morton 44, 85–88, 106–110, 171
Statham, Col. Winfield S. 112–120, 121–132
Stephens, Col. William H. 103, 112, 121–132
Stephenson, Pvt. Phillip 13
Stevens, Col. William H. 111
Stewart, Brig. Gen. Alexander P. 65, 79, 80, 90, 104
Stewart County, TN 6
Stillwell, Cpl. Leander 50–54
St. Louis, MO 2, 5, 11, 4
St. Louis, USS 8
Stones River 192
Stoney Lonesome, TN 38, 153, 154
Story, Newton 87
Stuart, Col. David 73, 111–120, 130
Sunken Road, The , 92, 95, 101–110, 96, 101–101, 111, 133, 149, 148, 76
Swan, William 187
Sweeny, Brig. Gen. Thomas 96, 101
Swett, Capt. Charles 41

T

Taylor, Maj. Ezra 58, 64, 71, 84, 89
Tennessee
 1TN 77
 1TN Btn 111, 112
 2TN 67–72
 4TN 79, 80, 82
 5TN 67–72, 83, 136
 6TN 103, 111
 9TN 111
 12TN 63, 64, 80, 82, 137
 13TN 63, 64, 71
 15TN 79, 112
 19TN 112
 20TN 111, 112, 181
 22TN 63, 80
 23TN 58, 67, 112, 136
 24TN 67–72, 136
 25TN 112
 33TN 79, 80, 83
 45TN 122, 124
 47TN 160, 191

52TN 118
54TN 112
154TN 64, 79, 80
Tennessee River, The 3-14, 15, 15-17, 34, 49, 125, 142, 187
Tennessee Valley, The 188
Terrill, Capt. William R. 164
Texas
  2TX 27, 171
  9TX 68
Texas Rangers 30, 136, 176-178, 176-176, 179, 183
Thayer, Col. John M. 153, 176
The Fighting Bishop. *See* Polk, Maj. Gen. Leonidas
The Great Creole 14
The Lost Opportunity 146
Thomas, Maj. Gen. George H. 190
Thompson, Capt. N.S. 173
Thulstrup, Thure de 108
Thurber, Lt. Charles 173, 174
Tigress, USS 23, 38, 43, 52, 148
Tilghman Branch 134, 139, 173, 178
Tilghman Branch Ravine 92
Tilghman, Gen. Lloyd 7
Timberclads 5, 8, 4
Timony, Lt. James P. 83
Tindall, Col. Jacob 52
Trabue, Col. Robert P. 90, 134, 181
Trenton, TN 160
Tucker, Pittser 15
Tupelo, MS 192
Tuttle, Col. James 96, 101
Tyconn, USS 23
Tyler, Lt. Col. R. C. 64
Tyler, USS 5, 8, 15, 140-152, 4

U

Uniform Militia Act of 1792 1
Upper Mississippi Valley 188
Urquhart, Col. David 146
US
  2nd U.S. Cavalry 12

V

Vaughn, Col. Alfred J. Jr. 64
Veatch, Col. James C. 76, 83, 84, 85, 95
Vertner, Pvt. A. V. 65
Vicksburg, MS 50, 74, 190, 192

W

Wagner, Col. George D. 181
Wallace, Ann 134, 139
Wallace, Brig. Gen. William H. L. 12, 13, 15-24, 38, 53, 76, 96, 101, 111-120, 121, 125-132, 133-134, 134, 139, 153
Wallace, Maj. Gen. Lewis 19, 38, 53, 128, 130, 139, 144, 153-158, 159, 160, 167, 173, 176, 76
Washington (LA) Artillery 27, 63, 68, 90, 134, 168, 170. *See also* Hodgson, Capt. W. Irving
Waterhouse, Capt. Allen C. 56-66, 70, 71
Waterloo 27, 28
Water Oaks Pond 76, 77, 83, 90, 179
Webster, Col. Joseph D. 140, 142
Western Corinth Road 55, 63, 67, 68, 73, 76, 79, 83
West Point 3, 14, , 21, 26, 74, 96, 192
Wharton, Col. John A. 136, 176-178
Whitaker, Col. W.C. 170
Whittlesey, Col. Charles 176
Whittlesey, Col. John 153
Wicker Field 125, 164
Wickham, Capt. Lee 126
Wickliffe, Col. Charles 181
Willard's Battery 125
Williams, Capt. John 93
Williams, Col. N. G. 95-100
Wilson Creek, Battle of 2-14
Wisconsin
  16WI 37, 41, 43, 47
  18WI 47, 51
Withers, Brig. Gen. Jones M. 47, 98, 146
W. Manse George Cabin 95-100, 164, 170
Wood, Brig. Gen. Sterling A. M. 41, 56, 80-88, 92, 179, 181
Wood, Lt. Peter P. 111, 112, 122
Wood's Brigade 34
Woods, Col. Joseph 108
Wood, Wilse 33, 34
Woolf Field 73, 74, 77, 83, 84, 90, 133, 134, 174, 179
Wyatt, Pvt. Jessie W. 137

Y

Yandell, Dr. D. W. 130
Yellow Creek 16
Yellow Creek Expedition 16

Z

Zollicoffer, Brig. Gen. Felix 13

www.ingramcontent.com/pod-product-compliance
Ingram Content Group UK Ltd.
Pitfield, Milton Keynes, MK11 3LW, UK
UKHW050418240426
12048UKWH00014B/697